Nonverbal Behavior
in Interpersonal Relations
Third Edition

Third Edition

Nonverbal Behavior in Interpersonal Relations

Virginia P. Richmond
James C. McCroskey
West Virginia University

Allyn and Bacon
Boston • London • Toronto • Sydney • Tokyo • Singapore

Series Editor: Carla Daves
Editorial Assistant: Mary Visco
Cover Administrator: Linda Knowles
Manufacturing Buyer: Megan Cochran
Marketing Manager: Lisa Kimball
Editorial-Production Service: Electronic Publishing Services Inc.
Cover designer: Suzanne Harbison

© 1995 by Allyn & Bacon
A Simon & Schuster Company
Needham Heights, Massachusetts 02194

The authors wish to acknowledge Harry Gwinn Peck Jr. for his photographic expertise, creativity, and development. All photos are the work of Mr. Peck.

Library of Congress Cataloging-in-Publication Data

Richmond, Virginia P.
   Nonverbal behavior in interpersonal relations / Virginia P.
Richmond, James C. McCroskey.—3rd ed.
      p.   cm
   Includes bibliographical references and index.
   ISBN 0-205-15388-7
   1. Nonverbal communication (Psychology)   2. Interpersonal
relations.   I. McCroskey, James C.   II. Title.
BF637.N66R53   1994
153.6'9—dc20   94-32740
                                                         CIP

Printed in the United States of America

10   9 8   7   6   5   4   3   98   97   96

▲ Contents

▲ PREFACE

This book represents what we believe the area of nonverbal communication is and should be—a unique blend of social, scientific, and humanistic study. More than any other area within the field of communication, nonverbal communication has generated scholarly investigations in a wide variety of academic disciplines and, therefore, has involved many epistemological models. What we know has been drawn from these diverse disciplines and orientations. We have attempted to integrate this knowledge while avoiding devotion to a specific epistemological position.

Nonverbal communication is the area of communication that simultaneously receives the most positive response from students and the most negative response from some professors in other areas of the field and some outside the communication discipline. For those of us who feel that the study of nonverbal communication is extremely valuable to students in all academic disciplines, it is difficult to reconcile these negative responses.

It is tempting to dismiss critics of the area as simply those who believe that if Aristotle didn't say it or Skinner didn't get rats to do it, it isn't worthy of scholarly study. Although some critics are guilty of such biases, many more are responding to the way nonverbal communication has been taught in the past and how it is sometimes taught today. Popular writers in the field often grossly overgeneralize research findings, and such generalizations too often find their way into nonverbal communication classes. In addition, many nonverbal communication classes, particularly in the late 1960s and 1970s, were developed as virtually content-free experiential courses, more commonly called "touchie-feelie" classes. Such distortions have not been conducive to generating respect for this area of study.

The teaching of nonverbal communication is plagued with a seeming dilemma. On one hand, we know that all of the categories of nonverbal behavior interact together to create communicative impact. To understand all of these behaviors, however, it seems necessary to look at the individual categories of behavior one by one. Thus, most textbooks and course instructors have chosen between a "variables" approach and a "functional" approach. The former leads to an excellent understanding of the individual behaviors that make up nonverbal communication but little understanding of how they interact with each other. The latter leads to an excellent understanding of the complexity of nonverbal communication but little understanding of the components of this complex communication system. To put it another way, the former leads to a good understanding of the trees but a poor understanding of the forest, and the latter leads to a good understanding of the forest but a poor understanding of the trees.

In this book, we have attempted to resolve that dilemma by including chapters devoted to the individual categories of nonverbal behavior as well as chapters that examine all of those variables in specific contexts. The book is divided into three sections. The first section includes only Chapter 1, in which we consider definition issues, challenge some common myths about nonverbal communication, look at the major communicative functions of nonverbal behavior, and note the major categories of nonverbal behavior. In the second section, we examine in detail the major categories of behavior—the trees, if you will. After nine chapters devoted to this purpose, we devote the final chapter in the second section to how each of these categories relates to immediacy, which we consider the primary outcome of the communicative impact of nonverbal behavior.

In the final section of this book, we consider four important contexts in which nonverbal behaviors have significant communicative impact: female–male relationships, superior–subordinate relationships, teacher–student relationships, and intercultural relationships. By examining these contexts with respect to the various categories of nonverbal behavior, we hope to help the reader to see the forest again. Through this combined functions–variables–contexts approach, we hope you will develop a full and well-rounded perspective on the role of nonverbal behavior in human communicative relationships.

This book could not have been produced without the help of thousands of people. Many hundreds of those are researchers in more than twenty disciplines whom we have consulted for our information. Equally important, however, are the more than 30,000 students, both graduate and undergraduate, who have studied nonverbal communication with us and our colleagues at West Virginia University over the past two decades. These students, many of whom were not required to take our courses, have made it clear to us what is worth studying and what is not. We deeply appreciate their ideas.

In addition, we would like to acknowledge the contributions of the following reviewers: Pat Kearney, California State University, Long Beach; Nina Jo Moore, Appalachian State University; and Richard W. Thomas, Central Michigan University.

For editorial assistance, our Acquisitions Editor Carla Daves, and her editorial assistant, Mary Visco, and others have been generous with their expertise. We welcome working with our new publisher, Allyn & Bacon.

We also appreciate the ideas of many teachers who have taught with and students who have studied from the first and second editions of this book. Many of their suggestions are reflected in modifications in this edition. One of the most common complaints about the first edition was what students perceived as constant citing of other authors. Students felt that it made the book harder to read; they disliked having the thoughts broken up by the citations. Although such citations are common in scholarly writing, students with little or no background in nonverbal communication are our intended readers, not other scholars. Therefore, in the second edition and this edition, we have reduced the number of citations in the text to only those we considered absolutely necessary. We believe this is appropriate for a book that is intended as an introduction to nonverbal behavior and communication. We have included extensive citations of references for each chapter at the end of the book for those who want to pursue a given topic more fully. We have also cited the works of several of our colleagues who have written books appropriate for advanced study in this field. We hope that when you read this introductory book, you will be motivated to move on to their excellent works.

Virginia P. Richmond
James C. McCroskey
Morgantown, West Virginia

1

Communication and Nonverbal Behavior

Interpersonal relationships are a central fact of our existence as human beings in modern society. We find ourselves in many kinds of relationships. Important to most of us are our relationships with our parents, our spouse, our children, and our friends. Early in life, we go to school and associate with teachers and peers. As we mature, we enter the world of work and find a new set of relationships— relationships with our manager, our coworkers, and our subordinates. The quality of those relationships, both individually and in combination, determines the quality of our lives and our communication determines the quality of those relationships. Communication, then, is the process that makes us what we are.

Human communication is the process of one person stimulating meaning in the mind of another person (or persons) by means of verbal or nonverbal messages. Because we have devoted several other books to explaining the nature of this process in considerable detail (McCroskey, 1993; McCroskey, Richmond, and Stewart, 1986; Richmond and McCroskey, 1993), we will not attempt to do so here. Our focus in this book is on the role of nonverbal behavior as messages in human communication. Our concern, then, is with nonverbal communication—the process of one person stimulating meaning in the mind of another person or persons by means of nonverbal messages.

MYTHS ABOUT NONVERBAL COMMUNICATION

For much of the history of the study of human communication, the nonverbal component was ignored. As increased attention has been directed toward this aspect

1

of communication, several myths have developed that have led to considerable confusion and, in some cases, to complete rejection of nonverbal behavior as an important component of communication. Let us examine a few of these myths.

1. *"Nonverbal communication" is nonsense. All communication involves language. Hence, all communication is verbal.* This is the traditional myth held by many people who center their attention on language and consider *language* and *communication* to be virtually interchangeable terms. Nonverbal behavior with potential for impact is always present in oral communication situations. We cannot even talk on the phone without introducing nonverbal elements to our message. The sound of our voice must be there, and no two people's voices are exactly alike. Therefore, no two people, even saying the same words, are sending the same message. Their voices cause the messages to differ from each other. In live interaction, of course, many more nonverbal messages are present. Nonverbal communication is not nonsense; in fact, nonverbal behavior affects all oral communication situations.

2. *Nonverbal behavior accounts for most of the communication in human interaction.* This myth is an overreaction to the falsity of the first myth. Early research into nonverbal communication, conducted in both laboratory and field settings, indicated that a very large portion of the variability in meaning communicated is a function of nonverbal rather than verbal messages. Although this research conclusively showed the falsity of the traditional myth, it was overinterpreted by many later writers. Authors of articles and books have commonly quoted this early research to conclude that 65 to 95 percent of all meaning communicated is attributable to nonverbal elements. Indeed, such was found to be the case in the studies cited. What is typically ignored is that these studies were specifically designed to prove the first myth incorrect. The human interaction studied was not presumed to be typical of all interaction. Such generalizations about the impact of nonverbal behavior are completely unjustified. Although nonverbal elements dominate communication in many circumstances, in some others nonverbal elements have far fewer significant effects. Both verbal and nonverbal elements are very important in most human interaction, and the meaning communicated usually depends on the interaction of the two, not on either element alone.

3. *You can read a person like a book.* Besides being the title of a popular book, this myth is held by many individuals who have never studied nonverbal communication. When we meet new people who learn that we have written a book on this topic, a common reaction is the concern that we probably can "read" their behavior. They needn't fear; we can't, and neither can anyone else. Human behavior is not structured like a language. It is highly variable and idiosyncratic to an individual. Although there are identifiable patterns, these are not nearly strong enough to tell us what a given nonverbal behavior means in all situations. Often nonverbal behavior cannot be translated to verbal definitions with any great degree of confidence. When a baby smiles, it may be that the baby is happy; it may also be that the baby has gas. When an adult smiles, it may be that the person is pleased; it may also be that the person is concealing anger or hatred. Read at your own risk!

4. *If a person does not look you in the eye while talking to you, he or she is not telling you the truth.* This myth is a variant of the previous myth and represents a whole range of myths about nonverbal behavior that we learned as children. Many of our nonverbal behaviors are subject to our control. Where we look is one of those behaviors. Because we learn that people think we are not telling the truth if we don't look them in the eye, we learn to look at them whether we are telling the truth or not! Some research shows that liars are more likely to look someone in the eye than to look away.

5. *Although nonverbal behavior differs from person to person, most nonverbal behaviors are natural to all people.* This myth is one that not everyone accepts when it is verbalized, but one that almost all of us behave as if we believe. We assume that the way we behave nonverbally is "normal" and that any substantial deviation from that pattern is not normal. This tendency is particularly problematic when we encounter people from another culture; people from different cultures learn very different nonverbal behaviors, and all perceive their own as "normal." There are also meaningful differences between males and females, between older people and younger people, and among people from various ethnic groups. Many stereotypes stem directly from adherence to the myth that our own nonverbal behavior patterns are normal and should be the norm for everyone.

6. *Nonverbal behavior stimulates the same meanings in different situations.* This myth assumes that nonverbal behaviors are meaningful in themselves. In other words, a handshake or a nose wrinkle means the same things in different contexts. Obviously, this is untrue. The meanings attributed to nonverbal behavior by others are always influenced by the context in which the behavior occurs. Nonverbal communication is contextual. We should never attempt to draw inferences based solely on nonverbal information without considering the entire verbal and nonverbal context. The meaning of any nonverbal behavior should be interpreted only in the context in which behavior takes place. Context must always be considered when attempting to explain communication based upon nonverbal behavior.

NONVERBAL VS. VERBAL MESSAGES

Throughout the almost 5,000 years of recorded history relating to the study of human communication, research and teaching about communication has been centered on verbal messages. Not until the eighteenth century did communication scholars begin to extend serious attention to the role of nonverbal behavior. By the mid-twentieth century, the study of nonverbal behavior and communication became the focus of intense interest in many scholarly disciplines, from anthropology to speech and from architecture to psychology. A tough issue facing nonverbal scholars has been drawing meaningful and clear distinctions between what is verbal and what is nonverbal. Such clear distinctions have been elusive. Although we are unable to provide an absolute distinction between verbal and nonverbal messages, we can draw several less-than-perfect distinctions that will help you to see the differences.

The Linguistic Distinction

Verbal messages clearly depend upon language, but nonverbal messages do not necessarily depend on the presence of any language. This has led some people to suggest that nonverbal communication is simply communication without words. Of course, much (if not most) nonverbal behavior exists in the presence of spoken words, so this distinction oversimplifies the matter. Nevertheless, the distinction is relevant. Verbal messages depend on language, and language is an arbitrary system of coding meaning so that it may be shared by people who share a common language. Most nonverbal behavior is not part of an arbitrary coding system. *Emblems* (a type of gesture we consider in Chapter 3) are an exception to this general rule. Similarly, some languages depend solely on nonverbal behavior and these languages are also arbitrary systems of coding meaning. Some examples are American sign language (the gestural language of the hearing impaired), drum languages in parts of Africa, smoke languages of American Indian tribes, the whistling language of the Canary Islands, semaphore (flag language), and the Morse code for telegraphic communication. Although there are many exceptions, it is still useful to realize that most verbal messages rely on a language whereas most nonverbal messages do not.

The Continuity Distinction

Verbal messages are discontinuous. That is, we say some words, then we stop saying words, then we say some more, and so on. Nonverbal messages are continuous. Nonverbal behavior never stops. Even when we are asleep, our bodies continue to emit nonverbal messages. The absence of behavior sends a message just as much as the presence, if not more so. (Have you ever received the "silent treatment?") This fact has led us to the grammatically imperfect but thought-provoking comment that when you are in the presence of another human being, you cannot not communicate.

Although the continuity distinction has fewer exceptions than the linguistic distinction, it is also less than perfect. Nonverbal messages may be considered continuous only if we take them as a whole. Individual nonverbal messages indeed do stop. Gestures begin and end. Eye contact begins and ends. Vocal tones begin and end. Touch begins and ends. Smiles begin and end. However, it is best to think of nonverbal behavior as a package of simultaneous messages rather than the discrete messages of gesture, voice, touch, and so on. In this sense, the continuity distinction is an important, if not fully accurate, one.

The Processing Distinction

In recent years, much has been made of the way the human brain processes incoming information. Early research in the United States provided strong evidence that most people process verbal stimuli on the left side of the brain while processing nonverbal stimuli on the right side of the brain. This suggests that verbal and nonverbal communication are really two separate and distinct communication systems. Subsequent research, however, has cast considerable doubt on this distinction. Humans are not all alike. People in some cultures, notably in Finland and Japan, process information in the sides of the brain opposite to those in the United States. Similarly, even within the United States, left-handed people do not consistently follow the pattern of right-handed ones. Some do, and others are more like the Finns and Japanese.

This distinction has not led to the insights researchers had hoped for. It is quite possible that as neurophysiological research advances, we will find an important distinction in this area. However, now the distinction is not very useful.

Like other writers in the area of nonverbal communication, we find ourselves unable to make an absolute distinction between verbal and nonverbal messages. We appreciate the feeling of a member of the U.S. Supreme Court when he found himself unable to define pornography. He begged off by saying, "I know it when I see it." We believe we know what nonverbal messages are when we see them. We hope that by examining the various categories of nonverbal behavior in Chapters 2 through 10, you can do so as well.

INTENTIONALITY AND NONVERBAL COMMUNICATION

We have used the terms *nonverbal behavior* and *nonverbal communication,* but we have not distinguished between them. It is important that we do so. Nonverbal behavior is any of a wide variety of behaviors in which humans can engage that also have the potential for forming communicative messages. Such nonverbal behavior becomes nonverbal communication if another person interprets the behavior as a message and attributes meaning to it. We can engage in nonverbal behavior whether we are alone or someone else is present. We can engage in nonverbal communication only in the presence of one or more others who interpret our behavior as messages and assign meaning to them. At a very mundane level, we can engage in the nonverbal behavior of scratching ourselves when we are alone. If we do so in the presence of another person and that person interprets our scratching as a message and interprets it as showing that we are nervous, for example, we have engaged in nonverbal communication.

For human communication to exist, whether verbal or nonverbal, a source must send a message and a receiver must receive and interpret that message. Sometimes we send messages intentionally, and sometimes we send them accidentally. Sometimes receivers perceive our verbal and nonverbal behavior as messages and sometimes they do not. Figure 1–1 illustrates these distinctions.

In the first box in Figure 1–1, the source engages in nonverbal behavior with the intention of sending a message and the receiver interprets the behavior as a message. When this occurs, nonverbal communication occurs. This does not mean that the receiver has interpreted the message the way the source intended, but communication has occurred whether the intended meaning was stimulated. In box 2 in Figure 1–1, the source has sent an intentional message, but the receiver did not interpret it as a message. Therefore, no nonverbal communication has occurred. This can happen when the receiver simply misses the message (is looking the other way, for example) or does not recognize the behavior as a message. The latter may be illustrated by the case of one spouse kicking the other spouse under the table to signal that it is time to leave, but the one kicked simply thinks it was accidental behavior and ignores it.

Box 3 in Figure 1–1 represents accidental communication. This is probably the most common type of nonverbal communication. People behave and others attribute meaning to the behavior without the source even being aware of it. Often people do things without considering their message potential for others. For example, a person may arrive a few minutes late for a meeting and think nothing of it. Other people in the meeting, however, may interpret this nonverbal behavior as showing lack of respect for them or a lack of interest in the topic of the meeting.

Box 4 in Figure 1–1 represents unintentional behavior that does not result in communication. The source behaves but the receiver pays no attention to the behavior. Unfortunately, people who have not studied nonverbal communication tend to overestimate the proportion that falls in this category. They often are insensitive to the accidental messages that they are sending and how receivers are responding to them. Much of box 3 is thought to be in box 4. Such a lack of understanding of the communicative potential of nonverbal behavior is what this book is designed to reduce.

CULTURE AND NONVERBAL COMMUNICATION

As we note throughout this book, and stress in detail in Chapter 15, the communicative potential of nonverbal behavior is heavily influenced by culture. We learn to behave in certain ways through our exposure to our culture. Similarly, our culture teaches us how to interpret the messages generated by other people's nonverbal behavior. Unfortunately, every culture has its own unique way of communicating nonverbally. Thus, a nonverbal behavior in one culture may send a strong message in that culture, but have little or no message potential in another culture. Similarly, the meanings of nonverbal messages may differ sharply from one culture to another; sometimes, virtually opposite meanings may be stimulated by the same behavior in two different cultures.

This book is written principally from the vantage point of the general U.S. culture. We do not apologize for this ethnocentric approach. To understand the relationship between nonverbal behavior and nonverbal communication, one must work within some cultural framework because little if any nonverbal behavior has pancultural communicative impact. Once one develops an understanding of nonverbal communication in one culture, one is ready to learn about nonverbal communication

		Source	
		Behaves to Send Message	**Behaves with No Intent to Send Message**
R e c e i	**Interprets Behavior as Message**	1 Nonverbal Communication	3 Nonverbal Communication
v e r	**Does Not Interpret Behavior as Message**	2 Nonverbal Behavior	4 Nonverbal Behavior

FIGURE 1–1   **Nonverbal Behavior and Nonverbal Communication**

in other cultures. Without such an understanding of nonverbal communication in one's own and another culture, extensive accidental communication is highly probable when communicating with people in another culture.

FUNCTIONS OF NONVERBAL MESSAGES

Nonverbal communication does not occur in a void. In most circumstances, nonverbal communication occurs jointly with verbal communication. Moreover, although single nonverbal behaviors can send independent messages, more typically nonverbal messages are composed of groups of nonverbal behaviors. Receivers may interpret the various messages independently, but usually they are interpreted together as a message system. Sometimes we draw most of the meaning from the verbal messages, sometimes we draw most from the nonverbal messages, and sometimes the meaning we draw comes from the combined impact of both verbal and nonverbal messages. Whether verbal or nonverbal messages are dominant, or neither is, depends on the situation. As we noted earlier, it is not possible to draw a valid

Verbal messages can communicate only when source and receiver share the same code.

generalization across all situations about the relative importance of verbal and nonverbal messages.

It is useful, therefore, to examine the functions of nonverbal messages in relation to verbal messages in communication. Such an examination will help us to see how verbal and nonverbal messages often are highly interrelated. These six functions are complementing, contradicting, repeating, regulating, substituting, and accenting.

Complementing.   Some nonverbal messages are consistent with accompanying verbal messages but add to, reinforce, clarify, or explain the meaning of the verbal message. Consider, for example, two lovers. One says to the other, "I love you." These words alone will probably be well-received by the other person. However, if the words are sent in a pleasant voice while the two people are seated closely together and accompanied by a warm embrace, the message is even stronger. In another vein, consider the person who says "I'll make your life miserable." Such a remark might upset us a bit, but it would be much more upsetting if the person who says it is standing before us, speaking in a loud voice, and waving an incriminating illicit love note!

Contradicting.   Instead of complementing the verbal message, some nonverbal messages contradict, dispute, conflict with, or counter the verbal. Consider, for example, the student who has just been reprimanded by a teacher. The teacher says, "Tell me you're going to behave." The student says the words, "Sure, I'm going to behave," but does so with an extreme pout or sneer and a whine while looking at her or his desk. Would you believe that student will behave for five minutes when the teacher isn't watching? Most people would not. People tend overwhelmingly to believe the nonverbal rather than the verbal message when the two are contradictory. The exceptions to this are younger children. By about age twelve, children learn most adult nonverbal norms and accept the nonverbal over the verbal message when they are in conflict. Usually, younger children have not learned this norm. If a parent whose child walked onto a clean carpet with muddy feet says, "That was really smart, Johnny," the child may take his parent at his or her word.

The latter illustration is an example of sarcasm. People often use sarcasm to make a point. Inherent in the use of sarcasm is the presentation of nonverbal messages that conflict with verbal messages. One must make sure that the nonverbal message clearly contradicts the verbal message if one wants the sarcasm to be understood. Even mature adults sometimes fail to sense the contradiction and sarcasm is lost on them. This, of course, is even more common in communication with young children.

Repeating.   A nonverbal message that serves the function of repeating, reiterating, or restating the verbal is one that could stand alone if the verbal were not present. Such messages usually are emblems and are discussed further in Chapter 3. As an example, however, consider the case where you are ordering two tacos at a fast food restaurant. You are likely to say you want two tacos and simultaneously hold up two fingers. The nonverbal repeats the verbal and vice versa.

Regulating.   Verbal interactions are coordinated through regulation. Such regulation and management are accomplished primarily through nonverbal messages. These messages include looking at or away from the other person, raising a finger while pausing to show that you are not finished, raising or lowering the inflection of the voice, and so on. For example, when we wish to signal that it is the other person's turn to talk, we finish our current statement with a lowered inflection, look directly at the other person, and stop gesturing. Such nonverbal behavior regulates or manages the flow of verbal messages.

Substituting.   Substitution occurs when nonverbal messages are sent instead of or in place of verbal messages. Waving at or beckoning another person are common examples. Glaring at another person may communicate the same thing as saying something negative. Often we let people know that we are angry with them by not sending them any verbal messages. Our nonverbal message of absence from their presence can express the same meaning, and it doesn't give them a chance to talk back!

Nonverbal communication can be used to substitute
for the verbal and still relay the same meaning.

Accenting.   Nonverbal messages can be used to accent, emphasize, or highlight a
verbal message. Pausing before saying something tends to make what is said next
appear more important. Saying something louder than usual also highlights the verbal message. Similarly, touching someone while talking emphasizes what is said. In
contrast, we can negatively accent a verbal message by presenting it unenthusiasti-
cally. When messages are presented in such a way, people tend to think of them as
unimportant and quickly forget them. You can probably think of a teacher you have
had who treated some material being taught this way. Would you remember it for
the test?

As you may have surmised by this point, these functions do not always occur
independently. It is quite possible for complementing, repeating, and accenting to
occur virtually simultaneously. This is an important point. Nonverbal messages can
serve to accomplish a variety of functions. Sometimes these functions can be
accomplished with a single nonverbal behavior, but more commonly a pattern of
behavior is used to accomplish a given function. Sometimes more than one function
is accomplished simultaneously. Sometimes verbal communication is involved.
Sometimes it is not. In short, although verbal messages can sometimes stand
virtually alone, as can individual nonverbal messages, more commonly there is

interaction between nonverbal behavior and verbal behavior to produce meaning in the minds of others.

For the most part, verbal messages serve primarily a content function whereas nonverbal messages serve primarily a relational function. The cognitive content of what we are sending to others usually is sent primarily via verbal messages. The affective, or emotional, meaning is sent primarily via nonverbal messages. This relational, or affective, meaning often is called *immediacy,* by which is meant a feeling of physical or psychological closeness to another person. Although verbal messages can have an impact on immediacy, nonverbal messages usually have a much greater impact. We consider immediacy in greater detail in Chapter 11.

CATEGORIES OF NONVERBAL MESSAGES

Individual nonverbal behavior serves as a communicative message only within contexts and often in the company of many other nonverbal behaviors and verbal messages. Communication is a process that involves a variety of messages within a given context. It is a dynamic, ongoing, interactive process, not a linear one. If you turn the light switch on, the light comes on. If you step on the brake, the car slows. If you press a word processor keyboard, a function takes place. These are linear processes.

Communication is not like these linear processes. No verbal or nonverbal behavior always produces the same outcome. Messages are processed by receivers within contexts. Therefore, it is rare that different receivers in different contexts interpret the same messages in the same way.

It is important to keep this in mind while reading the next nine chapters. We will break nonverbal behavior down into several categories and examine each category in some detail. Messages generated by each category do not exist in isolation but exist in the company of messages from other categories, verbal messages, contexts, and people functioning as message receivers. Although we discuss some effects of messages in each category, you must remember that these effects are influenced by more than the message from the given category alone. After we have broken down the forest of nonverbal behavior into its constituent trees we devote the final chapters in the book to viewing these parts in broader contexts. We hope that this structure helps you to understand how the individual parts work together to produce the total effect.

At this point, we need to outline the various categories of nonverbal messages that are considered in detail in the following chapters. Each category is listed and briefly explained below.

Physical Appearance

The first message we send to anyone with whom we come in contact is conveyed by our physical appearance. If that message is deplored by the other person, he or she may not even consider further communication. There are many aspects of physical appearance that produce potential messages—body size, body shape, facial features, the clothing and other objects we wear. Each of these can have an important impact on our communication with others.

Gesture and Movement

The study of the communicative aspects of gesture and bodily movement is known as *kinesics*. This research focuses on the movements of hands and arms, posture, and bodily movements (such as walking). Messages generated by this type of behavior have often been called *body language,* but this term is a misnomer. Although the body is sending messages, such messages do not form a linguistic system (except the gestural language of the hearing impaired) and thus do not represent a language in any formal sense of that term. Viewing all bodily movements and gestures as if they constitute a language may lead one to exaggerate the importance of a given behavior.

Face and Eye Behavior

The study of the communicative aspects of eye behavior is known as *oculesics*. Because it is virtually impossible to separate the messages sent by the eyes and those sent by the face, we prefer to consider these together. These messages have a major influence on expressing emotions and regulating interactions between people.

Vocal Behavior

The study of the communicative aspects of the voice has been variously known as *vocalics* or the study of *paralanguage*. Characteristics of the voice and its use, including the accent with which we speak, have a major impact on how verbal messages are received. Some researchers argue that more of the meaning in interpersonal communication is stimulated by vocalic messages than the verbal messages themselves. This is often true.

Space

The study of the communicative aspects of space is known as *proxemics*. There are two important areas in this research—territoriality and use of personal space. Each has an important bearing on the kinds of messages we send as we use and exist in space. There is reason to believe that our basic approach to space is, at least in part, instinctual. Nevertheless, humans differ greatly in their use of space and, as a result, send very different nonverbal messages.

Touch

The study of the communicative aspects of touch is known as *haptics*. Touch has been called the most potent message in human communication. Although this may not be universally true, it is very true in the general United States, where touch is so uncommon. Touch, in this culture at least, does indeed send a potent message, one that can rarely be ignored.

Environment

Researchers in many disciplines have examined the impact of environment on human behavior and its impact on communication specifically. Because this is not human behavior per se, it may seem strange to include this category in a book such as this. However, because environment can have a major influence on communication and we can exert considerable control over our environment through our behavior, we have chosen to include it. We look at such things as architecture, spatial arrangements, music, lighting, color, and temperature and how these can be used to send nonverbal messages.

Scent and Smell

The limited research involving the study of the communicative aspects of scent and smell has been called *olfactics*. If beauty is in the eye of the beholder, then scent is in the nose of the sniffer. People react very differently to scents and smells. Often we can send important nonverbal messages through our use of scents and smells. U.S. society shows its concern with this nonverbal category by the millions of dollars it spends annually on deodorants and perfumes.

Time

The study of the communicative aspects of time is called *chronemics*. Few cultures are as dependent upon time as the general U.S. culture. Our use of time sends strong messages about how we feel about ideas and people. Because people in this culture are so time-bound, they fail to realize what their response to time communicates to others. It has been said that time talks. "Time shouts" might be a more accurate statement.

These, then, are the trees that make up our nonverbal forest. In the following nine chapters, we examine each in considerable detail.

A GLOSSARY OF TERMINOLOGY

Accenting is the use of nonverbal messages to accent, emphasize, or highlight the verbal message.

Accidental communication occurs when people behave and others attribute meaning to the behavior without the behaver intending it.

Chronemics is the study of the communicative aspects of time.

Complementing is the use of nonverbal messages that are consistent with, reinforce, clarify, or add to the meaning of the verbal message.

Contradicting is the use of a nonverbal message that contradicts or conflicts with the verbal message.

Haptics is the study of the communicative aspects of touch.

Human communication is the process of stimulating meaning in the mind of another person or persons by means of verbal or nonverbal messages.

Kinesics is the study of the communicative aspects of gestures and bodily movements.

Nonverbal behavior is any of a wide variety of human behavior that also has the potential for forming communicative messages.

Nonverbal communication is the process of stimulating meaning in the mind of another person or persons by means of nonverbal messages.

Oculesics is the study of the eye behavior.

Olfactics is the study of the communicative aspects of scent and smell.

Proxemics is the study of the communicative aspects of space and territoriality.

Regulating is the use of nonverbal messages to coordinate, manage, or regulate verbal interactions.

Repeating is the use of a nonverbal message that repeats the verbal message but can also stand alone and still have the same meaning as the verbal message.

Substituting is the use of nonverbal messages in place of verbal messages.

Vocalics or **paralanguage** is the study of the communicative aspects of the voice.

▲ 2

Physical Appearance

Randy felt confident as he began his first day at college. He knew how to size people up. You can tell a person by what they wear, what they look like, he thought. As Randy strolled across campus, he spotted a young woman with a black leather jacket, bright white, cropped hair, dark stockings under her very tight jeans, and red high-heeled shoes. Wow! She's a loose one. Crossing College Avenue and ascending the steps to the student union, he saw "Mr. Jock" wearing a football jersey with the number 34 on the back, expensive Nike shoes, and a pair of Guess jeans. He's a dumb jock, thought Randy. A running back in high school; probably knows lots of young women. It may be to my benefit to get acquainted with him!

At 9:57 A.M., Randy arrived at 110 Jones Hall for his first class. In the center of the front row, he noticed a young man, obviously a senior, wearing a pair of "lawyer glasses," dress slacks, a button-down shirt, a tie, a V-neck sweater, and well-polished oxblood loafers. Although shorter than the average man and a bit frail looking, this young man seemed more than likely quite intelligent. Randy figured him to be shy and withdrawn. He could be an economics or accounting major, maybe engineering. At any rate, he would make a good partner if the professor assigned any group projects. Randy took a seat near the door next to an attractive, amicable woman. She appeared to be friendly and sociable, but Randy felt a little uncomfortable about the thought of introducing himself. She might tell him to get lost; she probably gets tired of men hitting on her.

At 10:00 the professor walked in hastily and placed her briefcase on the lectern. So, this is Dr. Hanson. Randy felt his stomach churn. She's not

Skin color needn't hinder positive communication.

going to be a pushover. The briefcase was scuffed and old, her grayish black hair was long enough to be arranged in a bun on top of her head. Dr. Hanson wore a drab green wool blazer and a long tan skirt. Reading glasses, those small black-rimmed half glasses, rested on her nose. Her dark piercing eyes were set in deep sockets under thick, bushy brows. Randy quickly resigned himself to the fact that he would have to work for a good grade; she was going to be strict, inflexible, and perhaps without a sense of humor, just like his high school English teacher, Mrs. Pierce.

Have we exaggerated the importance of physical appearance in our account? Like Randy, many of us develop expectations about people we meet based upon the way they look, what they wear, whether we think they are attractive, and what objects they use to adorn their bodies. It may seem to you that Randy jumped too hastily to conclusions about people he had seen only once. He has determined that individuals possess certain characteristics and behave in particular ways, and his only source of information was the way they looked. Furthermore, he has begun to establish the foundations for his interactions with these people.

Nonverbal messages based on physical appearance may be as important as any nonverbal messages we receive from other people. These messages are generally the first received and initially have a strong influence on the relationships developed. In this chapter, we discuss the significance of physical appearance as it influences our perceptions of attractiveness, our perceptions of others based upon the size and shape of their bodies, and the way we react to clothing and artifacts individuals use.

ATTRACTIVENESS

When someone says that someone is attractive, what do they really mean? Do people possess something called attractiveness? Is it a characteristic of certain individuals? We prefer to think of attractiveness as perception. Granted, such perceptions are based on the physical attributes of the people we are considering. Nevertheless, attractiveness is something we perceive in someone else; it doesn't exist on its own. Beauty or non-beauty is in the eye of the beholder.

Types of Attractiveness

In general terms, *attractiveness* is the degree to which we perceive another person as someone with whom we would want to associate. From this perspective, three different types of attractiveness may be identified. The first type, the one with which we are primarily concerned here, is *physical attractiveness*. This type of attractiveness is an assessment of a person's physical attributes. Although writers in nonverbal communication have been hard-pressed to formulate a specific definition of physical attractiveness, clearly this type of attractiveness plays a very important role in determining our interactions with others, particularly with strangers. Research has shown, for instance, that we usually prefer to converse with strangers we perceive to be good looking, pretty, or handsome. People often attempt to avoid contact with those whom they find physically unattractive.

The second type of attractiveness is *social attractiveness*. Social attractiveness is the degree to which we perceive another person as someone with whom we would like to socialize. The final type of attractiveness is *task attractiveness*. This is the degree to which we perceive another person as someone with whom we would like to work. Although perceptions of physical attractiveness are distinct from perceptions of social and task attractiveness, this does not mean these are totally unrelated perceptions. Often, particularly during initial encounters, we perceive another person as physically appealing and then see him or her as socially or task attractive as well. On the other hand, we tend to judge unattractive persons as less sociable and less desirable to work with. Although these are initial impressions, they often affect future interactions with new acquaintances and decisions regarding future communication. Perceptions of social and task attractiveness may change over time. These changes may occur despite the physical attraction. However, in a newly formed relationship, physical attractiveness may determine one's level of task or social attraction for another.

What Is Attractive Today May Be Out Tomorrow

Who or what we consider attractive is highly dependent on cultural and historical influences and current trends. In North American culture, recent trends for women suggest that the well-toned, athletic look is in; just a few years ago, the super-thin look was in, and earlier generations found the plump look more appealing.

Joya Patterson (1993) holds seminars on buying guidelines for purchasing the correct bra. She suggests that 85 percent of women wear the wrong bra. Her seminars focus on figuring out your body size and cup size, trying on the bra, and studying it. Now one might ask, why are the above relevant? The answer is simple—many American women want comfort as well as a fit that enhances their appearance.

Hair styles for men and women have changed considerably and, we suspect, will continue to do so as people's ideas of physical attractiveness evolve. Fair skin was once not only a mark of beauty, but a significant sign of social status as well. Only wealthy women had enough money not to have to go out into the sun and work. More recently, however, tanned skin has become a sign that the individual can afford the leisure time to sunbathe and, sometimes, the cost of traveling to where it is warm enough to do so. Even more recently, for health-conscious individuals at least, fair skin has become attractive again. The concern about skin cancer caused by exposure to the sun has influenced the perception of what is attractive.

During the 1920s, American women went to great lengths to make their chests appear flat and their hips small. In more recent times, padded bras and breast implants have been used to enhance these features. In the 1990s, American men are having chest implants to make their chests appear more "manly" and strong. What is in today may be out tomorrow.

What is physically attractive is not just a function of time; it also depends on culture. In one culture, men look with great pleasure at women whose necks have been stretched to twelve inches since birth and whose noses or lips are pierced with wooden jewelry. The Chinese once believed that small feet on women were a sign of fertility. Therefore, Chinese females from infancy would have their feet bound tightly to thwart growth. Although such binding is no longer common and fertility is not even in for many Chinese people, small feet are still seen as attractive by many Chinese. In a few African cultures, people bind their heads to flatten them, stretch their lips with wooden plates, and scar their bodies in various places to make them more appealing. In their book on nonverbal communication, Malandro, Barker, and Barker (1989) described the phenomenon most appropriately by suggesting that "the human body has been twisted, pulled, and pushed into a myriad of shapes for the sake of beauty and in order to be perceived as a visual symbol of group identification" (p. 28).

Although it would be easy to laugh at these behaviors in other cultures and muse about the lack of sophistication of such people, we must take care, for the last laugh may be on us. Such manipulation of the body is common in U.S. culture. Breast implants, face lifts and other forms of plastic surgery, hair implants, contact lenses, capped teeth, braces, tattoos, high-heeled pumps, girdles, padded bras, shaved legs and faces, and tight jeans are all examples of ways North Americans have penalized their bodies and endured unnecessary pain for the sake of making themselves more appealing, well-liked, sociable, and acceptable—in short, more physically attractive to their fellow human beings. Our phobia against unshaven underarms on women causes howls of laughter from people in most other parts of the world. Never let us forget our culture's addiction to diets, diets, and more diets, or the "healthy lifestyle," as it is commonly known today. If the diets and so-called healthy life changes do not work, there's always liposuction! In the last decade, liposuction has become the most popular plastic surgery for both men and women. We call ourselves civilized! Why then is attractiveness so important? Why do we go to such extreme lengths to be perceived as attractive?

It may be true that beauty is only skin deep. It may also be that often all we are interested in is the skin; we get involved in appearance and give it too much attention. However, a very important question we should consider is this: Why do humans go to so much trouble, endure such discomfort, and spend so much time, money, and energy to make themselves more physically attractive? The answer lies in the nonverbal messages our appearance communicates to others. Others use our appearance as an important source of information about us. They attribute to us certain characteristics, predict our social behavior, and make judgments about our success, failure, competence, and character in our business and professional lives. Think for a moment about your own reactions. When you see someone who is physically attractive, do you automatically make certain judgments about that person? In a class focusing on nonverbal communication, one young man responded anonymously to this question in this way:

> *I tend to judge a book by its cover and a person by his or her looks. When I see somebody who is unattractive I tend to lose interest in wanting to meet them. Sometimes I even try to avoid them. In brief, it seems like these men and women don't care much about what other people think about them. Unattractive people also tend to be sloppy. I wonder sometimes how they think they are going to get by in this world. I know they can't help the way they look, but they could stay at home.*

A female student in the same class in response to the same question made the following observations:

> *The way a person looks says a lot about them. I find myself being more interested in people (especially men) I think are attractive. They seem more sure of themselves and confident. They don't get as nervous around other people because they don't have to be self-conscious about their looks. Since they have more experience around lots of other people, they probably know more about how to act at parties. They're cool!*

Although these are responses selected to represent extreme views, they represent the views many of us hold. Most of us are guilty of judging books by their covers. Research in this area also suggests that we make evaluations based upon a person's attractiveness. People who are rated as more attractive are often judged to be more socially desirable in many ways. One study found that beautiful people are evaluated as more successful in their careers, more sexually active, happier about their life situations, and even better at persuading others. Sometimes we go as far as to perceive them as holding more prestigious jobs, having more friends, and having better marriages.

Attractiveness: A Double-Edged Sword?

It should be no surprise to you that many of us also assume that attractive women are frequently being asked for dates and attractive men seldom have trouble finding women to accompany them to movies, parties, and other social functions. Although sometimes these perceptions are true, sometimes they are not. Studies of extremely attractive males and females show that they are often lonely and rejected by members of the opposite sex. They are seen as too attractive, or as one person put it, "too good to be true." Clearly, many of our perceptions of others based upon their physical attractiveness may prove to be correct. However, we sometimes completely misperceive the situation.

Perceptions of physical attractiveness are associated with many personality characteristics. One study asked subjects to rate attractive and unattractive persons on a variety of personality variables. The attractive people were judged as warmer, more genuine, sincere, mentally stable, sociable, and affable. It seems evident from this list that most of these perceptions are positive and desirable.

However, to the attractive person, life is not always a bed of roses. Many report having to overcome negative judgments of others. An extremely attractive male graduate student (dimples and all) once complained, "I am constantly accused of getting by only on my looks. Some people assume I'm lazy and conceited and automatically don't like me." A young woman with a Ph.D. complained, "No one would believe I could look like I do and be competent. I had to wear my hair up, put on glasses and not wear makeup, and wear some suit two sizes too large to get someone to listen to me in an interview. When I showed up for work looking like I normally do, some of my colleagues assumed I must have slept with the boss to get the job! To this day, none of my married female colleagues have invited me to their homes. I guess they think I'll steal their husbands." Whether attractive or unattractive, we sometimes find ourselves stereotyped in ways that significantly influence our interactions with others.

Another major issue related to attractiveness involves interaction behavior itself. We have seen from the preceding discussion how attractiveness affects perceptions. Now let us consider the effects of attractiveness on interaction in different contexts.

Effects of Attractiveness

In the educational environment, scholars have found some very interesting relationships between physical attractiveness and student–teacher interaction. Attractive students have been found to receive higher grades than their less attractive counterparts. Observations in classrooms show that teachers engage in less interaction with unattractive students and initiate more communication and respond to comments from their more attractive students more readily. Not only do we see such behavior from teachers, but classmates are also less likely to communicate with the less attractive classmates. The physically unattractive student begins to experience in early grades the importance our culture places on good looks. Others have reported that even misbehavior in the classroom is interpreted differently depending on the child's attractiveness. Teachers generally perceive the unattractive child as having a chronic behavior problem whereas the attractive child is more likely to be judged to have a temporary problem. We should stress here that teachers usually do not engage in such behavior maliciously. They, like others, are not immune to the stereotypes and expectations we all have of others' physical appearance. This does not, however, negate the significance of the impact that teachers' actions and reactions have upon their students' success or failure.

We stated earlier that often physically attractive people are perceived as more persuasive. Research on attractiveness and persuasion has shown that attractive people have greater success at getting others to do what they want them to do. Attractive women, in particular, are better at changing the attitudes of males. Important work has shown that attractiveness even pays off in the American court system. Not only are attractive persons more likely to be found innocent of charges brought against them, but when they are found guilty, their chances are better of receiving lighter sentences. With these kinds of results, it is no mystery why most actors in television commercials are physically appealing people. Their job is to get you, the consumer, to buy their product. Sales training consultants place great importance on an attractive physical appearance. They realize the impact first impressions have on a potential customer's decision to purchase the goods.

An author was acquainted with a manager of a regional office of a life insurance company in a large city in California. At a luncheon engagement one day, this manager introduced the author to a young man the manager claimed was his best salesperson. The young sales agent had a striking appearance: blond, tanned, tall, and lean, with a most charming smile. His resemblance to a young Robert Redford was remarkable. Because the young man had been a life insurance salesman for only a short time, the author was curious about the salesman's quick success with a product that is usually quite difficult to sell. The agent's response was not surprising.

I sell only to women. When marketing individual policies, I either identify households run by single women or make sure the wife is present when I give my sales pitch to her husband. When selling group policies, I try to

find companies who have women in charge of such decisions. After that, my
job is easy.

This young sales agent was not arrogant or self-centered, but he did realize that
his best asset at guaranteeing success was his personal physical attractiveness to
women.

Before you jump to the conclusion that only women are susceptible to such
influences, be assured that males are equally susceptible. How else can we explain
the effectiveness of advertisements for male-oriented products that prominently display female models? Many, many beer ads feature very attractive and appealing
women. Why?

Physically attractive people seem to have an edge on other people when it
comes to interviewing for a job, although the comments of the attractive female
Ph.D. quoted above might suggest the opposite. In his recent book, *Molloy's Live for
Success* (1983), John Molloy refers to his own research that has shown there are
four types of people who have the big advantage during job interviews. The first
type he mentions is beautiful people. According to Molloy, "people who are good-
looking have a three to four times greater chance of being hired for almost any position, whether it is typing, sales, or management" (p. 69). Molloy would be the first
to agree that looks alone do not guarantee you a job, but when all else is considered,
it generally helps. Whether in business or social contexts, we seem to want to be surrounded by the beautiful people. Some nonverbal scholars have even suggested that
one important consideration for executives when making choices of a secretary
involves her (and sometimes today, his) potential to decorate the office environment
with her or his appearance.

Our perceptions of physical attractiveness no doubt have an important influence
on our dating and marriage decisions as well. In a very early study, Baber (1939)
asked his subjects whether they would marry a person they would rank low on one
of several qualities. The results showed that men would more likely reject women
who were not good-looking, but women did not seem quite as concerned about the
physical appearance of potential marriage partners. Because this study was conducted more than fifty years ago, it may be that things have changed. In contemporary culture, it is much more acceptable for women to talk about the physical
attractiveness of men than it was in the pre–World War II era. Another interesting
finding in the research literature is that men are reported to want wives who are
more attractive than they perceive themselves to be, whereas women would rather
marry men who are similar to them in attractiveness.

Because such general preferences would lead to constant conflicts if everyone
shared the same standards of judgment for physical attractiveness, we are left to
speculate about the importance of self-esteem in such decisions. We should stress
that in dating and marriage decisions, physical attractiveness is not always the num-
ber-one priority. However, sometimes it is. Studies have shown that, within the context of a blind date between college students, the person's physical attractiveness

was the primary predictor of whether a person said they liked their date. Subsequent research revealed that perceptions of a date's attractiveness also predicted whether the subjects would want to ask the person out again. We suspect that physical attractiveness continues to be a dominant predictor for the first few dates, but as the relationship develops, it gradually begins to take a back seat to other considerations. Of course, if the attractiveness is not there in the first place, the relationship may not continue long enough for those other considerations to come into play.

In summary, physical attractiveness has a substantial impact upon our communication with our fellow human beings. These powerful nonverbal messages influence our decisions about approaching or avoiding others, dating or not dating, marrying or not marrying, hiring or not hiring, and our expectations about the future success or failure of others. Let us now turn to a discussion of the particular aspects of physical appearance. Our perceptions of the physical attractiveness of others and of ourselves are determined by body shape and size, weight, height, hair and skin color, and the clothing we use to protect, adorn, conceal, and display our bodies.

PERSONAL BODY CONCEPT

Ask yourself these questions: What parts of bodies of others do I think are the most important? Are they the same as the ones I choose for myself in terms of my satisfaction with my own body? Is there any relationship between the two? It shouldn't surprise you that the body parts of others you find most important in judging attractiveness may also be the ones you are either extremely satisfied with or extremely dissatisfied with in yourself.

How you feel about your body has an impact on your self-concept as a whole. Your *personal body concept* is the perception you have of how attractive your body is and what you perceive to be the attributes of your body. The importance of the personal body concept to our discussion of nonverbal communication is twofold. First, the concept is developed because of our communication with others, and second, it influences our communication with others. Let us look at these reasons more closely.

The thoughts and feelings we have about our bodies did not simply materialize in our minds at some magic age. Personal body concept, whether positive or negative, develops gradually. The influencing factors involve our interactions with other people, particularly if those people are important to us. Significant others provide us with many verbal and nonverbal messages that communicate the feelings and attitudes they have about our bodies, and we eventually take their judgments as our own judgments of ourselves.

Research shows the significant impact peer and parental judgments have on children's personal body concepts. One study has shown that children with predominantly negative concepts about their own attractiveness and abilities received negative messages from their parents. Let us consider an illustration. Ten-year-old Jimmy was not an attractive child. He was quite plump and his nose was a bit large. Jimmy's parents were often self-conscious about his appearance while around their friends and acquaintances. One day, he overheard his mother lamenting to a neighbor, "I'm afraid Jimmy will never be very popular, the way he looks. He's not at all athletic looking, you know. I constantly worry that the other kids at school tease him about his weight. On top of that, his father makes me so angry sometimes when he calls him 'chubby cheeks' or says he has the four biggest cheeks on the block. I think he's embarrassed about his own son's appearance!"

Feelings of inadequacy are influenced by our communication, and they also affect future interactions. Jimmy's feelings about his body will eventually affect his communication behavior. He may choose to withdraw from or avoid associations with peers at school for fear that they will ridicule him. His feelings may influence his decisions about sports, leisure activities, friends, dating, and even his ultimate career choice.

In summary, satisfaction with our bodies is important to both our self-esteem and our interpersonal relationships. One does not have to be a "hunk" or a "fox" to be satisfied with his or her body's appearance and attributes. One rule does tend to hold true, however: The more satisfied people are with their bodies (regardless of their actual appearance) the better their chances of being happy about themselves. This, in turn, probably contributes to healthy interactions with others.

NONVERBAL MESSAGES OF BODY SHAPE AND SIZE

Whether you realize it or not, the general shape and size of your body communicates nonverbal messages. Figure 2–1 is a self-description test. Follow the instructions and work your way through the test. After you have done so, we will discuss its meaning to the body and nonverbal messages.

Many writers have shown that body shape and general temperament are closely related. William Sheldon is usually credited for originating this idea. Sheldon believed that there are three classifications of body types and worked to develop a method called *somatoyping* to categorize individuals into one of three major types. There has been considerable criticism of some of Sheldon's experimental methods, his original conceptualization of temperament, and some of his mathematical calculations, but others have taken Sheldon's work and improved on it, and many writers in nonverbal communication now feel there is merit to his work.

According to Sheldon, the first general body shape is called the *endomorphic* type. Persons who are endomorphs (endos) have rounded, oval-shaped bodies, are usually heavy (though not necessarily obese), and often are described as pear-shaped. The second type is the *mesomorph*. Mesomorphs (mesos) are characterized by a triangular body shape that is broad at the shoulders and tapers to the hips. Their shape is firm and muscular in appearance with all the curves and angles "in the

Purpose: To demonstrate how body type affects behavior and communication. Directions: Fill in each blank with a word from the suggested list following each statement. For any blank, three in each statement, you may select any word from the list of twelve immediately below. An exact word to fit you may not be in the list, but select words that seem to fit most closely the way you are.

1. I feel most of the time _____, _____, and _____.

calm	relaxed	complacent
anxious	confident	reticent
cheerful	tense	energetic
contented	impetuous	self-conscious

2. When I study or work, I seem to be _____, _____, and _____.

efficient	sluggish	precise
enthusiastic	competitive	determined
reflective	leisurely	thoughtful
placid	meticulous	cooperative

3. Socially, I am _____, _____, and _____.

outgoing	considerate	argumentative
affable	awkward	shy
tolerant	affected	talkative
gentle-tempered	soft-tempered	hot-tempered

4. I am rather _____, _____, and _____.

active	forgiving	sympathetic
warm	courageous	serious
domineering	suspicious	soft-hearted
introspective	cool	enterprising

5. Other people consider me rather _____, _____, and _____.

generous	optimistic	sensitive
adventurous	affectionate	kind
withdrawn	reckless	cautious
dominant	detached	dependent

6. Underline one word out of three in each of the following lines that most closely describes the way you are:
   (a) assertive, relaxed, tense
   (b) hot-tempered, cool, warm
   (c) withdrawn, sociable, active
   (d) confident, tactful, kind
   (e) dependent, dominant, detached
   (f) enterprising, affable, anxious

FIGURE 2–1 **Body Type Survey**

Source: Cortés, J. B., and Gatti, F. M. (1965), "Physique and Self-Description of Temperament," *Journal of Consulting Psychology* 29, 432–439. Copyright © 1965 by the American Psychological Association. Adapted by permission of the publisher and the author.

right places," at least for U.S. culture. They are frequently described as athletic in appearance. The third type is the *ectomorph*. Ectomorphs (ectos) are characterized as bony, thin, and tall, have a fragile-looking physique, a flat chest, and underdeveloped muscular tone. (See Figure 2–2.)

1 ENDOMORPHIC	2 MESOMORPHIC	3 ECTOMORPHIC
dependent	dominant	detached
calm	cheerful	tense
relaxed	confident	anxious
complacent	energetic	reticent
contented	impetuous	self-conscious
sluggish	efficient	meticulous
placid	enthusiastic	reflective
leisurely	competitive	precise
cooperative	determined	thoughtful
affable	outgoing	considerate
tolerant	argumentative	shy
affected	talkative	awkward
warm	active	cool
forgiving	domineering	suspicious
sympathetic	courageous	introspective
soft-hearted	enterprising	serious
generous	adventurous	cautious
affectionate	reckless	tactful
kind	assertive	sensitive
sociable	optimistic	withdrawn
soft-tempered	hot-tempered	gentle-tempered

Discussion:
1. Discuss how your body type affects your behavior.
2. Discuss how you communicate with others based on their body type.

FIGURE 2–2   **Body Type Self-Descriptors**

Source: Cortés, J. B., and Gatti, F. M. (1965), "Physique and Self-Description of Temperament," *Journal of Consulting Psychology* 29, 432–439. Copyright © 1965 by the American Psychological Association. Adapted by permission of the publisher and the author.

Can you think of anyone you know who fits into one of the three categories? What about yourself? Nell Carter, Delta Burke, John Goodman, Roseanne, and Charles Durning have endomorphic characteristics. Tom Selleck, Linda Evans, Jerry Seinfeld, Clint Eastwood, Denzell Washington, Harrison Ford, Sylvester Stallone, Mel Gibson, Michael Jordan, Ann-Margaret, and Candice Bergen are appropriate examples of the mesomorph. Joan Rivers, Pee Wee Herman, Don Knotts, and Bob Denver have obvious ectomorphic features.

Return to the self-description test in Figure 2–1. This inquiry has been used in several studies investigating the relationship between body type and temperament. Cortés and Gatti developed this instrument in the 1960s, and they found that the adjectives subjects chose to describe themselves were highly associated with their body types. In Figure 2–2, you will find three columns of the adjectives found on the self-description test. Place a check mark beside each adjective you chose earlier. After checking the adjectives, count the number of checks for each column and write the totals underneath. You should have three numbers. These numbers should add up to 21.

From these three numbers, you can now determine your general temperament or psychological type. Let us take you through a couple of examples. Heather checked 3 adjectives in the first column, 14 adjectives in the second column, and 4 in the third. Her overall temperament score is 3/14/4. Miles checked 11 adjectives in the first column, 5 in the second, and 5 in the third. His overall temperament score is 11/5/5.

According to Sheldon's theory, endomorphs have a corresponding psychological type called *viscerotonic*. The viscerotonic psychological type is characterized by the self-descriptors in Column 1 of Figure 2–2. In other words, endomorphs tend to characterize themselves as slow, sociable, submissive, forgiving, relaxed, and so on. Mesomorphs have a corresponding psychological type called *somatotonic*. The somatotonic type is described as dominant, confident, energetic, competitive, assertive, hot-tempered, enthusiastic, and optimistic. The ectomorphic type is associated with the *cerebrotonic* psychological type represented by adjectives such as tense, self-conscious, meticulous, precise, sensitive, awkward, and withdrawn.

Heather, having a temperament score of 3/14/4, would have a somatotonic psychological type and more than likely have mesomorphic physical features. By contrast, Miles' score of 11/5/5 would indicate that he has a viscerotonic psychological type and an endomorphic body.

It has been suggested that individuals' body shapes correspond with their own psychological descriptions of themselves. A major question is this: Do others perceive certain psychological characteristics in persons who are endomorphs, mesomorphs, and ectomorphs? According to one well-cited study using silhouette drawings, we do make psychological judgments of others based on body shape. We describe them in much the same way they describe themselves. In this study, the researchers showed 120 adults the silhouettes of the three body types and asked them to rate the drawing on several adjectives. The results showed that endomorphs were rated as older, shorter, more warm-hearted, more talkative, weaker, lazier, and more old-fashioned. The mesomorphs were perceived as taller, younger, stronger, more adventurous, more masculine, better looking, more mature in behavior, and more self-reliant. Finally, the ectomorphs were seen as more tense and nervous, more ambitious, thinner, younger, quieter, more inclined to be difficult, more suspicious of others, less masculine, and more stubborn.

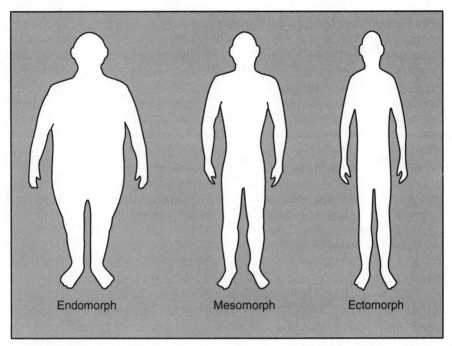

Sheldon's System

Body Type	Psychological Type
Endomorph (oval-shaped body; heavy, large abdomen)	**Viscerotonic** (slow, sociable, emotional, forgiving, relaxed)
Mesomorph (triangular body shape; muscular, hard, firm, upright body quality)	**Somatotonic** (confident, energetic, dominant, enterprising, hot-tempered)
Ectomorph (fragile physique; flatness of chest; poorly muscled limbs)	**Cerebrotonic** (tense, awkward, meticulous, tactful, detached)

FIGURE 2–3 **Sheldon's System and Body Types**

There is little doubt that our culture values the mesomorphic body more than the other two, although recent trends would show that ectomorphs are beginning to gain ground in positive social judgments. The mesomorph has many physical features we rate as physically attractive. As such, we often assume they are socially and task attractive as well. That is, we perceive them during initial encounters as more likely to be very sociable and desirable to work with. Although we tend to perceive endomorphs as socially attractive at the outset, we rarely indicate that they are physically attractive or task attractive. Ectomorphs are more likely to be seen as task attractive, particularly because we consider them meticulous, precise, and considerate. On the other hand, they are not generally perceived as socially attractive during initial interactions because we characterize them as detached and more inclined to be difficult.

Our discussion about the correspondence between body shape and temperament has important implications for our communication with others. The relationship between the two is not airtight. Nonetheless, the evidence would lead us to believe that social impressions based upon body type alone do exist, and these impressions are at least somewhat accurate. Moreover, the fact that any correspondence exists at all is more than likely a function of our interactions with others. We stereotype people by the size and shape of their bodies. We develop expectations about the personalities and behaviors of endomorphs, mesomorphs, and ectomorphs and then interact with them as if they possessed the very qualities we expect. As we suggested earlier, people develop their self-concepts largely by the way others respond to them. If we expect the oval-shaped endomorphs to be lazy and submissive, then we will communicate with them in a way that is consistent with those expectations. We are contributing to their self-concepts, and they often submit to the role we force on them. They accept others evaluations of them as their own evaluations.

NONVERBAL MESSAGES OF HEIGHT, WEIGHT, AND SKIN COLOR

Height

Taller is preferred, particularly where males are concerned. Our culture values tallness in men, and only slightly less in women. The military and law enforcement agencies have only recently begun to relax the height standards for their recruits. Surveys reveal that the overwhelming majority of male executives in the Fortune 500 companies are over six feet tall. Women want "tall, dark, and handsome" men. We tell our children to "stand tall." The taller of the two presidential candidates has won almost every election since the turn of the century.

What does height communicate? Height is often associated with power and dominance. Those persons with a height advantage can tower over others and may appear to be overpowering and dominating the other individual during conversations. It is not difficult to imagine the power and authority a tall supervisor communicates while reprimanding a short subordinate. Shorter men have reported that one major reason they refuse to date tall women is their fear that she may dominate the relationship. Taller individuals may have a general advantage in persuading others and influencing their behavior.

One study investigated the interpersonal impact of height from the point of view of the receiver. In this study, one person was introduced to five groups of students at different times. With each introduction, the person introduced was ascribed a different status (student, lecturer, doctor, full professor). The results revealed that the students distorted the height of the person introduced depending upon that individual's ascribed role. In short, the higher the ascribed status, the higher the students' judgments of height.

Weight

It is estimated that at any time, approximately 75 percent of women in the United States feel unhappy about their weight and want to be thinner. In addition, most of these women are either on some type of diet or have dieted in the past. The heavy, overweight woman is the most maligned individual in our culture. Heavy women are perceived to be slow, unattractive, and perhaps even lazy. Often they are not even viewed as "jolly," as overweight men often are. Furthermore, the range between the "ideal" weight and the weight at which one is perceived to be overweight is much smaller for women than for men. Therefore, most women in the United States spend a lifetime attempting to stay slim. It is no wonder that anorexia nervosa and bulimia are so common today. Generally, in this culture, when a woman's weight increases, her self-esteem decreases and the pressure is strong for that woman to lose weight.

This is not to suggest that men do not suffer from weight consciousness, too. They do. More than ever, men are enrolling in diet courses and workout programs to stay slim, virile, and young-looking. In this culture, slim and trim (despite gender) is associated with success, good self-concept, physical well-being, and acceptability. Overweight is associated with apathy, sluggishness, physical slowness, unattractiveness, and perhaps even mental slowness.

Skin Color

Another body dimension that has the potential to communicate is skin color. Much attention has been given to racial issues in the last century. Prejudices and stereotypes are perpetuated and individuals categorized solely on the color of their skin. The 1960s saw our culture take strides against the negative images so long a burden for blacks. The cry came forth that "Black is beautiful," and the rally revolved around the color of skin. Black civil rights leader Martin Luther King painted a powerful message for the vast crowd in Washington, D.C. in 1963 when he spoke these words: "I have a dream that one day my little children will not be judged by the color of their skin, but by the content of their character." Unfortunately, that dream is yet to be fully realized. To decide just how far we have yet to go, respond quickly to the following questions: What color skin do a people have who are good at math? Good at basketball? Good at dancing? Good at leading others? Good at medicine? Good at computers? How many of your friends do you think would give the same answers you did?

NONVERBAL MESSAGES OF HAIR

Look at the list below. What stereotypes do you associate with individuals who have the following characteristics?

Males	*Females*
oily, uncombed hair	unshaven legs or armpits
full beards	red hair
goatee beards	blonde hair
graying temples	oily hair
crewcut or flattop	hairy arms
mohawk	punk haircut
hairy chest and arms	short cropped hair
clean shaven with short hair	salt-and-pepper hair
silver, flowing hair	bouncy ponytail
short, tight curls	pigtails
the wet look	hair stacked high on head
one-day beard stubble	long, loose curls
ponytail	big hair
hair flowing below shoulders	spiky hair
moussed hair	moussed hair

If anything changes with the times, it is the way people wear their hair. In the late 1950s and early 1960s, the fashion for high school- and college-aged males was the crewcut or flattop. Females stiffened their hair with sticky sprays and wore it up. Students today might be heard saying, "I wouldn't be caught dead looking like that!" All right, how about the hippie look of the late 1960s and early 1970s—a stark contrast to styles only a few years before? "No way! Too long!" Can you believe flattops and crewcuts were back again by the late 1980s?

Hairstyles have much to do with our perceptions of attractiveness and social competence. Hairstyles give us cues about social norms. Nonverbal messages of hair result from hair color, hair length, facial hair, and hair manipulation.

Let's first look at hair color. With little effort you can probably come up with several stereotypes associated with hair color. Sally is a blonde woman. Does she really have more fun? Mark has coal-black hair. Is he really more mysterious? Do redheads have hot tempers? Maybe not, but that does not mean we do not think so. According to one popular women's magazine, most of us perceive red hair as tempestuous, brown hair as wholesome, and black hair as sultry, but the blondes still have all the fun. A survey in 1969 showed that most men would prefer to have blondes for their mistresses, but would rather marry a brown-haired woman. Another survey showed most women would prefer their men to have hair (color was not an issue), but a significant minority preferred bald men.

Length of hair has been associated with perceptions of credibility. One study conducted during the 1970s asked subjects in two different classrooms to assess a speaker's credibility. The speaker was the same man for each of the two classes of students. In one condition, the speaker's hair was arranged to make it appear long; in the other, the hair was arranged to appear short. On the credibility dimensions of competence and dynamism, the speaker was rated significantly higher with short hair. Some writers have suggested that the results of this study may indicate that men are perceived as less serious and less mature when wearing longer hair. Think of all the U.S. presidents who had long hair! Obviously, perceptions based on hair length vary with the times.

Career and job placement personnel have been reported as suggesting that long hair on men is detrimental to their chances of getting hired. They contend that the longer the hair, the more restrictive the job opportunities become. Women as well may influence their chances for jobs by the length of their hair. Long hair on women is usually perceived as sexy or rebellious. Contrary to some popular notions, women who enhance their sex appeal for the office may create feelings of resentment from their female coworkers and perpetuate perceptions of incompetence and low intelligence among the men. In short, one popular writer may have been right when he warned his female readers that long hair on women may work wonders in the bedroom, but is a real killer in the boardroom. For this reason, many women who have long hair wear their hair up for work and down after work.

A study conducted in the early 1970s explored people's perceptions of facial hair on men. The results revealed that the more hair on the face, the more the men were evaluated as mature, masculine, good-looking, dominant, courageous, industrious, self-confident, and liberal. An earlier study showed that both men and women describe clean-shaven men as youthful. For women only, bearded men were perceived as mature, sophisticated, masculine, and more sexually appealing. Men, however, responded that they felt less tense with clean-shaven men than with bearded men. It seems that perceptions of facial hair differ depending on the gender of the perceiver. Women may find beards a more positive characteristic for men, whereas men may perceive them as cues that stimulate withdrawal and avoidance, possibly the result of apprehension or fear. Whether this two-decade-old research still applies in the 1990s is an unanswered question at this point.

Hair manipulation may also create strong social impressions. Consider Martha for a moment. She sits in a dimly lit lounge. She soon spots Charles across the room at another table. Charles has been watching her for some time, seemingly waiting for an opportunity to get acquainted. Finding him to her liking, Martha runs her fingers through her hair, intermittently curling the ends around a finger. Such hair manipulations are called preening behavior and, according to some experts, are usually engaged in while in the presence of members of the opposite sex. Preening behavior is a nonverbal cue to potential courtship partners informing them that it is all right to approach and possibly engage in more intimate interaction. It is, of course, quite as possible that individuals perform this behavior out of habit or as adaptive behavior while anxious or nervous. In such cases, hair manipulations may be misinterpreted as approach messages or perhaps even invitations for sexual inter-action. Other examples of hair manipulation include beard stroking, chewing on one's hair, pulling of the arm hair, and brushing hair away from the eyes.

DRESS AND ARTIFACTS

The way we dress communicates a great deal of information about us. The fabric, colors, textures, and styles adorning our bodies send messages about what we think, who we are, our relationship to others, our values, attitudes, preferences, goals, and aspirations. Think about the money, time, and effort you spend choosing your own clothing. You probably had specific reasons for buying that particular pair of shoes, suit, or sweater. Often we communicate highly intentional messages with our clothes. Prostitutes, for example, know the signals they are capable of sending; they dress the part so that potential clients can easily identify them (check out the movie *Pretty Woman*). These signals eliminate what may be a waste of time for the client and, for the prostitute, a waste of money.

We intentionally clothe our law enforcement officers and military personnel in readily identifiable uniforms. Law enforcement and the military go to great pains to publish and enforce their rules for "tailoring for success" for both men and women. Personnel in these positions who do not tailor for success are not likely to be pro-moted or recommended for promotion.

Those of us who are not assigned a dress code still attempt to dress for success. For example, we take great pains and fuss over details before job interviews. The youthful high school English teacher wears a jacket and tie to offset his "baby face." After all, he is only a few years older than his senior students, and he wants to give the impression of status and competence. These are obvious examples of how peo-ple intentionally encode specific meaning into their dress.

However, the vast majority of our messages of dress are not nearly as deliberate as the above examples suggest. Many of our dress cues are transmitted without our awareness. Similarly, we receive many messages from others without realizing that their clothing stimulated the meaning. During the 1960 presidential election, Richard Nixon and John Kennedy held a series of presidential debates. In one of those debates, millions of television viewers saw Nixon in a gray suit that, on the black-and-white TV sets of those days, provided little contrast to the drab gray back-ground. Kennedy, on the other hand, contrasted quite well in his dark suit, so well that several commentators have attributed much of his success in that debate to the fact that his clothing allowed him to stand out, creating a favorable impression with the viewers.

Consider for a moment society's preoccupation with designer clothing during the early 1980s—the Izod and Polo shirts, the designer jeans, the Gucci loafers, and the Christian Dior tie. Surely we were aware of the acceptance and the perceptions of social competence that resulted from adorning our bodies with this fashionable wear. Are we always conscious, however, of the perceptions we may be creating in others? An anonymous source once complained, "My, my, ye all in equal attire! Do you not think in unison as well?" Unaware, can we not through our dress tell the world we are conformists?

There are several reasons why people wear clothes. The following discussion addresses the question Why do people dress the way they do?

Why Do People Dress the Way They Do?

According to Desmond Morris, one reason we dress the way we do is for comfort and protection. This hardly needs a lengthy explanation. The act of protecting our bodies from the elements evolved when human beings began to move about the world, traveling into areas where climatic conditions required more protection than their bodies alone could supply. Concealment is a second function of dress. Morris notes that the loincloth is culturally the most widespread of all garments.

These two functions probably satisfy the basic human motivations—the drive for survival and shelter and the psychological comfort of modesty. Recent thinking, however, leads us to conclude that protection and concealment may not be the primary reasons we wear clothing. Many cultures, for example, do not conceal their bodies to satisfy standards of modesty. People in some cultures do not clothe their bodies even though they live in taxing weather conditions. This would indicate that other motivations influence the wearing of clothing.

Morris claims that the third function of clothing is cultural display. "It is impossible," says Morris, " to wear clothing without transmitting social signals." When our dress serves this function, our clothes become important sources of information about us. Articles of clothing are essentially sociocultural badges communicating our status, economic level, social class, morality, educational background, trustworthiness, level of sophistication, level of success, and social background. Researchers Sybers and Roach summarized the sociocultural messages of dress through the following conclusions: Clothing serves as a symbol of our status; if we fail to dress as expected, we tend to believe that our occupational mobility is negatively affected; we feel that we have to dress according to our job to impress other people; and we feel that others associate our clothing choices with our socioeconomic status, goals, and satisfaction.

Clothing Characteristics and Personality.   Is it possible that our clothing reveals messages about our characteristics and personality? Does our use of dress give any clues about what characteristics are a part of our social and psychological orientations? According to many writers, it does. Let's review several studies that have investigated the relationships between the characteristics of wearers and the actual clothing they wear.

Compton was interested in establishing an association between the characteristics of individuals and their preferences for particular clothing designs and colors. Her research showed that people who preferred saturated colors and deep shades tended to be outgoing, forward, and sociable. Individuals who preferred small designs, on the other hand, were more interested in making a good impression. Compton concluded that people choose colors, fabrics, and designs that are consistent with the ideal image they hold of themselves. Our clothing choices, then, allow us to conform to that perfect picture.

In the same year, Rosencranz studied the clothing attitudes of married women. The results showed that women who were high in dress awareness usually belonged to many organizations, were in the upper social classes, had higher verbal skills, were more educated, and married white-collar men with higher than average incomes. According to Rosencranz, the higher classes of society probably place a great deal of emphasis upon the physical appearance of their members, thus making clothing awareness a high priority. It would also seem that women in upper socioeconomic brackets have the time and financial resources to focus more attention on their dress.

One of the more famous and extensive studies in relationship to wearer characteristics and clothing is that of Aiken. This researcher was interested in whether clothing selections were associated with personality traits. Aiken's survey questionnaire was developed to identify five dimensions of clothing selections. In brief, people select their articles of clothing because they have an interest in dress; they are concerned about economy in dress; they use their clothing for decoration; they dress for conformity; and they dress for comfort. Essentially, the Aiken study attempted to determine what personality traits best predicted how individuals select their clothing.

Using only females in the investigation, Aiken found that women who had an interest in dress were conventional, conscientious, compliant before authority, persistent, suspicious, insecure, tense, and stereotyped in thinking. Women who were concerned about economy in their clothing selection scored as more responsible, alert, efficient, precise, intelligent, conscientious, and controlled. Those who used their dress for decoration were conscientious, conventional, stereotyped, nonintellectual, sympathetic, sociable, and submissive. Women who dress for conformity were characterized by several conformity-type traits. They were more socially conscientious, moral, traditional, and submissive, and exercised restraint. These women also emphasized economic, social, and religious values and tended to deemphasize aesthetic values. Finally, Aiken found that women who chose their clothing for the sake of comfort were self-controlled, socially cooperative, sociable, thorough, and deferent to authority.

Various researchers have conducted follow-up investigations, and they appear to confirm Aiken's original findings. Notable among these studies is that of Rosenfeld and Plax. A major improvement here is that the researchers used both female and male respondents in exploring the relationship between four clothing orientations and personality characteristics.

The first clothing orientation Rosenfeld and Plax looked at was clothing consciousness. People who have a high clothing consciousness would, for example, feel that it is important if others "always noticed what they wore." The second dimension or orientation toward clothing was exhibitionism. Those scoring high in exhibitionism would, for instance, "approve of skimpy bathing suits and wouldn't mind wearing one myself." The third dimension identified by Rosenfeld and Plax was practicality. Subjects who responded very agreeably to such statements as "When buying clothes, I am more interested in practicality than beauty," would score high on this dimension. The fourth dimension, designer, referred to the degree to which subjects would "love to be a clothes designer." In Figure 2–4, we have provided the results of Rosenfeld's and Plax's study. Listed are the personality characteristics for both females and males who were either high or low on the four clothing orientations.

Popularity, Liking, and Homophily. Some people dress the way they do to enhance their popularity or because they feel that others will like them better. Still others feel that they can use their clothing to create perceptions of homophily, which

We tend to communicate more with people whom we
perceive as similar to us in dress and clothing styles.

CLOTHING CONSCIOUSNESS

High Females: inhibited, anxious, compliant before authority, kind, sympathetic, loyal to friends.
High Males: deliberate, guarded, deferential to authority, custom, and tradition.
Low Females: forceful, independent, dominant, clear thinking, low motivation for heterosexual relationships, low motivation to manipulate others.
Low Males: aggressive, independent, did not believe people are easily manipulated.

EXHIBITIONISM

High Females: radical, detached from interpersonal relationships, high opinion of self-worth.
High Males: aggressive, confident, outgoing, unsympathetic, unaffectionate, moody, impulsive, low self-concept regarding familial interactions.
Low Females: timid, sincere, accepting of others, patient, feelings of inferiority, low motivation for heterosexual relationships.
Low Males: believe people are easily manipulated, guarded against revealing themselves, low self-concept regarding familial interactions.

PRACTICALITY

High Females: enthusiastic, outgoing, clever, confident, guarded against revealing themselves, feelings of superiority, no desire to lead.
High Males: dissatisfied, cautious, rebellious, inhibited, also had little motivation for sustaining relationships, gaining recognition from authority figures, or making friends.
Low Females: detached, self-centered, independent.
Low Males: analytical, serious, forceful, success oriented, mature.

DESIGNER

High Females: stereotyped in thinking, irrational, uncritical, expressive, ebullient, quick.
High Males: conforming, demanding, irritable, cooperative, sympathetic, warm, helpful, sought encouragement, worried about their behavior.
Low Females: persistent, resourceful, clear thinking, efficient, when under pressure became easily disorganized, pessimistic about future in career.
Low Males: egotistical, dissatisfied, adventurous, anxious, feelings of superiority, little motivation to make friends.

FIGURE 2–4 **Personality and Clothing Orientation**

they hope will lead to increased popularity and liking. Can our clothing affect others' feelings about us?

Creating homophily with others can be quite beneficial to our interpersonal relationships. *Homophily* is perceived similarity in appearance, background, attitudes, and values. Some experts suggest that similarity in appearance (in the clothing we wear) may ease perceptions of similarity in other ways as well. One thing seems to hold true: We tend to like people more whom we perceive are similar, and this includes similarity in dress.

Research has found that conforming to the dress of others is related to our desire to be liked and accepted. The research also shows that people do like us and accept us more based on the way we dress. Popularity and liking are related to clothing. For women, wearing the right clothing is more important than either personality or looks when aspiring to become popular. The women studied also considered clothing the most important consideration when describing the attributes of popular females.

Rank and Status.   We suggested earlier that clothing serves as a symbol of our status. Research in the area tells us that dressing formally rather than casually increases perceptions of status. In many situations, we can enhance or minimize our status with others by the clothes we wear. Some writers report that dress is the most important consideration during initial encounters.

The young and inexperienced classroom teacher finds that if he wears a tie and coat, or if she wears a suited skirt or blazer with skirt, students will behave differently toward him or her. Think about your own college instructors for a moment. If you attend a large university, chances are very good that some of your teachers have been graduate teaching assistants. You remember them! They are more than likely the most formally dressed instructors you will ever have. Why? Most of them are only two or three years older than you, and they have probably been well-coached by their own professors about the importance of creating a perceived status differential in your minds. They are told, and rightly so, that higher-status clothing often engenders more respect.

Some experts suggest that clothing is very important in the business world when it comes to giving off messages of rank and status. The vested suit, we are told, denotes upper-level management.

Power and Success.   Closely related to rank and status are the nonverbal messages of power and success. In the world of high finance and big business, corporate men and women struggle daily to achieve the rewards that come with the successful climb up the ladder. Popular writers such as Korda and Molloy have stressed the importance of the symbols of power and success that are necessary in our places of business. According to Molloy's book *Dress for Success,* the men's business suit is designed to send powerful messages of authority and credibility. Although solid black three-piece suits may communicate too much power, Molloy suggests that the darker suits create perceptions of more authority. Although dark blue and gray pinstripes are acceptable, solid colors are strongly recommended.

In a later book, Molloy stressed the importance of the navy blue, charcoal, or beige skirted suit for women. He cautions women, however, to avoid imitating the dress of their male counterparts. This could be seen as a threat and eventually reduce the woman's power and authority in the corporate office. Molloy also offers advice to the businesswoman about wearing sweaters. He says "Any woman at any level who wants to move up should not wear a sweater to work. Sweaters give out nothing but negative impulses. They say lower middle class or lower." Away from the work environment, of course, is another matter altogether. Thus, although some clothing may make a woman more attractive, it may not enhance her value in the company. Some well-controlled research shows that attractiveness (at least after initial hiring) is not an asset to women employed above the clerical rank. Physical attractiveness was found to be negatively related to performance evaluations.

The popular media also have made much of the "power colors" for men's ties. For a while, the power color was dark red. Then it became yellow. If you want to know what it is now, enter any major business organization and look at what the middle-level businessmen are wearing. Odds are, they are wearing the color that is "in" today.

Group Identification. Closely associated with popularity and liking, group identification is another reason people dress the way they do. We are often told, "If you want to belong to the group, you have to do what the group does." In other words, "When in Rome, do as the Romans!" Singer and Singer (1985) found that when police officers were in uniform they were perceived to be more competent, reliable, and intelligent than when dressed casually. Hewitt and German (1987) found that a male Marine sergeant and a male Navy lieutenant were perceived as more attractive and intelligent when in uniform than when dressed casually.

Try this small test: *Go to a bank where you are not known, dress informally and somewhat sloppy, then attempt to cash a check. Watch the reaction. Later, go back to the same bank dressed in a suit or formal attire, and watch the reaction.*

People have always strived to belong, to be identified with a certain group of individuals. The young man begs his parents to buy him a sports shirt with his favorite football team's colors and his favorite player's jersey number. Young women imitate the clothing fashions of famous actresses and models. Even on our college campuses men and women aspiring to become members of fraternities and sororities attempt to prove themselves worthy by identifying with the clothing and actions of their potential brothers and sisters. An older man once boasted that he could tell a Republican from a Democrat by the very clothing the person wore. Whether we know it or not, we wear the uniforms of the groups with which we associate (or even aspire to associate). Informal uniforms though they may be, Leathers suggests that by wearing the uniform of a particular group, a person shows that he or she has given up the right to act freely as an individual and must follow the limitations and rules of the group. Other researchers would agree that the clothes we wear tells a great deal about our social and political attitudes.

GENERALIZATIONS ABOUT DRESS

We have discussed several important functions of clothing, including the fact that we use the dress of others to perceive and stereotype them in many ways. Before we move on, it is necessary to outline important generalizations about judgments we make based on dress.

Generalization 1: The accuracy of our judgments about others based on dress varies as a function of what type of judgment we make. Malandro and Barker (1989) suggest that greater accuracy is found in judging sex, age, nationality, socioeconomic status, identification of group, occupational status, and official status. In other words, we are generally much better at judging demographic characteristics based on dress. Less accuracy is found in judging personality, moods, values, and attitudes. That is, we are usually not as good at using the dress of others to evaluate psychological characteristics.

Generalization 2: Whether the dress of others influences our perceptions of them is in part a function of whether they are strangers or acquaintances. Basically, impressions based on dress tend to be most important during the initial and early stages of interaction.

Two studies conducted by Hoult seem to support this rule. He asked subjects in the first study to rate male models on several social dimensions. The models receiving the lowest ratings were then instructed to dress up; those with the highest ratings were told to dress down. The models were then rated a second time, but Hoult found no change in the ratings. The clothing had no influence on social judgments. Upon realizing that his research might be confounded because the subjects were closely acquainted with the models, he conducted another study using models who were complete strangers to the subjects. The results of the second study showed that clothing did influence the ratings. The models who dressed up increased in social ranking and those who dressed down lost ground in their ranking.

Generalization 3: The perception we have of others is initially influenced by their dress. We judge and will continue to judge others based on their dress. Often we decide whether to initiate interaction based on a person's dress and general physical appearance.

Generalization 4: If one dresses like or similar to us then we are more likely to approach her or him and initiate interaction. Again, the principle of homophily emerges. The more two people perceive themselves to be similar (based on dress) the more likely they are to communicate with one another.

In short, when we know someone, her or his clothing has little influence on our perceptions. We see the real person even if the clothing is not consistent with that perception. With strangers, however, clothing takes on an extremely important role in our judgments. As with other physical appearance factors, the clothes of strangers are a rich source of information about them when no other source exists. If we don't know the real person, what we see is what we assume is real.

ARTIFACTS

Look at your body and dress. Search well. Do you find anything else adorning, decorating, serving, or identifying you other than your clothing? The accessories used to adorn our bodies and clothing are called personal artifacts and can tell as much about you as your dress. Jewelry, glasses, hats, the writing pen you carry in your shirt pocket, purses, briefcases, and even smoking utensils communicate to others the personality underneath it all.

Many individuals are so closely identified with their personal artifacts that it is virtually impossible to divorce them. Many people have personalized artifacts—accessories that define who they are. During World War II, General George S. Patton was as famous for his ivory-handled pistol and swagger stick as he was for his successful military campaigns. It is quite difficult to imagine General Douglas MacArthur without his aviator sunglasses and corncob pipe. Where would George Burns be without his monstrous cigar? Country humorist Minnie Pearl would have lost her charm were it not for her lovable hat with the dangling price tag. A few years ago, any true-blue Michael Jackson fan would never have thought of leaving for school without his white sequined glove.

Molloy (1988) is a professional image consultant and does not hesitate to give guidelines for artifact choice. He even has a "Your Image I. Q. Test," in which he asks "For which professionals are bow ties acceptable?" The answer is waiters, clowns, college professors, and commentators. Almost all professions have personalized artifacts that associates can adorn their attire with. For example, many groups have lapel pins, brooches, tie tacs and other badgelike artifacts that identify the status of the individual.

Quite common among the artifacts we use are our articles of jewelry. The type of watch you wear may say much more than you realize. A self-proclaimed preppie recently commented to his psychology professor that a plain, ordinary Timex watch is an essential item for the hardcore preppie. A Rolex, however, can transmit a strong signal about your socioeconomic status. Molloy has suggested that the amount and type of jewelry the businessperson wears can make or break her or his business image. Molloy's recommendation includes a simple (preferably thin) gold watch with a wedding band. Any more is overdoing it. As for businesswomen, adding more than simple gold post earrings to the watch and wedding ring is going too far. Although things may change in the future, for now even one of those simple gold post earrings is too many for the businessman!

Another type of artifact by which many Americans have expressed themselves is the hat. The cowboy hat, whether straw or gray felt, is a popular means of self-expression in parts of the West. One cannot step onto a university campus without observing a myriad of caps of many types, shapes, and forms. Sports caps, painter's caps, and farmer's caps are just a few. Of course, wearing a baseball hat backwards is currently a sign that you are "with it." This too shall pass. They help to define, typecast, and stereotype the wearer. Although it is not currently popular, the "business" hat has often been used by men to create perceptions of maturity, status, and authority.

The most prominent, and probably the most researched, artifacts of all are eyeglasses. Since their invention, eyeglasses have been associated with particular personality characteristics. One study has shown that people who wear glasses are thought to be more intelligent, industrious, and honest. Another study found that females who wear glasses were seen as more religious, conventional, and unimaginative. At least for women, general perceptions related to eyeglasses are somewhat negative. This may explain why an estimated 75 percent of all contact lens wearers are female. Since the early 1980s, however, manufacturers of glasses frames have become highly imaginative with their products. Designer frames and other innovations, as well as the changing perceptions and uses of eyeglasses, allow the wearer to express herself or himself in ways that were impossible only a few years ago.

Eyeglasses can also communicate messages by the way we manipulate them. One of the most widely cited sources concerning the message value of glasses manipulation is Levy and Poll. According to this noted review, people who wear glasses can send a variety of signals about their self-images and emotional states. Chewing on the temple tips, for example, is usually a sign of nervousness, tension, or stress. Deep concentration can be communicated when wearers touch the temple tips together. Boredom may be shown by the individual who continually folds and unfolds his glasses. Poll also suggests that persons who prop their glasses on the forehead and look at another with the naked eye may well demonstrate honesty and willingness to be open. However, says Poll, resting them on the tip of the nose and looking over the top of the frames may send the message "You're putting me on."

When one watches an old movie, one made at least twenty years ago, it is often striking to note the amount of smoking present. Smoking is far less prominent in contemporary films. Also, in old movies the "good" characters smoked, but in contemporary movies smoking is usually restricted to actors portraying evil characters. In years gone by, college professor characters were usually seen with pipes, but today any smoking by such a character (except a villain) would be unthinkable. Filmmakers use artifacts to stimulate perceptions of characters, and smoking paraphernalia are often used. To create the intended perception, the filmmaker must be tuned in to contemporary stereotypes. Research conducted more than a decade ago suggested that the stereotype of cigarette and cigar smoking was a negative one, but smoking a pipe was still positive. If similar research were done today, it most likely would show a very negative stereotype for all forms of smoking and smoking artifacts. One would be wise, therefore, not to smoke or appear with smoking artifacts in the presence of others. Such artifacts are very likely to stimulate negative perceptions in today's society.

We have discussed just a few of the many artifacts that contribute to the social and cultural cues you transmit every day. Little things they may be. However, you should never dismiss the smallest lapel pin, the simplest necklace, or the plainest earrings when taking an inventory of the potential nonverbal messages you send others through your physical appearance. Others judge you by your artifacts as well as your clothing. Your artifacts communicate your self-image, your affiliations, and your social and political attitudes. The next time you think about putting on one of your favorite T-shirts, look at that shirt. Read what it says. It may be saying much more than just "Just do me!"

A GLOSSARY OF TERMINOLOGY

Artifacts are accessories used to adorn our bodies and clothing.

Attractiveness is something we perceive in someone else; it doesn't exist on its own. It is in the eye of the beholder.

Ectomorphs (ectos) are bony, thin, tall people with a fragile-looking physique, flat chest, and underdeveloped muscle tone.

Endomorphs (endos) are people with rounded, oval-shaped bodies who are somewhat heavy (not necessarily obese) and are often described as pear-shaped.

Mesomorphs (mesos) are people with a triangular body shape that is broad at the shoulders and tapers to the hips. Their shape is firm and muscular in appearance with all the curves and angles "in the right places," at least for U.S. culture.

Personal body concept is the perceptions you have of how attractive your body is and what you perceive the attributes of your body to be.

Physical attractiveness is the degree to which we perceive another attractive because of her or his physical attributes.

Social attractiveness is the degree to which we perceive another person as someone with whom we would like to socialize.

Somatyping is used to categorize individuals into one of three major body types (endomorphic, mesomorphic, ectomorphic).

Task attractiveness is the degree to which we perceive another person as someone with whom we would like to work.

▲ 3
Gesture and Movement

Joe felt uncomfortable, nervous, and anxious. He had never interviewed for a real, long-term job in his life. His prior positions had all been part-time or transient work. Never before had he really wanted to impress someone so he could obtain a permanent, future-oriented job. He kept thinking, "Will they like me? Did I remember to check my appearance? Do I look too young? Do I look confident? How should I appear?" Joe had spent a large portion of the morning making sure his navy business suit was form-fitting without being too snug, making sure the coat fit well in shoulders and back, tie correct, and slacks smooth. He looked at his shoes to make sure they were polished, not scuffed. The longer he waited, the more he fidgeted, squirmed, and wiggled. What could go wrong? He had studied all the information he could obtain on the Patterson Corporation. Why was he worried?

He sat in an outer waiting room with several other applicants, all of whom looked similar to him and equally anxious. The interviewer had been calling them in one at a time to meet with a committee.

"Sit up straight. Look alert. Look calm. Don't bite your nails. Stop running your hands through your hair. The interview committee will think you're a putz if you don't calm down," Joe told himself. "And stop drumming your fingers on the chair arm!" Joe then realized that he had been running his hands through his hair again, and his crossed leg was twitching rapidly. He folded his arms loosely across his chest, breathed deeply, and forced himself to sit calmly.

*In the next chair, a well-dressed woman sat calmly reading a maga-
zine. She slumped and yawned. A man to her right continually looked at his
watch. Toward the other side of the room, Joe noticed another woman pacing in front of a bulletin board. Occasionally, she flipped a posted notice or
brochure then looked anxiously down the hall where several interviewees
had disappeared with the Patterson representative.*

*"Joseph M. Richmond," came the words from a strong, serious, firm
voice. Joe turned to see the representative gesturing for him to follow. He
approached, smiled, extended a trembling hand, and bent from his waist.
"Not nervous, are you Mr. Richmond?" asked the representative. "Oh, no,
no, sir . . . I mean madam . . . I mean ma'am. . . . Not at all. Very good to
meet you." Joe bit his lower lip for fear that his general behavior and mannerisms had betrayed him.*

It is said that actions speak louder than words. The gestures and movements of
our body express our feelings so powerfully that what we say is hardly processed.
Because of popular books and articles in mass circulation magazines, body movements have become commonly known as body language. Although such writings
have helped to raise awareness of nonverbal behavior and of gesture and movement
in particular, these writings also have led to some misconceptions about nonverbal
communication. The movements, actions, gestures, motions, displays, twitches,
swingings, and swayings of our body do not constitute a language. They are simply
behaviors to which another person may attribute some meaning. In short, they may
communicate, but they do not do so in the manner of real language.

There are functions of movement and gesture, or more technically the skeletal
and muscular systems. The first is called the *instrumental function*. In this capacity,
the skeletal and muscular systems contribute directly to the accomplishment of
some task. The second (and in this context more important) is the *referential function*. This is the potential our movements and gestures have to communicate nonverbal messages. *Kinesics* is the study of the communicative impact of body movement
and gesture. In Chapter 1, we introduced the various functions of nonverbal communication: complementing, accenting, contradicting, repeating, substituting, and regulating. Our body movements provide many messages that serve these functions.

Kinesic behaviors include all gestures, head movements, eye behavior, facial
expression, posture, and movements of the trunk, arms, legs, feet, hands, and fingers. Researchers have studied these motions from a wide range of perspectives, but
most nonverbal scholars today would agree that it is virtually meaningless, and
probably inappropriate, to study them apart from their context. It is rare that a particular body movement symbolizes a specific message outside the restrictive environs
of the context or culture in which it occurs.

Consider Joe's behavior in our illustration. Had you not known his particular
situation, the impending interview, could you have assigned specific meaning to
those behaviors? Probably not. Some may have guessed that he was bored, others

that he was irritated. It is only because we understand his predicament that we know his behaviors are signs of nervousness.

Besides the situation surrounding body motions, it is also essential to understand that our culture, upbringing, ethnic and geographic origins, social status, and even our educational background contribute to the meaning of gesture and movement. The way a male walks in our culture may lead some individuals to question his masculinity. In other cultures, the same gait would not. The A-OK sign North Americans use may tell that all is well in Oklahoma City and Buffalo, but don't rely on the same reactions in some Latin cultures. Decades of extensive research and formal observation have shown us the error of our ways when we attempt to "alphabetize" the nonverbal behavior of human beings. Crossing your legs away from another while talking with them may not mean that you are rejecting them. You may simply be more comfortable with your left leg over your right than the other way around.

We would like to discuss gesture and movements in several ways. First, we present a section on the theoretical views. Second, we present a discussion on the types or categories of gestures and movements. Third, the idea of posture is discussed in terms of its potential to communicate. Finally, we review the effects of gesture and movements on our communication with others.

A THEORETICAL LOOK AT GESTURE AND MOVEMENT

We have always known intuitively that body movements tell us much about another person. Gestures and movements can illustrate and regulate our verbal dialogue. Through our bodily motions, we can communicate our emotions, reinforce and accent the language, and even contradict what we have said. It is only quite recently, however, that theorists and researchers have developed scientific ways of studying kinesic behavior of humans. There are two general approaches to the study of kinesics. The first is the structural approach, the second, the external variable approach. As we will see, researchers from each perspective make different assumptions about the communicative potential of kinesic behavior.

Structural Approach to Kinesics

The common thread among the writers who take the *structural approach* to kinesics is that they view communication as a structured system, and this system is presumed to be independent of the specific behaviors people engage in during particular interactions. They believe that all behavior should be presumed to be learned socially and have communicative value. Birdwhistell (1952, 1970) is one of the most famous structuralist writers. Birdwhistell believed that the context in which behavior occurred was very important. However, behavior can also be seen as meeting many criteria for language. In other words, there is an underlying structure to behaviors, a rule system that can be discovered. Behaviors can be broken into parts like sentences or words, and they can be categorized. Additionally, Birdwhistell thought that it was meaningless to make distinctions between verbal and nonverbal communication. He is well-known for his linguistic approach to movements.

Birdwhistell's method for studying body motions involved identifying the smallest and most basic units of behavior, called *allokines*. We usually cannot detect these microbehaviors in ongoing interaction with others. They are performed rapidly and usually must be detected by mechanical means, such as video tape. Several allokines together make up larger units of behavior called *kines*. According to Birdwhistell, even kines may not be meaningful. A still larger unit of behavior, *kinemes,* are combinations of kines. These movement sequences are the smallest set of body movements with differential meaning and are analogous to the linguistic phoneme. Kinemes make up *kinemorphemes,* which are analogous to the linguistic morphemes, the smallest meaningful unit of language. Thus, Birdwhistell based his category system of behavior on a model taken from the categories of verbal communication (allophone, phone, phoneme, morpheme).

A major critic of Birdwhistell's approach to the study of kinesics is Dittman (1971). He did not believe that all behavior could be treated in the same way we treat language. According to Dittman, "the basic hypothesis of kinesics as a communication system with the same structure as spoken language is not a viable one" (p. 341). He claims that all words are discontinuous and discrete pieces of information. However, only certain body motions and gestures can meet this criterion. Many, if not most, must be considered continuous and therefore cannot be treated or studied as a linguistic system. Dittman says, "there is no evidence that movement elements are assembled into groupings based upon any set of rules internal to the movements themselves" (p. 341). Other critics of Birdwhistell have cautioned that such an approach may lead researchers to impose a structure on the body movements they observe that may not exist but fits a presupposed model of the researchers.

It should be noted that Dittman and others strongly agree with Birdwhistell that gestures and movements are valuable sources of information. However, they would disagree that no distinction between verbal and nonverbal behavior can and should be made. As you probably have surmised, we find ourselves firmly in Dittman's corner in this controversy. The distinctions we noted in Chapter 1 between verbal and nonverbal behavior are important. The stream of research that was based on the linguistic model has been not particularly useful to our understanding of human communication.

External Variable Approach to Kinesics

Unlike the research of Birdwhistell that began with commitment to his theoretical models (which frequently were not in agreement with the research that followed from them), other researchers have taken an external variable approach to the study of bodily motion. Paul Ekman is one of the more famous researchers who have taken this perspective. He started by observing behavior experimentally and then developed his theory based on his findings. Ekman and his colleagues were not interested in microbehaviors that could not be seen by the unaided eye. They saw no real use in hypothesizing the existence of allokines and kines because they had no significance in relationship to social meaning and communication. Ekman and Friesen (1972) state that "our interest in how nonverbal behavior functions in social interaction has required our examining molar units of behavior" (p. 354). According to Ekman and Friesen, any classification of human gesture and movement should be based on motions that are easily seen by any observer. If movements cannot be discerned by the average observer, then how can they potentially communicate?

Ekman and Friesen were also interested in the type of information certain nonverbal acts conveyed. Movements can convey idiosyncratic information or shared information. Moments and gestures that can be understood only in relation to one individual generate idiosyncratic meaning. That is, the meanings of these nonverbal acts are seen as different if engaged in by different people within the same group. Furthermore, the knowledge of the particular circumstances surrounding such behavior are essential to understanding what they may mean. Nonverbal acts that generate shared meaning are those that most persons in a given group or culture would interpret similarly. The "middle finger" or the "victory sign" are examples of behavior that generate shared meaning in the American culture. Conversely, one person may engage in a particular movement in response to feelings of stress, such as stroking one arm, that may stimulate no meaning in most others nearby, but one observer (such as a spouse) could see this behavior as a sign of anxiety. This would be idiosyncratic meaning.

In an extension of their idiosyncratic–shared distinction, Ekman and Friesen distinguished between inborn, or innate, behavior and behavior that is learned through social interaction and cultural influences. From their research and thinking, they also devised the most commonly accepted system to categorize gestures and movements. Let us now turn to a discussion of the types of bodily motions using the categories they developed.

TYPES OF GESTURE AND MOVEMENT

Gestures and movements of human beings may be separated into five different types. The five types are emblems, illustrators, regulators, affect displays, and adaptors. The following discussion presents each type and describes them in terms of their characteristics.

Emblems

The first type of body motion is called the emblem. *Emblems* are gestures and movements that have a direct verbal translation. Emblems are known by most or all of a group, class, culture, or subculture. They can be used to stimulate specific meanings in the minds of others in place of verbal communication. Giving someone "the finger" or "the bird" typically produces a precise shared meaning, and few in our culture would miss the message it transmits. This is about as close as most of us can get to a body language. However, those who know American Sign Language (ASL) can communicate much more fully with an emblematic language based on gesture.

Emblems are used intentionally by the sender to communicate a specific message to an individual or group. Rarely do individuals unconsciously wave goodbye or use their thumbs along the roadside to signal for a passerby to pick them up. Users of emblems are aware of their actions and are in control of the movement or gesture. The sender, in essence, takes the responsibility for the message.

Though generally classified as nonverbal behavior, emblems have more in common with verbal communication than any other nonverbal behavior. Besides having direct verbal translations and usually being used intentionally, emblems are socially learned in much the same manner as language. Furthermore, emblems are much like language itself. The meanings we assign to them are arbitrary, and the way we associate meaning with the action is highly similar to the way we associate meaning with words. Finally, as with words, emblems may stimulate entirely different meanings, or no meanings at all, in the minds of people from different cultures. Given the closeness of emblems to language, it may be better to think of nonverbal and verbal behavior as a continuum than as a dichotomy. Emblems would fall somewhere in the middle of the continuum, with verbal and nonverbal behavior representing the polar extremes.

Verbal behavior——————Emblems——————Nonverbal behavior

Illustrators

Gestures and movements that are closely linked with spoken language and help to illustrate what is being said are called *illustrators*. Like emblems, illustrators are usually intentional. Unlike emblems, however, they cannot stand alone and have the same meaning of the verbal. That is, illustrators generate little or no meaning when not accompanying speech. Try turning down the volume on your television and observe the actions of the people on the screen. Unless you are an excellent lip reader, you will find it extremely difficult to understand. Seldom can we assign specific meaning to illustrative behavior without the accompanying speech. Illustrators make little sense without the words they accompany.

Cohen (1977) found that illustrators were used more often in face-to-face interaction. This is because in face-to-face communication, we as senders often use illustrators to make our meaning clearer. In non-face-to-face interaction, we need other forms of nonverbal behavior to clarify our speech. Lastly, we often use illustrators in face-to-face interaction even if we suspect that the other knows what we mean. In other words, we like to clarify, so we use illustrators.

There are various types of illustrators, depending upon the function they serve.

Batons are used to accent the words, phases, or sentences that are spoken. You are using batons, for example, when you slam your hand on a table to emphasize the urgency of what you are saying. *Ideographs,* according to most writers, represent the cognitive processing of the speaker. Ideographs are usually quite prevalent when individuals are having difficulty putting their thoughts into words. Snapping your fingers repeatedly while trying to think of an answer is an example of an ideograph. *Pictographs* are movements or gestures that serve as pictures or drawings of objects of the speech. Young men often draw the outline of a sexy "girlish figure" in the air while describing an attractive woman to their friends, for example.

Regulators

Think for a moment about what it would be like to interact daily with others and not be able to see them. Some research has shown that if interactants are not allowed to observe one another while conversing, the interaction becomes difficult. This happens because we use movements and gestures (and observe those of others) to help us regulate our conversations. This is also part of the reason we find it difficult at first to interact with a visually-impaired person. We unconsciously expect the person to respond to our gestures and movements, but he or she is not aware of them. Once we recognize this fact, we may still have a problem because we have to figure out how to regulate the interaction without these nonverbal aids.

Regulators are gestures and movements that, along with eye and vocal cues, maintain and regulate the back-and-forth interaction between speakers and listeners during spoken dialogue. Regulators are not nearly as intentional as emblems and illustrators. They are learned gradually and are an integral part of the socialization process. Usually, they are learned to such a degree that they become ingrained habits. We are rarely conscious of the behavior we use to control and regulate our conversations with other people.

Kendon and Ferber (1973) identified six stages of general interaction to regulate or act in the regulative mode in greeting situations. They are as follows:

1. Sighting, orientation, and initiation of the approach.

2. The distant salutation, or movements and gestures that signal official ratification and acknowledge that a greeting sequence has been initiated and who the participants are. Smiles, waves, head nods, and so on can all be part of this "official acknowledgement" stage.

3. The head dip, which signifies transitions between acts and shifts in psychological orientation. This stage may not be observed if the greeter did not continue to pursue the partner.

4. The approach, which assumes that the greeting process continues. In this step, the greeters use several nonverbal behaviors that signify approach, such as moving toward one another, gazing, grooming, and extending one or both arms somewhat in front of body.

5. The final approach, where participants are less than ten feet apart. There is smiling, mutual gazing, much face-to-face interaction.

6. The close salutation, when the participants of the greeting ceremony negotiate a standing position. They use ritualistic speech (Hi, how are you?) and if the situation calls for body contact (such as handshake, shoulder slap, or embraces), it takes place here.

Consider the behavior you use to cue others that you are finished talking. What particular actions are signals that you want to speak? That you do not want to speak?

Managing turn-taking is the primary function of regulators. It is necessary during our conversations to exchange roles as the speaker and the listener. The goal, of course, is to switch those roles smoothly and fluidly. *Turn-taking behaviors* can be categorized into those that the speaker uses to maintain or yield her or his talking turn, or those that the listener uses to request or decline an invitation to talk. *Turn-yielding cues* are given by speakers who wish to discontinue talking and give the listener the opportunity to take the speaking role. These movements may include direct body orientation, a forward lean, a beckoning gesture with the hand or head that says "Come on, I'll listen to you now," and many eye and vocal cues (increased eye contact, raised inflection, or simply a long silent pause). *Yielding cues* can be seen as behaviorally "putting on the brakes," communicating to your fellow interactants that you are coming to a verbal stop.

Turn-maintaining cues are used by speakers who want to continue talking. They are especially observable when the listener is trying to interrupt. Keeping eye contact to a minimum, increasing the rate and loudness of speech, indirect body orientation, filled pauses, and "halting" gestures (holding your hand out with palm facing the listener as a traffic officer would while stopping traffic) are all examples of turn-maintaining cues. They communicate to the listener that you still have more to say.

Turn-requesting regulators are used by the listener to signal the speaker that he or she would like to talk. Examples of requesting cues include raising the hand, a raised index finger, an audible intake of breath, tensing and straightening of posture, or any other behavior that may get the speaker's attention. Vocally, we can use a throat-clearing sound or a "stutter start" to request a speaking turn. One writer has also suggested that requesting cues may also be those that are used to hurry the speaker to the "talking finish line." Rapid head nods that signal agreement or a rolling gesture with the hand may get the speaker to make her or his point much sooner than she or he normally would.

Finally, there are cues listeners use to signal the turn-yielder that we do not wish to talk. We decline our turn to speak. These are called, simply enough, *turn-denying behaviors*. Sustaining a relaxed posture while remaining silent, slow and frequent positive head nods, and positive vocal utterances such as "uh-hum" usually encourage the speaker to continue talking.

Affect Displays

The fourth category of bodily motion is called *affect displays.* These cues involve primarily facial expressions but also include a person's posture, the way he or she walks, limb movements, and other behavior that provides information about the person's emotional state or mood. Affect displays indicate both our emotional reactions to what is going on and the strength of those reactions.

It is quite possible for many, if not most, people to portray an emotion they do not actually feel. That is the essence of acting, also a central component in good social skills. Similarly, it is possible for many people to repress the expression of an emotion they feel would be inappropriate for others to be aware of. However, behaviors that reveal true emotional states are usually unintentional, even when we are

The smile is a generally interpretable sign in most of the world. It is usually associated with friendliness or pleasantness.

aware of them. For instance, when we feel our knees shaking and see our hands trembling while experiencing fear or anxiety, we often cannot control them.

Deception, for example, can sometimes be detected in body movements even though speakers may believe they have effectively concealed any cues that might give them away. Research on deception and movement indicates that people are better able to conceal lying cues in the face and head areas than in other body areas. In several studies, observers who observed only the body of the deceiver were more likely to detect falsehoods than observers who keyed on the face and head. But don't assume that you can always catch liars. Even with videotape and unlimited time to review observations, subjects could detect deception by observing bodily movements only slightly better than by pure guessing.

DePaulo (1988) suggests that a liar has to care about keeping a secret or telling a lie. She states, "When liars are not overly concerned about getting caught telling their lies, then they often can control some of their nonverbal behavior—particularly their facial expressions—so that their lies will not be apparent" (p. 154). DePaulo (1988) citing DePaulo and Kirkendol (1988) suggests that when liars are "highly motivated to succeed in their lies, it becomes more likely that their nonverbal behaviors will betray them" (p. 154). She suggests that this betrayal occurs not despite their best efforts to conceal a lie, but *because of their efforts to conceal a lie.*

Some conclusions about detecting deception are needed at this juncture. As nonverbal encoders and decoders, we can safely conclude the following about deception:

> The particular behavior that is likely to show that one is lying depends on the characteristics of the lie, the liar, the receiver of the lie, and the context.
>
> Liars probably do learn to control their head and facial movements when deceiving, but it is difficult for them to control all nonverbal behavior.
>
> If you think someone is deceiving you, look at other parts of the body for *leakage cues*—cues that demonstrate that someone is being untruthful.
>
> Leakage cues are not the same for all; they differ from person to person, context to context, and for different emotions.
>
> With certain liars (deceivers) it is almost impossible to detect the lie. Some people are highly skilled deceivers and are effective liars who do not feel guilty about a lie, have convinced themselves that they are not lying, or are confident that the target of their lies will believe them.
>
> Attractive people are more likely to be able to convince others of untruths than unattractive people. The reasoning here is that attractive persons receive more opportunities to communicate, gain confidence in a variety of communication situations, and therefore can control their verbal and nonverbal behavior more easily when lying.

Children and adults who have honest-looking features and affect displays are often given the benefit of the doubt even if someone thinks they are lying. People in this culture often say, "this person can't be lying, he (or she) looks too honest." Deception is difficult to discern. We must be cautious in assuming that someone is lying because they display negative affective displays or in assuming that someone is telling the truth because they have honest affect displays. When in doubt, check out the context and circumstances surrounding the assumed liar before making any conclusions.

We return to a more extensive discussion of emotional messages and facial expression in the next chapter. Because facial and eye behavior represent distinct nonverbal cues, we have chosen to treat them separately.

Adaptors

The fifth category of nonverbal behavior is adaptors. *Adaptors* are highly unintentional behavior that are usually responses to boredom or stress or are closely linked with negative feelings toward ourselves or someone else. These behaviors are vestiges of coping behavior that we learn very early in life. According to several writers, they were once part of our efforts to cope with physical and emotional needs and the need to learn instrumental behavior. They are, in essence, behavior that once allowed us to adapt to situational, social, and cultural influences. They can be described as "leftovers" of goal-directed behavior that later became automatic habitual actions.

Commonly behaviors that people use every day may actually be adaptors. Are you, for instance, aware when you pick your nose, tap your pen or pencil on your desk, pull at your ear lobe, rub your arms, or fiddle with an object in your hand? Lip biting and nail biting are not generally well-accepted behaviors but we often see people do them in front of total strangers. Chances are that such lip or nail biting is an adaptor.

Many researchers characterize adaptors as falling into three different types. *Self-adaptors* are nonverbal acts in which an individual manipulates her or his own body. Scratching, rubbing, and hair twisting are common self-adaptors. *Alter-directed adaptors* are movements that are designed to protect oneself from other interactants. Folding arms may indicate protection against some sort of verbal or nonverbal attack. Unconscious leg movements during interaction may represent a thinly repressed desire to keep others away. Finally, there are *object-focused adaptors.* These acts include the unconscious manipulation of a particular object such as tapping a pen, smoking a cigarette, rubbing a worry stone, twirling a ring around your finger. One of the authors feels it necessary to have a piece of chalk in hand while lecturing. By the end of the class, there generally is more chalk on clothing, face, and under the fingernails than on the chalkboard!

POSTURE

Helen walked into the office Monday morning. Smiling, she waved good morning to her coworkers, and crossed to the coat rack, hanging up her jacket and gloves. Helen then went to the water cooler and drew a cupful of water. She poured the contents of the cup into a heating pot to boil for her morning tea. Checking her mailbox, she grabbed a pile of miscellaneous memos and letters, thumbed through them causally, and placed them on the edge of her desk. Helen sat and placed her purse in the bottom drawer. After reading a note from the custodian taped to her typewriter, she looked over to Harriet and, smiling again, exclaimed, "Hi, Harriet. Did you get an eyeful of that great weather?"

"Yes," replied Harriet. "Nice change." Somewhat puzzled, Harriet scrutinized Helen and said, "Helen, are you feeling all right this morning?"

"Why, I feel fine. Why?"

Body position can tell us a lot about a person.

> *Dismissing the entire matter, Harriet replied, "Oh, nothing. Just curious. Guess we'd better get started on our work."*

Reading the above scenario, you are probably wondering why Harriet seemed concerned. It may not be apparent to you that she was keying in on visible cues that Helen may not have been aware of transmitting. Harriet was receiving messages from Helen's posture. This Monday morning, Helen's shoulders were drawn downward much more than usual. Her head was turned a bit downward and she seemed to slump. As she walked through the office, her feet moved slowly and dragged on the floor. Usually, Helen had a crisp and commanding stride. Not today. In Harriet's mind, it was definitely a slow, painstaking gait.

As we said earlier, posture can be a rich source of information about emotional states and relationships. The way we walk, whether with a bounce or a saunter, sends messages to others. The way we sit can indicate interest or boredom. Our body orientation toward others during conversation may say much about our relationship, orientation, and feelings about other persons. You can receive social signals from a person by the way he or she stands, lies, leans, lounges, reclines, or rests.

How Does Posture Communicate?

A leading writer on body movements and gestures, Albert Mehrabian, posits that there are two primary dimensions of posture. Through these dimensions, we transmit messages about our attitudes. The first dimension is called *immediacy*. The concept of immediacy is discussed in depth in Chapter 11. For now, the behavior that represents an immediate attitude includes direct body orientation, symmetric positioning, forward leans, and a host of other nonverbal acts such as increased touch, greater eye contact, and approach cues.

The second dimension identified by Mehrabian is called *relaxation*. Relaxed behavior includes backward leans, reduced tension in the arms and legs, and asymmetry of positioning.

The basic idea of Mehrabian's work is that we can communicate an openness and willingness to communicate, along with a positive attitude, by exhibiting immediacy and relaxation in our postural positions. On the other hand, our posture can close out another person and shut off communication. Postural cues that reduce visibility and increase perceptions of distance tend to discourage interaction and cues that facilitate the opposite perceptions enhance interaction potential.

Scheflen (1964), another notable writer and researcher in the area of kinesics, contends that we can communicate with our posture in many ways. Scheflen divides all postures of interacting persons into three major categories: inclusive or noninclusive, face-to-face or parallel body orientation, and congruence or incongruence.

Inclusive vs. Noninclusive.   Postural cues in this category are acts or positions that either include or block out other people. Imagine you're at a party held by a social organization. It may be in a large hall or ballroom, and the attending crowd may be large. As you look around the room, you see that small groups, or conversation pockets, have formed. You particularly notice a group of four people who are enjoying their private interaction immensely while virtually ignoring the other partygoers. With their posture, this little group has communicated to others that they are not included. You are well-acquainted with each of the four but may hesitate to approach and become a part of their interaction because of the noninclusive postural cues they are transmitting.

Face-to-Face vs. Parallel Body Orientation.   This category refers primarily to the postural relationship between two people during conversation. Essentially, two people can engage in conversation while facing one another or while sitting or standing side-by-side. These postural orientations can tell a great deal about a relationship. For instance, the face-to-face position may indicate a more formal or professional interaction. It may also suggest that each person feels a need to continually monitor the other. The face-to-face positioning also may be a sign of a more active interaction, whereas the parallel orientation may indicate neutral or passive interaction.

Congruence vs. Incongruence.   Scheflen's last category, congruence vs.incongruence, refers to whether two people imitate or share a similar posture. If people share a similar posture and tend to imitate the positioning and movements of each other, they are exhibiting congruent body positions. If there is a marked difference in the postures of interactants, they are engaging in incongruent body positioning.

When the postures of two people are congruent, this may signal agreement, equality, and liking between them. A primary message transmitted when postures are incongruent is that there is a status differential between the interactants. The higher-status individual exhibits a more relaxed posture with indirect orientation, backward leans, and asymmetric leg and arm positions. The lower-status person usually maintains a more formal posture with direct orientation, forward leans, more muscle tension, and straightened spine. Therefore, people of perceived equal status, such as friends, may strive to maintain that equality through their posture whereas those of different status (such as teachers and students, doctors and patients, bosses and subordinates) may exhibit postural cues that signal the inequality.

Communicative Potential of Posture

Many psychiatrists, therapists, and psychologists believe that attitudes, predispositions, and emotional states may be manifested as enduring postural patterns. They contend that the structure and orientation of the body seldom lie. Practitioners, such as some chiropractors, believe that our history of emotions, deep-rooted feelings, and personality can be identified by the way we hold our bodies, move our bodies, and exhibit tension in our bodies.

As we noted in our Harriet and Helen scenario earlier, the way we walk can betray our outlook on life, our attitudes, or our emotions. It may even tell others a lot about our cultural or ethnic background. Others suggest that our stride is closely linked to our personality. We may be able to change other people's perceptions of us by changing the pace or rhythm with which we walk.

It is not surprising that our posture is most effective at reflecting our gender. In fact, many behaviors that go into "separating the boys from the girls" can be seen in the way we hold, carry, and orient our bodies. For centuries, females in American culture have been socialized to exhibit "shrinkage" in their postures. Shrinkage cues include such things as the lowering of head and eyes, tilting the head to one side, and pulling the body and limbs inward to take up less space (knees and feet together and arms held closely to the trunk). Males, on the other hand, have been socialized to engage in "expanding" nonverbal acts. A stereotypical masculine posture is characterized by positions and movements that take up more space. Such expansive behavior includes such things as positioning the legs apart while standing or sitting, carrying arms away from the trunk, and taking longer strides.

It should be noted that individuals begin to develop the postures considered appropriate to their genders as early as infancy, leading some to believe that they are natural. In actuality, we learn them. We model the appropriate posture (accidentally) and our parents reward us. We show indications of postural positions and movement that are typically associated with the other gender, and we may get punished or ignored. Consider the stereotypes associated with males who exhibit the shrinking behavior generally accepted as feminine. How about the female who has the masculine expanding posture, walk, or body orientation?

MOVEMENT AND COMMUNICATOR STYLE

Norton published a comprehensive book on different styles of communicators. His definition of *communicator style* is "the way one verbally and paraverbally interacts to signal how literal meaning should be taken, interpreted, filtered, or understood in the communicative process." To Norton, communicator style is what gives form to the content of messages. According to Norton, several verbal and nonverbal factors discriminate among the various styles. One of these factors is the different patterns of body movements and gestures that are used by the communicator. Norton suggests that the major types of communicator style are dramatic, dominant, animated, open, contentious, relaxed, friendly, attentive, and impression-leaving. Let us consider the behaviors that go into each style.

The Dramatic Style.   You probably know someone who is quite dramatic when he or she speaks. These individuals are usually masters at exaggeration, tell the most fascinating stories, and often have a rhythm to their voice. Dramatizing, according to Norton, is the most physically visible of all the communicator styles. It is usually not enough for the "dramatist" to say something in an interesting way. He or she generally relies on a wide range of illustrative behaviors. Common illustrators that represent the dramatic style are pictographs, drawings of forms and figures in space, also moving dramatically from one location to another. In short, the world is a stage. An interesting characteristic of dramatic style is that the behavioral cues signal deviations from normal behavior. The abnormality of dramatic behavior is probably the major reason it successfully captures the interest of listeners. Additionally, perceptions of popularity, attractiveness, and status are often enhanced by the dramatic communicator style.

The Dominant Style.   The dominant communicator uses nonverbal cues to dominate listeners. Some writers have likened the too-dominant style to a big stick that beats the listener into a submissive posture. Expansive body posture and movements that fill space are often associated with dominance. People who quickly approach fellow interactants are generally seen as dominant. Although these behaviors are more commonly used by males, females with dominant styles use them as well, along with more reciprocal eye contact. Research shows that dominant communicators are perceived as more confident, conceited, self-assured, competitive, forceful, active, and enthusiastic.

The Animated Style.   The animated communicator engages in exaggerated bodily motions and gestures actively while speaking. Comedian and talk-show host Joan Rivers illustrates the animated style well. Frequent and repetitive head nods and frequent smiles are commonly used with this style. In an early work, Scheflen suggested that preening, intimate positioning, and "reading oneself" are essentially animated behaviors that pervade courtship and dating.

The Relaxed Style.   The relaxed communicator seems to remain collected and calm internally in anxiety-producing situations; he or she also manifests relaxation in posture, movement, and gesture. Rarely do relaxed speakers unconsciously engage in adaptive-type behaviors. They seem immune to nervous mannerisms, and seldom allow their gestures to get out of control. Communicators with a relaxed style transmit a variety of messages. According to one investigation, a relaxed style communicates calmness, serenity, peace, confidence, and comfortableness. A lack of tension in the body and movements may also indicate an enviable self-assurance.

The Attentive Style.   The attentive style of communication more adequately characterizes a style of listening to or receiving messages from others than a style of speaking. Some writers have referred to attentiveness as active listening. Norton contends that the attentive style is inversely related to the dominant and dramatic styles. Attentiveness is characterized by a more immediate posture, forward leans, head nods that indicate agreement, a direct body orientation, and gestures that encourage the speaker to continue. These also are cues that signal interest and empathy. The attentive communicator can make the speaker feel that what he or she is saying is worth hearing. Good listeners do not ordinarily get their honorable labels because they process information well. When we think of good listeners, we usually think in terms of their nonverbal behavior of attentiveness toward us.

The Open Style.   Norton contends that the open communicator uses bodily activity that is expansive, unreserved, extroverted, and approach-oriented. Other characteristics of the open style include those that are affable, friendly, frank, gregarious, unsecretive, and conversational. The primary function of behavior used by open-style communicators is to signal to individuals that they can communicate openly and freely. Think for a moment about how difficult it would be to share your feelings with someone who hardly looked at you, seemed more interested in a cup of coffee, positioned their body away from you, and folded their arms across their chest. Add to that a plethora of adaptors (tapping a cup with their fingers, playing with a napkin) that start just about the time you begin "spilling your guts." Chances are that you would quickly become discouraged and change the topic of conversation to less personal matters. The next time you find yourself easily revealing to a friend or acquaintance, check the person's behavior. Through openness in positioning and orientation, the person may have "pulled it out of you."

The Friendly Style.   Norton says that the friendly style ranges from an absence of hostility to signals of deep intimacy. To the extent that communicators strive to neutralize or avoid being perceived as hostile, they use a friendly style of communication. This dimension of style is closely related to the open and attentive styles. Body movements that serve to reduce distance such as approach, forward leans, and other immediacy behavior may help to create a friendly style. In addition, communicators with a friendly style continually confirm their fellow interactants' wishes, often touch in an affectionate stroking manner, and behave in a way that positively and uniquely acknowledges the other.

The Contentious Style.   This style is similar to the dominant style, but it might better be thought of as aggressive dominance. People exhibiting this style are argumentative. They are likely to accompany their assertive tone of voice with forward leans and a substantial amount of arm waving. They sound like they want to fight, and often intimidate their less assertive interaction partners.

The Impression-Leaving Style.   This is the least researched of the various communication styles and may be simply a combination of the rest. The name refers to the impression a person projects or leaves: not just how a person is remembered after communication, but also whether the person leaves an impression at all.

GENERAL COMMUNICATOR STYLES

Norton's dimensions of communicator style have received considerable attention from many writers. However, others have suggested that many styles can be combined because they involve common communicative behavior. There are three general dimensions of communication style: assertiveness, responsiveness, and versatility. Let us consider each in turn.

Assertiveness is a communicator's use of control and ability to maintain the interest and attention of listeners. Common to the assertive communicator are factors such as dominance, forcefulness, independence, presence, taking charge, and willingness to defend one's own beliefs. The assertive communicator is an initiator. He or she is actively engaged in maintaining the attention of others through a dynamic delivery, vocal variety, and frequent movements and gestures.

The communicator who uses a responsive style is characterized as emotional, understanding, sensitive, and approachable. Through her or his actions, the responsive communicator projects friendliness, warmth, sincerity, and tenderness. Responsive communicators are eager to soothe hurt feelings and often show sympathy to others. They are willing to be helpful through their liberal use of positive feedback, and may continually reward others for open communication. The responsive style is a combination of the open, attentive, and friendly styles.

The third general communication dimension is versatility. Highly versatile communicators are those who adapt to the communicative behavior of the other. They often let others know of their willingness to be adaptive through an attentive posture. The versatile manager, for instance, can adapt her or his style of behavior and interaction to the needs of each employee. He or she uses dominating and assertive behavior with employees who require more control or direction, while using a more responsive style with those who need encouragement and supportive interaction. Behavior is flexible depending on the person or situation. The person who is capable of this style is the one who can project a high or low level of all, or nearly all, of the styles described by Norton. Clearly, this individual has considerable communicative competence.

Now that we have discussed the concept of communicator style and the body movement and gesture associated with each dimension, let's turn to an analysis of some effects our bodily motions have on us and others.

EFFECTS OF MOVEMENT AND GESTURE

In the final section of this chapter, we look at some effects of body movements on perceptions and interaction. Because the concept of communicator style is fresh in your mind, let's begin with a brief review of some studies that have been conducted in this area.

Communicator Style.   Do the dramatic style, the animated style, the contentious style, or the versatile style affect people's perceptions of you in any way? Research shows that they do. For example, in one study the researchers were interested in whether students' perception of teachers' effectiveness was affected by perceived assertiveness, responsiveness, and versatility in the behavior of the teachers. They found that students who saw their teachers as assertive also reported a more positive attitude toward the class and had a greater behavioral commitment to the teacher and the subject matter. The authors suggested that teachers who use assertive behavior are well-liked. Students who judged their teachers to be highly versatile and responsive also reported a more positive attitude and greater behavioral commitment. In another study, teachers who were perceived as more dramatic by their students were rated as more effective instructors. In brief, within the educational environment, more animated and lively styles of presenting material make it more interesting and provide a touch of entertainment. Similarly, teachers who use open and attentive positioning and encouraging movements can influence their students to view them as concerned and supportive.

Simplifying Encoding and Decoding.   Many writers believe that the use of illustrative gestures actually helps us to more easily encode our thoughts into spoken words. When you see someone who is having difficulty finding the right words, you probably notice that her or his gesturing increases considerably. Research tells us that, for one reason or another, the gesturing is aiding the speaker in her or his attempt to "spit it out."

Illustrators also help in the decoding of verbal messages. Body movements can elaborate the meaning of the words spoken and provide a second way of processing the information. People who paint pictures with their gestures or visually place imaginary objects in the space around them while speaking are giving their listeners cues they can process spatially and temporally while they are digesting the words. This may have important implications in the classroom. It is likely that students with dramatic teachers retain more class material and perform better on exams. One study was conducted to determine whether listeners who were provided visual cues by speakers were better at comprehending verbal messages. The results indicated that when listeners had the opportunity to see the speaker's body movements, their comprehension scores increased. Even when the speaker's lip and facial cues were hidden from the listeners view, kinesic cues alone positively affected comprehension.

Positive and Negative Perceptions.   We have already discussed many perceptions others have of us based on our bodily motions. We said, for instance, that open and attentive posture can affect perceptions of responsiveness and friendliness; closing ourselves off by blocking movements or indirect body orientation may produce perceptions of aloofness or an unwillingness to get too deeply involved. Other studies have shown that the positive or negative movements can influence others' judgments of our attractiveness. Positive head nods and other approval-type gestures are positively related to attractiveness. On the other hand, people who use self-manipulation behaviors are generally rated as less attractive.

Research on immediacy has shown that movement such as forward leans, closer proximity, more openness of arms and body, more direct body orientation, and postural relaxation can influence whether a person likes you. Closely related to liking, perceptions of warmth can be enhanced with shifts in posture toward the fellow interactant and keeping the hands still while smiling. You can, however, communicate a cold attitude by drumming your fingers, slumping in your chair, and moving your eyes as you look around the room.

As we conclude this chapter, it is important to note that gesture and movement are at the heart of the study of nonverbal communication. We have summarized many ways by which nonverbal messages are encoded into and decoded from the bodily actions of human beings. They provide particularly effective means for complementing, accenting, regulating, contradicting, and substituting verbal utterances. Caution should be exercised however, in assigning specific meaning to behavior without considering the context within which the nonverbal action occurs.

A GLOSSARY OF TERMINOLOGY

Adaptors are highly unintentional behaviors that are usually responses to boredom or stress or responses closely linked with negative feelings toward ourselves or someone else.

Affect displays are cues that involve primarily facial expressions but also include a person's posture, gait, limb movements, and other behaviors that provide information about the person's emotional state or mood.

Communicator style is the way one verbally and paraverbally interacts to signal how literal meaning should be taken, interpreted, filtered, or understood in the communicative process.

Emblems are gestures and movements that have a direct verbal translation. Emblems are known by most or all of a group, class, culture, or subculture. They can be used to stimulate specific meanings in the minds of others in place of verbal communication.

Illustrators are gestures and movements that are closely linked with spoken language and help to illustrate what is being said.

Instrumental function is the use of the skeletal and muscular in the accomplishment of some task.

Kinesics is the study of the communicative impact of body movement and gesture.

Referential function is the potential that our movements and gestures have to communicate nonverbal messages.

Regulators include gestures and movements that, along with eye and vocal cues, maintain and regulate the back-and-forth interaction between speakers and listeners during spoken dialogue.

Turn-denying behavior is behavior we use to decline our turn to speak.

Turn-maintaining cues are used by speakers who want to continue talking.

Turn-requesting regulators are used by the listener to signal the speaker that he or she would like to talk.

Turn-taking behavior is behavior that either the speaker uses to maintain or yield her or his talking turn or that the listener uses to request or decline an invitation to talk.

Turn-yielding cues are emitted by speakers who wish to cease talking and give the listener the opportunity to speak.

▲ 4

Face and Eye Behavior

The face, particularly the area around the eyes, probably is the most significant area of the body for communicating nonverbal messages. If research has taught us anything, it has helped us to understand that the human face is the primary tool used for transmitting expressions of emotion. The facial muscles provide such a complex repertoire of configurations that most of us, if we worked at it, could move our faces into more than a thousand different looks.

The major reason the face is so important in human communication is that it is usually visible during interaction. When you converse with others, where do you usually look? At their feet, their waist, their hands, shoulders, chests, or elbows? Of course, we might be more observant when communicating with others, but most of us look at the face, often to the exclusion of other parts of the body. When asked to describe an attractive man or woman, we generally begin with facial features. When we are engaged in serious dialogue with friends, acquaintances, and strangers, we turn to their faces for evidence that supports or contradicts their verbal messages.

It has been suggested that the eyes are the windows to the soul and our faces a marquee advertising our emotions, moods, and attitudes. Some view the study of facial expressions as the study of emotion itself. What this really suggests is that our emotions and the facial expression of those feelings are so closely connected to one another as to be inseparable. Although we believe that expressions and emotions are not totally linked, we do feel that people can find a plethora of cues on the faces of their fellow interactants that provide rich information about feelings toward self, toward others, and probably toward life.

Facial expression and eye behavior can say it all.

The face is important in other ways as well. By looking at the face and eyes, we often make judgments about personality characteristics. We can think of a variety of facial features that are stereotypically associated with certain personalities. Many performers complain of being typecast in particular types of television or movie roles because of the shape, profile, size, width, or narrowness of their faces. The crook, the family man, even the innocent victim must have the facial characteristics that convince the viewing audience that they are really "nasty vermin" or "good ol' boys."

The face and eyes are also important because they help us to manage and regulate our interactions with others. With our faces we can signal our disapproval, disbelief, or sincere interest in the messages of others. Our expressions can set the mood or tone of the conversation.

Our face and eyes influence our day-to-day communication at least as much as any other nonverbal behavior. To develop a clear perspective on the role of the face and eyes in nonverbal communication, it is useful to examine some perspectives others have advanced.

PERSPECTIVES ON ACQUISITION AND DEVELOPMENT

Are our facial expressions somehow inherently linked with our feelings? Do we have to learn how to smile when we are happy, to frown when we are sad or angry? Are facial expressions a product of social and cultural influences, or is there something universal and innate about the way we express our feelings on our faces? The debate over whether facial expressions are innate or learned (or both) is not new.

Charles Darwin (1872), who is most famous for his theories of evolution and the origins of the species, was quite interested in facial expression of animals as well as human beings. Darwin believed that expressive facial behaviors are essentially survival mechanisms and therefore evolved in much the same way as other physical characteristics. From this evolutionary perspective, facial expressions were acquired through the process of natural selection for establishing successful interaction. Long before the human species mastered the higher-level communicative skills required by verbal exchange, facial expressions allowed the higher-order primates to transmit their feelings, attitudes, and emotional states.

Results of research are increasingly supportive of the hypothesis that some facial expressions are inborn characteristics of human beings. Even without access to that research, if one travels the world, one can see that for many facial expressions and the meanings they convey appear to successfully cut across many cultural boundaries. This pattern is not present for other aspects of human behavior.

Eibl-Eibesfeld (1972), a researcher in the area of expressive behavior, holds closely to the position that facial expressions are innate. Much of his claim is based on his observations of children who were born both deaf and blind. Eibl-Eibesfeld's research has shown that the fundamental expressions of emotion on the face can be seen in such individuals. Says Eibl-Eibesfeld (1972), "they laugh, smile, sulk, cry, show surprise, and anger. The probability that they acquired all these facial expressions by learning is practically nil" (p. 305). In response to the argument that such deaf and blind children may have acquired expressions similar to normal children through the sense of touch, Eibl-Eibesfeld suggests that brain-damaged deaf and blind children also exhibit the typical facial expressions. In conclusion, he states:

> *It is difficult to imagine how they [blind and deaf brain-damaged children] could have learned social expressions without deliberate training. If anyone insists in such cases on the learning theory, the burden of proof for such an improbable hypothesis lies on his (or her) side. It seems more reasonable to assume that the neuronal and motor structures underlying these motor patterns developed in a process of self-differentiation by decoding genetically stored information. (p. 306)*

Therefore, according to the Darwin and Eibl-Eibesfeld perspective, facial expressions are inherently linked with moods and feelings, they are innate products of the evolutionary process, and they are generally universal in that emotions and feelings are expressed similarly whether you are Native American, European, Asian, African, or Indian.

Before we accept this position as the only explanation for how we acquire our facial expressions, let's think about other possible influences. Although much research supports the innate view, and although many basic or primary facial expressions are similarly decoded in many cultures, there are probably external factors such as the environment, social rules, and culture that contribute to our facial behavior.

Although no credible research shows that facial expressions are entirely learned, that does not mean that learning perspectives have no place in our understanding of facial expressions.

The other major perspective on the acquisition of facial expression is that such behaviors are both innate and learned. Many theorists hold to this position. Let us summarize very briefly what this position is. First, it is generally accepted there are primary facial expressions that, when we are born, are very closely linked to our primary emotions. These primary emotions are sadness, anger, disgust, fear, interest, surprise, and happiness. An effective and entertaining way to remember these primary emotions is to create an acronym: *SADFISH.*

As we observe infants and very young children, we see that they do spontaneously express the emotions they feel. As they grow older, however, they become socialized into the adult world of their cultures. As with anything else, they learn certain facial display rules that they must follow during particular social situations. As this learning process begins to take hold, facial expressions and feelings become somewhat divorced from one another. In short, we learn what is acceptable and what is unacceptable in terms of expressive behavior. For instance, it is natural to smile and laugh when something strikes us as funny. However, you soon learn that smiling and laughing at someone's off-key singing during the Star Spangled Banner at a baseball game is a behavior that often elicits a poke in the ribs from a friend or relative near you. You've learned rule number one: Thou shall not smile at some things that are funny.

The culture-specific differences that eventually appear in our facial expressions arise primarily from three factors. First, cultures differ concerning circumstances that elicit certain emotions. Second, cultures differ about the consequences that follow certain emotional expressions. Third, different cultures have different display rules that their members must learn, which govern the use of facial behavior. For instance, even today in North American culture, men are discouraged from expressing extreme sadness or happiness. American males are expected to be more composed. It is no wonder! You can surely remember that all-important rule you learned as a child: Big boys don't cry! Consider other consequences that might befall the male who is too expressive. Females, on the other hand, are generally allowed to be more emotional than males, whether they feel extremely sad or tremendously happy. In other cultures, we may find the rules reversed. Some Arabic peoples view it as perfectly acceptable for their men to be overcome with joy and excitement at the reunion of an old friend or to weep openly when saddened or disappointed.

EXPRESSION OF EMOTION AND FACIAL MANAGEMENT

We suggested earlier that some researchers believe that a study of the face and its expressions is a study of emotion itself. Although the face is a vital source of information about the *type* of emotion a person is experiencing, some writers claim that body tension is a better indicator of the *intensity* with which an emotion is felt. Furthermore, cultural and social influences may have taught us to divorce our emotions from our actual facial behavior. Controlling our facial behavior is an ability we learn very early in life. We master display rules, rules that tell us how to display our emotions in various social settings. The term used to describe these prescribed behaviors is *facial management techniques.*

Facial management techniques are not only learned very early but often are learned so thoroughly they become habitual. That is, we learn them to such a degree that they become automatic responses. We can modify facial expressions of primary emotions to the point that normally universal expressions can differ from culture to culture. In addition, social norms decide which facial management techniques are appropriate for each emotion when expressed by individuals of varying status, gender, age, and social role. Let's review the four most common facial management techniques: intensification, deintensification, neutralization, and masking.

Intensification

Intensification of our expressions is accomplished by exaggerating what we feel. Sometimes we have to build the external expression of the emotion far beyond what we feel in order to meet the expressed concern of others. Have you ever been in a situation where social pressures required that you exaggerate a facial expression? Consider the following scenario:

> *Jim's fraternity brothers had decided to surprise him with a birthday party. They had planned the party well in advance to ensure that Jim's girlfriend from home could be there. Friday afternoon finally arrived and Jim decided to go home for the weekend to visit his girlfriend. As he packed a few articles of clothing into a backpack, Damon bounded into the room.*
>
> *"Where do you think you're going?"*
>
> *"Thought I'd spend the weekend at home. I haven't seen Heather in two months," Jim replied. He grabbed his backpack, put the strap over his shoulder, and headed for the door. "See you Sunday night."*
>
> *"Whoa! Hold on a minute! You can't leave!"*
>
> *"What do you mean I can't leave! I'm outta here, buddy."*
>
> *No doubt Damon had to explain the surprise party to Jim. Jim was certainly excited and happy. That evening at the fraternity house, no one ever guessed that he had been told of the big surprise because Jim's face was filled with wonder and amazement when the lights popped on and everyone yelled "Surprise!" He over-exaggerated his facial expression so his fraternity brothers and Heather would not be disappointed. Jim felt happy and surprised, but not nearly as much as his friends expected him to be. He had to intensify his expression to meet their expectations.*

In some cultures, such as those in several Mediterranean countries, sadness or grief responses commonly are exaggerated. In others, such intensification would appear very much out of place. Similarly, some people habitually engage in intensification, such as those who employ a dramatic communication style, whereas others do not. Most of us who live in the United States find intensification an appropriate technique from time to time.

Deintensification

There are situations and social events, some of which are near opposites to those discussed above, that call for us to *deintensify* or deemphasize the facial expression of a particular emotion. The circumstances require us to downplay how we truly feel. Usually, deintensification of expression occurs when we experience feelings that our culture has taught us are unacceptable. The British, as you may know, are well-known for understating almost any emotion. In our culture, men are generally not permitted to express strong feelings of fear or sadness. At the funeral of a loved one, the American man is permitted to express some grief, but because he is the "man of the family" and is expected to be "strong" for everyone else, he may deintensify those expressions to meet the expectations of his family members.

People in controlling positions, such as teachers, physicians, and supervisors, often find themselves in situations where it would be most inappropriate to express their emotions to the true extent to which they are felt. Managers often find themselves in situations with employees that require them to downplay facial expressions. A manager might be outraged at the behavior of one subordinate during a departmental meeting, but recognize that expressing those emotions in that setting would be very counterproductive. After the meeting is over, the manager expresses his or her concern in a controlled manner and the wayward subordinate is appropriately reprimanded. However, if the manager had expressed the emotions to the extent that he or she really experienced them, the poor employee may have ended dangling by the toes from the ceiling as the manager flailed away with a bullwhip!

Neutralization

You have probably heard someone described as a "poker face." Chances are that these emotionless individuals are engaging in the facial management technique called *neutralization.* When we neutralize our facial expressions, we essentially eliminate any expression of emotion. The poker player does not want her or his face to tell the world the draw just hit an inside straight. To express elation at this point would frighten the other players, and they would fold. Conversely, the player does not want a bad hand of cards showing on the face, either. If the other players were to read her or his face and discern that the hand contained nothing, the player could no longer bluff them. Consequently, the successful poker player learns to neutralize all facial expressions and keep opponents confused.

It is not only in poker games in which we may wish to neutralize our facial expressions. In many circumstances, we may experience emotions when expressing any emotion might be against our best interests. Although we cannot usually avoid negative emotions such as fear and anger, we often can prevent undesirable reactions of others by neutralizing our expression of those emotions. When our expressions are neutralized, others are unaware that we experience any emotion, much less which emotion.

Masking

The fourth facial management technique we learn to use under certain cultural or social influence is *masking*. This technique involves repression of the expressions related to the emotion felt and their replacement with expressions that are acceptable under the circumstances. Think for a moment how people feel when they lose a contest to another person. How do you think they really feel? How would you feel? Not too great, most likely. However, in American culture we are expected to show happiness and pleasure for the winner and avoid any expressions of our own disappointment. That is part of being a "good loser" or a "good sport."

An elementary school principal recently told a story about a second-grade boy who had been sent to the office for telling an unacceptable joke during class. After several long minutes of talking with the young boy and explaining the inappropriateness of such behavior, the principal asked the boy if he had understood the situation. Looking puzzled, the boy asked, "Don't you want to hear the joke? It's a very good one." The boy proceeded to tell the joke, whereupon the principal scolded him. The circumstances dictated that the principal show sternness, although he actually found the entire situation humorous.

In some cultures, expression of negative emotions is more of a taboo than it is in others. This often causes communication problems when people from different cultures interact. When American businesspeople do not like something, it is considered appropriate that they express this displeasure. For Japanese businesspeople, the opposite is true. The Japanese are often considered masters of masking. Americans, then, have great difficulty understanding how their Japanese counterparts are responding because the external expressions of emotion may always be positive. A friend of the authors returned from a very unsuccessful trip to Japan with this comment: "There is no word in the Japanese language for 'no,' but there are a hundred words for 'yes.' Unfortunately they all really mean 'no.'" Clearly, he had not yet learned the art of masking in the Japanese culture.

Styles of Facial Expression

Based on these facial management techniques, Ekman and Friesen (1975) devised a classification of various styles of facial expression. The techniques we have discussed are often used during a particular situation at a particular time. However,

Ekman and Friesen contend that some people display a certain style of expression consistently no matter what the circumstances may be. These styles represent enduring predispositions toward making certain emotional displays. Let us look at eight different styles that some people consistently use. Keep in mind that these "facial sets" are generally outside the conscious awareness of the people displaying them.

The *withholder* style is characterized by individuals who seldom have any facial movement. The face inhibits the display of actual feelings. We might say that withholders use the neutralizing display rule almost constantly.

The *revealer* style is essentially the reverse of the withholder style. Revealers always show their true feelings. They are often described as wearing their heart on their faces, and they generally admit that they "just can't help expressing themselves." They often have a highly dramatic communication style.

The *unwitting expressor* often believes that he or she is doing a good job of masking true feelings. He or she unknowingly leaks information about the actual emotion that is being experienced. This person is a poor neutralizer. Thus, he or she is often in trouble for expressing inappropriate emotions such as laughing when someone else falls down or spills food.

Blanked expressors have ambiguous or neutral expressions even when they believe they are displaying their emotions. They think they have moved their faces into a smile, but the only thing that others see is a blank face. For these people, the feeling of emotion and the expression of emotion are two unconnected phenomena.

The *substitute expressor* substitutes one emotional expression for another. The person may think that he or she is showing happiness but actually is expressing disgust. The substitute expressor will not believe it when told what her or his expression really communicates.

The *frozen-affect expressor* manifests at least a part of a particular emotional expression always. During a neutral state, frozen-affect expressors look naturally sad, happy, or angry under all circumstances. One emotion is carved forever in their faces. This person wears a permanent mask.

Ever-ready expressors tend to display one particular emotion as the initial response to almost any situation. They may first smile, whether they receive good news or bad news. Whether the situation provokes anger, surprise, fear, or sadness, the first response is always the same and is then followed by a more revealing expression.

Finally, *flooded-affect expressors* flood their faces constantly with a particular emotion. These individuals never appear neutral. One person, for instance, may have an extreme look of fear all the time; even during situations that cause them to express happiness, the fearful expression does not fade completely. Any temporary expressions are generally tempered by the expression of fear.

Our discussion of facial management techniques and facial styles brings up an important point about the expression of emotion. We do not always express one emotion. In other words, our facial expressions are not purely ones of sadness, happiness, or disgust. Sometimes, we express two or three emotions simultaneously. At other times, we are neutral in our expression but one area of the face reveals our feelings. The following discussion addresses this issue.

Affect Blends and Partials

Ekman, Friesen, and Tomkins (1971) devised a way of locating and evaluating the facial expressions of individuals. Their technique is called the *Facial Affect Scoring Technique (FAST),* and it separates the face into three areas: the lower face including cheeks, nose, and mouth; the eyes and eyelid area; and the brows and forehead area. Designed for use with both still photographs and motion picture film, the FAST technique decides which emotions are being expressed in the three different areas.

The lower face. Desmond Morris (1985) suggests that "the cheek is also the region most likely to expose the true emotions of its owners. For it is here that emotional changes of color are most conspicuously displayed" (p. 85). He further suggests that shame and embarrassment can be seen on the cheeks when two small points on the cheeks turn deep red. Cheeks are also indicators of anger. In anger, there is a different pattern of reddening. The red color spreads all over the cheeks and even to the top of the skull (although the cheeks of a truly aggressive person may turn very pale, almost white, because the blood is drained away from the skin). If a person is truly frightened, the color may drain from the cheeks and the person's cheeks look blanched.

The human mouth, Desmond points out, "works overtime. Other animals use their mouths a great deal—to bite, lick, suck, taste, chew, swallow, cough, yawn, snarl, scream, and grunt—but we have added to this list. We also use it for talking, whistling, smiling, laughing, kissing, and smoking. It is hardly surprising that the mouth has been described as 'the battleground of the face'" (p. 93). He goes on to suggest that the mouth is not only one of the busiest parts of the body but one of the "most expressive." The mouth can be used to express boredom, interest, erotic emotions, sadness, happiness, contempt, disgust, fear, anger, bodily needs, insubordination, surprise, and many other emotions. Because the mouth is such a focal point on the face, cultures have often modified, exaggerated, improved, reshaped, colored, stained, tattooed, or altered the appearance of the mouth.

The nose, according to Desmond, is unique. Other species "have nothing quite like it" (p. 65). The nose can be seen as a resonator, a shield to protect the eyes against injury, a shield against water, a shield against dust and dirt, or an air filter. If we lose the use of our nose as a filter, we experience serious respiratory difficulty within a few days. The nose also aids us in scent. If we lose our scent function, we may cease to enjoy food and certain forms of entertainment. As with the mouth and cheeks, many cultures have gone to extreme lengths to change, reshape, or decorate the nose. Michael Jackson is noted for having his nose reshaped and reduced through cosmetic surgery. Some persons pierce their noses and attach jewelry through the pierced holes.

Eye and eyelid region. Desmond Morris suggests about the eyes that "it has been estimated that 80 percent of our information about the outside world enters through these remarkable structures" (p. 49). We are visual animals—if we can see it, we are likely to remember it. The entire "primate order is a vision-dominated group, with the two eyes brought to the front of the head, providing a binocular view of the world" (p. 49).

The brows and forehead region. Morris suggests that "to have a brow like a human being you have to be a very intelligent animal indeed. For the human brow, made up of forehead, temples and eyebrows, was the direct result of our ancestors' dramatic brain enlargement" (p. 37). The brows and forehead region can express many messages. Lowering the eyebrows is a frown and can be a sign of displeasure. Raising the eyebrows can be a sign of interest, hence the term "an eye-opening experience." An extreme eyebrow raise can express surprise or fear, depending on the situation. Raising one eyebrow while keeping one steady (the eyebrow cock) is a questioning expression. Knitted eyebrows can be associated with chronic pain, headaches, anxiety, grief, or extreme frustration. Flashing eyebrows (eyebrows are raised and lowered in a second) could mean acknowledgement, greeting, friendly recognition, or surprise. Like the other regions of the face, this region can communicate multiple expressions and emotions.

Researchers in the area of facial expression have used the FAST and similar methods and found that some primary emotions can be judged accurately and consistently. No one area of an individual's face is best at revealing an emotion. The information one gets from any particular area depends a great deal on the emotion being judged. Research in this area has revealed a number of interesting findings. Fear and sadness are best identified from the eyes and eyelid area (67 percent accuracy); happiness can be judged accurately 98 percent of the time from the lower face and 99 percent of the time from the eyes and lids; and surprise is accurately identified from all three areas fairly well (brows/forehead, 79 percent; eyes/eyelids, 63 percent; and lower face, 52 percent). Anger, however, is not accurately perceived from any one area alone. At least two areas of the face must be seen for anger to be judged. The facts seem to show that it depends on which emotion is being judged whether one area of the face best reveals that emotion.

Ekman contends that at any given time, an individual may show two or more emotions, one in the lower face and another in the eyes, for example. These multiple facial expressions are called *affect blends*. When someone plays a nasty trick on you, you may respond by showing anger in the eyes and disgust in the lower face. When Jim walked into his surprise birthday party, chances are he expressed both happiness and surprise simultaneously but in different areas.

Affect blends may be responsible for many cultural differences found in emotional expression. In one culture, sadness expressed at a funeral may be combined with expressions of fear, while in another expressions of sadness may be combined with anger. Although primary facial expressions may be universal, affect blends are not. The way we combine displays of affect are generally dictated by cultural and social constraints.

According to Knapp and Hall (1992), affect blends appear on the face in several ways. First, one emotion appears in one area of the face and another emotion appears in another area. An example of this type of blend would be raised brows for surprise while the corners of the mouth are lifted into a smile to show happiness. Second, two emotions appear in one area of the face. They suggest that we sometimes show surprise and anger with the eyebrows—one raised and one pulled down toward the eye. Third, and more complicated, a given facial expression may be produced by "muscle action associated with two emotions, but containing specific elements of neither" (p. 268).

Another facial behavior that is commonly seen involves showing an emotion in only one area while successfully controlling the other two areas. Emotional expressions in only one area are called *partials* and are more than likely the result of emotional leakage. During a tornado, a mother hurries to comfort her young child. While her lower face and forehead appear calm, her eyes may express fear.

Katsikitis, Pilowsky, and Innes (1990) tested whether line drawings of faces generated by a computer produced the same responses in decoders as the photographs from which the line drawings were derived. The computer-generated line drawings were of the mouth, nose, eyes, eyebrows, and facial outline and were not gender-specific. Twelve facial measures were generated by the computer. They were named End-Lip Raise, Mouth-Width, Mouth-Opening, Mid-Top-Lip Raise, Mid-Low-Lip Raise, Top-Lip Thickness, Lower-Lip Thickness, Eye-Opening, Top-Eyelid/Iris Intersect, Lower-Eyelid/Iris Intersect, Inner-Eyebrow Separation, and Mid-Eyebrow Raise. These twelve represented landmark facial points relevant to emotional signals and were chosen because they accounted for a wide range of emotional expression. The subjects viewed the computer-generated images and the photographs and made judgments. The conclusions are as follows: The judges could recognize and decode facial expressions from computer-generated line drawings and real photographs with fairly equal ability. Human judges are in tune to the common emotions and the common expressions that correlate with the emotion, whether it is a computer-generated line drawing or a photograph. Subjects could reliably distinguish expressions of smiles from neutral looks. Therefore, whether they are computer-generated or real-life, most of us can fairly accurately judge the primary facial emotional expressions commonly used within this culture.

Tucker and Riggio (1988) found that "the ability to pose emotions was possibly facilitated in those individuals skilled in verbal expression" (p. 94). In other words, individuals with higher verbal ability might also be the ones who can portray emotions more readily. Or they might be the persons who can mask emotions better. Much of this research warrants further examination.

Brownlow and Zebrowitz (1990) found that "mature-faced" spokespersons on television were viewed by judges as more expert than "baby-faced" spokespersons, although baby-faced spokespersons were viewed as more trustworthy than mature-faced spokespersons. Women were viewed as slightly more trustworthy than men and men were viewed as slightly more expert than women by the judges. Therefore, they conclude that "the results of this study reveal that actors' facial maturity and gender influence the type of commercial communications they are chosen to deliver" (p. 58). The relationship between baby-faced spokespersons and mature-faced spokespersons must be examined extensively before conclusions can be etched in stone. However, the results do affirm some past research on the effects of facial appearance on interviewer impressions and real-world experiences.

THE IMPORTANCE OF EYE BEHAVIOR

Oculesics is the study of eye behavior, eye contact, eye movement, and the functions of eye behavior. Of all of the features of the face, the eyes are probably the most important in the human communication process. The human eye is capable of "responding to one-and-a-half-million simultaneous messages, and yet it is no bigger than a table-tennis ball" (Morris, 1985, p. 49). Some writers claim that the eyes provide signals concerning emotions, attitudes, and relationships when no other body cues may be found. The initial contact made between people usually is eye contact. If that contact is not pleasing to one or both of the individuals, it is quite possible that no additional contact will take place.

With our eyes we can love, hate, attack, avoid, or insult our fellow human beings without uttering a word. Eye gaze can, as the philosopher Emerson once said, transcend the spoken word. One of the authors recalls the sharp glance of a strict person to silence the misbehavior of the children at the annual Thanksgiving gathering at Aunt Virginia's house. All the children used to laugh and tease one another with old Uncle Henry's frightening glare. Molly stared daggers at Tiffany; Paul made eyes at Heather; Tony saw blood in Peter's eyes; Ms. Albright silenced the class with a cold hard glance; Mary had the evil eye; Bill would not look her in the eye. All these illustrate the power of eye contact and mutual gaze. "So small are the glistening spheres; so large is their message."

Eye behavior has been defined in many ways depending on the particular type of "looking" that is being studied. There are several types of eye behavior. *Mutual look* or *mutual gaze* refers to two people looking in the direction of one another's faces. Eye contact is characterized by mutual gaze that is centered on the eyes. On the other hand, a *one-sided look* is a gaze of one individual in the direction of another person's face. Here, the gaze is not reciprocated. When someone avoids looking at another during an interpersonal encounter, even when the other is looking at him or her, then *gaze aversion* has occurred.

Gaze aversion typically is an intentional act. People who avert their eyes from another normally do so consciously and are somehow motivated not to look. Gaze aversion may signal that you are not interested in what the other has to say. You may be unsure of yourself and not want the other to read this in your eyes. You may also use gaze aversion as a regulator when you do not wish to communicate any further (see Chapter 3 for a discussion of regulators). For whatever reason it occurs, gaze aversion is normally is taken as some kind of avoidance.

Looking at someone can send nonverbal messages.

Gaze aversion should not be confused with gaze omission. *Gaze omission* describes a situation where one person does not look at the other but is not intentionally avoiding eye contact. The confusion between aversion and omission may lead to interpersonal misunderstanding. Although the actual behavior may be similar, different messages are communicated. See if you can figure out whether aversion or omission is represented in each case below.

1. Mary and John are quarreling over what television program to watch. Finally, Mary turns off the set and stares out the window while John continues to argue.

2. Harry is a constant troublemaker in class. Mr. Baker has finally had enough of Harry's misbehavior, and asks him to stay after class. As Mr. Baker scolds him, Harry looks toward the floor and smiles.

3. *Melanie sits at the end of the bar. Stephen enters the lounge and glances at her. Occasionally, Stephen looks toward her, hoping to catch her eye. Each time he looks toward her, she is happily engaged in conversation with someone else. He eventually becomes dismayed and concludes that Melanie is not interested in him.*

Well? What did you decide in each case? If you said that Mary was engaged in gaze aversion, you are probably right. Her intention was to end the verbal dispute and conclude the interaction. She had enough. What about Harry? He was also intentionally averting his gaze from Mr. Baker. By looking away, he may have intentionally transmitted a message to Mr. Baker that he was unconcerned, unshaken, and not a bit threatened by the dressing-down he was receiving. Melanie, on the other hand, was more than likely unaware of Stephen. Although Stephen may have taken her lack of eye contact as a signal of rejection, chances are that she was completely oblivious to Stephen's apparent advances. Her eye behavior involved gaze omission rather than aversion.

The Functions of Eye Behavior

You have probably developed an appreciation for the importance of our eyes in the interaction process. Let us now turn to the properties and functions of eye behavior.

There are three important properties of eye behavior. The first property is salience. Because eye behavior, such as a direct gaze, has a high probability of being noticed, it is usually a much more salient interaction signal than most other bodily motions. That is, the behavior of our eyes plays an extremely important role in managing our interactions, in eliciting the attention of others, and in communicating our interest in what others have to say. We generally expect people to respond to our gaze and often become frustrated when they do not do so immediately.

The second important property of eye behavior is its extraordinary capability to stimulate arousal. It is virtually impossible not to experience some degree of arousal when we see another person. This arousal may be negative, such as when we catch the glance of someone we would rather not interact with, or it may be positive, as with two lovers at a cozy table in a dimly lit restaurant.

The final important property of eye behavior is involvement. In our culture, it is difficult to establish eye contact with someone and not interact with her or him. Even with a stranger we meet for the briefest of moments while passing on the sidewalk, eye contact seems to oblige us to nod our heads and smile, if nothing else. Eye contact with another virtually commands involvement with that other.

Many scholars have been interested in these properties of eye behavior and have learned that the eyes serve many functions in our communicative exchanges. Kendon, a notable writer in the area of visual behavior, first described these functions in 1967. Since then, other writers in nonverbal communication have expanded and elaborated on the ways our eyes serve to hinder, help, or otherwise influence interaction. Eye behavior appears to serve four primary functions. Let us consider each.

Eye behavior functions to establish and define the nature of interpersonal relationships. As we suggested above, eye contact often obliges us to interact with others. Looking at another person is often an invitation to interact. Interpersonal encounters usually begin with the two parties mutually gazing and establishing eye contact. We challenge you to strike up a conversation with a friend or stranger in a public area without looking at her or him. You may, with a great deal of effort, do so, but it feels quite unnatural and it is difficult to maintain the interaction.

If you recall the case of Melanie and Stephen (in the bar), you remember that a relationship never was actually established. Stephen repeatedly looked in Melanie's direction hoping to catch her gaze. Like Stephen, many of us find it difficult to approach another person and begin to interact without first having received the appropriate signals. You may meet a stranger on the sidewalk with every intention of saying "hello," but you find that without their return glance the words escape you. The stranger has essentially communicated, through gaze avoidance, that he or she does not wish to exchange cordialities.

The type and amount of eye behavior can also reveal the nature of a relationship. Two conversants who differ in status usually engage in different visual behavior toward one another. The higher-status individual generally receives more eye gaze from the lower-status person than the other way around. Both men and women look less at speakers who are lower in status than themselves. The relationship between status and eye behavior may indicate one of several things. First, it may suggest that lower-status individuals show their respect by gazing at their higher-status counterparts. Second, the higher-status person may simply feel less of a need to monitor the lower-status person, whereas the lower-status person may feel it important to do so.

The amount we look at others may be a function of how much we like them. In dyads where interactants report liking one another, mutual gaze tends to be more prominent. Eye contact is also greater among persons engaging in intimate relationships. You can be perceived as too "fast" or forward if you look more than the other person deems appropriate. In such cases, you may be using eye contact to let the other know you would like to become more intimate, and he or she may use substantially less eye contact to tell you to "back off."

Increasing our gaze to a speaker also functions to signal the speaker that we are paying attention and are interested in what he or she has to say. This is a culture-specific visual activity, however. North Americans equate looking with interest and attention, but this is not true in all other cultures. One North American teacher became extremely frustrated with an Asian student and held him after class. While talking to the young student, the teacher became upset because the student constantly looked at the floor. Little did the teacher realize that the student was attending to her message, but had been socialized to not look at higher-status individuals. To gaze at an authority figure while she spoke would, to the student, have been disrespectful. This unfortunate student was doing his best to behave appropriately, but was being punished because the teacher was unfamiliar with the cultural differences in expected gaze behavior. It would be easy to criticize that teacher for her "insensitivity" to the child from another culture, but it must be recognized that very few teacher education programs include instruction in nonverbal and intercultural communication.

Eye behavior functions to express emotion. In an earlier section of this chapter, we explained how the eyes are a valuable source of information about emotional states. The eye area of the face generally is considered the least controllable of the facial areas and, as a result, probably shows more accurate emotional states than other areas. Paul Ekman and his associates have conducted much research in eye behavior and emotions, and they suggest that the eyes provide a great deal of information about the emotions of fear, disgust, anger, happiness, and sadness. They note, however, that there is considerable change in the eyes with fear and surprise, whereas there is little change during states of happiness and disgust. We make our best judgments of emotion when we can see the other's entire face.

Eye behavior functions to regulate and coordinate our interactions with others. Along with many other nonverbal cues, the eyes are quite effective in regulating the back-and-forth interaction between speakers and listeners. Research has shown that interactants look more while listening than while speaking. Gaze avoidance is increased by speakers who are using turn-maintaining cues. Those who want to continue talking often signal their intention by dramatically reducing their eye gaze toward the listener. Furthermore, listeners who wish for the speaker to continue usually gaze toward the speaker. A primary turn-yielding cue used by speakers as they finish talking involves a head-turn in the direction of the listener accompanied by increased eye contact. In contrast, listeners request a turn by turning the head away from the speaker to reduce eye gaze.

Breaking eye contact and sustaining the break is a good clue that one is ready to end an interaction. For instance, if you are in an interview and feel that all is going well, check the eye behavior of the interviewer. He or she may be telling you, by breaking eye contact, that the time is up. Your failure to heed this signal may have a negative impact on the interviewer and negate all those wonderful qualities you have been rolling smoothly out of your mouth.

Regulating and controlling interaction involves power displays. The sustained gaze or stare is an effective means by which individuals can display power. Furthermore, these power gazes generally elicit one of two visual responses. Either the other person will stare back to communicate that your power display is being defied, or the other will use gaze avoidance for escape. Surely, you have played the childhood game of "stare down." What starts out as fun and games may quickly deteriorate into an out-and-out struggle for interpersonal supremacy. The one who stares the longest gains control of the other. Even among children and during harmless play, the result of a session of "stare down" can have long-lasting interpersonal consequences. Often, however, more powerful individuals give less visual attention to lower-status speakers than the other way around.

Gaze avoidance behavior functions to reduce distractions. Many believe that the reason speakers avert their gaze from their listeners more than they look at them is because they must reduce such monitoring behavior while putting their thoughts into words. By looking away, we are better able to concentrate on our verbal messages, putting them together in a more comprehensible fashion.

Avoiding gaze with others in order to reduce distractions tends to increase when the other asks us a difficult question. The more difficult the question, the longer we are likely to avert our gaze.

> *Try a little experiment with a friend or roommate. Sit facing one another, and ask your friend a series of questions. Ask some easy ones and some difficult ones. Observe his or her eyes. Next, ask your friend to look at you while answering, without looking away. It is probably very hard for him or her to think about an answer and watch you simultaneously.*

Closely related to gaze avoidance and the reducing of distractions are eye behaviors called *conjugate lateral eye movements.* These movements, usually referred to by the acronym *CLEMS,* are involuntary lateral shifts of the eyes to the right or left. CLEMS are thought to be closely associated with cognitive processing; that is, we look away to the left or right while we are thinking but look forward again when we stop processing information. People can be categorized as either right-lookers or left-lookers because approximately 75 percent of an individual's conjugate lateral eye movements are in one direction. CLEM movement is usually quite prominent when someone is working on a task that requires him or her to think or reflect. Asking will more than likely cause an involuntary shift. There is some speculation that when we call attention to a person's CLEM movement and ask that person to control it, stopping the shifts may make it so difficult for her or him to concentrate that it may distract from the person's cognitive processing.

The Importance of Pupil Dilation

The pupils of the eyes can dilate (increase in size) or constrict (decrease in size). This fact has been known for centuries. Whether pupil dilation and constriction are important to the communication process, however, is still open to question. The impact of pupil dilation and constriction on interpersonal interactions, and vice versa, is hardly clear-cut. Many factors influence this involuntary pupil response. Physical conditions such as the brightness or dimness of lighting invariably affect the size of someone's pupils. Neurophysiological factors and chemical stimulants or depressants are known to affect pupil size as well. Nevertheless, research has provided some interesting findings that may have implications for social interactions.

As early as 1960, researchers Hess and Polt were interested in the effects of certain visual material on pupil size. They found that men's pupils dilated when they viewed posters of women and women's pupils dilated when they observed photographs of men. Another study found that the pupils of gay men dilated when they were shown photographs of men. Still another study found that women's pupils dilated when they were shown photographs of newborn infants.

These studies suggest that pupil dilation may be a good indicant of positive emotional arousal and interest in what is being observed. Pupil constriction, on the other hand, seems to indicate an aversion to the thing or person being observed. Thus, it is not too great a leap to speculate that if we see that the eyes are dilated in the person with whom we are talking, it may be a sign that person is interested in what we are saying, or even in us.

Indeed, one study found that dilated pupils in photographs of women enhanced perceptions of attractiveness. Long before this research, several hundred years ago, women used the drug belladonna to cause their eyes to dilate. (This is essentially the same drug eye doctors use during examinations today to dilate our eyes.) Dilated pupils, they believed, made them more appealing to men. A study was conducted in which two exact pictures of the same women were used, one picture with pupils retouched to appear dilated and the other retouched to appear constricted. Men who evaluated the pictures attributed more positive characteristics to the one with dilated pupils and more negative characteristics to the picture with constricted pupils.

Another study recently found that deception may be detected through pupillary activity. Clark (1975) had his subjects memorize a secret code while playing the role of secret agents. He later exposed them to the secret code while giving them a lie-detector test. Clark found that subjects' pupils would dilate more often while observing the secret code than when observing other codes. He reported detection 80 percent of the time.

A very interesting phenomenon that has been discovered in the pupillometric research above is that there tends to be a reciprocal effect on individuals who observe dilated pupils. That is, when viewing the dilated pupils of someone, the other's pupils tend to dilate as well. This seems to suggest that dilated pupils enhance positive responses and create perceptions of attractiveness. Constricted pupils, on the other hand, do not generally elicit positive arousal and may reduce perceptions of attractiveness.

Now, as to the importance of pupil dilation in human interaction, we leave the decision up to you. You usually cannot see the pupils of others' eyes in a context in which emotional reactions are the primary determinant of pupil size; ambient lighting is always a factor. Under controlled conditions, however, it probably is possible to gain some emotional information from this aspect of human eye behavior. At least, that is what some poker players appear to believe. We are told that is why many professionals prefer to wear sunglasses to conceal their eyes or eye shades or caps to cause their eyes to remain dilated despite the hand they draw. So can pupil dilation be important? We wouldn't want to bet against it!

EYE BEHAVIOR AND INDIVIDUAL DIFFERENCES

One researcher has reported that the "normal" gazing duration during interpersonal interaction ranges from 28 to 70 percent. Another reports that "normal" variation in looking ranges from 8 to 73 percent. What these findings suggest is that what is "normal" depends largely on the many individual differences among people. We must always keep in mind that normal behavior for some may be abnormal for others, depending on their gender, personality characteristics, and ethnic and cultural background as well as the context in which the interaction occurs. Let us consider some of these individual differences as they affect the eye behavior of people during communication.

Cultural Differences

A person's culture is the atmosphere in which he or she learns the social norms for what is appropriate or inappropriate behavior. The influence of the ethnic and cultural environment on eye behavior has been observed by many scholars.

In an extensive investigation involving members of several different cultures, Watson (1970) found that Latin Americans, Southern Europeans, and Arabs tended to focus their gaze directly on the eyes or face while talking and listening. On the other hand, Northern Europeans, Indian-Pakistanis, and Asians tended more toward a peripheral gaze or no gaze at all. By *peripheral gaze,* Watson meant an orientation toward the other without actually focusing on the face or eyes. When they did not gaze at all, they either looked toward the floor or gazed into space.

Knapp and Hall (1992) suggest that many cultural differences are best seen in terms of duration rather than frequency of gaze. He noted, for instance, that Swedes do not look as frequently as the English during conversations, but when they do look they gaze for a longer period. Malandro, Barker, and Barker (1989) suggest that some cultures, such as the Korean, place much more emphasis on the observance of the eyes than do others. That is, Koreans are highly aware of eye behavior because it is believed that "real answers" to questions they ask may be found there, although the other's words say something else.

Contextual Differences

Often the context or topic of discussion affects the amount and duration of looking behavior during interaction. When we are attempting to persuade another, for instance, we tend to look more at our fellow interactant. Speakers who use more eye contact are judged by listeners to be more persuasive, credible, and sincere. Furthermore, when we find the situation comfortable, interesting, and happy we tend to establish more eye contact with our partners. Conversely, eye gazes in the direction of the partner are found to decrease during moments of embarrassment, guilt, or sadness.

Personality Differences

It should not surprise you that the personality characteristics of individuals are closely related to the amount of eye contact they use during conversations. People who have a high need for affiliation, inclusion, or affection gaze more steadily at others. People who are dominant, authoritative, and extroverted have also been found to look more frequently.

Although there has been little research bearing directly on this question, what there is suggests that such characteristics as shyness, communication apprehension, or unwillingness to communicate may affect eye behavior. Individuals who have these negative orientations toward communication tend to establish less eye contact. Because eye contact, in our culture, almost obliges us to engage in interaction with others, those who experience anxiety about communicating use behaviors such as gaze aversion or omission that allow them to avoid interaction when possible.

Gender Differences

If one finding seems clear concerning gender differences in eye behavior, it is that, overall, women engage in more looking behavior than do men. Not only do females look more at their conversational partners while listening, they also look more while speaking. However, the amount of actual eye contact is greater in male–male and female–female dyads than in mixed-gender dyads. One study has suggested that women appear to use shifts in gaze while speaking as a cue for liking whereas men generally use gaze for listening.

Much of the difference in looking behavior between women and men may be due to personality differences. Some studies, for example, indicate that females generally report higher needs for inclusion, affiliation, and affection during interaction and may use more looking to fulfill those needs. It has also been suggested that females probably rely more heavily on visual stimuli than do males because they are more sensitive to the social impact their eye behavior has on interpersonal exchange.

Given that much of the research on gender differences in eye behavior was conducted more than 25 years ago, we must accept these distinctions with caution. There has since been a revolution in gender roles that may have had a major impact on what is considered "normal" female eye behavior. It is probable that the high female needs for inclusion, affiliation, and affection noted in the 1960s, needs that are commonly acknowledged to be at least partially culturally determined, are lower for today's females. Similarly, characteristics of dominance and assertiveness, which were considered appropriate only for males a quarter-century ago, are now considered less aversive for females. Because these personality factors have been found to be highly related to gaze behavior, it is entirely possible that the differences between male and female eye behavior observed in the past are much reduced or even missing in today's society. We cannot be certain about such speculation, of course, until some of the classic studies of the 1960s are replicated with females and males of the 1990s.

To summarize, normal eye behavior includes a wide range of looking frequency and duration. It is generally necessary to consider personality, gender, culture, and contextual influences in evaluating the gazing activity of other people. Neglecting these influences may lead to interpersonal misunderstandings. Remember: Nonverbal cues do not occur in a vacuum. Often, their true significance is apparent only when we consider all the factors surrounding the nonverbal activity.

A GLOSSARY OF TERMINOLOGY

Affect blends are multiple simultaneous facial expressions.

CLEMS (Conjugate Lateral Eye Movements) are involuntary lateral shifts of the eyes to the right or left. CLEMS are thought to be closely associated with cognitive processing; that is, we look away to the left or right while we are thinking but look forward again when we stop processing information. People can be categorized as either right-lookers or left-lookers because approximately 75 percent of an individual's conjugate lateral eye movements are in one direction.

Deintensification is the deemphasizing or downplaying of the facial expression of emotion.

Facial Affect Scoring Technique (FAST) separates the face into three areas: the lower face, including cheeks, nose, and mouth; the eyes and eyelid area; and the brows and forehead area.

Facial management techniques are behaviors used to control facial expressions, and are divided into four common types: intensification, deintensification, neutralization, and masking.

Gaze aversion is when someone avoids looking at another during an interpersonal encounter.

Gaze omission occurs when one person does not look at the other but is not intentionally avoiding eye contact.

Intensification is an exaggeration of facial expressions.

Masking is the facial management technique that involves repressing the expression of the emotion actually felt and replacing it with expressions that are acceptable under the circumstances.

Mutual look or **mutual gaze** refers to two people looking in the direction of one another's faces.

Neutralization is when people eliminate any expression of emotion.

Oculesics is the study of eye behavior, eye contact, eye movement, and the functions of eye behavior.

One-sided look or glance is a gaze of one individual toward another person's face.

Partials are emotional expressions in only one area of the face.

▲5

Vocal Behavior

Vocal behavior provides listeners with valuable information about a speaker. Often, the actual verbal message means very little to the receiver without the vocal cues that accompany it. Often, the entire meaning is determined by the way something is said. In one study, only 7 percent of the meaning in an interaction was conveyed by the verbal content of spoken utterances and 38 percent was conveyed through other vocal cues.

The study of the communicative value of vocal behavior, or paralanguage, is called *vocalics. Paralanguage* includes all oral cues in the stream of spoken utterances except the words themselves. The importance of vocal behavior as a type of nonverbal communication lies in the impact it has on perceptions of the verbal content of our messages.

The functions of nonverbal communication (see Chapter 1) are often performed by vocal cues. For example, vocal cues may reinforce what is said. Consider the verbal phrase "I love you." No one doubts the powerful meaning that can be transmitted by the words alone. However, if you are intimately involved with someone, you probably have heard this phrase repeatedly. The way your sweetheart says "I love you" can make all the difference in the world. How would you say it that would leave no doubt in your lover's mind about your true affections? Stop a moment and think about the vocal cues that validate the verbal statement.

Vocal cues can also contradict the verbal message. Look at the list of verbal phrases below. Repeat them aloud so that your vocal cues communicate the opposite of what the phrases appear to mean.

> *Gee, thanks!*
> *This turned out to be a fine day.*

Vocal communication can overlap.

I just love it when you do that.
Way to go, dude.
I would like nothing better.
Wow, this is fun.
Wonderful.
That's my favorite!
Truly awesome!
Real nice.
This stinks!
Rhonda's a real winner, isn't she?

If you have spoken these phrases as we have asked you to do, you have probably concluded that they are sarcastic remarks. You are exactly right. *Sarcasm* is saying one thing and communicating something else. We are sarcastic when our words say one thing and our vocal cues say the opposite. This brings up a very important point about vocal behavior. Sarcasm is something we learn to communicate. It is also something we learn to understand. Small children often do not understand sarcasm. Some studies have shown that small children tend to believe the face value (verbal content) of a message rather than the meaning signaled by the contradicting vocal cues. Furthermore, we usually cannot appreciate the sarcasm of people from other cultures. The way we say something is influenced considerably by cultural factors.

As we shall discuss more extensively later in this chapter, vocal behavior plays an extremely important role in regulating our interactions with others. Not only do we control the flow of conversations with our body movements and eye behavior, but we can signal to listeners with our voices as well. Regulative behaviors involved in turn-taking are rich with vocal information.

Vocal cues transmit many other messages as well. The way we speak can tell others about our background, gender, age, socioeconomic status, where we grew up, what part of the country we are from, and a variety of other demographic data. By listening to the vocal cues, receivers can glean accurate pieces of information, and may use such information to stereotype the sender in several ways. For example, if we think a person sounds like they are from Princeton, New Jersey, we might have certain stereotypes that go along with our perceptions of New Jersey.

CATEGORIES OF VOCAL BEHAVIOR

The study of what someone says is virtually meaningless without a study of the vocal cues that surround the words. This *vocal atmosphere* is what paralanguage is all about. The primary difference between speaking and writing is the presence of paralanguage. Although the verbal message (the text) may be the same, what is communicated can be, and usually is, very different. To study a speech is to study a text within its vocal atmosphere. The texts of long-deceased speakers, of course, may be studied by scholars today, but these texts cannot be studied as speeches unless a vocalic record is available for simultaneous study. Paralinguistic cues did not just emerge in recent years; they always have been critical.

As we said earlier, *how* you say something may be more meaningful than what you actually say. Vocal behavior, however, is more than just how something is said. It includes a variety of vocal activity that emanates from the oral cavity of human beings. In 1958, Trager classified all paralinguistic activity as falling into one of several categories. Trager is widely credited for delineating the relationship between spoken language and paralanguage. It is useful to examine some of Trager's categories.

Voice Set

When we speak, we do so in what Trager describes as the "setting of an act of speech." This vocal environment around the talking activity is in some measure a result of the speaker's voice, which involves several of the speaker's personal characteristics. Included among these factors are age, gender, present condition of health, state of enthusiasm, fatigue, sadness, and other emotions. Even seemingly irrelevant factors such as social status, education level, and group identification may play an important role in contributing to the speaker's voice set. *Voice set* is closely related to who the speaker is; such information helps us to interpret the speaker's words more accurately.

We realize that the idea of voice set may be difficult to grasp. It becomes quite apparent to listeners, however, when different speakers say the same phrase with the same emphasis and express the same emotions. The remaining difference in their vocal activity can be attributed to their different voice sets. Consider several very different individuals: an elderly woman, a truck driver, a Presbyterian minister, a Hispanic school teacher, and a successful male businessperson. Think of how each of these individuals would sound while speaking the following phrases with the same amount of enthusiasm and emotion.

> *It is certainly a nice day.*
> *Hello, Myrtle.*
> *That tastes great!*

You probably visualized differences in the vocal cues of these four individuals even before you considered the phrases. If you did, you were keying in on the phenomenon of voice set. For many successful performers, the key to playing any given role realistically is creating a voice set they feel is consistent with their character's identity.

Vocalizations and Voice Qualities

Trager distinguishes between two other categories of vocal behavior that he sees as the actual objects of study in paralanguage. The first category is called *voice qualities,* and includes tempo, resonance, rhythm control, articulation control, pitch control, glottis control, vocal lip control, and pitch range. Voice qualities are seen as modifications of all the vocal cues that accompany spoken words. Changes in voice qualities can often signal very important messages to others. Although they are considered content-free speech, you can surely see that a change in tempo, such as speaking rapidly, may communicate a sense of urgency or excitement. Maria tells you she is angry; her extremely resonant vocal burst tells you exactly *how* angry she is.

Closely related to voice qualities are vocalizations. According to Trager, *vocalizations* are audible vocal cues that do not have the structure of language and may or may not be accompanied by spoken words. There are three different kinds of vocalizations. First, *vocal characterizers* involve nonlanguage sounds such as laughing, crying, whimpering, giggling, snickering, and sobs. We might also consider many audible meditative chants as vocal characterizers. Other characterizers include groaning, moaning, yawning, growling, muttering, whining, and sighing. Many people are well-recognized and closely associated with the characterizers they frequently use. A recent graduate student, addressing his classmates in open discussion, would invariably end his comments with a long, audible sigh. Not only did this cue his classmates that he had finally finished one of his long and frequent oral commentaries, it also became so closely identified with him that everyone would sigh loudly in imitating him.

Trager's second type of vocalizations are called vocal qualifiers. *Vocal qualifiers* are quite similar to voice qualities but are considered separately for basically one reason. Whereas voice qualities usually modify an entire stream of speech, vocal qualifiers serve to qualify or regulate specific portions of the verbal utterance. In other words, qualifiers provide variety within a specific spoken sentence. Vocal qualifiers include intensity, pitch height, and extent. Vocal cues that vary the rate, loudness, or softness during a given utterance are also qualifiers. The nonverbal function of accenting is effectively served by these vocal qualifiers. Janet emphasized the word "now" in her statement "Put that kitten down . . . NOW" by pausing briefly before the last word, then increasing the loudness of her voice. This left no doubt in her son's mind as to when he should leave the poor kitty alone!

The last category of vocal behavior is *vocal segregates.* Again, these vocal cues are audible but are not linguistic. Some segregates have been described as nonwords that are used as words. These cues include vocalizations such as "Shhh," "uh-huh," and "uh-uh." Furthermore, vocal segregates include many common filler sounds such as "uh-uh-uh," "er," "ah," and even seeming words such as "and-ah," and "y'know." You probably can think of an acquaintance who uses more than her or his share of segregates. See if you can identify the vocal segregates in the following conversation:

Freckles: I, uh, I think, you know, we ought to go to class, and, uh. . . .

Fathead: Duh. . . . What for? Ya know . . . we have better things to do, like, ya know, smoking in the boys' room or terrorizing someone's pet, ha, ha.

Freckles: Uh-uh-uh, because we're having a test next week, ya know, we should go to class.

Fathead: Uh-uh. I ain't goin'. No way.

Freckles: So, like what you want to do?

Vocal segregates such as "uh-uh" and "uh-huh" function as substitutes for verbal utterances, but we also find them in the stream of speech of people who are thinking about what they are going to say next. While teaching a public speaking course a few years ago, one speech professor counted 67 "and-uhs" in one student's five-minute speech. The speech began with one of these vocal segregates and each sentence ended with one. After noting how many athletes make excessive use of segregates during their interviews on radio and television, one of our students suggested that we should change the term for these vocalizations to "athlegates!"

Silence and Pauses

Although not always considered a category of vocal behavior, silence is an important aspect of the communicative value of vocal activity. You have no doubt heard the phrase "silence is golden." Can saying nothing say something? Ask the disruptive student in the last row who settled down when the teacher fell silent. Ask the "bad little kid" whose father said nothing when asked "Are you mad at me?"

Contrary to what many believe, silence is not the opposite of speech. Silence should not be equated with not communicating. It is an integral part of our vocal behavior and, depending on the situation, can provide a great deal of information about our thoughts, emotions, attitudes, and relationships with others.

Bruneau (1973) has been widely quoted as an authority on the importance of silence in communication. He states:

> *Silence is to speech as white paper is to this print. Physiologically, silence appears to be the mirror image of the shape of discernible sound for each person. Speech signs, created by necessity or will, appear to be mentally imposed figures on mentally imposed grounds of silence. The entire system of spoken language would fail without man's ability to both tolerate and create sign sequences of silence–sound–silence units. (p. 18)*

Silence is generally discussed in terms of pauses in the stream of speech. These pauses can be identified as either unfilled pauses or filled pauses. *Unfilled pauses,* or silence, are periods where a lack of vocal activity occurs during the spoken utterance. *Filled pauses,* on the other hand, are interruptions in the stream of speech content that are filled with audible sounds such as "uh," "er," "ah," stuttering, and even slips of the tongue or repetitions.

According to Bruneau (1973), filled and unfilled pauses can be classified as three different silence phenomena: hesitation silence, psycholinguistic silence, and interactive silence. Hesitation silences are generally pauses during speech caused by some kind of anxiety or uncertainty about what to say next. Psycholinguistic silences, on the other hand, are pauses related to the encoding and decoding of speech. Pausing is most prevalent at the beginning of a grammatical stream of speech. It often is necessary to pause while translating thoughts into words. Finally, interactive silences or pauses are products of the interaction itself and can communicate various messages about the relationship between two interactants. The silent moments two lovers share, the silence that signifies respect for an elder, the cold silence between individuals in conflict, and the silence that ignores are all examples of interactive pauses.

Pauses can also be classified as grammatical or nongrammatical. According to often-cited author Goldman-Eisler, pauses are grammatical when they occur at the following junctures: natural punctuation points such as the end of a sentence; just before a conjunction (but, and, or); just before relative and interrogative pronouns

A person's vocal quality can punctuate the message.

(who, which, why); in association with an indirect or implied question ("I'm not sure about that"); just before adverbial clauses of time, manner, and place ("I will leave when I'm ready"); or when complete parenthetical references are used ("I am sure my students—those in my nonverbal communication class—will vote for you").

Pauses may also be nongrammatical. Nongrammatical pauses occur in the middle or at the end of a verbal phrase; as gaps or breaks between words and phrases that are repeated ("I think you will find /pause/ will find that /pause/ that I am right"); as gaps or breaks between verbal compounds ("I have /pause/ talked until I'm blue in the face"); and as a disruption or false start ("I am concerned /pause/ the problem is your rotten attitude").

Knapp and Hall (1992) have made an interesting observation regarding spontaneous speech: Only about 55 percent of all pauses in such speech are grammatical, whereas well-prepared presentations, such as oral readings of texts, are generally characterized by a high consistency in grammatical pausing.

Uses of Silence in Communication

Silence can be used in four major ways. First, silence can establish distance in interpersonal relationships. Sometimes we wish to put distance between ourselves and others around us. Although we may not physically remove ourselves, we can create a psychological distance by remaining silent. Second, silence is often necessary in order for a person to put her or his thoughts together. As we suggested earlier, encoding messages is facilitated by silent moments during the process of putting thoughts into words. A third use of silence is to show respect to another person. Not only do we show respect through silence, but those in authority often use silent pauses to command the respect of others. Finally, silence can be used to modify another's behavior. Mothers and fathers throughout the ages have used the silent treatment on their children to get them to behave. Spouses and friends also have been known to use this approach.

> *Kevin finally decided to give in. Sandy had given him the old silent treatment from the moment he told her he would not be able to take her skiing this weekend. "Okay, I give up," says Kevin, "I'll do anything you want, if you'll just talk to me!" Sandy smiles and replies, "How about taking me for a pizza?"*

VOCAL BEHAVIOR AND INTERACTION MANAGEMENT

In previous chapters, we introduced the concept of turn-taking during conversations. We suggested that many gestures and eye behaviors are used to regulate the back-and-forth interaction between speakers and listeners. Such behaviors are usually used with a variety of vocal cues that signal to others our speaking or listening intentions during conversations. Recall that there are four types of turn-taking behavior: turn-maintaining, turn-yielding, turn-requesting, and turn-denying.

Turn-Maintaining

There are times in our interactions with others when we wish to continue talking. That is, we wish to maintain our turn in the speaking posture. Cues that speakers use to signal their listeners that they want to keep the floor are called *turn-maintaining cues.* These cues are most prominent in situations where the listener may be trying to interrupt. Vocal cues involved in turn-maintaining may include an increase in the loudness of speech. Such increases usually serve to drown out a listener who may be requesting a turn. Another turn-maintaining vocal cue is an increase in the rate of speech. It is generally difficult for others to break in to a stream of speech that is moving quickly. It decreases the chances that a listener can get a word in edgewise.

Other effective vocal cues in turn-maintaining include the use of more filled pauses. Filling pauses with vocal segregates rather than leaving them unfilled can cue the listener that you may be at the end of a particular thought but you are not finished talking. Mr. Jones, Jake's boss, scolds him for coming in to work late. As Jake tries to explain, Mr. Jones increases his rate and volume because he wants to add, "It should not happen again."

Turn-Yielding

When we are finished speaking and wish to signal our listening partner that he or she can now begin talking, we generally engage in *turn-yielding behavior.* Asking your listener a question is certainly a yielding cue. Questioning generally calls for us to raise the pitch of our voices at the end of the utterance. Another vocal cue that signals turn-yielding is an emphatic drop in voice pitch. Often the drop in pitch is used together with trailing off of the utterance. Such end phrases as "you know" and "or something" may be tacked on after the drop in pitch to trail off the comments. Trailing-off phrases are usually more prevalent when the speaker is coaxing the listener to begin talking.

Intonation changes that deviate from the normal rising and falling of the voice during an utterance usually are signals of turn-yielding. Furthermore, your speaking rate can signal the listener that you are relinquishing the speaking turn. Of course, a long unfilled pause (silence) also serves the turn-yielding function. Long silences during a conversation can be uncomfortable for those involved. Although a listener may not have something important to say, he or she may begin speaking simply to break the silence. As an exercise, try a little experiment with silence. Get with an acquaintance and strike up a conversation. Insert a few silent pauses after a few of your comments and see how long your partner lets the silence remain unfilled. Chances are good that he or she will fill the silence with almost anything before too many seconds have ticked away.

The time that it takes a person to begin speaking after another stops is called their *response latency.* People differ greatly in the length of their response latencies. People with very short response latencies often overtalk their partners. That is, they start speaking before their partner is finished. They take the slightest pause as a sign to take over the conversation. In contrast, people with very long response latencies can cause their partners to be very uncomfortable. If we pause to let our partner take a turn, but our partner does not do so right away, we may feel forced to begin talking again. When a person with a short response latency interacts with a person with a long latency, the former usually dominates the interaction.

Turn-Requesting

Think for a moment of a time when you were listening to someone speaking. As that person continued, you found yourself wanting to speak. You wait for them to pause, if only for a brief second, so that you can begin. To your dismay and increasing frustration, the pause never comes. You know you have to speak soon or you will forget what you were going to say. What do you do? If you are like most folks, you start to use *turn-requesting signals* in the hope that the speaker will wrap things up. In essence, you nonverbally help them put on the "speaking brakes." Turn-requesting vocal cues include the *stutter start* ("But . . . but . . . but," "I . . . I . . . I"), which may be inserted into the conversation even while the speaker is still talking. Stutter starts and other vocal cues such as *vocal buffers* (vocalizations such as "Er . . . ah," or "Uh . . . well") tend to encourage the speaker to finish in less time. Increasing the rate of responses such as "mm-hmm" or "yes . . . yes" also serves as an effective turn-requesting signal.

Turn-Denying

Finally, there are times when listeners transmit signals to speakers that they do not wish to take a speaking turn. *Turn-denying behavior,* or back-channel cues, occur most often when the listener has nothing to say although the speaker begins to yield the turn. Turn-denying includes a slower rate of responses and vocal cues that tend to reward the speaker for talking. Positive nonlanguage vocalizations such as "mm-hmm" delivered at a slowed pace and accompanied by a positive head nod generally signal the speaker, "Please go on, I like what you're saying."

As university professors, the authors often exchange stories about how students effectively use rewarding turn-denying cues to keep them talking. "When your professor is talking," commented one college junior, "you know you're not going to be asked any questions, right?" The student went on to say, "You have to act very interested in what they're saying. Give them a good nod of the head and throw in a 'Mmm' or 'yeah' every so often, and they'll talk a twenty-minute streak."

It should be noted that vocal behavior used in interaction management seldom occurs alone. Often, gestures and other body movements, as well as our eye behavior, accompany the vocalizations. For instance, raising a finger along with the eyebrows, leaning forward, and inhaling audibly communicates a request to speak. Conversely, by accelerating your rate of speech, looking away, turning your body, increasing loudness, and exhibiting a "halting gesture" toward the listener, you maintain your speaking turn. Similarly, verbal comments may function to decline turns. If listeners complete sentences for the speakers or request clarification on earlier comments, they may more easily maintain their position as listeners.

Accent and Dialect

What is an accent or a dialect? What is it about the speech of others that causes you to conclude that they talk differently? Do accents or dialects have any impact on our interactions with people? *Accent* refers to the different ways words are said. *Dialect,* on the other hand, refers to use of different words to reference similar meanings. Accent, then, is a paralinguistic concern, whereas dialect is a concern of linguistics. People from different regions of the United States or from different cultural groups within a given region are likely to differ from each other in terms of accent, dialect, or both.

If you are like most people, you do not think of yourself as having an accent or speaking in a dialect. We tend to see others, those who speak differently, as having an accent or dialect. Accent and dialect, then, can be viewed as perceptions one has of another's way of speaking. If you are from the New York borough of Brooklyn and speak with the stereotypical Brooklyn accent, you would probably not be considered to have a dialect by your Brooklyn neighbors. That is, you and your neighbor would characterize one another's speech as "normal." But both of you would say that the person down the block who moved in from New England "talks funny."

Similarly, a person who was born and raised in Balls Gap, West Virginia and speaks with a southern Appalachian drawl would not be perceived by his fellow Balls Gappians as having an accent. Should the Brooklynite go to West Virginia, or the southern Appalachian travel to New York, each would have an accent and a dialect in relation to the local speakers. The fact is that we never think of our own speech as different or funny; rather, it is the other who "talks funny." It is the other person who has the dialect. One author's brother is from southern West Virginia and has an Appalachian accent and dialect. Some vowel sounds that are familiar to most people in the United States are virtually unrecognizable to him. Although he has lived in other accent and dialect communities for most of his life, he still pushes a "buggy" through the grocery store and occasionally takes his lunch to work in a "poke." He often is mistaken for a Southerner or a Texan, but not by true Southerners or Texans!

Essentially, perceptions of accent and dialect arise when one encounters speech patterns that are not consistent with the way in which that individual has been socialized to speak. Factors that contribute to perceptions of dialect include many vocal phenomena. First, vocal qualities are perceived as different. For instance, the Southern accent is often characterized by a slower rate of vocal delivery, the Texas drawl even slower. Generally, Northerners describe Southerners' speech as containing more syllables. One Southerner at a national communication conference recently commented in a humorous vein that the word *cowboy* does not have two syllables; it has four: ca'-o-bo'-ah. Another Southerner in the audience noted that such a word is very different from a true two-syllable word such as "fit" (pronounced fee'-it)!

Another vocal phenomenon that contributes to perceptions of dialect is differences in pronunciation of words. The word *Mary* is pronounced as "merry" in some regions, "marry" in others, and "mury" in still others. Take the three words *I'll, all,* and *oil.* Say them aloud several times. Do you say each differently? People from most parts of the United States do. However, if you are from Lubbock, Texas, chances are you pronounce all three words the same way—"all." Do you say "bird," "boid," or "bud" when referring to one of our feathered friends? When you point to a distant hillside, do you say "over yonder," "over yonda," or "ova yawner?" Do you put a "nyu tyube in yer tire" or a "noo toob in yer tar?"

Can perception of dialect lead to other judgments as well? According to some research, it does. In the educational environment, teachers have been found to rate children with different patterns of speech as culturally disadvantaged and to judge those with foreign accents as lower on the social status ladder. Still others have shown that English speaking Hispanics are perceived by non-Hispanic Americans to be less successful, lower in intelligence, lower in social awareness, and lower in ability when they speak with a Spanish accent. Some research suggests that the slower rate of Southern speech can create perceptions of low intelligence and slowness of thought in other parts of the United States. The Brooklyn accent has been known to connote arrogance and other negative perceptions with Americans in the West and South.

You may be asking yourself, "Why does it seem so common to make such unfavorable judgments about people because of their dialect?" It doesn't seem fair, does it? However, it does happen, and often negative consequences arise because of dialect perceptions. Those consequences can range from relatively unimportant social disadvantages to not being considered for particular jobs. Particular regional vocal patterns and ethnic accents are often associated with peoples' ability to socialize, to perform, and to behave appropriately. No, it is not fair to discriminate against people because of the way they speak. It is not fair to judge an individual's intelligence by her or his accent. It occurs every day. Our best advice is to be aware that even you are often guilty of this. It is always wise to suspend judgment until you can validate them with other sources of information. Know that everyone has a dialect and an accent. This becomes obvious only when you interact with people of other regions, cultures, or subcultures. As with most things, we tend to consider our own accent and dialect as the "right," "best," and "normal" one. That is part of what may make others refer to us as ethnocentric. When they do, be assured, they do not intend it as a compliment!

It is worthwhile to consider the words of Phillips, Kougl, and Kelly (1985) in their book on speaking:

> *It is important to remember that people are entitled to choose how they wish to talk and what language communities they wish to seek membership in. . . . Learning language styles of various groups is not an easy task, but it is a mark of respect shown for one's origins and one's new affiliations. (p. 241)*

Consider the vocal cues that contribute to the accents or dialects of the following cultural or ethnic groups. On a piece of paper, write down the specific vocal qualities, vocalizations, and word pronunciations you believe are characteristic of each group. After completing this task, get with one of your classmates and compare your lists. What stereotypes do you associate with each? Also, ask yourself how your perceptions of accents and dialects may influence your communication with a member of each group. Finally, decide whether such judgments are appropriate, fair, and accurate.

Russian	California teenager
Hispanic	New York Jewish lawyer
Japanese	African-American (urban)
Southern male	African-American (rural)
Southern female	Italian-American male
Englishman	Irishman
European-born person	Young male athlete from Alabama

Now that you have completed this task, consider the accents of the following famous people. What vocal behaviors are characteristic of their accents?

Jimmy Carter	George Bush
Joan Rivers	Cher
Jesse Jackson	David Letterman
Richard Nixon	Tom Brokaw
Madonna	Tim Allen
Ronald Reagan	Martin Luther King, Jr.
Barbara Walters	Michael Jackson
Al Gore	Hillary Rodham-Clinton

EFFECTS OF VOCAL BEHAVIOR

Vocal behavior can affect our interactions with others in several ways. The following pages present a discussion of the effects of vocal cues on the expression of emotion, judgments of personality, learning, ability to persuade others, and effective delivery.

Vocal Behavior and Emotions

Choose a partner, classmate, or roommate to participate in this exercise. One of you should close your book while the other attempts to communicate the following list of emotions. There are a couple of rules. Rule number one: Turn away from one another so that you are back-to-back. Rule number two: The person with the job of communicating the emotion is allowed to use only one statement. The only phrase you may use is this: "Onions taste great in the morning." With this phrase only, see if you can get your partner to guess each of these emotions:

anger	excitement	disgust
concern	love	sadness
affection	sympathy	pleasure
fear	protection	dejection
joy	hate	frustration

Although you may not have guessed the exact emotion every time, you probably were quite successful with this activity. Given the restrictions of the rules, some people are surprised they can get any right! Vocal behavior, apart from actual verbal content, carries much information about emotions. The vocal expression of emotion is found in the paralinguistic cues rather than the content of the spoken utterance. Research on the vocal expression of emotion often uses content-free speech techniques. That is, listeners are asked to judge which emotion is being expressed in the voices of others while the actual content of speech is made to be incomprehensible. This is similar to hearing your neighbors arguing without being able to discern what they are saying to one another. You certainly can tell they are angry, but you can't tell why!

Studies that use the content-free speech approach have been quite helpful to our understanding of which vocal cues communicate a given emotion. Whether a speaker is excited or calm is associated with the extent and type of change in pitch and loudness. However, some emotions are more accurately judged than others. Nervousness, anger, sadness, and happiness are the easiest emotions to interpret from vocal cues alone. On the other hand, surprise, fear, and love are very often quite difficult to judge. Although their voices usually are very different from one another, males and females use the same vocal activity to express the same emotions. For example, both sexes use increased volume while expressing anger, increase rate and pitch during impatience, and so on. Most of the research on vocal cues and emotional expression appears to indicate three consistent findings:

1. Negative emotions are more accurately identified than positive emotions.
2. The ability of listeners to identify emotions in the voice is greatly affected by the speaker's ability to encode emotions into his or her voice.
3. Individuals who monitor and control their own emotions are better able to identify the emotion of others through vocal cues.

The last of these three generalizations may need some explanation. People who are considered high self-monitors (unusually aware or attentive toward what they do) are much more sensitive to the vocal expressions of others. This probably is a result of their having practiced observing how they express their own emotions and worked to control the vocal cues. Knowing which vocal cues contribute to the expression of particular emotions has made them more competent judges of others' vocal expressions. Not only do high self-monitors surpass others in judging vocal expression, they also are better at intentionally encoding certain emotions into the voice.

Vocal Behavior and Personality

There has surely been a time when you have formed impressions of others' personalities simply by the way their voices sound. You can probably think of someone who talks too fast or whines, or whose voice constantly trembles. What do you generally think of people who have tense voices, breathy voices, deep raspy voices, or throaty voices? Are there any stereotypical judgments we make about them? Consistent vocal quality of others' speech is often associated with particular personality characteristics. Let us consider the extensive work conducted by David Addington back in the late 1960s and early 1970s.

Addington (1968, 1971) was extremely interested in whether our vocal cues consistently created stereotypical personality judgments in others. He identified nine qualities present in voices: breathiness, thinness, flatness, nasality, tenseness, throatiness, orotundity, increased rate, and increased pitch variety. Addington used both males and females considered to have these types of vocal qualities. The following paragraphs provide a general summary of Addington's findings.

Breathiness.　A breathy voice is characterized by audible exhalation during speech. Although breathiness is not usually associated with males, there are males whose voices have this quality. Generally, men with breathy voices are perceived by others as younger and more artistic. Extreme breathiness in males may often be associated with perceptions of femininity and homosexuality. Breathiness in females tends to elicit judgments of femininity and petiteness. Women are also perceived as prettier, more effervescent, and more high-strung. Often, females with this vocal quality are seen as more shallow.

Thinness.　For the most part, thinness of voice in males does not seem to be associated highly with any particular personality judgments. For females, however, a somewhat different picture emerges. Women with thin voices are more likely to be seen as socially and physically immature. They are also perceived as more immature emotionally and mentally. These perceptions of immaturity are generally considered to be negative judgments. However, two positive perceptions were also associated with thinness in female voices: a better sense of humor and greater sensitivity.

Flatness.　A flat voice, whether in a male or female, tends to be associated with the same perceptions. Flatness of voice for both sexes is more likely to create perceptions of masculinity and sluggishness. Furthermore, persons with flatter voices are seen as colder and more withdrawn.

Nasality.　There is probably no vocal quality that is less desirable in our culture than nasality. People who "talk through their noses" are not seen as a whole lot of fun. However, this is a common voice problem among Americans. According to Addington's research, nasality in both males and females provokes a wide array of socially negative characteristics, such as laziness, low intelligence, and boredom. This is not a good set of characteristics for anyone to be stuck with, unless, of course, you have no interest in having friends or a social life and making a good impression during job interviews.

Tenseness.   If you tense the muscles in your throat and around your jaw, you will notice that as you speak, you are putting a strain on your voice. Vocal tenseness has also been found to relate to judgments others make of us. In Addington's work, men were generally seen as older if they had tense voices. Furthermore, they were perceived to be less yielding in conversations. On the other hand, women were seen much differently. Voice tenseness in females was more likely to provoke ratings of being younger, more emotional, more feminine, and more high-strung. Women with tense voices were also perceived as less intelligent.

Throatiness.   The increased throatiness in the vocal quality of male voices tended to cause judges to stereotype them as older, more mature, and sophisticated. They were also seen as more realistic in their outlook and more well-adjusted. What this seems to suggest is that throatiness in males is a positive and desirable characteristic. For females, the perceptions caused by this vocal quality are almost exactly the opposite. They were seen as unemotional, ugly, boorish, lazy, more masculine, less intelligent, careless, inartistic, naive, neurotic, apathetic, humble, and uninteresting.

Orotundity.   This quality refers to the robustness, clearness, and strongness of the voice. Males with increased orotundity were perceived as energetic, more sophisticated, interesting, proud, enthusiastic, and artistic. The general perceptions of males are that they are more expressive, open, and aesthetically driven. Many similar personality characteristics were also attributed to females. Women with robust and strong voices were seen as more gregarious, more lively, and aesthetically sensitive. According to Addington, however, they are also perceived as humorless and proud.

Increased Rate.   Addington's research showed that increased vocal rate tended to create the same perceptions whether the speaker was male or female. Essentially, speakers with faster rates of speech were seen as more animated and extroverted than those who spoke at slower rates. That probably means that faster talkers are perceived as more socially oriented. Increased rate, then, is a socially desirable characteristic of vocal behavior because it seems related to positive perceptions. Others have noted that increased speaking rate is related to perceptions of competence or credibility of the speaker. People who can speak at quicker rates with few or no disfluencies in the stream of speech may seem more sure of what they are saying and, as such, appear more confident.

Increased Variety in Pitch.   We commonly associate pitch variety as a feminine behavior rather than a masculine behavior. Males do not generally see the advantages that may result by incorporating a variety in their pitch. Addington's findings indicate that males who used more pitch variety were perceived as dynamic, feminine, and aesthetically inclined. Females were seen as more dynamic and extroverted.

Vocal Behavior and Learning

A major concern of scholars who study communication in the classroom environment is the impact of vocal behavior on student learning, comprehension, and retention of material. There is probably no worse an enemy to the classroom teacher than a monotone voice. Our own research shows that having a monotone voice is more closely related to negative evaluations of teachers by students than any other factor. *Monotone* voices are simply those that incorporate little variety in vocal qualities during verbal utterances. Monotone speakers have little or no inflectional variety or rate variety when speaking. Much like the dull moan of distant environmental sounds, monotonous speech tends to thwart the attention and interest of the listeners. One thing is certainly clear: Students cannot learn anything that does not capture their attention. Not only does monotone contribute nothing to a teacher's presentation, it works against the teacher's efforts to stimulate student attention.

Many studies, in fact, suggest that vocal variety contributes to the comprehension and later recall of presented material. Seven decades ago, in one if the earliest empirical studies in the field of communication, Woolbert (1920) showed that vocal variety in tempo, force, and pitch contributed to higher retention of material. More recent studies have found that monotone actually reduces listeners' comprehension of orally delivered readings. Others have even found that qualities such as nasality and breathiness hinder comprehension and retention.

The impact of the rate of speech on learning has been studied extensively. It may surprise you to learn that, up to a point, increased rate tends to increase the amount that listeners comprehend and later recall of oral presentations. Many experts believe we can process and comprehend information much more quickly than we can normally speak. For this reason, we often let our minds wander between particular points the speaker is presenting. Should the speaker talk at a faster rate, there is less chance that we will turn our attention away from the speaker's presentation. Of course, it is possible to talk too fast. Listeners may simply be unwilling to put in the effort to stay with the extremely fast talker. Excessive speed may also conjure up the stereotype of the used-car salesperson and lead to reductions in perceived credibility.

Warm positive vocal behavior of teachers is important to classroom learning. Positive vocal cues can serve as reinforcers that encourage students to participate more actively in their own learning by talking more and seeking clarifications from teachers. Positive vocal cues of teachers also tend to create positive attitudes in the student toward the material and the teacher. Some research indicates that positive vocal behavior contributes even more to improved interest and learning for lower-class than for middle-class students, although improvement is generally seen in both groups.

Vocal behavior can enhance the clarity of verbal messages. The clarity of a verbal message directly contributes to listeners' ability to understand oral presentations. Verbal utterances are clear to listeners in part because the speaker has used her or his vocal qualities to emphasize, accent, or point up certain parts of the message. Vocal cues can signal to the listener which portions may be most important, for example. Vocal cues highlight, underline, boldface, or italicize words or phrases and subsequently contribute to the listeners' ability to retain the material.

Vocal Behavior and Persuasion

When we use the word *persuasion,* we are referring primarily to influencing the attitudes, values, and beliefs of others. Generally speaking, we can persuade by generating a new attitude in our listeners, reinforcing an attitude already held, or actually changing someone's attitude from one orientation to another. Can vocal behavior ease our ability to influence others? Can the qualities and vocalizations that surround what we say make the difference between changing and not changing an attitude, between someone believing us or not, or between selling or not selling a product? It should be obvious to you that many factors affect our ability to influence others and that they often interact to enhance persuasion. However, much research has shown that vocal behavior plays an extremely important role.

One study of vocal behavior and persuasion found that the speed with which we speak may influence our ability to persuade others. In short, the faster we talk (within reason, of course), the more likely we are to influence our listeners. Maybe there is something to the stereotype of the fast-talking salesperson! The probable explanation for this finding is that faster speech rates are often associated with perceptions of competence, expertise, and intelligence. If we as listeners see those characteristics in speakers, we are more likely to perceive them as credible sources and consequently believe their message. Recall Addington's research. Often, the perceptions we hold of others greatly affects their ability to influence us.

Although studies have failed to find any relationship between nonfluencies in a person's speech the person's impact on attitude changes, several studies have found that nonfluencies influence ratings of a speaker's credibility. According to these researchers, such vocal nonfluencies as tongue slips, stuttering, repetitions, and vocal buffers can harm perceptions of the competence and dynamism of the speaker. Although these studies have not demonstrated an immediate impact on persuasion, because they found the nonfluencies to hurt speakers' credibility, it is likely that these negative impressions of credibility would affect the speaker's persuasiveness.

Vocal Behavior and Attractiveness

Recently, Zuckerman and Driver (1989) conducted two studies that examined the impact of attractiveness of voice on observers. Their assumption was that "individual differences in vocal attractiveness may elicit different impressions of personality" (p. 28). They found that observers agreed on what the vocally attractive voice was. They also found that observers agreed that senders with the more attractive voices rated more favorably than senders with less attractive voices. Attractive voices were perceived as sounding dominant, likeable, and achievement-oriented.

Vocal Behavior and Confidence

It has been a given for years that if a speaker sounds confident, he or she will be perceived as confident. There are many ways in which a speaker can demonstrate confidence in what he or she is saying. It is often done with verbal statements such as "I am positive of this," "I know this well," and "I am the expert in this area." It is also possible to display confidence through nonverbal means, such as speaking faster, louder, more forcibly, and with dominance. Kimble and Seidel (1991) studied two paralinguistic variables, vocal loudness and response latency, to determine whether they were associated with perceived speaker confidence in answers to trivia questions. Their results showed the following: When people are confident in what they are saying, they exude confidence vocally and verbally; this confidence is shown by louder speech and faster response times; the more assertive a person is, the more likely he or she will respond with confidence; and confident responses were given more loudly, more enthusiastically, and more energetically. Therefore, in order to appear more confident, we should speak confidently. Work on it.

Vocal Characteristics of Good Delivery

In another book, one directed toward presentational speaking, we summarized research and theory relating to the use of voice in such communication (McCroskey, 1993). We concluded there were six specific vocal qualities that may directly affect your ability to be a persuasive speaker. Because these qualities are valuable beyond the narrow confines of presentational speaking, we repeat them here.

First, *volume control* is essential when considering the audience and circumstances surrounding your speaking. It is important to realize that "you should speak loudly enough to be heard but not so loudly that you will overpower your audience" (p. 238). Loudness of voice is actually relative. What is too loud or too soft depends on where you are speaking. The thing to remember is that talking too loudly can offend or turn off your listeners, and not speaking loudly enough can also irritate them. They will eventually give up trying to understand you, ending your chances for influencing them.

We have already discussed *rate of speech* as a factor that affects your ability to persuade others. Although it does appear that faster rates enhance your persuasiveness, you can reach a point of diminishing returns. Good rate is characterized by speech that is "rapid enough to hold attention and yet slow enough for the audience to digest one idea before it is bombarded by more" (p. 239).

A third important quality of voice is the *use of pitch* to clarify and accentuate the important points of the verbal message. To ensure that you are stimulating the desired meaning, you must incorporate appropriate variations of pitch in your messages. Remember, monotones are no fun! Monotonous speech is uninteresting and, according to some, is difficult to listen to. Whether the pitch is too high, too low, or somewhere in the middle range, remaining at the same level with little or no inflectional change may require your listeners to exert too much effort to pay attention.

Good articulation is a fourth element of the voice to consider in your persuasive messages. Poor articulation or misarticulation can indirectly affect your ability to persuade others because it can work against listeners' perceptions of your competence, intelligence, and expertise. Our culture values good articulators and looks with disdain on those who do not appropriately articulate their words. What is good articulation? "Good articulation merely includes all the sounds that normally should be in a word without stressing them too much" (p. 240). If you can speak a word without calling undue attention to how you say it, you are articulating appropriately. However, slurring or butchering verbal messages may cause others to conclude that you are careless with other aspects of your message as well.

Speech that persuades others should also be *fluent*. A fluent speech "is one that flows smoothly" (p. 240). A nonfluent utterance, as you may recall, includes vocal activity such as hesitations, vocal buffers, repetitions, stutters, and conspicuous pauses. We have already suggested that these vocal cues can negatively affect your listeners' perceptions of your credibility.

Finally, *effective pauses* can be used to call attention to particular ideas. A "pregnant pause" just before or after a statement can make that statement seem very important, a key element of your message. Unfilled pauses used in strategic locations can enhance a speech. However, filled pauses, those that interrupt the smooth flow of messages, serve no useful purpose but tend only to detract from fluency. They may signal that you are grasping for ideas that are not there, and subsequently may cause your listeners to conclude that you were not prepared to deliver the persuasive message.

A GLOSSARY OF TERMINOLOGY

Accent is the different ways words are said. Accent is thus a paralinguistic concern.

Dialect is the use of different words to reference similar meanings. Dialect is thus a concern of linguistics.

Filled pauses are interruptions in the stream of speech that are filled with audible sounds such as "uh," "er," "ah," stuttering, and even slips of the tongue or repetitions.

Response latency is the time that it takes a person to begin speaking after another stops.

Sarcasm is saying one thing and communicating something else.

Turn-denying cues or **back-channel cues** are vocal cues the listener transmits to signal that they do not wish to speak. Turn-denying behavior, or back-channel cues, occur most often when the listener has nothing to say when the speaker begins to yield the turn.

Turn-maintaining cues are used by speakers to signal listeners that they want to keep the floor.

Turn-requesting cues show others that it is our time to speak or that we want to enter the conversation.

Turn-taking in conversations involves the following four techniques: turn-maintaining, turn-yielding, turn-requesting, and turn-denying.

Turn-yielding cues are used to signal that we are finished speaking and wish to prompt our listening partner to speak.

Vocal characterizers are nonlanguage sounds such as laughing, crying, whimpering, giggling, snickering, and sobbing.

Vocal qualifiers are similar to voice qualities but are considered separately for one main reason: Whereas voice qualities modify an entire stream of speech, vocal qualifiers qualify or regulate specific portions of the utterance. In other words, qualifiers provide variety within a spoken sentence. Vocal qualifiers include intensity, pitch height, and extent.

Vocal segregates include many common filler sounds such as "uh-uh-uh," "er," "ah," and even seeming words such as "and-ah" and "y'know."

Vocalics or **paralanguage** is the study of the communicative value of vocal behavior. Paralanguage includes all oral cues in the stream of spoken utterances except the words themselves.

Vocalizations are audible vocal cues that do not have the structure of language that may or may not be accompanied by spoken words.

Voice qualities are characteristics including tempo, resonance, rhythm control, articulation control, pitch control, glottis control, vocal lip control, and pitch range. Voice qualities are modifications of the vocal cues that accompany spoken words.

Voice set is closely related to who the speaker is; such information about speakers helps us to interpret their words more accurately.

Unfilled pauses, or **silence,** is an absence of vocal activity that occurs during the spoken utterance.

▲ 6

Space and Territoriality

Human beings, much like other animals, seem to have a need to claim and stake out space to call their own. We defend territory, invade that of others, put distance between others and ourselves, and avoid using certain space. As a culture, we use our space differently from other cultures. As individuals, we may differ depending on our age, gender, personality, and background. The way we use space, claim it, defend it, or allow others to enter it has a great deal to do with the nonverbal messages we transmit. As Edward T. Hall (1959) put it, "space speaks." Look around you. Are you in your space or in someone else's? If you are in your own, take note of the ways you have claimed it. What have you done to tell others, "This table is mine"? Take a walk up and down your street. How do your neighbors communicate their space? Do they use fencing, hedges, signs, or unique little markers to enhance the dividing line between their territory and the rest of the world?

Return to your home. Walk around the house. How have members of your family divided the rooms? What about the room you and your roommate share? Is there a "your side" and a "my side?" Whether we realize it or not, we spend a great deal of time negotiating the space we must share with our fellow human beings. The difference between war and peace, success and failure, good relationships and bad, often comes down to the way we use space. The way we interact spatially with others and the respect we show for others' sacred spots or space can be a critical component in effective communication. Furthermore, our ignorance of the spatial needs or behavior of others does not excuse our abuse or misuse of space. Effective interaction requires that we understand not only our own spatial behavior, but that of others.

People have a way of creating space for themselves.

The study of the ways humans use and communicate with space is called *prox-emics*. Use of space and territory is highly related to culture. To a major degree, we cannot fully understand use of space and territory without understanding culture, and we cannot fully understand culture without understanding use of space and territory. The way a person uses space, then, is determined by the dictates of the individual's cultural values. Although humans may have an inherent tendency to express territorial and spatial behavior, the specific ways they go about doing so are learned.

The work of anthropologists such as Hall leads us to believe that a major way cultures can be distinguished is by their proxemic patterns. This work also shows that spatial norms are learned to such an extent that they become habitual and unconscious. That is, once we learn the appropriate distance for conversation, we do not have to continually remember to maintain this distance with every new conversation.

This chapter discusses the concept of proxemics in three basic ways. First, the phenomenon of territoriality is presented. Second, the concept of personal space is discussed. Third, we consider the area of proxemics called *crowding and density*.

TERRITORIALITY

Most of the research on territoriality, and conclusions subsequently drawn, has been based upon studies with different species. You are probably aware of the many accounts of territorial behavior in a variety of species, particularly those of birds and fish. You have a pet that daily exhibits some form of territoriality in and around your home. Dogs, for example, are known to urinate on objects at the boundaries of their masters' property and defend those boundaries from invasion by other dogs.

In the animal kingdom, territory serves a variety of functions. Two primary reasons animals claim and defend territory are to ensure a food supply and to provide an area for mating. The first of these is self-explanatory. Concerning the second reason, Rosenfeld and Civikly (1976) explain:

> *Females mate only with males who occupy certain prime territories. Since it is the strongest and most intelligent who occupy such places, this means that only the best members breed. . . . This also helps regulate population density. If only those animals with territory mate, the number of potential young is limited. (pp. 148–149)*

Those who have studied intensively the territorial behavior of animals contend that territoriality is innate behavior that has been developed and fine-tuned through the process of evolution. Such behavior may be somewhat innate for humans as well.

Humans do exhibit behaviors that are considered territorial in nature, although the innateness of human territoriality can be questioned. There are similarities in the territorial behavior of humans and other animals, although humans are called on to defend our territory much less frequently. Human territoriality, therefore, is seen by some as primarily a passive activity, whereas for animals it is quite active and often necessary for survival.

Human territoriality is a human's presumptive claim of a geographic area with or without a formal, legal basis for that claim. The claim is most commonly established through continuous occupation of that area.

Territory is semifixed or fixed space whose perceived owners can move in and out of it without giving up their claim to it. It is claimed, staked out in some way, and defended by the individual against encroachment from others. Furthermore, those claims are respected by other people.

Categories of Territory

Territories, as we have identified them here, can be classified into several types. Let us consider six types: primary, secondary, public, home, interactional, and body.

1. *Primary territory.* Territory that is considered the exclusive domain of its owner is called primary territory. Your dormitory room, or at least "your side" of it, is your primary territory. Other examples include personal offices, Dad's chair, and Mom's study. If the territory is used by its owner virtually every day, then it would fall into this category. Primary territories are most often respected by others and not violated by encroachers without the permission of the owner. There is little or not doubt about who the rightful claimant is.

2. *Secondary territory.* This type of territory usually is not central to the daily functioning of the owner. It is not under the owner's exclusive control. However, secondary territories are generally associated with a particular person or group, and they are frequently seen in and around it. You can probably think of a popular university hangout, such as a bar or restaurant, that is frequented by a certain group of students. Possibly, this group even sits at the same table every time they patronize the establishment. Here, the table in the bar or restaurant would be so closely associated with that group it is perceived as their territory. Unlike primary territories, secondary territories are more vulnerable to invasion and takeover by others. They are a little more difficult to hold onto because the perceived owner does not generally use and control this space with the same frequency as he or she does primary space.

Take, for example, the big-screen television in the family room. If Dad is disposed to sit in his chair and watch television every evening, the television may be seen as his secondary territory. However, it is more likely that there will be conflicts regarding who gets to control the channel selector (secondary territory) than about who sits in Dad's chair (primary territory).

3. *Public territory.* The third type of territory identified by Altman is public territory. Public territory spots are open to anyone and are seldom under the constant control of any one person or group. They are, however, subject to temporary ownership and are often protected with as much vigor as personal property. Spring break may have found you at one of the many beaches of Florida, Texas, California, or Mexico. If so, you may recall the different ways individuals stake out and claim a small portion of the sand for themselves, if only for the day. CD players, towels, umbrellas, bottles of suntan oil, sunglasses, and books are placed in strategic locations to tell other vacationers, "Find another place in the sun—this one's mine!"

Other examples of public territory include parking spaces, theater seats, restaurant tables, library tables, park benches, bus stop shelters, and many other public properties that can be temporarily owned. It is with public territory that most disputes over ownership usually occur. They are the most difficult of all territories to maintain control over. How often have you pulled into the parking lot of malls, spotted a parking space, and just before you get to it someone else slipped in ahead of you? Although this space is available to anyone, you probably felt you had been wronged because "some jerk took my place!"

4. *Home territory.* When a group of people colonize a public territory by taking it over and using it continuously, it becomes home territory. Regular patrons of a neighborhood bar, street gangs in a large city subdistrict, and children who claim a huge elm tree for club meetings all represent groups who have taken a public place and made it their own. The major characteristic of home territory is the claimants have a sense of freedom in terms of their behavior, and their control over the territory is somewhat continuous. Although the territory technically remains public, it functionally becomes secondary territory. It would not be uncommon for the owners to feel as comfortable and intimate in their home territories as they would in their own homes.

5. *Interactional territory.* These special places can develop anywhere persons congregate for purposes of social exchange. Although there may be no visible boundary markers for these conversational zones, they exist nonetheless. Consider two people standing in the middle of a hallway carrying on a conversation with one another. Have you ever noticed how passers-by go to great lengths to avoid intruding? Rarely does someone pass between these interactants. To do so would constitute a gross violation of the interactional territory of those conversing. At social functions, such as parties or get-togethers, one can usually observe pockets of four or five people engaged in communication. These individuals have established an interactional territory. Newcomers to the interaction are expected to approach cautiously and often apologetically, realizing they are guests of the owners of this arbitrary turf.

6. *Body territory.* Body territory also is known as personal space. Unlike other types of territory, body territory is portable; we carry it with us everywhere we go. It is probably easier to think of this personal space as an invisible bubble surrounding the human body. It is the most inviolate form of territory to the individual. Strict control is maintained by the owner, and defense is usually not required because most people have a great respect for the personal space of others. We discuss personal space in more detail later in this chapter as a special topic of proxemics.

Territorial Defense and Encroachment

Methods of Territorial Defense. Territorial defense can involve one of two primary methods. The first method of defense is preventive measures. Prevention is something that someone does before encroachment occurs. Usually, this method involves individuals staking out their territories by using markers to establish boundaries.

Preventive Method 1: Markers are usually personal artifacts or belongings such as purses, umbrellas, overcoats, books, hats, and briefcases. Sommer (1969) contends that in order for markers to be effective in preventing encroachment, "the object must be perceived as a marker and not as litter. This requires the item either to have symbolic meaning or some intrinsic value" (p. 53). That is, the potential encroacher must perceive in the marker an indication that someone, not just something, has laid claim to the space in question.

A bartender once showed one of the authors an effective method of reserving a table or place at a bar. He told us to buy a drink and place it at the space we wanted to reserve with a napkin or drink stirrer over the top. Sure enough, just as he had suggested, that table with marking was still empty when all of the other tables were occupied. Only then did a couple venture to sit there, and then they carefully avoided sitting right where the drink was placed. We can't guarantee that this reservation method will always work. Someone may come in who has met the same bartender—or has read this chapter!

Preventive Method 2: A second type of prevention is markers with symbolic meaning. These are commonly called *labels*. Examples of labels include signs saying "Keep Out" or "Reserved," or even nameplates on office doors, pens, computer disks, and so on.

Preventive Method 3: Another way individuals use prevention as a form of territorial defense is through a combination of postures, stances, and gestures known as *offensive displays*. This form of defense reflects the old adage that the best defense is a good offense. Offensive display simply calls for the owner to look aggressive and formidable to potential encroachers. One major drawback of this preventive measure is that the individual obviously has to be present within the territory, whereas markers can hold spaces in the owner's absence. Another drawback, according to Sommer (1969), is that in some situations offensive displays can backfire. Let us illustrate this point. Suppose you are one of the first passengers aboard an airplane, train, or bus with open seating. You settle in to a window seat and hope that no one decides to sit next to you. As the other passengers come aboard, you incorporate in your posture and position some behaviors that you hope others perceive as formidable. Sommer suggests that you will probably be quite successful at driving away the timid and introverted individuals, but this may leave you with a seatmate who is overbearing and highly aggressive because he or she perceived no potential threat in your offensive display.

Preventive Method 4: A third prevention technique is called *tenure*. People who have become associated with a particular territory over a long period can effectively lay claim to that territory. Sommer (1969) states:

> *Their rights to this space will be supported by their neighbors even when they are not physically present. At a meeting it is not surprising to find a newcomer cautioned against sitting in a certain chair at the table. (p. 52)*

One teacher in a continuing education class recently related a story in which she unknowingly offended another more veteran teacher. She had just been transferred to a different school and, being the new person in the teacher's lounge, had no knowledge of the unspoken rules and norms the veteran teachers had established long ago. After a long lecture, she retired to the lounge for a brief respite. Upon entering, she spotted a large cushioned chair in the corner unoccupied. She could not imagine why none of the others present had taken this inviting place to relax. She gladly crossed over to the chair and sat. A young basketball coach quickly warned her to find another seat in case Mrs. Jones entered. Before she could ask who Mrs. Jones was, an older woman appeared at the door. Mrs. Jones had arrived. The new teacher quickly learned that she had taken the wrong chair. Later, the young coach told her that Mrs. Jones had claimed that chair since before anyone could remember. "It took three months," said the new teacher, "before Mrs. Jones would speak to me and stop giving me the evil eye."

In summary, the four preventive techniques of territorial defense are the use of markers, labels, offensive display, and tenure. The second method of territorial defense is important if prevention has failed. This method is *reaction*. When our territories are encroached on by others, we become physiologically aroused. When we become aroused because of encroachment, we label that arousal as either positive or negative. That is, not all encroachment is interpreted as a bad thing. Sometimes it makes us feel good, relieved, or warm, as often happens with two close companions. At other times, however, encroachment is interpreted negatively because it creates stress, anxiety, or even embarrassment.

Depending on whether we decide that the arousal caused by encroachment is positive or negative, the reaction we make will take one of two forms. If we see the encroachment as positive, we will reciprocate. This means essentially that we encroach on the person who encroached on us, also in some positive way. For example, Bart finally gets up the nerve to put his arm around Sheila while watching a movie. Sheila interprets this encroachment positively and reciprocates by resting her head on Bart's shoulder.

Types of Encroachment.   Often, however, we perceive the encroachment in a negative manner. There are three general types of encroachment that we usually perceive negatively: invasion, violation, and contamination.

Encroachment 1: *Invasion* is a drastic and permanent type of encroachment in which the invader actually crosses the territorial boundaries of others with the intention of taking over and keeping it for herself or himself. When invasion occurs, the encroacher imposes her or his physical presence on the territory of the owner and usually wants to propel that owner out. Of course, invasion can occur on a large scale or small scale. One country invading another to expand its own territorial boundaries represents large-scale invasion. On the other hand, the school bully who invades the area of the playground claimed by others illustrates a small-scale invasion.

Invasion may take on rather subtle disguises as well. Two people sharing a table in a restaurant usually claim parts of that table as their own. It is not uncommon in instances such as this for one person to slowly move "their" objects into the space of the other to increase their share. Many American women have unknowingly fallen victim to the invasion of female relatives who come to visit. Hall (1959) relates a story of a woman who became infuriated each time her mother or sisters came to visit. Invariably, her relatives would take over her kitchen as if it were their own. Hall concludes:

> *Even a mother can't come in and wash the dishes in her daughter's kitchen without annoying her. The kitchen is the place where "who will dominate" is settled. . . . Daughters who can't keep control of their own kitchens will forever be under the thumb of any woman who can move into this area.* (p. 148)

Encroachment 2: Violation is the unwarranted use of someone else's territory. Unlike invasion, violation usually is temporary in nature. The encroacher uses someone else's sacred spots without permission. While Dad is out, little Tonya feels free to sit in his chair. A major complaint of many college students about their room-mates is that they are always using a CD player, hairdryer, or television without first getting permission. Newlywed couples often have difficulty adjusting to married life because, for the first time in their lives, someone violates their possessions regularly.

Encroachment 3: Contamination is rendering the territory of another impure with respect to its definition and usage. As one student so aptly put it, "This means going into someone's territory and stinking up the place." It is not so much that you encroach with your physical presence as much as it is leaving something of yours in the territory. Miles, for instance, did not mind so much that his grandparents Betty and Harry were given his room to use during their weekend visit. He was used to let-ting relatives stay there. What irritated him so much was what they left behind on their departure. Grandmother Betty had left two ashtrays full of cigarette butts on the dresser and night stand and a stack of newspapers on the foot of the bed. Grand-father Harry's deodorant had been smudged on the dresser, and used tissues over-flowed from the waste basket in the corner. One of Grandfather Harry's socks was draped over an open drawer while Grandmother Betty's bra dangled from the closet doorknob. Miles' desk had evidently been turned into a preening stand because a small mirror and brushes cluttered its surface, along with a few strands of Grand-mother Betty's hair. His room reeked of cigarette smoke and sweet perfume.

Encroachment Reactions. When our territory has been encroached on either through invasion, violation, or contamination, and we interpret that encroachment negatively, we may compensate (adjust our behavior) in several different ways. Negative encroachment prompts classic flight-or-fight responses. These responses can be classified as withdrawal, insulation, or turf defense.

Encroachment Reaction 1: Withdrawal means that we compensate by moving away from the encroacher and letting him or her take over. In short, we flee without a fight. This is the classic flight response, a normal reaction to something fearful. Although most encroachment does not actually create fear, what we may fear is what will happen if we make a fuss (in other words, fight). We are most likely to find withdrawal the best form of reaction when someone invades a public territory that we have occupied temporarily. If someone sits too close to us on a park bench, we will more likely move over or get up and walk away than ask the encroacher to move. One study conducted in a library showed that when invaders encroached on the tables of students who were studying, every student moved to another location rather than actively defend the territory. In another library study, a female researcher invaded the tables of females already seated in the library. She also found that most took flight. In fact, only one of the eighty females she invaded asked her to move.

Encroachment Reaction 2: Insulation is a second type of reaction owners may make when their territory is invaded. This response can be thought of as sophisticated fighting. When we perceive another encroaching on our territory, we may build visible boundaries to stop others. This may take the form of markers, as discussed earlier, or body movements and gestures that block the invader's advances. In our example with Bart and Sheila at the movies, Sheila could have interpreted Bart's encroachment as negative. Instead of reciprocating by putting her head on his shoulder, she might have placed her purse on the arm rest between their seats and moved her own arm into a position between them that would have stopped Bart's advancement. Several years ago while attending a conference in Chicago, one of the authors boarded a city bus to see the sights. The behavior of the bus riders became more fascinating, however. Sitting across the aisle was an elderly woman with a package and an overcoat resting in her lap. The seats on each side of her were vacant. At the next stop, several passengers came aboard. Noticing that they were looking for places to sit, the woman placed her package on the one side and her coat on the other. The unfortunate newcomers stood while the elderly woman sat quite contented that she had well-insulated herself from potential encroachers.

Insulation often is accomplished by use of markers. Some markers are more effective that others. A study was conducted in which personal and nonpersonal markers were used to protect areas of a study hall in a school. Personal markers such as sports jackets and combinations of pens, notebooks, and texts seemed to signal the potential invaders that someone would return. On the other hand, nonpersonal markers such as magazines and newspapers often were ignored. The personal marker could hold off encroachers for as long as two hours, whereas randomly scattered magazines worked for only thirty-two minutes.

The gender associated with markers may also be important. Some research has found that feminine markers are not as effective at discouraging encroachment as are masculine markers. In one study, tables in barrooms marked with women's sweaters, purses, and jackets were taken over more frequently and in less time by arriving customers than were tables marked with masculine objects. This outcome, of course, may be the simple result of the assumption that males would be more likely to react in an aggressive, physical manner when their territory is invaded— perhaps a reasonable assumption in most cases.

Encroachment Reaction 3: *Turf defense* is the third type of reaction to territorial invasion, and is closest to the classic fight response. This is the most active form of defense available. Turf defense calls for the owner to repel the invader out of her or his territory. Children often play a game called "King of the Mountain." This usually involves one individual claiming a piece of high ground, such as a mound or small hill, and protecting it from approaching invaders from all directions. The object of the game is to keep control of the mountain by fighting off intruders. One wins the game by taking the high territory and keeping it. Turf defense is an adult version of "King of the Mountain."

Turf defense is seen among animal species. It is represented by a dog fight, for example. For humans, however, this reaction to encroachment generally is used as a last resort. Fighting back, repelling, and standing one's ground are most common in situations where the invasion is very intense and persistent or the territory is unusually highly valued. Highly desirable territories may cause many of us to forgo social etiquette and, instead, give in to a more selfish disposition to obtain or retain the best territories. Less desirable territories may be seen as not worth fighting for.

Factors Influencing Territorial Defense

Several factors influence the defense of territory. These factors determine the defensive methods we use and the success or failure of those methods. Knapp and Hall (1992) suggest that the intensity of our reactions to encroachment depends mostly on at least seven considerations (p. 151):

1. *Who violated our territory?*
2. *Why did they violate our territory?*
3. *What type of territory was it?*
4. *How was the violation accomplished?*
5. *How long did the encroachment last?*
6. *Do we expect further violations in the future?*
7. *Where did the violation occur?*

You would probably react more forcefully if the invader was a lower-status person. On the other hand, you may tolerate and endure intrusions of your manager. You are less likely to react aggressively with a friend than with a stranger. Furthermore, you may choose to withdraw from a public space when encroached but insulate or actively defend a primary, more private territory. You may realize that the encroachment was unintentional or could not be helped, in which case you would react less forcefully or decide to tolerate it. Small children, for example, do not understand the idea of territoriality as it applies to others (however, they react when others invade their territory). An understanding neighbor may see the children playing hide-and-seek in her yard as harmless. Her reaction may be quite different with two adults who have stopped to strike up a conversation under her beautiful weeping willow tree.

The intensity with which someone invades a territory usually affects the way the owner reacts. One investigation showed that if invaders intrude and simply move the belongings of the occupant of a public space, the occupant will more likely withdraw. The study also indicated that, when invaders approached and sat across from an occupant, withdrawal rarely occurred. It is more common to resort to withdrawal if one is encroached on quickly and aggressively in public settings. A quick response is called for, and retreat is simpler than anything else. Only people with very strong aggressive and defensive tendencies are likely to react differently. Gradual intrusion is less likely to be seen as threatening because it is not as likely to be startling. Therefore, a more reasoned response is likely.

Another factor influencing territorial invasion and defense is density conditions. Under high-density conditions, territorial defense is less effective than in low-density conditions. The reason for this is simple. The more people there are, the less space available per person, so the less likely it is that any one individual can hold onto a larger amount of space. We consider density in more detail later in this chapter.

PERSONAL SPACE

Although territoriality is seen as a fixed area of space, *personal space* is an invisible bubble that surrounds us that expands or contracts depending on personalities, situations, and types of relationships. Furthermore, personal space is portable; we take ours with us everywhere we go.

The two major considerations about the variability of personal space are as follows: Appropriate space distancing is socially learned though communication with other people in our culture; and our choices of space distancing communicate information about ourselves, our relationships, and our needs. With these considerations in mind, let us consider the many factors that influence the invisible bubbles or space cushions we carry with us constantly.

Interpersonal Distance

Edward T. Hall (1966) suggests that the type of interpersonal relationship in which we are involved affects the distance we place between ourselves and those with whom we interact. Our comfort level during interaction varies depending on our spatial orientation with others and their relationships to us. Hall describes four interpersonal distance zones that are characterized by the type of communication relationship involved. It should be noted that Hall's distance zones represent North American norms. Other cultures differ considerably from the distance norms described here. The four interpersonal distance zones are intimate, casual-personal, social-consultive, and public.

The *intimate zone* of our personal space bubbles represents the innermost interaction region. It ranges from touching to a distance of eighteen inches. This zone usually is reserved for the very few special people in our lives. Lovers, very close friends, and intimate family members are the only ones we voluntarily allow into this zone for any length of time. We often find ourselves in public places and situations, such as crowded elevators or long waiting lines, where complete strangers or children with no awareness of appropriate interpersonal distances encroach on the intimate zone. Although these cases generally are brief encounters, they can be very stressful. Our desire may be to push those people away, but the situation demands that we tolerate the intrusion.

The *casual-personal zone* is the next region of the personal space bubble. It ranges from eighteen inches to about four feet. The casual-personal distance is used during conversations with close friends and interactions with relatives. Long-time business associates often are permitted into this range because it is a signal that we see them as friends.

Spatial distance in the classroom is often learned.

However, most must remain in the third distance zone, the *socio-consultive zone*. Ranging from four feet to eight feet, this region of personal space has often been called the distance at which Americans transact business. Salespersons are often trained to keep within the socio-consultive area when dealing with potential buyers. A stroll through a corporate office complex reveals that when business is the topic of discussion, the socio-consultive distance usually is strictly observed. When the topic turns to casual or personal matters, it is quite common to see the interactants move closer to one another.

The socio-consultive distance is also used when teachers communicate with older students, with other teachers, and with parents or principals. Teachers of young children, however, learn quickly that little children have no sense of these interaction zones. They also learn to wear easily cleaned clothes, and that children love to rub nylons!

The *public zone* represents the outer region of the personal space bubble. This zone begins at eight feet and extends to the outer limits of interaction potential. The outer limit can vary depending on the situation. At a public speech, for example, it is quite possible to have several thousand people present, and because of broadcast systems they are all within the zone.

Gender Differences

Gender is a major factor that influences personal space. Females, for instance, tend to interact with others at a closer distance than do males. However, male–female dyads interact more closely than either male–male or female–female dyads. Other studies have shown that the relationship between gender and personal space is dependent on other factors. Females allow others to approach them from the sides more closely than from the front whereas males allow the opposite. At least one study, however, has found the results reversed. It would also appear that the degree of the acquaintance and the social setting also affect gender and personal space. Females approach their best friends very closely, but not as closely as males approach "just friends."

Other nonverbal behavior has been found to affect the relationship between gender and personal space. Several studies have shown that males and females approach differently depending on whether the other person is looking at them. Males, for instance, are more likely to stand closer to nonlookers, whereas for females it depends on the other person's gender. When approaching males, females stand closer to nonlookers. When approaching females, they are more likely to stand closer to lookers than to nonlookers.

Cultural Differences

According to Hall (1959), differences in the ways other cultures use space is a major reason Americans often experience culture shock when traveling abroad. In short, many problems two people from different cultures experience when communicating can be attributed to differences in personal space norms. Hall (1959) describes one situation in particular:

> *In Latin America the interaction distance is much less than it is in the United States. Indeed, people cannot talk comfortably unless they are very close to the distance that evokes either sexual or hostile feelings in North Americans. The result is that when they move close, we withdraw and back away. As a consequence, they think we are distant and cold. . . . We, on the other hand, are constantly accusing them of breathing down our necks, crowding us, and spraying our faces. (p. 164)*

Research has shown that North Americans feel more comfortable when interacting at greater distances. For this reason, our culture is commonly referred to as a *noncontact culture*. Others that have been labeled noncontact cultures include northern Europe, Asia, Pakistan, and India. On the other hand, many cultures interact at much closer distances and are referred to as *contact cultures*. Those that have been labeled contact cultures include Latin America, southern Europe, and Arab countries.

Several investigations have shown that the above classifications into noncontact and contact cultures do not always hold true. To assume, for instance, that people in all Latin American countries prefer close distances when interacting is a mistake. For example, Shuter's (1976) research suggests that Panamanian and Colombian Latin Americans interact at greater distances than do Costa Ricans. Malandro, Barker, and Barker (1989) suggest that the stereotypes associated with Italians and

Germans hold only for males in these cultures. Generalizations, therefore, probably should not be made beyond the single-country level, and often there are substantial differences between groups within a single country.

Age Differences

When it comes to personal space, little children are the real space invaders. Spatial orientations are culturally learned, but that learning does not occur quickly. It is, therefore, no surprise that small children in our culture would just as soon crawl up into the lap of Mrs. Witherspoon from down the street as they would Grandma's. After all, both laps are soft and warm. By the age of twelve, however, most children have reached adulthood concerning personal space orientations. This is probably a result of differing expectations adults have about twelve-year-olds in relation to younger children.

One study used five-, eight-, and ten-year-old children to investigate adult reactions to the invasion behavior of children. That study revealed that the older children who invaded adults' personal space in a line at a movie were perceived in a negative manner. On the other hand, the five-year-old children were actually received positively. Essentially, the older children were treated as adults would have been and were expected to know better than to invade the space of others.

Although age differences have received little attention in the research literature, other writers have posited two generalizations. First, Knapp (1980) contends that "it is reasonable to assume that we would interact closer to people in our own general age range" (p. 81). This may be a simple function of people of the same age being more likely to have more things in common than people of substantially different ages. Second, Baxter (1970) suggests that, up to a point, there appears to be a direct relationship between age and distance when comparing personal space orientations of children, adolescents, and adults during conversations. Children converse more closely and adults converse at greater distances. Again, children are likely to have more in common generally than are adults. Thus, the observed differences in interpersonal space usage sometimes attributed to age may just be a function of interpersonal similarity. Whether this is the case must be tested in future research.

Personality Differences

Do people with certain personality characteristics use personal space in ways that are different from others? In their comprehensive book on nonverbal communication, Harper, Wiens, and Matarazzo (1978) have summarized research that suggests that extroverts require less space than introverts during conversations. Introverts are particularly likely to stand further away if the situation is an intimate one.

Persons with general anxiety predispositions have also been reported to require greater distances while interacting. An interesting study showed that highly anxious individuals tended to recall previous interactions as significantly closer than did nonanxious individuals. Others have also found high social anxiety scores to be positively related to interaction distance. The closer a person stands to another, the more the situation demands communication, so it is not surprising that shy people have been found to prefer greater interpersonal distances.

Some studies indicate that individuals with a high need for affiliations are likely to move closer to their interaction partners. It also appears that persons with an internal locus of control establish closer spatial orientations to strangers than do those with an external locus of control. Less distance has also been associated with self-directed people, low authoritarians, and individuals with high self-concepts.

Stigmas

Hickson and Stacks (1993) suggest that "an area that has received less attention is the finding that people maintain greater distances from others who have stigmas. These stigmas can be of two basic types: physical and social. *Physical stigmas* include being in a wheelchair; using crutches, a cane, or a walkers; being blind; being an amputee; and having a burned, scarred face or body. Conigliaro, Cullerton, Flynn, and Rueder (1989) found that pedestrians gave a legally blind person with a white cane 33.8 inches of space as opposed to 5.6 inches when the person had no cane. Social stigma includes such things as a reputation of being an ex-convict, an ex-stripper, an ex-killer, or having sexually transmitted diseases such as herpes or AIDS. In this culture at least, we seem to maintain greater distances between ourselves and those with physical or social stigmas.

Psychiatric and Deviant Differences

Malandro, Barker, and Barker (1989) identify deviant populations as including "[those with] histories of mental illness such as schizophrenia, prisoners, other individuals with criminal records, and disruptive high school students" (p. 192). One major commonality among these populations is that their members generally require more space than nondeviant members of society. It appears that deviants, whether criminal, schizophrenic, disruptive, or violent, depend on their spatial distancing to provide a means of protection. That is, they require larger body-buffer zones between themselves and others than do nondeviant members of society.

CROWDING AND DENSITY

Frank left his hotel room to see the sights of the Big Apple. Seldom did his job bring him to such large metropolitan areas as this one. Being from a small city in southern California, Frank had often longed for a few days between big buildings and large numbers of people hurrying about the streets. As he approached the elevator at the end of the corridor, his excitement and anticipation began to rise.

Frank pressed the down button and waited patiently as the light flashed each floor number until it finally reached the twenty-fifth floor. The elevator stopped and the doors opened. To his amazement, the small cubicle was crammed with people. He stepped inside as the crowd shifted to make room. Before he could step back out to wait for another elevator, the doors closed and the descent began. He quickly realized that he had no room to turn around. He would have to face the man in front of him, their noses only inches apart.

His hands clasped tightly behind his back, Frank closed his eyes. His heart began to beat rapidly and a feeling of extreme discomfort overcame him. "So slow, this damned elevator!" he thought. He looked around at the others. No one else appeared to be bothered by this ordeal. Their faces were solemn, their eyes gazed toward the ceiling or floor. Frank began breathing more quickly and wondered if the man directly in front of him was becoming annoyed with him. After an eternity, the elevator jolted to a stop and the doors slid open. He quickly escaped to the spaciousness of the lobby. The discomfort subsided and he felt relieved.

After a brief respite in the open lobby, Frank made his way to the revolving glass door, beyond which was the excitement of the hustle and bustle of a large metropolis. With new experiences in mind, he regained his confidence and boldly revolved through the door onto the crowded sidewalk outside. Horns honked, street vendors yelled, and the stench of exhaust from a wave of taxis and buses filled his nostrils. "It's so dark for the middle of the afternoon," he thought. Looking upward, he noticed the tall buildings rising forever on each side of the street, blocking out the warm rays of the sun.

A continuous flow of pedestrians walked quickly by, surrounding him on all sides. Several expressed disgust and made gestures at Frank for not moving along. Others pushed past him, nudging him into others. Frank closed his eyes again; the discomfort was coming back. Through the mass of moving bodies, he searched frantically for the hotel's revolving door. Only then did he realize that he had been forced several yards down the sidewalk. He wildly fought his way against the flow and sprang into the hotel lobby. He dashed toward the elevator, pressed the button, and waited. Finally, the door opened to a crammed cubicle. Frank decided to take the stairs to his room on the twenty-fifth floor!

Our story about Frank's visit to the city may not be as exaggerated as at first you may think. It illustrates an important point about personal space. Too much invasion can lead us to feel a great deal of discomfort and often cause us to behave somewhat irrationally. *Density* is the number of people in an area of space. High density, therefore, is a large number of people per given area. Because there is less personal space available for each individual, high-density conditions often create much involuntary encroachment.

Density should not be confused with crowding. *Crowding* is a perception experienced by an individual when that person becomes aware of spatial restrictions. High density does not always cause people to feel crowded. Notice in our story that the other individuals did not react as Frank did. Living and working in high-density conditions, these people have learned to cope with constant invasion and spatial restriction. Frank, on the other hand, was from a small town with less dense conditions and more open spaces. Given time to adapt to the large city, he might develop ways of coping as well. The point here is that density may or may not lead to crowding. It may depend more on what we are used to in our day-to-day encounters with others than how dense the physical conditions actually are.

Three factors can cause people to feel the discomfort associated with crowding. *Surveillance,* the first factor, is the degree to which you sense that strangers are watching you. When you perceive that surveillance is high, you may become uneasy and seek to escape that condition. In Frank's case, the stranger face-to-face with him in the elevator may have caused him to perceive that surveillance was high. This alone could have created the feeling of crowding.

However, Frank's movement was also extremely restricted. *Behavioral constraint,* the second factor, refers to a reduction in the freedom of movement. The more constrained one's activity becomes, the greater the probability that individual has of experiencing crowding. The third factor that leads to crowding, *stimuli overload,* refers to the plethora of noises, sounds, sights, and other stimuli that bombard the senses simultaneously. If the individual is not able to cope with the myriad of stimuli in a given condition, her or his reaction may be to withdraw and find refuge in quieter places. When Frank stepped out into the street, the many stimuli emanating from the environment probably contributed to his feeling of being closed in although he was outside.

Any one of these factors, or a combination of them, can lead to crowding. The major point is that individuals differ in the amount of surveillance, stimulus overload, or behavioral constraint they can experience before the feelings of crowding set in. An individual has to perceive the factors of surveillance, constraint, or stimulus overload as present, whether they are or not, in order for high density to cause feelings of crowding.

The Impact of High Density

It probably is not surprising for you to hear that crime is more prevalent in large urban areas where density is high than in low-density rural regions of the country. One study has shown that urban dwellers more frequently commit vandalism. The same study also showed that city people are less willing to help others than are people who live in rural areas. Results such as these have led many experts to conclude than high density causes criminal behavior. Although there may be some truth to that assertion, other researchers suggest that negative activity such as crime and delinquency in urban areas may be attributable to education, social status, and income level rather than density.

Other writers have maintained that higher death rates, increased health problems, and greater fertility rates are closely related to high density (summarized in Knapp and Hall, 1992). Overall, the research literature seems consistent in one major respect: High-density areas are generally plagued with a greater number of human woes per capita than low-density areas. Furthermore, people who dwell in large urban centers spend much of their day coping with the stimulus overload, surveillance, and behavioral constraint caused by density conditions. The behavior that city dwellers use to cope with crowding can lead others to feel that they are noncaring. According to Knapp and Hall (1992, pp. 157–158), coping methods used by such people include the following:

1. *Spending less time with each input (i.e., shorter conversations)*
2. *Disregarding low-priority inputs (i.e., ignoring other people on the street, subway, elevator, or commuter train)*
3. *Shifting the responsibility for some transactions to others (i.e., not requiring bus drivers to make change)*
4. *Blocking inputs (i.e., having guards protect apartments and limiting accessibility)*

It is unfair for those who live in smaller communities to label people from other large cities as unfriendly, cold, and distant. The behaviors we observe when we visit their cities are quite probably the very methods they use to survive the continuous conditions of high density. If Frank learns to act "unfriendly, cold, and distant," he might enjoy his next trip to the city much more than his last one.

A GLOSSARY OF TERMINOLOGY

Behavioral constraint is a reduction in the freedom of movement. The more constrained one's activity becomes, the more likely that individual is to experience crowding.

Body territory also is known as personal space, the most inviolate form of territory to the individual. Unlike other types of territory, it is portable, and can be thought of as an invisible bubble surrounding the human body.

Casual-personal zone is the region of personal space that ranges from eighteen inches out to about four feet.

Contamination is rendering the territory of another impure with respect to its definition and usage.

Crowding is the perception of spatial restrictions.

Density is the number of people in a space. High density, therefore, is a large number of people in a given area. High density does not always cause people to feel crowded.

Home territory is a public territory colonized by a group that takes it over and uses it continuously.

Human territoriality is a human's presumptive claim of a geographic area with or without a formal, legal basis for that claim.

Insulation is a reaction to an invasion of territory that includes building formidable boundaries. This response can be thought of as sophisticated fighting.

Interactional territories are special places that develop wherever people congregate for social exchange.

Intimate zone of our personal space is the innermost interaction region. It ranges from touching to eighteen inches.

Invasion is a drastic and permanent encroachment in which the invader crosses a territorial boundary with the intention of taking over.

Labels are a type of prevention. Labels include signs or nameplates that are used to prevent takeover of space.

Markers are usually personal artifacts used to mark ownership of space.

Offensive displays are assertive or aggressive postures, stances, stares, and gestures that are meant to prevent encroachment.

Personal space is an invisible bubble that surrounds us that expands or contracts depending on personalities, situations, and types of relationships. Personal space is portable; we take it everywhere we go.

Primary territory is territory that is considered to be the exclusive domain of its owner.

Proxemics is the study of the ways in which humans use and communicate with space.

Public territory is open to anyone and is seldom under constant control of any one person or group. It is subject to temporary ownership and is often protected with as much vigor as personal property.

Public zone is the outer region of the personal space bubble. This zone begins at eight feet and extends to the outer limits of interaction potential.

Secondary territory is generally associated with a person or group that is frequently seen in the territory. Secondary territories are more vulnerable to invasion and takeover than primary territory.

Socio-consultive zone is the region of the space zone that ranges from four feet to eight feet. This region is often called the distance at which Americans transact business.

Stimuli overload is a reaction to a plethora of noises, sounds, sights, and other stimuli that bombard the senses simultaneously.

Surveillance is the degree to which you sense that strangers are watching you.

Tenure is a form of prevention from encroachment; when people have become associated with a particular territory over a long period, they can effectively lay claim to that territory.

Territory is semifixed or fixed space whose owners can move in and out of it without giving up their claim to it. It is claimed, staked out in some way, and defended against encroachment.

Turf defense calls for the owner to repel the invader out of her or his territory.

Violation is the unwarranted use of someone else's territory. Unlike invasion, violation usually is temporary in nature. The encroacher uses someone else's sacred spots without permission.

Withdrawal means that we compensate by moving away from the encroacher and letting them take over. In short, we flee without a fight.

▲ 7

Touch

In the previous chapter, we discussed the idea that human beings use spatial orientations to communicate a variety of messages. Proxemic behavior in humans tells us a great deal about relationships, attitudes, and feelings. One proxemic phenomenon that we have reserved for this chapter is probably one of the most important and controversial of all nonverbal codes associated with the process of communication. *Haptics* is the study of the type, amount, uses of, and the results of tactile behavior. Touch and body contact provide rich and powerful tools for communication, and are vital to the survival and normal development of animals and human beings.

In their book on interpersonal communication, Adler and Towne stressed that touch was essential to life itself:

> *Besides being the earliest means we have of making contact with others, touching is essential to our healthy development. During the nineteenth and early twentieth centuries many children born every year died of a disease then called marasmus, which translated from the Greek means "wasting away." In some orphanages the mortality rate was nearly one hundred percent, but even children in the most "progressive" homes, hospitals, and other institutions died regularly from the ailment.... They hadn't enough touch, and as a result they died. (pp. 225–226)*

Other writers have emphasized the extraordinary function of touch in the relationship between parents and their children. Even the unconscious feelings of parents are received by children through touch and can sometimes create confusion and conflict. Many experts contend that touch deprivation may eventually lead to a myriad

Touch can be a nonverbal expression of closeness.

of problems related to communication, such as reduced learning of speech and symbol recognition.

Furthermore, touch is very important because it is the most effective means by which we communicate many of our feelings and emotions. Body contact is a signal of liking and acceptance. Withholding touch, on the other hand, may communicate an assortment of negative feelings such as resentment, hostility, anger, or distrust. Touching others can help to fulfill our need for closeness. Can you imagine having a romantic relationship with someone without the assistance of a good dose of touching?

Edward T. Hall (1966) contends that the study of touch is an integral part of keeping people within the context of their cultures. He laments that much of the touch research "has failed to grasp the significance of touch, particularly active touch. They have not understood how important it is to keep the person related to the world in which he (she) lives" (p. 57). The point Hall is making is a very important one. The way we touch, the amount we touch, and what we use touch for is largely a consequence of our culture's norms.

Tactile communication is the earliest and probably the most basic form of communication. The most primitive life forms rely almost exclusively on touch to interact with the environment around them. Human beings depend on tactile sensitivity as their first and possibly most important form of contact with other human beings. Even before the infant is born, it is nurtured, caressed, and usually held secure in the mother's womb. The omnipresent heartbeat of the mother provides a comforting life rhythm that soothes and satisfies the infant.

In this chapter, we discuss the impact of touch on the process of communication in several ways. First, we present the functions of touch, particularly in our society. Second, we discuss touch norms, followed by a section on life-span development and touch.

TYPES AND FUNCTIONS OF TOUCH

Morris (1977) defined between touching others and touching oneself. He concluded from field observation that there are "457 types of body contact" (p. 92). He also suggests that there are fourteen major types of public contact that could occur between two people. He refers to these as "tie signs" because this contact signals that some type of relationship is present between the two persons. Table 7–1 lists Morris's major categories of touching.

Our touch behavior functions in a variety of ways. Depending on our interpersonal relationships with others, the way we touch and amount we touch serve different functions. The following discussion centers on five categories of touch, each of which serves different functions: professional, social, friendship, intimate, and sexual.

Professional-Functional Touch

You have had the experience of being examined by a physician. If you are smart, you have regular checkups with your doctor and dentist. In such professional interactions, the professional must touch the patient to provide a thorough examination. Often, these encounters involve body contact that in any other situation might appear extremely intimate and inappropriate. However, we generally accept the doctor's probing and jabbing as necessary. In situations such as this, touch is used on an impersonal level. The professional touches the client as an "object" rather than as a person. It is a cold and unsympathetic form of touch that has little more interpersonal involvement than a person manipulating an inanimate machine. Even in extreme cases such as a breast examination, the breast and the patient are not regarded as anything more than objects. It is not only in medical contexts that professional touch occurs. It may occur when you are trying on shoes, when you visit your barber or beautician, or when you are exchanging money with others. All these situations have in common the fact that the touch is incidental to the purpose of the transaction between you and the other person.

TABLE 7–1   **Morris's Major Categories of Touch**

1. **The Handskake.** The strength of the tie or desired tie between the participants often can be observed by watching the nonshaking hand.
2. **The Body Guide.** Here, touching is a substitute for pointing. The person guiding the other's body is frequently in charge during that encounter.
3. **The Pat.** Morris says when adults pat other adults it is often a condescending gesture or a sexual one. The well-known exception is the congratulatory pat (often on the buttocks) following a successful performance in men's team sports.
4. **The Arm-Link.** This form of touching may be used for support when one person is infirm, but it is also frequently used to indicate a close relationship. The person in charge, says Morris, is less likely to be the person grasping the other's arm.
5. **The Shoulder Embrace.** This "half embrace" is used in male–female romantic relationships as well as to signify "buddies" in male–male relationships.
6. **The Full Embrace.** This gesture, sometimes called a hug, frequently occurs during moments of intense emotion, sporting events, romance, greetings, farewells. It is also used ritualistically to show a relationship closer than a handshake would indicate.
7. **The Hand-in-Hand.** When adults hold hands with children it is designed for support, to keep the child close, or to protect the child. As adults, hand-holding (because both parties are performing the same act) suggests an equality within the relationship. It is often thought of in opposite-sex relationships, but same-sex hand-holding is not uncommon, particularly in groups.
8. **The Waist Embrace.** This, according to Morris, is frequently substituted for the full embrace when the participants wish to signal more intimacy than hand-holding or a shoulder embrace yet still remain mobile.
9. **The Kiss.** The location, pressure, duration, and openness of a kiss help to signal the closeness or desired closeness of a relationship at a particular moment.
10. **The Hand-to-Head.** Given the highly vulnerable nature of the head area, letting someone touch you on the head shows a trusting and often intimate relationship.
11. **The Head-to-Head.** Two people touching heads renders them incapable of regarding other ongoing activities in a normal manner, so this form of touching is usually thought of as an agreement by both parties to shut out the rest of the world — a condition common to young lovers especially.
12. **The Caress.** This is a signal associated with romantic feelings for one's partner, although, like any signal, it can be used by nonintimates who are trying to deceive others about the depth of their relationship.
13. **The Body Support.** As children, our parents often support us by carrying, lifting, or letting us sit in their lap. As adults, such support may be sought in playful situations or when one person feels physically helpless.
14. **The Mock Attack.** These are aggressive-looking behaviors performed in a nonaggressive manner, e.g., arm punches, hair rufflings, pushes, pinches, ear nibbles, etc. We sometimes allow or even encourage such gestures with friends to show the range of behavioral understanding between us. And sometimes these mock-attack touches are substitutes for more loving touches that, in the case of some fathers wishing to show love for their sons, may be too embarrassing.

Social-Polite Touch

The type of touch used for the social function serves to communicate a limited form of interpersonal involvement. When this form of touch is used, we touch one another as more than mere objects. Rather, our body contact serves to acknowledge the other in a social role. Social touch, however, is quite restricted by the social rules of the culture. As a result, we find that cultures may differ widely about what is proper social touch. In North American culture, the handshake is a largely accepted way to acknowledge another person. In other cultures, we see shoulder clasps and kisses on each cheek serving the same function. Social touch is a form of tactile behavior that neutralizes the status differential between two persons.

Friendship-Warmth Touch

Friendship touch is a means by which we let others know that we care for and value them. This form of touch is probably the most difficult to interpret, both for the receiver of the touch and for an outside observer. One reason is that relationships in which friendship touch occurs are often so close as to be confused with intimacy and sexual attraction. Another reason is that this type of touch often is unique to the relationship itself. Interpersonal involvement at this level sees interactants touching for more than professional or social reasons. Here, two people touch one another as people, not objects, and as people who know each other, not as strangers passing in the night.

More cross-cultural variability occurs with friendship touch than any other type. In our culture, for example, touch that signals friendship-warmth is handled with great care. Because we are members of a noncontact-oriented society, we appear to have many unwritten rules that dictate when it is appropriate to use touch in this fashion. In this culture, when close friends are alone together, there is substantially less friendship touch between them than in other cultures. This is because in our culture we tend to associate touching in privacy with intimacy and sexuality. In an open public area, as with two friends meeting at an airport after months or years apart, this type of touch is more appropriate. Later, when the two are alone, it seems less appropriate.

Love-Intimacy Touch

In relationships between intimate lovers and spouses, touch takes on more important characteristics. *Intimate touch* may include caressing the cheek, holding another around the waist, hugging, embracing, kissing, and many other forms that signal a particularly close and involved association between individuals. Intimate touch is highly communicative. It is used to communicate love and closeness, and it is accompanied by many other nonverbal cues to make sure its intent is clear. We also use intimate touch to satisfy the touch needs of our loved ones, even if we ourselves are inconvenienced in doing so.

Intimate touch can convey some of our most important interpersonal messages. Through this kind of touch we complement and validate our verbal messages that say "I love you," "You are very special to me," and "You are a very important part of my life." An important point to remember is that intimate touching does not necessarily involve sexual activity. These relationships usually do include sexual contact, but the sex is not what makes two people intimate. This confusion has lead many couples to become dissatisfied with their special relationships. One of them may not understand that frequent sexual contact does not fulfill the needs of the other. Although sexual activity is pleasurable, it also is important to have quiet, intimate moments of cuddling, caressing, or simply holding hands.

Sexual-Arousal Touch

As implied above, sexual arousal is often equated with intimate touch. Think about it for a moment. Can you have sexual intercourse with someone without being intimate? How about the prostitute and her or his client? The client may be satisfying an intense personal drive whereas the prostitute views the entire ordeal as purely a business transaction. Furthermore, the prostitute most likely will see the touch involved as professional in nature. We could hardly describe this encounter as loving and intimate. How about another purely sexual phenomenon called the one-night stand? Although it is possible for a one-night rendezvous to involve a temporary form of "instant intimacy," most are strictly pleasurable experiences. The relationship between the participants can barely be described as friendship, much less intimacy.

Sexual touch is the most intense form of touch. It may also be the most communicative. Famous sex therapists Masters and Johnson have been quoted as saying, "We believe that effective sexual intercourse is the ultimate in communication" (cited in Knapp, 1980, p. 149). We feel that Masters and Johnson may be correct, if they are looking to the ideal. However, because it is quite possible to have sexual intercourse without intimacy, it is also possible to have virtually uncommunicative sexual intercourse.

TOUCH NORMS

What is normal touch? The answer to that question depends on many factors. Your normal may not be my normal—at least if we are not from the same culture, are not approximately the same age, are not of the same gender, and so on. "Normal" is highly individualized, which has made research in this area so difficult.

One of the most widely cited researchers in this area is Jourard. In his first study (1966) on the touch behavior of humans, he devised and administered a body-accessibility survey to unmarried American college students. This survey instrument included figures of human beings that were divided into several areas. The subjects were asked to indicate the amount of touch they received from significant others, such as parents and close friends, in each of the body areas and the extent to which they touched others in those areas. Jourard's investigation revealed, not surprisingly, that the hands, arms, shoulders, back, and head were body parts that were most frequently involved in touch. Other interesting results included the following: Males in the study touched their mothers less than they were touched by their mothers; people (both male and female) who considered themselves unattractive indicated that they were touched less in all body areas; and Jewish females reported less touch with their boyfriends than did Protestant and Catholic females.

To ascertain whether the touch norms had changed over the years, a group of researchers conducted a study similar to Jourard's a decade later, after the so-called sexual revolution of the late 1960s and early 1970s. They found much the same results concerning touching between subjects and their mothers, fathers, and same-sex friends. However, two major differences in the results of this study did emerge: Males had increased the amount of touch they initiated with female friends in the body areas ranging from chest to knees; and females touched their male friends more frequently about the chest, stomach, and hips. It is speculated that these differences were a reflection of changes stemming from the sexual revolution, but it would be interesting to see yet a second replication conducted today to see whether these changes are still reflected in the behavior of young people.

Touch norms depend on the type of situation in which interpersonal interactions take place. Touching is likely to be more frequent in some situations than in others. The contexts in which touching is more likely and more frequent include the following: attempts to persuade rather than being persuaded; getting "worry" or "concern" messages from others rather than sending them; more involving and deeper conversation than superficial and casual conversation; signaling excitement and enthusiasm rather than receiving such messages; giving rather than asking for advice; giving rather than taking orders; and at social gatherings such as parties rather than in professional situations such as at the office. If these situational constraints seem normal to you, it is a sign that you have assimilated the norms of the culture around you. If they do not, you may find your touching behavior (or lack of it) communicating something very negative to others.

Cultural Differences

What is considered normal in the amount and type of touch an individual gives or receives depends not only on the situation but also on the culture in which he or she lives. According to Argyle (1975), several types of tactile behavior are common to Western culture. Table 7–2 summarizes the types of touch and the area of the body usually touched, as shown in Argyle's work.

Jourard (1968) has shown that body contact is less frequent among North Americans than among individuals in other cultures. We are often called noncontact-oriented. This study by Jourard found that the rates of touch per hour among

TABLE 7–2   **Type of Touch**

TYPE OF TOUCH	BODY REGION
Patting	Head, back
Slapping	Bottom, hand, face
Punching	Chest, face
Pinching	Cheek
Stroking	Hair, face, upper body, knee, genitals
Shaking	Hands, shoulders
Kissing	Mouth, cheeks, breast, hand, foot, genitals
Licking	Face, genitals
Holding	Hand, arm, knee, genitals
Guiding	Hand, arm
Embracing	Shoulder, body
Linking	Arms
Laying-on	Hands
Kicking	Legs, bottom
Grooming	Hair, face
Tickling	Almost anywhere

adults in several cultures differed considerably. The results showed that in coffee shops, adult couples in San Juan touched 180 times per hour; those in Paris touched 110 times; in London, 1; and in Gainesville, Florida, 2. According to this study, at least, North Americans are not among the world's greatest touchers!

Although North Americans are not frequent touchers compared to most cultures, at least one study has shown that we engage in body contact more often than the Japanese. Barnlund (1975) conducted a study using a similar technique to that used by Jourard. He asked both Americans and Japanese to indicate the amount and frequency of touch they give and receive in various body areas. The results showed that for nearly all areas, Americans touched their partners more.

We stereotypically view macrocultures as either contact or noncontact oriented. One such stereotype is that all Latin Americans touch a great deal of the time. Research has shown, however, that even within the macroculture of Latin America, subculture differences for touch are evident. Shuter (1976), for example, observed the three Latin cultures of Panama, Costa Rica, and Columbia. According to this study, the amount of touching and holding behavior decreases the farther south the culture is. Before this research, there were some who argued that there was a world-wide pattern about touch. The belief was that the closer to the equator, the more the people touch. Although this was an interesting speculation, and many cultures conform to this pattern, the Shuter study indicates that touch patterns are more complex than this speculation would allow.

Gender Differences

Touch behavior differs between males and females in our culture. Not surprisingly, females usually are seen as more touch-oriented than males. This has been a general and consistent observation (Andersen and Leibowitz, 1978; Larsen and LeRoux, 1984; and D. Fromme, Jaynes, Taylor, Hanold, Daniell, Rountree, and M. Fromme, 1989). What is more interesting, however, is that males and females perceive touch differently. Females discriminate among their body parts in terms of touchability more than males. Females feel that hand-squeezing is a sign of love and friendliness, and they do not see the squeezing of their chests as playful! Males, on the other hand, are not as concerned about specific parts of their bodies. Males are not as likely to apply specific meaning to specific kinds of touch, but they are more concerned about the type of touch they receive than about the areas of the body that receive the touch.

Touch Avoidance

Do you have some friends who touch you and others constantly without regard for your personal space or touch norms? We shall call this group the "touchies." Do you have some friends who rarely touch and do not appreciate it when others touch them? We shall call this group the "untouchables." They are very conscious about whom, when, and where they touch or receive touch. The "touchies" constantly touch and often are told by others to stop touching. Despite the situation or the person, these "touchie" people touch others. These people do not seem to be aware of the touch norms of others around them, nor do they seem to realize that their constant touching can be annoying to those they touch.

On the other extreme, there are the "untouchables." Again, it matters little whom they interact with or what the situation is; these people generally avoid touching. They are called *touch avoiders*. Are you a high toucher or a touch avoider? Does it depend on the people and situation?

Touch avoidance is when a person does not initiate touch and prefers that others not initiate touch with her or him. Research on touch avoidance is quite sparse. However, what is available shows that males typically are more touch-avoidant than females with members of the same sex. Females, on the other hand, are more touch avoidant than males are with individuals of the other sex. Religious affiliation and age are also related to touching behavior. Protestants, for example, are more touch-avoidant than non-Protestants. Also, individuals who are older and married tend to be highly avoidant of members of the opposite sex.

Sorensen (1979) had confederates approach and touch subjects to study the perceptions that subjects developed. Using the Touch Avoidance Measure developed by Andersen and Leibowitz (1978) to identify touch avoiders and high touchers, she found that high touchers consistently rated the confederates more positively, and touch avoiders consistently rated them negatively. Sex differences were also found. In general, touch from females was seen as more acceptable than touch from males.

LIFE SPAN DEVELOPMENT AND TOUCH

Tactile stimulation is a highly necessary form of interaction throughout the life span of animals and humans. In this section, we discuss the nature of touch during human development. Much of the research in touch has been done in animal populations and has provided considerable insight into the effects of touch on growth and development.

Touch in Animals

We suggested earlier that tactile communication is the primary, if not the only, means of interaction for many basic forms of animal life. Consider the communication among social insects such as bees and ants that is highly dependent on touch. Through their antennae, these insects transmit the messages that ensure the smooth operation of their microsocieties. Touch signals in most animal species generally are coupled with chemical signals detected through smells.

Two important tactile phenomena that occur among various species are gentling and licking. These are kinds of touch adult animals use with their offspring just after birth. Gentling behavior is the stroking and touching of newborns. Licking, on the other hand, is used for cleaning the offspring. Licking also plays a very important role in stimulating the physiological functions of newborn animals and, as a result, contributes dramatically to their survival.

Results of studies on the gentling behavior of rats showed that gentling played a vital role. Rats that had been stroked and touched were gentler and less prone to become frightened. During this experiment, both gentled and nongentled rodents were subjected to an operation to remove their thyroid and parathyroid glands. The gentled rats had a much higher rate of survival: 79 percent of nongentled rats died compared to only 13 percent of the gentled rats survived the operation.

Probably some most notable research concerning the effects of touch on animals was conducted by psychologist Harry Harlow and his associates (1958, 1963) using monkeys. Harlow was interested in the bodily contact between mother monkeys and their offspring. Under tightly controlled laboratory conditions, the investigators observed that infant monkeys separated from their mothers grew fond of, and essentially attached themselves to, gauze pads that covered the cages. Upon removing the pads, Harlow and his colleagues noticed that the infant monkeys became violent. They also found that infants reared in bare wire-mesh enclosures had considerable difficulty surviving during the first several days after birth.

In a later study, the researchers placed two surrogate mothers in the cages with the infant monkeys. One surrogate mother was made of terry cloth with a lightbulb behind the head to give off heat. The second surrogate mother was constructed out of wire-mesh material. The cloth mother lactated in half the conditions, and the wire mother lactated in the other half. The conditions were such that the baby monkeys had equal access to both mothers and were allowed to spend any amount of time they wanted with either. The results were somewhat surprising. Even where the wire mother lactated, the infant monkeys preferred the cloth mother. The researchers concluded that the attraction to the cloth mother was a result of the tactile comfort she provided. Harlow and his colleagues were surprised to observe that the affection and love stemming from the tactile comfort seemed to far exceed the need for the infant monkeys to nurse. At least in some circumstances, touch may be more important than food.

Human Development

Children. Just as tactile stimulation is crucial to animals, it also is highly necessary for human growth and development. Knapp and Hall (1992) comment on the vital role touch plays in the human communication process:

> *Tactile communication is probably the most basic or primitive form of communication. In fact, tactile sensitivity may be the first sensory process to become functional. In fetal life, the child begins to respond to vibrations of mother's pulsating heartbeat, which impinge on the child's entire body and are magnified by the amniotic fluid. . . . In one sense, our first input about what "life" is going to be like comes from the sense of touch. (p. 231)*

The implication of these remarks and those of other experts is that tactile communication (D. Maurer and C. Maurer, 1988) in the very early stages of life may establish the foundation of all other forms of communication humans later develop. As we suggested at the beginning of this chapter, touch in the infant years is necessary for the subsequent development of the abilities to learn speech and recognize symbols.

Around the turn of the century, *marasmus,* the "wasting away" disease among infants, was determined to be the result of a lack of tactile stimulation. However, it was not until years later that the medical community accepted touch as a treatment. A dramatic illustration of how important touch was to the survival of infants occurred shortly after the end of World War II in Europe. The death rate of babies in orphanages was extremely high, although they were well-fed and technically very well cared-for. When older women were hired to hold, rock, and feed the babies, however, the death rate dropped to almost nothing. Touching the babies literally saved their lives.

It should not surprise you that as infants you received more touch from other human beings than you will receive for the rest of your life. Both the frequency of touch and the duration of touch between mothers and their infants is at its peak between the ages of fourteen months and two years. Touch decreases consistently after this period. Although male infants actually receive more touch than females in the first six months, after this time females receive more touch and are encouraged to engage in greater amounts of touch than are their male counterparts. This suggests that as early as the first year of life, parents are socializing their children's tactile behavior to conform to the expectations of adult gender roles. Boys are encouraged to play away from parents, to let go, whereas girls are often rewarded for doing the opposite.

According to Burgoon and Saine (1978), touch is valuable to development during infancy for several reasons. First, touch has a biological value. "The newborn is very vulnerable and is totally dependent on others for its protection and comfort, which the mother supplies through physical contact" (p. 66). Second, touch provides communication value. At this early stage, "contact is necessary for communication between mother and child" (p. 66). Third, touch has psychological value. Burgoon and Saine explain that touch is the primary means by which the child develops an identity. The child learns to separate herself or himself from the rest of the world. His or her environmental awareness "will depend on how much direct tactile exploration is permitted. Children learn spatial dimensions, sizes, shapes, and textures through touching and manipulating things" (p. 66). Finally, Burgoon and Saine contend that touch during infancy and childhood has social value. They suggest that "physical contact appears to be necessary for the development of satisfactory interpersonal relationships" (p. 67).

As the child moves from infancy into later childhood, the frequency with which he or she gives and receives touch appears to make a steady decline. Willis and Hofman (1975) found this trend among children from kindergarten to sixth grade. Once adolescence is reached, the amount of physical contact falls to about half that observed in the early elementary grades. These writers note, however, that even adolescents' touch is more frequent than adult touch. In short, older children are experiencing less touch than they ever have before, but they are also experiencing more than they will for the rest of their lives. Some writers suggest, however, that in the adolescence stage children reach a latency period during which touch is greatly reduced. Once sex becomes significant, physical contact increases sharply.

Adults.   When humans reach adulthood, tactile behavior becomes considerably more restricted. Much of the adult's touch is restricted to greetings and goodbyes. Furthermore, it appears that touching becomes more rule-governed. Most societies, if not all, hold adults accountable for the amount and type of touch they use. As a result, our culture requires that grownups exercise caution when engaging in physical contact with others. It is during adulthood that cultures enforce their touch norms. Violation of these norms can have extensive social consequences. It is also during this stage that the cultural differences become quite prominent. A particular restriction on physical contact, according to many writers in nonverbal communication, is that between two adult males in our society. Malandro, L. Barker, and D. Barker (1989) comment:

> *Physical contact by a man with another man remains so potentially*
> *dangerous and unspeakable for many American males that other than a*

constrained handshake, no touch by any male (other than the dentist and the doctor) is permitted. (p. 212)

Many current researchers suggest that because women are involved with the physical care of children and others in their surroundings, they are less likely to have negative feelings about touch. Unlike most men, many women perform touch behavior such as bathing, drying, powdering, kissing, dressing, undressing, lifting, carrying, combing, grooming, feeding, holding, smoothing, caressing, and comforting on a routine basis. Men who share equally in such touching routines may be less fearful or anxious about touch.

As adolescents grow into adults, tactile communication gradually gives way to other forms of communication. Because adults may experience a great deal of frustration from a lack of physical contact with others, it is quite common to see them resort to a variety of substitutes. According to Desmond Morris (1976), adults often use the services of "licensed touchers" to fulfill the body contact needs that result from decreased adult contact in our society. We hire masseuses, barbers, and beauty specialists, and may even increase our visits to the doctor sometimes merely to get a good dose of "tactile medicine."

According to Morris, North American adults are so touch-starved that we may resort to many different forms of substitute touch.

Most of us solve the problem to some extent by using substitutes such as petting a dog or stroking a cat. . . . [We] suck our thumbs or smoke cigarettes; we drink out of bottles that are the same size as baby bottles, we will hug ourselves when we're in distress . . . attempting to get back some kind of infantile comfort. (Rosenfeld and Civikly, 1976, p. 130)

Substitute touch may be the primary way that adults meet their touch needs. Your family's pet may be more important to the daily comfort of the grownups than it is for the pleasure of the children. It is not uncommon for pets originally purchased for a child to become more Mom's or Dad's. Usually it is explained that the child is negligent in caring for the pet, so the adult is forced to step in. One may wonder which came first, the child's negligence or the adult's caring!

As humans grow older, the decline in touch continues. Senior citizens, for the most part, have begun to decrease even the sexual contact that gained full strength during early adulthood. One study investigating touch in senior citizens found that the rules governing touch may be more restrictive at this age than any other. Results of a study of older persons in senior housing led to the following conclusions: When the elderly are touched, it is far away from the genital area; touch is highly restricted between residents and staff members of the other sex; the initiator of any touch is usually of high status; and residents who are physically impaired received less touch. The researcher noted that the extremely impaired males in such institutions are the least touched of all because most staff members are female. One might question whether the impairment presaged the lack of touch, or the reverse. Without a doubt, our senior citizens are the most touch-deprived of any age group in our culture. This acute lack of touch in the later years is a major contributor to seniors' growing feelings of isolation.

WHAT DOES TOUCH COMMUNICATE?

Touch and Emotion

Positive Affect Created. Tactile communication is an effective means by which we communicate emotion. Immediacy (see Chapter 11) is closely related to touch. As with other immediacy cues, we see more touch occurring between individuals who like one another and a greater amount of avoidance behavior between persons who dislike one another. Touching, like other immediacy cues, tends to help interpersonal attraction. When research confederates touch and reveal to subjects, more positive affect toward the confederate was shown by the subjects.

Increase in Touch as Emotions Increase. Touch also tends to increase between persons when the situation becomes more emotional. Observations of people in airports found that when it came to greetings and goodbyes, 60 percent of those observed engaged in touch. Other studies have shown that touch enables us to better discriminate among the emotions of others.

Attitudes Communicated. A variety of interpersonal attitudes can be communicated through physical contact. Touch can signal sexual interest, affiliation, friendliness, and even negative attitudes such as aggression, disrespect, or disgust. It should be noted, however, that the specific emotional messages communicated may depend to a large extent on the individual. Recall the earlier discussion on gender differences. What may be perceived as playfulness, friendliness, love, or sexuality depends on the gender of the individual as well as the area touched and kinds of touch (pat, stroke, or squeeze, for example). Generally, however, we tend to associate stroking with love, warmth, and sexual desire whereas the pat is usually perceived as playfulness.

Touch and Status

Henley (1977) has advanced three general conclusions concerning the literature on touch and status:

1. Individuals have certain expectations about touching and being touched in particular role relationships. For example, individuals expect to touch subordinates

Touch can show our caring for one another.

more than they touch superiors and to be touched more by superiors than by subordinates.

2. Touching depends on the situational context.
3. Touching and dominance are related. Specifically, dominant persons are more likely to initiate touch.

Consistent with Henley's conclusions, it has been observed that people who initiate touch are more likely to be attributed higher status. We would then expect the doctor rather than the nurse to be the touch initiator, the professor rather than the student, the manager rather than the assembly-line worker.

Touch and Self-Intimacy

Have you ever found yourself in a traumatic situation and realized that you were in some way attempting to comfort or reassure yourself by self-touching? Desmond Morris (1971) suggests that these self-intimacy behaviors represent a psychological need for someone to soothe us during moments of crisis. These behaviors are quite similar to the self-adaptive behaviors discussed in Chapter 3. They generally are most prevalent when we feel nervous, lonely, frightened, or depressed. According to Morris and other writers, self-touching includes shielding actions (covering ears or mouth), cleaning actions (wiping, rubbing, picking, scratching), and self-intimacy (hugging yourself, holding your own hand, masturbating).

Intimate self-touching may indicate a need or wish to be held by someone. Touch is such a strong need of humans. If that need is not satisfied by others, we may be driven to satisfy it ourselves.

EFFECTS OF TOUCH DEPRIVATION

We conclude this chapter by summarizing what we believe may be one of the most acute problems of human beings and their interactions. Throughout this chapter, we have touched on a variety of ways in which physical contact influences communication. The effects of touch deprivation, however, go far beyond social exchange itself. Lack of touch can negatively affect our ability to develop normal speech, reading skills, and symbol recognition; furthermore, many have claimed that touch deprivation in early life can result in a variety of health problems, including skin diseases and allergies.

Skin hunger is a strongly felt need for touch, just as regular hunger is a strongly felt need for food. It results from insufficient body contact for psychological, and possibly physical, well-being. Not only can touch deprivation lead to psychological problems, it may also negatively influence our ability to withstand stress. Hite (1977) reports the work of Seymour Levine, who studied the effects of three conditions of touch on a sample of newborn rats. In the first condition, the infant rats were allowed physical contact with their mothers. In the second, the rodents were completely deprived of touch. In the third condition, electric shocks were administered to the infant rats. After a period of time had elapsed, the touch-deprived group was found to be weak and suffering from illness. The rats allowed to have physical contact with their mothers, on the other hand, were healthy and vital.

What most surprised Levine was the condition of the rats that had been shocked. They were as lively and healthy as those in the mother-contact group! These findings may suggest a rather startling effect. Could it be that "bad" touch is better for normal biological development than no touch at all? That may be a bit far-fetched, but these dramatic results illustrate that touch deprivation is not good.

A GLOSSARY OF TERMINOLOGY

Friendship-warmth touch is touching behavior that recognizes the other person's uniqueness and expresses liking for that person. The person is perceived as a friend.

Functional-professional touch is impersonal, businesslike touch used to accomplish or perform some task or service.

Gentling behavior is the stroking and touching of newborns.

Haptics is the study of the type, amount, uses of, and the results of tactile behavior.

Licensed touchers are professionals we hire to fulfill the body-contact needs that result from decreased adult contact. They include masseuses, barbers, beauty specialists, and even doctors.

Licking is used in the animal world to clean newborn offspring.

Love-intimacy touch is touch that expresses emotional and affective attachment and caring. It is usually a hug, caress, or stroke.

Marasmus is the "wasting away" disease among infants that was determined to result from a lack of tactile stimulation.

Sexual arousal touch can be a part of love-intimacy, but it can also be distinct from love-intimacy. Sexual arousal touch can include the use of a person as an object of attraction or lust.

Skin hunger is a strongly felt need for touch, just as regular hunger is a strongly felt need for food. It results from insufficient body contact for psychological and possibly physical well-being.

Social-polite touch is the type of touch that affirms or acknowledges the other person's identity. This type of touch follows strict cultural codes. In North America, it is normally the classic handshake.

Touch avoidance is the avoidance of touch from others and the unwillingness to reciprocate touch.

Touch avoiders are people who do not like to receive touch or be expected to give touch in most situations.

▲ 8

Environment and Physical Surroundings

What does environment have to do with human communication? What is so important about the physical surroundings of individuals when they come together for social interaction? Do environmental factors such as spatial arrangement, design, color, lighting, and temperature really affect how people feel, what they discuss, how they perceive messages, how they behave? Can the way individuals use and manipulate environments transmit messages about their personalities, intentions, moods, and other characteristics? The research suggests that the answer to these questions is a resounding "Yes!"

The study of environment in relation to human communication is yet another aspect of proxemics dealt with in the previous two chapters. Hall (1966) referred to environment as *fixed-feature space* that involves primarily the arrangement of physical features in our homes, offices, rooms, schools, and even the layout of our cities and towns. We also include in our discussion of environment what Hall calls *semi-fixed features,* or the movable objects in our environments. Among these objects are tables, chairs, desks, and other furniture and accessories that adorn, accent, highlight, and personalize the physical areas in our world.

Why does it matter how environments are arranged? If you find yourself asking this question, then consider the following story related by McCroskey, Larson, and Knapp (1971).

> The United States and South Vietnam wanted a seating arrangement in which only two sides were identified. They did not want to recognize the National Liberation Front as an "equal" partner in the negotiations. North

Structures can have an environmental message of their own.

Viet Nam and the NLF wanted "equal" status given to all parties—repre- sented by a four-sided table. The final arrangement was such that both par- ties could claim victory. The round table minus the dividing lines allowed North Viet Nam and the NLF to claim all four delegations as equal. (p. 97)

The debate among these four groups concerning a mere seating arrangement showed how important the environmental setting was for the negotiations to end the war in Vietnam. The table issue was argued for eight long months before an agree- ment was made. Meanwhile, thousands of soldiers on both sides were killed in the ongoing conflict raging in Southeast Asia.

A more recent international situation has shown that the importance of physical arrangements for negotiations has not declined since the Vietnam conflict. It continues to be an all-important consideration. In early 1985, talks began between the United States and the Soviet Union to reduce nuclear weapons. Before the actual negotiations began, however, talks about the talks were held to set the ground rules for the meeting. A primary consideration in these preliminary negotiations was the arrangement of the physical setting in which the nuclear weapons reduction meeting was to be held.

Consider for a moment the layout of your home, your dorm room, or your

People's environments can transmit many messages about them.

apartment. Think of what your furnishings, color choices, and arrangement say about you. Are you comfortable in your environment? Do others feel at ease, or have you set up your surroundings so that visitors conform to your wishes? Do you find that one room is your favorite and another is seldom used? We asked our own students questions such as these. One young woman responded that her favorite room in her apartment was the sun porch:

> *It's so light and the plants add much warmth and color. I have wicker chairs in it and multi-colored green cushions. That is where I spend almost all of my time when I'm home. My bedroom is too dark. It's somewhat ugly, and I only go in there to change my clothes.*

It is not surprising that some environments, even different rooms in the same house, are more frequented than others. Psychologists have found that our environmental surroundings affect our emotional states. Environments can create arousal in us, and depending on how we interpret that arousal, can make us feel stimulated, alert, frenzied, or active. We may experience pleasure or displeasure because of the influence of physical surroundings. Some surroundings evoke feelings of happiness, joy, and contentment and others produce discomfort, uneasiness, and dissatisfaction.

In this chapter, we look at environment in several ways. First, we discuss the perceptual characteristics of environment. Second, we consider the relationship between architectural design and the impact of environment. Third, we deal with spatial arrangements and individual differences associated with them. Fourth, we present a discussion of the impact on human interaction of environmental factors such as attractiveness, color, lighting, and temperature.

PERCEPTUAL CHARACTERISTICS OF ENVIRONMENT

Our physical surroundings can be perceived in a variety of ways. Perceptions of the environments in which we interact affect our communicative behavior. Often we create our environments in such ways as to intentionally create certain perceptions in the people who use them. Let's consider the six perceptual characteristics of environments advanced by Knapp (1978) and the communication behaviors that generally are associated with each. The six perceptual characteristics of environment are formality, warmth, privacy, familiarity, constraint, and distance.

Perception of Formality

Think for a moment about the church buildings and sanctuaries with which you are familiar. Are there common characteristics of these particular environments? Generally, churches, synagogues, and temples are constructed and furnished in a way that creates a perception of formality. As with many other environments, the more formal a church is, the more formal the communication behavior in it will be. That is, if we perceive the environment to be formal, our communication behavior is likely to be less relaxed and more superficial, hesitant, and stylized (see diagram).

Perception of Formality

Formal ————————————————————————— Informal

It is no accident that some environments produce a more formal atmosphere. We would expect that the more one wishes to have individuals conform to rules and norms, the more likely one will strive to make the environment more formal. Knapp (1980, p. 59) has referred to what may be called the *unliving living room.* Surely you have seen such formal rooms in either your own or another's home. It more realistically resembles a showcase than a place to relax and interact with fellow human beings. This is the room into which guests are ushered during more ritualistic or formal, and sometimes unpleasant, occasions— meetings with angry neighbors, talking to an unfamiliar salesperson, waiting with acquaintances to attend a funeral, and the like.

Any American male knows the feelings that rise when he sits in the unliving room waiting for his date to come downstairs for their first evening out. Later, if the dating continues, the young woman's parents get to know the young man better and may eventually invite him to share the more relaxed and less formal family den. The more informal the physical surroundings are perceived, the more we expect the interaction to be relaxed, open, and inviting.

Perception of Warmth

Environments can also create perceptions of warmth or coldness. Consider the cold, hard marble walls of a bank building or courthouse. In contrast, think of the warmth associated with the family den or the kitchen. The degree to which environments create a psychological feeling of warmth is the degree to which we feel comfortable and relaxed and want to linger in those physical surroundings (see diagram). Warm environments tend to encourage interaction among individuals. Through color, lighting, and textures in rooms, one can ease interaction and keep people from taking their leave. On the other hand, we can move people along by "cooling off" the physical surroundings. Fast-food chains such as McDonald's, Wendy's, Burger King, and Taco Bell have found a winning combination by manipulating the warmth or coldness of their restaurants. Because these businesses rely on a rapid rate of customer turnover, their establishments must display enough warmth to invite the customer in but include enough coldness to discourage them from staying around and taking up seats after they have finished that jumbo burger or taco and drink.

Perception of Warmth
Psychologically Warm ——————— Psychologically Cold

One author of the text recently visited a fast-food restaurant in an Alabama city. She noticed that the decor was unusually attractive and the seats more comfortable than in most restaurants. Evidently, the increased display of warmth was their way of dealing with the heavy competition in the area. However, the management still wanted customers to move through quickly (and the warmer environment was not helping). The problem was solved by displaying a sign on the wall that read "Fifteen-minute limit for consuming food on the premises!"

Perception of Privacy

The degree to which an environment is enclosed and small (allowing few people to enter) is the extent to which it may be perceived as private. Privacy is enhanced when individuals feel that there is less opportunity for their conversations to be overheard by others (see diagram). Eating establishments can lose their regular customers by changing their dining room into a large expansive area from a smaller and more private one, a realization many formerly busy restaurants have come to after expanding to meet high demand. Some restaurants prefer to keep customers within their establishments, unlike fast-food chains. The finer places enhance their profits not so much by rapid turnover but by attracting an affluent clientele that lingers and continues to spend more money. The longer the customers remain, the more drinks they will buy. Getting the people to linger often means providing an environment that allows them to talk privately in an intimate atmosphere. People often select restaurants and lounges to patronize because their environment encourages and permits intimate interactions. A loud band can put such an establishment out of business almost overnight!

Perception of Privacy
Perception of Privacy ————— **Perception of Nonprivacy**

Perception of Familiarity

A fourth perceptual characteristic of environments is the degree of familiarity or unfamiliarity. Physical surroundings that are very unfamiliar to us often create feelings of uneasiness (see diagram). Because we do not know what to expect in such unfamiliar situations, we tend to be rather cautious, deliberate, and conventional in our communication behavior. Unfamiliarity often generates high levels of arousal as a function of our trying to figure out how we should behave. We are unsure of the norms and rituals of unfamiliar places. We are apt to engage in many adaptor behaviors.

Perception of Familiarity
Familiarity ————————————————— **Unfamiliarity**

Imagine getting in your car to take a long trip. You drive onto the interstate highway and set your cruise control at 55 or 65 miles per hour. After a few hours, you become hungry and begin to look for places to stop. If you are like many individuals, you will pass by several restaurants because they are unfamiliar to you. You want to relax, not worry how to behave. After a while, you see a welcome and familiar sight. Beckoning you to approach are the two golden arches. You can already taste that Big Mac and fries. You know what to expect. You probably can even guess where the restrooms are going to be.

Most chain restaurants, hotels, convenience stores, and gas stations count on you making this kind of decision. They know that most people want to avoid hassles when they travel. They go out of their way to make you feel at home when you enter their establishment. If you have learned that you can count on a chain to be reliable, even if their food, room, or whatever is not the very best, you are much more likely to stop there than to go to their competitor across the street. Have you ever stopped at what you thought was a familiar chain operation only to learn that it was not what you had come to expect? If you have, you know the frustration, even anger, of unexpectedly encountering an unfamiliar environment.

Perception of Constraint

Constraint is the opposite of feeling free to easily enter or leave an environment. Perceptions of constraint can become intense if there is a realization that very little space is available to us. If we are granted a small portion of the space and simultaneously find it difficult to leave (along with no privacy), we feel extremely constrained (see diagram). Riding in a crowded subway with the knowledge that your stop is forty-five minutes down the line may influence you to take your leave sooner, if you can get to the door before it closes at the upcoming station.

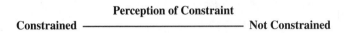

Perception of Constraint
Constrained ——————————————————— **Not Constrained**

Many have commented that we can more easily tolerate temporary constraint (as in the subway ride) if we are aware that it is only temporary. Sometimes constraint is of a more permanent nature, such as being locked up in a prison. You can imagine how traumatic that would be! Crowded classrooms sometimes give students a similar feeling, particularly if they are required to take the class. They feel that there is little or no hope of escaping soon, much like the person confined in prison. In Chapter 6, we discussed the idea of crowding. Essentially, environments that are constraining tend to produce the factors that lead to this feeling of psychological discomfort: stimuli overload, behavior restriction, and increased surveillance.

Perception of Distance

Finally, environmental factors can create perceptions of distance. Distance perceptions can influence the type of response we make to others because of how close or far away we are from them (see diagram). Actually, perceptions of distance in environments depend on other nonverbal cues. We can establish physical distance by placing ourselves far away from others. In large environments with several other people, this may require that we speak more loudly (which, of course, causes our interactions to be less personal or private).

We can also create psychological distance, although we may be physically near another person. In the crowded subway or elevator, we may turn away from others or engage in gaze avoidance to establish a distance that otherwise would not be possible.

Perception of Distance
Physically or ——————————————————— **Physically or**
Psychologically Close   **Psychologically Far**

Our proximity to the center of power in an organization affects other people's perceptions of our power. That is, the closer we are, the more powerful we are perceived. The person whose office is next to the president's office is perceived as powerful, and even more powerful if there is a private door between the two offices.

ARCHITECTURE AND ENVIRONMENT

Winston Churchill has been quoted as saying "We shape our buildings, thereafter they shape us." Little could Churchill have realized how much research would be devoted in subsequent years to studying the impact of environmental factors on human behavior and communication.

Buildings, landscaping, positions of walls, partitions, rooms, and stairways all influence human interaction in one way or another. Often, the perceptual character-istics are considered before the architect and building engineer even start to design a new shopping mall, office building, or even a home. Take a few minutes to try this activity:

> *If you could design your own home, what environmental characteristics would you incorporate? Where would the living room be located? What about the bedroom? What colors will you choose to decorate your home? Is the exterior going to be brick, wood, aluminum siding, stone? Will the interior walls be paneled? Will the inside be open and airy or closed and private? Think of the choices you made and explain why you made the ones you did.*

Buildings are designed to express feelings and impressions to those who see them as well as those who enter them. Is it any wonder, then, that banks of the past were built of stone with marble walls and floors, many of which incorporated tall concrete pillars on the facades? What were the bank owners attempting to communi-cate to the public? They wanted to create the impression of endurance, stability, and security. Can you imagine a family in the early 1930s selling their farm, loading the truck with all their belongings, and driving into the big city to look for a new way of life? Can you imagine them pulling up to a flimsy-looking drive-through bank? After all, the truck could just about knock the thing over, exposing all that money! If you were in their place, would you feel safe depositing your life's savings into a vacuum-powered air chute? Building designs can have a great impact not only on people's behavior but also on their impressions of the owners of those buildings.

Benson and Frandsen (1982) observe that the impressions evoked by architec-tural design were of utmost importance to Adolf Hitler:

> *When Hitler commissioned the great monuments of the Third Reich, he wanted them to symbolize the massiveness, the grandeur, and the durability of his vision. Beyond looking impressive, the buildings were designed to force people to relate to each other in ways consistent with the propagan-distic purposes of the state. The great stadium at Nuremberg, for instance, was a symbol of the Reich . . . the huge stadium encouraged people to "translate" themselves into a mass of cheering followers. (p. 24)*

Have you ever wondered why almost any courtroom you have ever seen tends to command from you and all who enter a sense of respect? It is by design that we are made aware of the seriousness and importance of the decisions that are made in our houses of justice. Status and power messages speak loudly in the courtroom. The elevated bench gives the judge a clear and visible position of dominance and control over all transactions. Even the opposing lawyers and their clients have carefully placed territorial boundaries that are respected by all. Only within the confines of the counselor's table can an attorney talk freely and openly with his or her client without intrusion by the opponent.

Bruneau (1972) studied the architectural design of office spaces in educational organizations. He was primarily interested in how the office designs controlled the communication of both owners and nonowners of the spaces. The following are the general findings of Bruneau's study. As the status of the owner of the office increased, the more control the design placed on students' behavior. The higher the status of the owner of the office space, the greater the number of offices nonowners had to pass through to reach the owner. Students moving too rapidly through offices of teachers and administrators appeared to be a gross violation of norms, and most office areas had prescribed routes for movement.

From Bruneau's work and that of many others, it is clear that people use architectural design to control the movement and the communication of visitors who enter their environment. When we enter an environment where we find it very difficult to decide where we are and are not supposed to go, it may be because the architect slipped up, or it may be that we have never been in that type of structure previously. Recall, if you can, the first time you entered a dormitory, a post office, a police station, a hospital, a church, a synagogue, or the lobby of a large hotel. Was it easier to know what to do in subsequent encounters with these types of environments?

SPATIAL ARRANGEMENT

The ways we arrange our environments for purposes of interaction can transmit a variety of signals. In this section, we discuss spatial arrangement in three ways. First, the impact of the shape of tables is discussed. Second, we present the topic of seating arrangement and its relationship to task situations and personality differences. Third, the topic of office arrangement and how it is related to professional and social interaction is reviewed. Although there is a significant body of literature regarding environment and classroom communication between teacher and student, we will not present it here. We feel that nonverbal communication in the classroom is substantial enough to merit a separate chapter. Therefore, Chapter 14 deals with spatial arrangement in the educational setting and its impact on interaction and learning.

The Shape of Tables

Consider for a moment the three different table structures in Figure 8–1. Can the shape alone affect the communication behavior of people sitting around it? Recall the story of the debate between the United States and North Vietnam earlier in this chapter. For eight long months, these parties argued over one major item—the shape of the table around which the negotiations would take place!

The round table is characterized by a circle. There are no distinct and visible edges to separate the sides. As a result, it often is taken as a symbol of equality and unity among the individuals that occupy it. The round table has taken on particular meaning concerning power and dominance. Although King Arthur used the round table to express unity and equality among his knights, there nonetheless developed a power message depending on where the knights were seated. The closer they were to the king, the more powerful they were seen to be. Do not be misled by the apparent equality projected by a round table. A powerful person at a round table, even in a very democratic society, is still a powerful person, and unlikely to be treated as an equal by others sitting at the same table, or to expect such treatment.

The square table is just that: square, or nearly so. Because it has four equal sides, it communicates equality of status and power. However, its distinct sides and prominent corners also suggest a separation among the interactants. The square shape facilities perceptions of equality but not unity. Square tables are excellent for interactions involving competition and negotiation.

The rectangular table is a quite common structural arrangement in the corporate boardroom. The impact of this type of table resembles that of the square table. That is, there are four separate sides that suggest to the interactants a lack of unity. However, two of the sides are short and the other two sides usually are twice as long or longer. One of the short sides is generally perceived as the head of the table, especially in instances where the other short side is left vacant. At the rectangular table, the center of power is at the head and gradually diminishes as the position gets farther and farther away. The person at the head usually controls the interaction at the table and normally is looked to for leadership by the group.

Seating Arrangement

Do our seating choices say anything about us? Research in this area suggests that our choice of a place to sit may be determined by several things. Even in the classroom, where it may appear that seating is little more than random behavior, researchers have determined that students choose their seats with considerable care. Factors such as the task before us, the kind of communicative relationship in which we are engaged, and even our personality characteristics contribute to where we decide to sit in relation to other people.

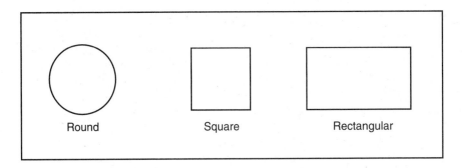

FIGURE 8–1 **Three Table Structures**

The Task Situation. Sommer (1969) was interested in the seating behavior of young people. In his investigation, Sommer asked his subjects to imagine that they were sitting at a table with a same-sex friend. He then asked them to consider four task situations. These situations were described as follows:

Conversation means sitting and talking for a few minutes before class.

Cooperation means sitting and studying together for the same test.

Co-action means sitting and studying for different tests.

Competition means competing in order to see who is the first to solve a series of puzzles.

All of Sommer's subjects were shown diagrams of two different types of tables—rectangular and round. Figure 8–2 displays the rectangular table arrangement, and Figure 8–3 displays the round table arrangement.

In the conversation task situation, the rectangular table appeared to elicit either corner seating (table 1) or opposite seating across the short distance (table 2). At the

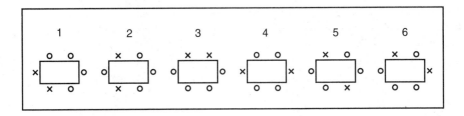

FIGURE 8–2 **Sommer's Rectangular Seating Arrangements for Task Situations**

round table during conversation, table 1 was chosen by 63 percent of the people in the study.

For the cooperation task situation, table 3 was chosen in the rectangular arrangement, and table 1 was chosen by 83 percent of the respondents in the round table arrangement. Evidently, working in cooperation with another person requires us to sit side-by-side, despite the table's shape.

The co-action situation, studying at the same table but for different tests, seemed to require a considerable amount of room for both parties. In the rectangular arrangement, table 5 was chosen by 43 percent and table 2 was chosen by 32 percent. At first glance, you might think that table 4 would have been a popular choice. We suspect, however, that studying may require a sufficient amount of lateral room on the table to spread books and notes. Tables 2 and 5 allow for this but table 4 does not. In the round table arrangement in Figure 8–3, table 3 with opposite seating allows the most room for both parties. This table was chosen by 51 percent of the respondents.

During competition situations, one arrangement is the predominant choice. Whether at a rectangular or round table, most respondents chose opposite seating. Forty-one percent chose table 2 in Figure 8–2 and 63 percent chose table 3 in Figure 8–3. It may be that during situations where two persons are competing against one another, they feel it necessary to keep their "opponent" in full view. Sitting at closer distances, such as rectangular table 2, rather than at greater distances, as with rectangular table 4, may allow for greater control and dominance over the opponent. At least one study has shown, however, that this may be true only for Americans. Cook (1970) replicated Sommer's study with a group of students and nonstudents in the United Kingdom. His respondents chose to have the greater distance allowed by rectangular table 4 during competitive task situations. Knapp (1980) has suggested that for Sommer's respondents, the closer opposite arrangement "would afford them an opportunity not only to see how the other person is progressing but would also allow them to use various gestures, body movements, and eye contact to upset their opponent" (p. 89).

Intimacy Level.   The intimate nature of the relationship also seems to have an impact on our choice of seating, or intimacy may be implied by our seating choice. In his study, Cook found that side-by-side seating was most preferred by very intimate friends while sitting in a restaurant and in a bar. However, corner seating is selected for same-sex friends and casual friends of the opposite sex when seated in a bar. Sommer found that the intimate level of the relationship may be the primary determinant of where we choose to sit. He concluded, on the other hand, that the topic of discussion probably has little impact. According to Sommer, "Apparently it is the nature of the relationship between individuals rather than the topic that characterizes a discussion as personal or impersonal. Two lovers discussing the weather can have an intimate conversation, but a zoology professor discussing sex in a lecture hall containing 300 students would be having an impersonal session despite topic" (p. 65). Therefore, greater intimacy is implied by closer seats (Gifford and O'Connor, 1986).

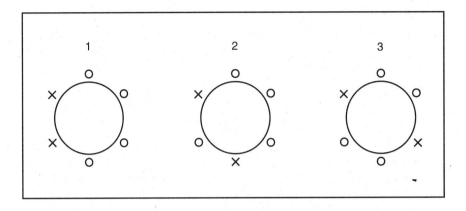

FIGURE 8–3   **Sommer's Round Seating Arrangements for Task Situations**

Personal and Personality Differences.   Personality characteristics and other individual differences have an impact on our seating preferences. Research has shown that people with different personalities prefer different seating positions if they are free to select where they want to sit. For example, students who choose to sit in the front of the class have been found more enthusiastic about school and learning. They also are more enthusiastic about reading, place more value on creativity and imagination, are more focused on their life goals, and desire to be alone more often than others.

In contrast, research suggests that students who prefer to sit in the back of the room are less likely to become leaders and organizers, see little value in being popular with other students, are less interested in making good grades, and generally are unhappy with school. A third group of students, those who choose to sit near a window, are more likely to dislike school and studying. Of course, there are some students who care little about where they sit. As with most individual-difference research, work in this area has found that those with more extreme characteristics are most driven by those characteristics.

Dominance has also been related to seating choices. Researchers have observed that people who score high on measures of dominance tend to select one of two seats at tables: the seat at the head of the table, or the seat at the center of one of the sides of the table. In either case, the position chosen by the dominant individual is central to the interaction and allows for high visibility and eye contact with other seated interactants. People who are highly willing to communicate, those who find communicating to be a pleasant experience in itself, have been found to behave much like people with dominant personalities. No doubt many of these people are both dominant and highly willing to communicate, but some are simply gregarious individuals who like to be in the center of communication activities.

Closely related to dominance is the quality of leadership. Research has revealed that leaders choose seating that is similar to that of dominant people. Leaders are more likely to sit at the end of a rectangular table, whereas individuals who sit at the corners contribute very little to the group. One may emerge as a leader of a group in large part because of where he or she is sitting. Seating position can and does determine communication flow. The flow of communication, furthermore, determines who emerges as the leader.

In one study of five-person decision-making groups, three of the individuals were assigned to sit on one side of a rectangular table while two sat on the other side. The results showed that the side with the two people could influence others more often, and those two people talked more than the others. As a result, leadership emerged from the two-person side in most cases.

The work of Russo (1967) has revealed several variables that are influenced by environmental arrangement. Russo was particularly interested in the seating preferences of friendly and talkative individuals. Figure 8–4 displays Russo's five different arrangements. Not surprisingly, she found that the friendliest people preferred the seating arrangement in table A. The most hostile individuals tended to choose arrangement E. In comparing all five arrangements on friendliness, level of acquaintance, and talkativeness, B was seen as more friendly, intimate, and talkative than C. C was seen as more so than D, and D more than E.

Introverts and extroverts also tend to display their differences from one another in a variety of ways. One major difference that has been found involves their seating preferences. Introverts are far more likely to choose seating that results in reduced visibility and greater physical distance from others. We suspect that the extreme introvert would prefer arrangement D in Figure 8–4 over any of the others. Table D provides for the greatest possible distance while simultaneously preventing the straightforward eye contact present at table E. Extroverts, conversely, tend to choose a seat opposite the other individual, as in table C and table E. Extreme extroverts also prefer to sit near others, which suggests that they would prefer table C as the most desirable arrangement.

Arrangement of Office Space

In recent years, much has been written to advise the owner of an office space how best to arrange the office for greater success and control. The editors of *Consumer Guide* magazine compiled a book in 1979 for the sole purpose of instructing upwardly mobile businesspeople how to decorate their work areas to achieve greater success. They emphasized that "the size and placement of furniture in your office is usually the prime factor in communicating your personality" (*Decorating Your Office for Success,* p. 4). These writers suggest that improving your office requires great care and planning. They present a planning process that involves two steps:

1. Develop a specific plan for projecting your personality and style.

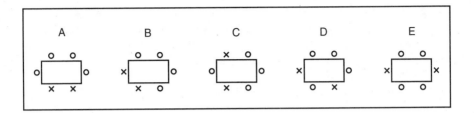

FIGURE 8–4   **Russo's Seating Arrangements**

2. Review the ways in which various aspects of an office can project character. Then plan the physical changes that express the qualities you wish. (p. 17)

Another popular writer, Korda, contends that a person can communicate power by the way he or she arranges the office. In fact, he places more importance on arrangement and use of office space than on the quality or size of things in the space:

Power lies in how you use what you have, not in the accoutrements per se. All the leather, chrome, glass, and expensive artwork in the world will not replace a truly well-thought-out power scheme. A large office is pointless unless it is arranged so a visitor has to walk the length of it before getting to the power desk, and it is valuable to put as many objects as possible in his path. (pp. 231–232)

Korda has also suggested that it is quite common to see large offices divided into two distinct areas—the pressure area and the semisocial area. According to Korda, different communication rules, although unwritten, apply to each area.

The *pressure area,* or the business transaction area, is centered on the desk of the office's occupant. It is here that firm decisions, hard negotiations, and tough bargaining take place. Korda contends that if the occupant of the office escorts the visitor away from this area and into the semisocial area, he or she is probably not very interested in discussing business on a serious level. The *semisocial area* is used primarily to "delay or placate a visitor" (p. 235).

Zweigenhaft (1976) investigated the office arrangements of faculty members in an academic setting. He was interested in how faculty of differing rank positioned the furniture in their offices to manage interaction with students. Zweigenhaft asked the teachers to make sketches of how their offices were currently arranged. The results of this study showed that most senior faculty members (associate and full professors) placed their desks between themselves and the visiting student. However, less than half the assistant professors and lecturers put their desks in the same "blocking" position. A more interesting result of this study involved students' perceptions of the faculty members. For teachers who did not place their desks in the "blocking" position, student perceptions were more positive. Students rated them as more willing to encourage different points-of-view, more willing to give students individual attention, and less likely to show favoritism unduly.

Our interactions with colleagues on several campuses suggest that the students' perceptions quite likely are accurate. Young colleagues tend to see students as more like them and as individuals with whom it is pleasant to interact. More senior colleagues suggest more negative experiences in their office interactions with students, suggesting that students usually come to their offices to complain. It is quite likely that as professors age they are seen by their students as having less in common and, therefore, as less desirable targets for interaction. Thus, it is less likely they would visit the professor's office for informal interaction. Student–professor office interactions, therefore, would become more likely to be related to problems the student was confronting. A cycle probably develops. The student interactions involve pleasant interactions less frequently, so structures are placed between the student and the professor. As these barriers go up, the likelihood of pleasant interactions decreases further, and so on.

OTHER ENVIRONMENTAL FACTORS

Besides spatial arrangement, other factors of environment have been found to influence communication behavior. In this final section, we discuss the impact of environmental attractiveness, color, lighting, and temperature on interaction among individuals.

Environmental Attractiveness

The decoration of rooms, whether attractive or ugly, tends to influence human behavior in several ways. One of the most widely cited studies investigating the effects of room attractiveness was conducted by Maslow and Mintz in 1956. In this study, the researchers selected three rooms in which to carry out an experiment. The first room involved a "beautiful" interior. There were two large windows, draperies, and carpeting, and the walls were a beige color. There also was indirect overhead lighting and the room was attractively furnished. The second room represented an "ugly" condition including gray walls and a single lightbulb overhead covered by a soiled lamp shade. The furnishings gave an impression that the room was a storage area. The third room, considered the neutral or average condition, was a professor's office. Subjects were placed in each of the three conditions and asked to rate photographs of people's faces. The researchers carefully controlled for noise, odor, seating, the time of day, and experimenter.

The results of this investigation showed that subjects in the beautiful condition gave substantially more positive ratings to the pictures than those in other two conditions. These findings are interesting, but were expected. What was not expected, however, was that both subjects and experimenters in the ugly room engaged in a variety of escape activities. The ugly room produced perceptions of monotony, headaches, hostility, and other negative reactions. The beautiful room, on the other hand, tended to elicit a myriad of positive reactions including a desire to continue and perceptions of comfort, importance, and enjoyment.

Other studies over the last three decades have indicated that the results of this classic study were not an accident. People react very strongly to the attractiveness level of the environment in which they must reside, even if only temporarily. People spend more time in their offices, given free choice, if their office is attractive. People are willing to wait longer without complaining if asked to wait in attractive places. People find others more attractive if they communicate with them in attractive places. Students even learn more in attractive classrooms than in unattractive ones.

Color in the Environment

Is environment color important to human interaction? Zell (1984) suggests that "If you're feeling depressed or harried, the color of the walls may be the reason." Red is the most arousing color, followed by orange, yellow, violet, blue, and green. According to many nonverbal specialists, colors have developed symbolic meaning throughout history. Table 8–1 shows an outline of colors and symbolic meanings that have come to be assigned to them.

Clearly, the mood and tone of an environment can be controlled to a major extent by manipulating the colors present in that environment. For over half a century, doctors have used colors to relax mentally disturbed patients. Similarly, restaurant and bar owners use color to stimulate or control the emotions of their patrons. In one of the more interesting studies on the impact of color, Ketcham (1958) examined the relationship between color and student achievement in the classroom.

Using kindergarten children as subjects, Ketcham selected three schools in which to conduct his experiments. The first school needed painting but was left unpainted. The second school was painted in standard institutional fashion—light buff walls and white ceilings. The third school was painted using the principles of color dynamics as a guideline. The hallways were painted a bright, cheerful yellow hue. Classrooms facing north were painted a pale rose color, and those facing south in cool shades such as blue and green. The front walls in the classroom were painted darker than the side walls, and the art room was done in a neutral gray so as not to interfere with the colorful work within it.

Ketcham's observations of the behavior in each school spanned a period of two years. According to Ketcham, the results were clear. The students in the colorful school showed the greatest amount of improvement in social habits, health and safety habits, language skills, arithmetic, social studies, science, and music. Those in the first school (the one left unpainted) showed the least amount of improvement and the one second only slightly more. When we first discussed this research with a

TABLE 8–1   **Colors and Meaning ***

Color	Meaning
Red	Excitement, happiness, vitality, vivaciousness, anger, rage, hostility, defiance, sin, blood, lust, energy, royalty, fun
Blue	Coolness, calmness, pleasantness, tenderness, dependability, dignity, truth, royalty, business-like attitude, softness, tranquility, acceptance
Yellow	Excitement, fun, boldness, glory, cheer, light, clarity, brilliance, softness
Orange	Activity, perhaps unpleasantness, excitement, disturbing stimulation, distress, fruits to consume
Purple	Royalty, control, demands, cool, calm, thoughtfulness, wisdom
Mauve	Calmness, respect, coolness, serenity, peace, acceptance
Green	Coolness, pleasantness, spring or summer, freshness, appeal, security, peace, tranquility, softness, crispness, cleanness, vegetables to consume
Gray	Dependability, coolness, calmness, business-like attitude, reliability, standards, faithfulness, sturdiness, stability
Black	Sadness, intensity, control, power, unhappiness, death, potency, strength, command, domination, masculinity, decay
Brown	Disappointment, sadness, down feelings, neutrality, humility, protection, acceptance,
White	Purity, cleanness, virtue, crystal, babyhood, innocence, joy, femininity, perhaps coldness or neutrality depending on shade, lightness

* Many of these standard colors have a variety of shades that can change the meaning. Here we are speaking only about the standard colors and meanings associated.

large class of public school teachers, one of them asked, "After all this time, why are so many schools in the United States still painted like the ugly room?" Good question.

Lighting in the Environment

Closely associated with color in the environment is the factor of lighting. Obviously, color would be immaterial without some form of illumination. Additionally, lighting may be colored itself. Certain colored lights are associated with particular emotional responses. Red lights are often related to danger, pale yellow lights to contentment, pale green with kindness, green with death, peacock-blue with sinister things, orange with warmth and excitement, blue with quiet, violet with delicacy, and lavender with wistfulness.

Not only does the color of lighting affect behavior, but the intensity of illumination seems to have an effect as well. High illuminations of gold and pink lighting produce a festive atmosphere and subdued lighting, particularly blue, tends to elicit a somber mood. Lighting that is too blue and subdued can actually create drowsiness.

Some studies have explored the effects of bright and dim lighting. One study placed subjects into either a room with bright lighting or room with dim lighting for period of one hour. Subjects were allowed to do whatever they pleased. Each room contained four females and four males, and both rooms were the same size—ten feet by twelve feet. The results showed that verbal output was strikingly different in the two rooms. In the lighted room, a continuous stream of speech was maintained, whereas in the darkened condition almost all talking had stopped after about thirty minutes.

Some have suggested that bright lighting and dim lighting differentially influence perceptions of intimacy and relaxation. Low lighting makes people want to linger because the environment is more relaxing, whereas extremely bright lights may create a desire to escape or produce fatigue. Dim lighting, coupled with intimate questions among nonintimates, has been found to produce hesitancy during responses, reduced eye contact, and a significant decrease in the duration of gaze.

Temperature and the Environment

Based on the research on environmental temperature, Rosenfeld and Civikly (1976, p. 168) conclude that 64 to 68 degrees F. may be the most optimal temperature for indoor environments. Knapp (1980) has provided an excellent summary of the research that has been conducted. He reports that Huntington "advanced a seemingly bizarre theory" in the early twentieth century that "an average outdoor temperature of 50 to 60 degrees F. is better than one above 70 degrees" (p. 58). According to Knapp, the experts have suggested the following effects of weather on human behavior.

   1. Monotonous weather is more apt to affect your spirits.

2. Seasonally, you do your best mental work in late winter, early spring, and fall.

3. A prolonged blue sky reduces your productivity.

4. The ideal temperature should average about 64 degrees F. (p. 58)

In his book *The Achieving Society,* McClelland (1976) reports that achievement motivation appears greatest in societies where the average yearly temperature is between 40 and 60 degrees F. McClelland also suggested that a variation of at least 15 degrees, either daily or seasonally, produced high achievement motivation. Other studies have suggested that temperature and aggression are related. We may be more likely to act aggressively in higher temperatures than in lower ones. Riots, for example, rarely occur in cold weather.

All of this appears to suggest that lower temperatures may affect human behavior in more positive ways than higher ones. Higher temperatures may also cause us to react more negatively toward other people. Although many of us who live in northern climates complain about cold weather and long for summer, we may not know what is best for us. Our desire for warm room temperatures may have just as negative an impact on our behavior.

Griffitt and Veitch (1971) explored such a possibility by looking at the effects of room temperature and room density. In the low-density conditions, there were an average of four subjects per room, whereas in the high-density conditions, the average was fourteen subjects. Two temperature conditions for both high- and low-density conditions were used (93.4 degrees F. and 73.4 degrees F.). The subjects in all conditions were asked to complete several questionnaires including a measure of attitude toward a hypothetical similar or dissimilar stranger. The results of the study indicated that the subjects in the high-temperature high-density room reported less liking, less positive personal reactions, and less positive social affective reactions toward strangers than in any of the other conditions.

In summary, environmental factors may be very important to human communication. Whether it is the attractiveness, the color, the lighting, or the temperature, these factors can affect our reactions to others, our emotional states, and our perceptions. If we understand the environmental factors present in a given situation, we may be better able to understand the communication that occurs in that situation.

A GLOSSARY OF TERMINOLOGY

Fixed feature space is space that is fixed or immovable, such as the physical features in our homes, offices, rooms, schools, and even the layout of our cities and towns.

Pressure area, or the business transaction area of an office, is centered around the desk of the office's occupant. It is here that firm decisions, hard negotiations, and tough bargaining take place.

Semifixed-feature space includes the movable objects in our environments, such as furniture and accessories that adorn, accent, highlight, and personalize the space.

Semisocial area is used primarily to delay or placate an office visitor, to socialize or to conduct less demanding talks, decisions, and bargaining.

Six perceptual characteristics of environment are formality, warmth, privacy, familiarity, constraint, and distance.

▲ 9

Scent, Smell, and Odor

The air around us is filled with scents and smells that express a variety of messages to us. Scents can communicate memories, fear, love, dominance, and excitement, and even arouse powerful feelings about another. If someone smells offensive or emits offensive odors (such as flatulent air) while we are interacting with them, we will probably end the conversation and think very negative thoughts about them.

Within the past fifteen years, researchers and scholars have started to acknowledge the powerful nature of scents in the communication process. The study of scents and smells and how we perceive them and process them is referred to as *olfactics*. Our olfactory senses often unconsciously help us to form opinions of others.

IMPORTANCE OF SCENTS

Scents are important in this culture: It is estimated that in 1993, the American public spent more than $2 billion on deodorants. This is an incredible amount of money to spend just to smell good! No other culture in the world spends near that amount to smell good. In fact, many other cultures prefer natural body scents to the artificial ones. In this culture, Winter (1976) notes:

> *We know that in society we can't have bad breath, sweaty underarms, or noticeable genital odor. You can tell people they need a haircut or to wash their faces, but if you tell them they smell, you are really insulting. (p. 16)*

171

Our sense of smell affects how we communicate with others and how we perceive them.

Research has clearly shown that animals have scents of their own and that they can smell other animals. Dogs have very distinctive scents and even mark their territory with their scents to keep other animals out. Cats have distinctive scents, and mark others with their scents. Cats' scent glands are near the base of the whiskers; when they rub their cheeks against a person's leg, they leave their scent behind. Other animals mark or carve out their territory by urinating around it. Wolves, bears, and many other animals leave their scents around their territory to keep others out.

We all have an individualized scent about us, what some call an *olfactory signature*. Like animals, humans use scents. It is a means of making us unique. We try to wear different perfumes that set us apart from others. Each person's odor is different.

Most living creatures have pheromones. However, none have been isolated in humans. *Pheromones* are chemical secretions that attract other animals for mates. This term originated from the Greek *pherein* (to carry) and *horman* (to excite or stimulate). Whereas animals exude scents when they are attracted to another, humans become more sensitive to scents when they are in a state of arousal.

The average person can recognize at least four thousand distinct scents. Some can recognize as many as ten thousand. Not only do people differ in their sensitivity to scents, they also differ in terms of their evaluation of a given scent. It is not uncommon, for example, for one person to find a scent pleasant, another to find it extremely unpleasant, and still another to not notice the scent at all. Nor, unfortunately, is it uncommon for a person who finds a scent pleasant to expect that everyone else should find it pleasant also.

Not only do individuals differ in their response to scent, but there is also evidence that scent is influenced to some extent by gender. Women and men may perceive odors differently. A perfume currently on the market and widely advertised is very popular with many women. Unfortunately, many men find the scent to be most unpleasant. The following interaction, overheard on an elevator, illustrates what can happen:

Man: Do you wear that perfume to make you smell good?

Woman: Yes, of course. Why?

Man: Well, it doesn't work!

Although few people, male or female, would make such a comment to a stranger, many have wanted to. Offensive odors in public places cause people to be very irritated and to perceive others in very negative ways.

Scents are invisible messages. What they communicate, as with other verbal and nonverbal messages, depends on the way the receiver perceives them. Scents are powerful messages and often determine whether communication will be initiated, continued, or terminated. Our reactions to others may be triggered by our conscious or unconscious awareness of the scents around us. The following sections review scent and smell in relation to attractiveness, touch, and environment.

Scent and Attraction

Some popular writings today suggest that there is a link between smell and attraction between sexual partners. Dr. Robert Henkin at Georgetown University's Taste and Smell Clinic found that 25 percent of people with smell and scent disorders lose interest in sex. He isn't sure why, but suggests that a similar thing happens when the olfactory sense of animals and insects is impaired. Alex Comfort, who wrote *The Joy of Sex,* suggests that the combined natural scents of a woman such as her hair, breasts, skin, armpits, and genital region may be a greater asset than her beauty.

Some researchers are trying to figure out whether males and females excrete something like animal pheromones that attract one another. Some people believe that alpha androstenol, a chemical found in male urine and sweat, might affect attraction. Androsterone, a male sex hormone that also is found in male urine, might also have an effect. Others are looking at the possibility that women exude scents from their genitals that attract men. The research here is very sparse and inconclusive. At this point, the search for human pheromones has yet to find anything even remotely similar to animal hormones in communicative power.

The desire to find such an element, however, appears very strong. As an example, Burton (1976) suggests that there is evidence supporting the idea that male pheromones might attract females. He cites the following apocryphal tale as evidence:

> *A young man was reputed to have great success with girls. After a dance he would wipe the perspiring brow of his partner with a handkerchief that had been carried in his armpit. Apparently his body odor acted as an aphrodisiac, and the young man claimed that his technique was highly successful. (p. 113)*

This is obviously very weak evidence that male pheromones can attract females. Until we have far better evidence than this, we should presume that pheromones are one thing that separate us from other animal life.

As suggested earlier, we use a variety of artificial scents to attract others or to make ourselves appealing. We are the most scent-conscious culture in the world. However, olfaction also is a very important means of communication in other cultures. As Hall (1966) notes:

> *Olfaction occupies a prominent place in Arab life. Not only is it one of the distance-setting mechanisms, but it is a vital part of a complex system of behavior. Arabs consistently breathe on people when they talk. However,*

this habit is more than a matter of different manners. To the Arab good smells are pleasing and a way of being involved with each other. To smell one's friend is not only nice but desirable, for to deny him your breath is to act ashamed. Americans, on the other hand, trained as they are not breathe in people's faces, automatically communicate shame in trying to be polite. (pp. 159–160)

We spend billions of dollars trying to smell appealing to others. The perfume industry employs people to be smell testers so they can come up with "the smell that will sell." These people are sensitive to more odors than the normal person and can sense odors that are appealing or unappealing. In the perfume business, "the nose has it." All fragrance companies have one goal in mind: to convey some message that sells their product. Check out your bathroom or makeup kit and you will find various messages given by colognes and perfumes.

Recently, one author was given a sample of Dioressence Esprit De Parfum by Christian Dior. The message inside was almost lyrical:

Dioressence Esprit de Parfum embodies curves of warm, sensuous florals enfused with a spellbinding twist of freshness. A composition so moderne, it envelops body and soul, gloriously adding to the luxury of daily wear. Esprit de Parfum is a new fragrance concentration, effusive and long-lasting. Wear it and celebrate life.

If the smell does not sell, maybe the poetry will! The perfume and cologne industry definitely knows how to communicate with the American public.

Some researchers suggest that perfume and attraction are related. However, the relationship, if it exists, must be very complex. For example, the woman who dresses elaborately may not require as much perfume as the woman who dresses down to be perceived as attractive. Does Miss America need to wear perfume to be seen as attractive? Will Meat Loaf be attractive if he wears cologne? The research in this area is insufficient to be sure, but we are reasonably certain that the impact of perfume and cologne is less than the advertisers would prefer we believe.

The norm of our culture is that if someone doesn't smell appealing, we are not attracted to them. However, what attracts one person might offend another person. Overpowering perfumes offend some people's senses, whereas others are turned on to the scent. We need to remember to stay within the norms of our culture and try to have a scent that is attractive to others. People can react very negatively to bad scents. There was a professor at a university in the South who rarely took a bath and insisted on wearing wool jackets year 'round. He seldom, if ever, took the jackets to the cleaners. He would hang them outside a few times a year and state that "wool cleans itself." Finally, students started to complain and faculty members were becoming offended. Some faculty members refused to sit near him in faculty meetings. They felt that they could not say anything. A colleague started placing cans of deodorant in the professor's mailbox. It helped. The professor started cleaning more and using the deodorant. Do not expect that the "subtle" approach will always work. Most people who smell very bad to others do not think they smell bad, and often it is very hard to change their minds.

Scent and Touch

Consider the following: An old woman is lying in the hospital bed looking worn, shallow, and weak. Her eyes are closed and breathing is shallow. At you reach out to touch her arm, she inhales deeply and exhales putrid breath into your face and simultaneously flatulates. Will you touch her? Will you unintentionally draw away? You will probably draw away.

The research in this area is scarce, but there is some related research from attraction literature that we reviewed in Chapter 2. People approach things and persons that are attractive. Therefore, if someone looks unpleasant or has bad breath or body odor, it is unlikely that we will want to touch them. Some parents refuse to touch their babies when they have vomited or messed their diapers because of the odor. In nursing homes and hospitals, the attractive patients get more and better care from the staff. Attractive people in society receive more touch. Attractiveness is related to scent. Those who smell attractive, pleasing, and good are much more likely to receive more touch than those who smell unattractive, unpleasant, and foul.

Recently, an author's mother was admitted to the hospital for chest pains. The mother said that she needed her perfume and cosmetics so she "wouldn't look and smell like death." The author understood and brought what her mother needed.

Hospitals are notorious for their distinctive scents and odors. Often, the staff and doctors are insensitive to them. The odors in hospitals can make patients feel bad and visitors feel frightened. Many hospitals are trying to improve their atmospheres by using scents that cover up the "hospital odor." They have to be cautious, however, so that the scents they use do not trigger people's allergies.

In conclusion, scent might determine whether someone will touch another person. Pleasant scents are much more likely to get another to touch than unpleasant scents.

Scent and the Environment

Our environment is flooded with a variety of odors that assault our olfactory senses. We have pollution in the air, cigarette smoke, strong perfumes, scented toilet tissue, scented underwear, scented yard sprays, and scented house and carpet cleaners. All environments in this culture are flooded with a variety of scents. Some scents are worse than the original odors. It is very difficult to purchase an unscented product on the market, and when they are available they are usually 10 to 15 percent more expensive. We must pay to keep the manufacturer from putting in the perfume!

Oddly enough, some "unscented" products actually contain scents to make them smell unscented.

Many people suffer from scent-related allergies. Because we have so many scents in the environment, it can take an allergist days and several types of tests to determine what someone is allergic to and where the scent is. One of the authors developed a rash under his arms. He switched to an "unscented" powder to see whether his powder causing the problem. The rash got much worse. The scent used to make the powder "unscented" was the culprit. His allergist was amused, but noted that this was a common problem.

In this culture, we are very sensitive to odors and may even react violently. In 1979 (before the Federal ban on smoking on domestic flights), a smoking war took place on Eastern Airlines flight 1410. Smoking and nonsmoking passengers got into an argument over the contamination of the air on the plane by the smoking passengers. Both wanted their rights to the air. The nonsmokers did not want their air contaminated by smoke, and the smokers wanted to smoke. The plane was forced to land early because of the confrontation that followed. This might seem amusing, but in a sense it isn't. Each of us feels that we should have a right to control the air in our space; when that air is invaded by undesirable scents, we are willing to fight to get the air clean. There are many stories of people becoming angered and enraged at others for flooding the environment with undesirable odors. Recall from Chapter 6 that one form of territorial invasion is contamination. When our air is fouled, our territory is fouled. We are very likely to respond with the fight response.

What we need to remember is that people do not prefer the same scents. A scent that smells good to one may smell foul to another. One of the authors' sons loves Ragu Spaghetti Sauce. The boy's father cannot stand the odor. So when they cook with Ragu, they consume it away from the father so that his "territory" is not invaded by the scent.

We must be sensitive to others around us and how our scents and the way we use environmental scents can effect others. Some people spray their homes with disinfectant spray and use strong carpet cleaners to hide pet odors. One of the authors of the text is allergic to most chemicals in these products. When she enters someone's home who has used these products, in a few minutes she can barely breathe.

In conclusion, we are flooded with environmental odors that communicate things to us about others. We react to environmental scents. We may even make judgments about others based on the scents they allow in their environments.

EFFECTS OF SCENT AND SMELL

Scent clearly is a means of communicating and interacting with others. We can use our scents to increase our communication with one another. We can also use our scents to guarantee that others do not communicate with us. Therefore, scent is

Scent and smell can cause us to recall memorable times in our lives.

a very powerful, although invisible, component of the nonverbal communication process.

First, scent can be used to increase perceived attraction between two people. People are attracted to others who exude pleasant odors. Heightening one's scent may entice others or repel others. Be careful what you do.

Second, scent can also influence the attractiveness of food. Often, smell is primarily responsible for creating flavor. Sometimes taste actually takes on a secondary role. Therefore, much of our taste is dependent on how good or bad or pleasant or unpleasant something smells. Unpleasant-smelling foods may never be tasted, much less eaten. We may know something will taste bad because it smells awful!

Taste sensations tend to be very intense and acute when we are young; as we age, our taste sensations tend to decline. This is often why many older people lose their appetite for foods they previously enjoyed.

Although smell plays a dramatic role in what we taste, there are other factors that must be considered. Other things that influence our preference for food beside smell are our expectations, our personality, the color of the food, the texture of the food, and frequency of ingestion.

Third, scent and smell can evoke meanings and memories of things, people, and environments from the past. Smell is one of the best senses for helping us to form meanings and to recall past instances. People who have *smell blindness,* who are not able to detect certain odors and scents, may be unaware of the scents around them and be unable to form meanings and memories of things and people. People with smell blindness also may have difficulty distinguishing certain scents, and this can affect their everyday lives. Every day we use what is called *smell adaptation.* This means that we adapt our smell senses every time we enter a new environment. For example, when we enter a chocolate factory, we instantly inhale the pleasant aroma of chocolate. Malandro, Barker, and Barker (1989) suggest that smell adaptation occurs

> *when an odor may have an effect on the perception of subsequent stimulations by the same or other odors. . . . [W]hen the same odor follows itself, or when one odor follows another, the second stimulation may be perceived as less intense than the first stimulation. (p. 269)*

Smell adaptation permits us to have pleasant scents linger longer and to keep unpleasant scents from lingering. Lastly, we experience what is called *smell memory.* This is when memories are recalled by the odors in the environment or on a person. We can all recall the smells in our parents' home and the pleasant memories associated with them. Smell blindness, smell adaptation, and smell memories are very important in finding our meanings and evoking memories.

Fourth, the use of scents and smell can be used to educate students to the world around them and to stimulate the learning processes or deaf and mute students. Winter (1976) reports that when researchers paired long lists of words with odors that matched the words, students could retain the words for a long period. The Braille Institute of America and the Perkins school for the Blind use scratch-and-sniff labels with learning tools that are written in braille. Smells and scents can definitely help such students learn about the world around them.

Fifth, smell and scent have recently become of scientific concern in many medical communities. The diagnosis of disease by smell is not a new technique, but one long practiced. Several patient odors have been associated with particular diseases. Yellow fever smelled like the butcher-shop odor. Scurvy and smallpox had putrid odors. Typhoid fever smelled like freshly baked bread. Diphtheria had a very sweet odor, and the plague had the odor of apples.

Many of these diseases do not exist in the United States now, but people should still be aware of the power of scent in diagnosing an illness. As a function of more recent research, for example, doctors can determine what type of alcoholism a patient is suffering, what type of poison a patient swallowed, and whether a patient is in a diabetic coma by the odor of acetone. All of the above can help a physician in making a diagnosis.

In conclusion, smells and scents communicate. They trigger emotions, reactions, feelings, and communication. As a society, we need to pay more attention to the scents around us and how they affect our communication with others.

A GLOSSARY OF TERMINOLOGY

Olfactics is the study of scents and smells and how people perceive them and process information about them.

Olfactory signature is the individualized, unique scent that each person has.

Pheromones are chemicals that animals excrete to attract other animals for mates. The term originated from the Greek *pherein* (to carry) and *horman* (to excite or stimulate).

Smell adaptation is the ability to adapt from one smell to the other, particularly from one strong scent to a stronger scent or to a less strong scent.

Smell blindness is an anatomical defect of the nose that impairs a person's ability to detect or distinguish certain scents.

Smell memory is the phenomenon by which scents and smells can trigger spontaneous recall of events that are associated with them.

▲ 10

Time

Perhaps more so than any other culture, the North American culture is time-conscious. Look around you. Wherever you go, you will find a clock or some type of timekeeping mechanism. We have clocks or some measure of time in our desk calendars, bathrooms, bedrooms, kitchens, classrooms, workplaces, pens, pencils, calculators, rings, necklaces, belt buckles, earrings, money clips, computers, cars, radios, TVs, VCRs, and on our desks and even in our exercise equipment. There is no other culture in the world that lets time rule as we do. There are other cultures with similar orientations about time, but there is no other culture in the world that has so many expressions of time. The person who does not wear a watch in this society is unusual. One of the most popular gifts for retirements, birthdays, graduations, and special occasions is a watch. Think of the number of watches you have had in your lifetime. One of the authors received a watch for his high school graduation. He has worn it every day for more than thirty-five years. It is the only watch he owns. His friends think he is strange. Most people have many more watches than one. Some have different watches to match dozens of different colors or styles of clothing.

Chronemics is how we perceive, use, study, structure, interpret, and react to messages of time. Hickson and Stacks (1993) say that the study of chronemics "is a significant area of nonverbal communication because we generally perceive our actions and reactions as a time sequence" (p. 175). The North American concern with time is evidenced in everything one says and does. We have nonverbal elements of time everywhere. We review this concern in two ways.

First, Americans are very scheduled people. Much of our communication, both verbal and nonverbal, is a result of a time schedule. We can see our *scheduling mania* in a variety of ways. For example, our schools and classrooms are on schedules; it is the rare one that isn't. Our workplaces have schedules. We schedule

Time can have many faces.

appointments with others and for ourselves. We eat at a certain time. We sleep at a certain time. We vacation at a certain time. If we miss that time, we miss our vacations because the other time factors have priority. We set priorities based on how much time a person or element in the work environment deserves.

Second, our oral language clearly makes time an overriding force. Let's look at a few of the things we say on a daily basis that reference time. How much longer will this take? What time is lunch? I don't have time for that. I will make time for that. Time is gone on this project. Time got away from me. Where has the time gone? I need more time. Can I have more time on this project? The time was well spent. I sure wasted a lot of time today. I wish I had more time. Can I get the deadline extended? You do it this time, I'll do it the next time. Time is money. We spent forty minutes studying for a test. I simply can't afford the time.

Time has become a part of nonverbal and verbal communication to such an extent that it literally rules what and when we do something. We are slaves to time.

TIME ORIENTATIONS

Hall (1959) made us aware of the importance of time. He said that "Time talks. It speaks more plainly than words" (p. 180). Hall (1984) says that we should examine the kinds of time we have. Hall states, "As people do quite different things (write books, play, schedule activities, travel, get hungry, sleep, dream, mediate, and perform ceremonies), they unconsciously and sometimes consciously express and participate in different categories of time" (p. 206). This section reviews the three time orientations to which Hall refers—the psychological, biological, and cultural—and their impact on communication.

Psychological Time Orientation

Psychological time orientation is how people feel, think, or perceive time and how it influences their daily communication and lives. Both individuals and cultures vary concerning their psychological time orientations. Throughout the study of psychological time, three psychological orientations have emerged. They are the past, present, and future. We discuss each psychological orientation here.

Past-oriented people place high regard on the past, the reliving of past events, and cherishing past happenings. Their motto could be "Remember the past, or it will come back to haunt you." Cultures that have a past-oriented philosophy tend to apply past events to similar new situations. These societies have respect for the elderly and listen to what their senior citizens have to say regarding the past. They use the past to shape the present. The traditional Chinese culture is very much a past-oriented society. They use the words of the elders to guide them. Native American tribes place great value on the past and tradition. They exert great effort to transmit the wisdom of the ages to the young. In general, one develops more of a past orientation as one ages, despite the general culture in which one lives. It seems that it is normal for people to value the learning they have gotten from their own experiences.

Present-oriented people live for today. The motto for these people could be "Eat, drink, and be merry for tomorrow you may die." They live very much for the present. They work for the present. They go to school for the present. They invest for the present. It is easy to understand why people in some impoverished nations would adopt such an orientation. It makes little sense to ponder the distant future if you are not sure where your next meal is coming from! In cultures with a strong present-orientation, senior citizens may receive less respect than they do in past-oriented societies. In fact, some young people say things like "What do they know, they lived back in the dark ages?" Some students feel this way about their teachers. Some children feel this way about their parents. American industry is coming under increasing criticism for its often too-present-oriented organizational culture. Critics claim that too many business decisions are made to enhance immediate profits at the expense of the long-term well-being of the company.

Future-oriented people base today's behavior on what they believe will occur in the future. The future-oriented motto could be "Tomorrow is just around the corner—be prepared." Future-oriented people believe that tomorrow is what we should work and strive toward. For example, they work so that their children can have a better place to live, play, and work. Future-oriented people tend to rely on what they think the future will bring. Many claim this is the orientation with which most immigrants identified when they came to this country. It represents a save-and-build approach to life, which many cite as the explanation for the success of this country.

Differences in time orientations can create many communication differences. Let's look at a fictitious example of past-, present-, and future-oriented executives trying to decide how to sell a product called Moment. Moment is a fragrance that is supposed to turn on another's significant other. The discussion might go something like this:

Past-Oriented Executive: Let's look at the past advertising campaigns and see what we can use. Perhaps we should talk to Ms. Smith, who was with the company when it started thirty years ago. Some of those old campaigns were real classics. They made the company what it is today.

Future-Oriented Executive: No way. Who cares what ads were like when Roosevelt was president? Let's determine what people will want in the future. Robots are the wave of the future. Let's have ads with talking robots. This is the trend of future advertising. We have to get ourselves in place for the next century.

Present-Oriented Executive: Wait a minute, you two. What we need is something that will sell today. Who cares about the next century? If we don't sell Moment now (this moment!), we won't have a job in the next century! Let's have some current up-to-date cool person be our spokesperson. We need someone who is hot with the in-people.

With these diverse orientations, our fictitious executives might never agree and the product might never be marketed. Because of their different psychological time orientations, they are making completely different assumptions based on different values. They cannot communicate to make good decisions because their differing views of time place their definitions of "good decisions" in different worlds.

In conclusion, the psychological time orientation of a person or a culture can determine the potential success of a communication transaction. People need to be aware of these time differences and their impact on communication.

Biological Time Orientation

A more popular (but less scientific) time orientation we have read about is biorhythms. These biorhythms come in three cycles: the physical cycle, the sensitivity cycle, and the intellectual cycle. Biorhythms vary in length. The physical cycle averages twenty-three days, the sensitivity cycle averages twenty-eight days, and the intellectual averages about thirty-three days. It is suggested that biorhythms begin at birth in the positive phase and are with us monthly until our deaths. According to biorhythm theory, a person's energy is high in the first half each cycle and low in the second half.

During the first phase of the physical cycle, we are at our strongest; our energy is at its height. We can accomplish more in less time. We work hard and feel good about working hard. We can expend a lot of energy and not feel exhausted. During the second phase of the physical cycle, we are at a low. We do not have much energy and spend a lot of time trying to get the energy to do something. People can have highs and lows during the day or throughout a month.

During the first phase of the sensitivity cycle, we experience positive emotions and we have a positive outlook on things. We get along with people better during this cycle. During the second phase of the sensitivity cycle, we are less positive, we are less cheerful, less happy, and have a less-than-positive outlook about others. We may even be grumpy and short-tempered with others. We spend a lot of time bolstering our emotional energies.

During the first phase of the intellectual cycle, we are more alert, attentive, and responsive to information. We process information better, can retrieve it better and apply it better. During the second phase of the intellectual cycle, we are slower at processing information, have difficulty retrieving it, and are less alert and less attentive. We may even have to force ourselves to concentrate. Our mental capacities are at a low ebb. In this phase, we spend time trying to recharge our mental capacities.

Advocates of biorhythm theory suggest that people can have critical days. These critical times are the days on which a cycle shifts. When a person's sensitivity cycle is shifting, they may be moody. When a person's intellectual day is shifting, they may have difficulty processing information. When a person's physical cycle is shifting, they may have less energy or seem tired.

Some people go to great lengths to chart their biorhythms so they can plan their lives to avoid making mistakes on critical days. Although it is a scientific fact that humans do have biological cycles, there is much less than solid evidence that such charting enables a person to plan communication better. As one of our colleagues once commented, "What difference does it make if I am not having a 'critical day' if the driver of that truck coming at me is?"

We think there is a much more important distinction to be made about biologically-based time orientations. This is the difference between people who are biologically more active in the evening and those who are biologically more active in the morning. This difference has been euphemistically called the difference between *owls* and *sparrows*.

Our own orientation in this regard is quite easily determined by most of us, in contrast to the difficulty most people have in figuring out their own biorhythms. Additionally, the orientations of our acquaintances can be judged fairly accurately by most of us. This distinction has been the subject of some social scientific research. The self-report measure we use to determine this orientation is presented in Figure 10–1. Circle your responses to the items on this scale and compute your score, using the instructions in Figure 10–2 before reading the next paragraph.

An average score on the MTO is 48. If your score is much higher than 48, you probably exhibit more owl than sparrow tendencies. In contrast, if your score is much lower than 48, you probably exhibit more sparrow than owl tendencies. Owls are at their best in the late afternoon and evenings. Sparrows are at their best in the mornings. This simple distinction has extensive implications for businesses and schools.

Owls are often punished by the 8-to-5 or 9-to-5 time schedule most of us are forced to follow. Owls have great difficulty functioning in the morning. They are just starting to be truly functional by noon. In other words, they do not do their best work between 8:00 and 11:00 A.M. Owls are the workers who want to work late and the students who like evening classes. Owls try not to do anything important early in the morning. They have learned that they do not function well in the morning. This is a biological fact. Even with the help of several cups of caffeine, their "heart just does not start beating" until later. What does the dominant time orientation in this culture do to owls? We force them to be in school and at work by 8:00 or 9:00 A.M. We force a heavy workload on them in the early hours when their eyes are just beginning to open and when their ears are just barely able to recognize sounds. It is no wonder that many owls do poorly in school and have a hard time holding a regular job.

We have had the opportunity of observing and talking with hundreds of owl schoolchildren and employees. The overwhelming majority of them say they do much better work in the afternoon. The schoolchildren suggest their concentration skills improve and their retention skills improve. They also say that they do better on assignments and tests in the afternoon, and they express a preference for their afternoon teachers. They say their afternoon teachers like them better, too. We think this is a result of teachers not liking or responding well to children who sleep or appear to be asleep in class. Owl children often fall asleep in morning classes; if they manage to stay awake, they do not function well. Therefore, their morning teachers do not respond to them as well as their afternoon teachers. By afternoon they are ready to answer questions and be responsive.

Sparrows do their best work in the mornings. Whereas owls are just waking up in the morning, sparrows are at their peak. Sparrows come into work or school at 7:00, 8:00, or 9:00 A.M. chirping loud and clear, while owls are barely functional. However, sparrow children don't do as well in their afternoon classes as they do in morning classes. They are less attentive, more tired, and do less well on tests and assignments in the afternoons.

As we can see, this can have broad impact on communication. The owl teacher has difficulty responding to the chirpy little sparrow, whereas the sparrow teacher has difficulty responding to the owl in the afternoon. Our time orientations deter-

Directions: Below are a series of questions concerning your time orientations. Please answer honestly. There are no right or wrong answers. Use the following to determine the time orientation that most closely approximates your feelings.

SA = Strongly Agree
A = Agree
N = Neutral or Undecided
D = Disagree
SD = Strongly Disagree

SD	D	N	A	SA	
1	2	3	4	5	1. I really dislike getting up in the mornings.
1	2	3	4	5	2. I like taking afternoon classes.
1	2	3	4	5	3. I prefer morning classes.
1	2	3	4	5	4. I am at my worst in the mornings.
1	2	3	4	5	5. I really like getting up in the mornings.
1	2	3	4	5	6. I dislike taking afternoon classes.
1	2	3	4	5	7. I am very irritable in the mornings.
1	2	3	4	5	8. I am very alert in the afternoons.
1	2	3	4	5	9. I am very irritable in the afternoons.
1	2	3	4	5	10. I am very alert in the mornings.
1	2	3	4	5	11. I rarely do well on tests in morning classes.
1	2	3	4	5	12. I usually do very well on tests in afternoon classes.
1	2	3	4	5	13. I usually do very well on tests in morning classes.
1	2	3	4	5	14. I rarely do well on tests in afternoon classes.
1	2	3	4	5	15. I like to do my studying late at night.
1	2	3	4	5	16. I like to do my studying early in the day.

F   I   G

Step 1: Add the numbers you circled for items 1, 2, 4, 7, 8, 11, 12, and 15. (Your score must be between 8 and 40 or you have made a mistake.)

Step 2: Add the numbers you circled for items 3, 5, 6, 9, 10, 13, 14, and 16. (Again, your score must be between 8 and 40.)

Step 3: Add 48 to your score from step 1.

Step 4: Subtract your score in step 2 from your total in step 3. This is your MTO score. (It must be between 16 and 80 or you have made a mistake.)

F   I   G mine how effective a communicator we can be at various times of the day. Most of the population has learned to function fairly well between nine and five. We call these people *sprowls*. They are neither sparrow nor owl. Much of the population fits into this sprowl time category, but at least 20 percent are owls or sparrows. This means that one in five persons is either an owl or sparrow. Businesses are just starting to recognize the impact of time scheduling. Many corporations are using *flextime,* which allows the individual employee to establish her or his hours within certain parameters. Organizations doing this have found production increasing and employee morale improved. In other words, owls can work owl shifts and sparrows can work sparrow shifts and there are still lots of sprowls to hold the down the fort. Many of our schools are attempting to let children enroll in classes that correlate with their body times. This should improve student production and teacher morale. College students have the advantage that they can generally, after their first year, choose a schedule that fits their body time.

Our biological time orientation influences our communication with others. It affects how we perceive others and how they perceive us. If we are aware of when we function best, we can make modifications in our schedule to capitalize on the times when we are at our best. We may also make strategic choices of when to talk with others if we can figure out their biological time orientations. It is the wise student who avoids asking owl parents for money at the breakfast table!

Cultural Time Orientation

This time orientation deals with the way cultures perceive and use time. Understanding time orientations of various cultures is not an easy task. Hall (1959) suggests there are three different time systems found in cultures. They are technical, formal, and informal time.

Technical time has the least correlation with interpersonal communication. It refers to precise, scientific measurements of time counted in precise, logical sequences. An example of technical time is the means of tracking time used by NASA. Technical time is a very ordered, scientific method of keeping time. It is noninterpersonal and nonemotional.

Formal time is the way in which a culture keeps track of time. For example, we keep track of days, months, years and so on. This is not scientific like technical time, but it is somewhat precise in that cultures have traditional means of keeping track of time. Farmers use formal time when planting crops and go by the seasons. People who live near the beach might go by the tide time. Therefore, each culture has a means of tracking time, and because cultures vary so much, their use of time varies.

Hall suggested seven components that distinguish formal time from other types. He suggested that the way one uses ordering, cycling, valuation, tangibility, synthesisity, duration, and depth all contribute to distinguishing formal time.

Ordering deals with the nature of time as fixed concerning the ordering of events. For example, "a week is a week not only because it has seven days but because they are in a fixed order" (Hall, 1973, p. 145). Hall notes that ordering of events can vary from culture to culture. Therefore, communication about ordering of events can lead to some misunderstandings. For example, some people say that Monday is the first day of the week; others say that Sunday is. Still others claim that it is Saturday.

Cycling focuses on the North American need to have time flowing in cycles. We group days into weeks, months, years, and so on. These units of time are cyclical; they are limited and eventually the cycle comes back to start over. Some other cultures do not believe in cycling. For example, Pueblo Indians are taught that things occur only when the time is right, so they wait until the time is right. They do not do things on a cyclical basis.

Americans place great emphasis on the next three components, valuation, tangibility, and synthesisity of time. *Valuation* is the value the culture places on time. *Tangibility* is the culture's consideration of time as a commodity. *Synthesisity* is the culture's desire or need to synthesize or add up time. For example, sixty minutes make an hour, twenty-four hours make a day, and so on. Hall suggests that North American culture places great value on time and how it is used and spent. We also consider time a valuable commodity that should be used wisely. Lastly, we synthesize time and use time to decide how we synthesize other elements in our culture. Hall suggests, "We are driven by our own way of looking at things to synthesize almost everything" (p. 147). Therefore, we have great difficulty communicating with people who don't place the same value on time as we do. We have great difficulty communicating with people who do not feel that time is a commodity and do not synthesize time and events the way we do. We often have misunderstandings about time and synthesis because of our inability to adapt to others.

Duration is usually measured by a clock in this culture. Duration may be relevant in other cultures and it may not. For example, the European tradition says that time is something that occurs between two points. The Hopi define duration as follows: "It is what happens when the corn matures or a sheep grows up—a characteristic sequence of events" (Hall, 1973, p. 146). In other words, the duration of length of time is considered differently by different cultures. Small children certainly have different meanings for duration from adults in any culture

Lastly, Hall reviews the depth of time. He suggests that *depth* is when the present emerges from some past. Even Americans feel that the present is heavily influenced by the past. Every time we have a presidential election, they draw on the past to predict the outcome. Stockbrokers try to predict the future trends based on past trends. Sports fans try to predict outcomes of present and future games based on past games.

To sum up, components of formal time determine how we use and perceive formal time. They also determine how we communicate with others around us. We cannot assume that others around us have the same value for time that we do. As Americans, we often presume this, only to find that is not so. We must also remember that children usually do not have a good grasp of the aspects of formal time in their culture until they are about twelve years old. By the age of twelve, they usually develop or are developing the norms of their culture concerning time.

Informal time is the most difficult cultural time orientation to understand and learn to use. This type of time can vary greatly from culture to culture. It is the casual time employed by a culture. It is often unconscious and determined by the situation or context in which it is used. For example, when we say "we'll be there in a minute," we might mean "in a while" or "in a little bit." These casual time orientations are the most difficult for people to learn and understand. There is no preciseness or logic to them. To a foreigner, when we say "in a minute," it could mean in a day.

Eight levels of duration exist in our informal time system. They are immediate, very short, short, neutral, long, very long, terribly long, and forever. Exactly how can we communicate these durations precisely? One of the authors of this text has communicated several times that she needs a letter sent to a student immediately. The secretary who preforms this duty knows precisely what she means because they have worked together for five years. *Immediately* to this author means "like yesterday." *Immediately* to others could mean in a while or shortly or tomorrow. The term *forever* has a very imprecise meaning. When students say, "I thought that class would never end. I felt like I was in there forever," what do they mean? Terribly long? Or terribly boring? Probably both. Their way of expressing it was by saying *forever.* What does the phrase "I'll love you forever" mean? To some people, it means "until death do us part." To others, it means "For tonight!" Our use of informal time is not only confusing in this culture but to others outside the culture. We need to remember that this is also very confusing for small children, so we need to have patience dealing with others who do not understand our use of informal time.

Punctuality has long created a communication problem in this culture. When we say we want someone to be punctual, we mean on time if not a little before. Punctuality is not a form of informal time, but it is often used in the informal sense. People seem confused about what punctual means. Little children do not understand the importance of being on time or punctual. After they are late several times and told by adults to start being on time or punctual, they learn what punctual is. Watch small children as they leave home to go to school or are on their way home from school. Most of them meander along without a care in the world. Their mothers or fathers are at home anxiously waiting for them to arrive. The child is late and the mother cannot understand why. Time has very little meaning for small children. By age six, the American child knows the days of the week and what they mean. If they don't know it by six, they will learn it when they enter school. By age eight, the child usually can tell time by a watch or clock and has learned the seasons and what they mean. All of you can probably remember the days when you were small and your parents or brothers or sisters helped you get ready for school. One of the biggest concerns was that you would be late. They probably said things like, "Hurry up and eat," "Don't miss the school bus," "Please hurry, teachers don't like it when you're late." This is how the idea of punctuality is learned.

Hall (1972) suggests that there are two ways of viewing punctuality: as a "displaced point pattern" and as a "diffused point pattern." The point is the time a person expects others to arrive for a social event. The point here is 8:00. People who view time as "displaced" will arrive before the appointed time. In other words, they will arrive about 7:30 to 7:57, with the majority arriving about 7:55. People who view time as "diffused" will arrive between 7:55 and 8:15. These people do not see time as fixed as the others and will arrive in a somewhat diffused pattern. This can be very disconcerting for people who expect others to arrive "on time." Sometimes, to arrive past the appointed time can be perceived as an insult or lack of respect. Variables that influence people's use of the time point are the type of social occasion, what is being served, the status of the individuals involved, and the individual's personal way of handling time. It is the rare person who would arrive late for a meeting with the president of the United States. However, the president might arrive late and no one thinks anything about it.

Trying to beat the informal time rules can lead people into mistakes that are somewhat amusing, although not immediately so. The authors of the book once were invited to what was announced as a two-hour get-acquainted social gathering. They didn't really want to be the first to arrive, so they intentionally set out to be late, assuming that they would miss the formal aspects of the gathering but could talk with friends on their arrival. Approximately 200 people were invited, so they knew they would probably not stand out if they arrived thirty minutes after the appointed hour. When they arrived thirty minutes late, no one appeared surprised or upset. However, they quickly learned that they had missed the cocktails, shrimp, lobster, and crab hors d'oeuvres. They were there "on time" to listen to the thirty-minute welcoming speech!

People make judgments about one another based on use of time and punctuality. For most Americans, it is almost unforgivable to be more than fifteen minutes late for any appointment without a very good excuse. Many teachers respond to this. If the student's excuse for being late was not life-threatening, the teacher will be very uncompromising about allowing the student to make up work. Businesses often deduct money from an employee's paycheck for lateness or tardiness. In order to be perceived in a positive manner in this culture, one must always be "on time."

Even if we are on time, there are two aspects of informal time that characterize how we use our time. Hall refers to these aspects as monochronic time and polychronic time.

Monochronic time (M-time) is the norm in the North American culture. M-time emphasizes the scheduling of activities one at a time, the segmentation of work, the promptness of work. Monochronic time means doing one thing at one time. Therefore, people in the general North American culture believe that things should have order, scheduling, and organization so that one thing is being worked on at a time. There is little room for flexibility.

Polychronic time (P-time) is the norm for many Latin cultures. P-time emphasizes the involvement of lots of people and is less rigid about the ordering of events and scheduling. People functioning on P-time believe in handling several transactions at one time. In parts of Latin America, it is not unusual to find several business meetings taking place simultaneously in the same room with many people involved. The person in charge is often walking from group to group and transacting business.

This difference in time orientations can create some very serious communication problems. American business executives are very insulted when they are expected to meet with several other groups simultaneously in the same room to transact business. They find the situation confusing, irritating, and insulting. Latins find monochronic business practices too rigid. They cannot understand the "one meeting, one time, one room" mentality of the American business executive. They like to involve lots of people. Some Arab cultures have similar time norms for business meetings. Often North Americans, Arabs, and Latins have very unsettling and stressful business transactions because of the differing time orientations.

In summary, clearly time talks, as Hall suggested. In fact, it talks so loudly that people misperceive others because of their differing uses of time. We expect others to conform to our time ideals. Often they do not. We must learn to understand the time orientations of others around us to become more effective communicators.

EFFECTS OF THE USE OF TIME

It is clear from the above discussions that time can influence our communication and perception of others. How we use time or let it use us determines several things.

First, time communicates our status to others. Higher-status persons are granted more time deviancies. They can be early or late for functions, whereas the rest of us cannot. For example, teachers can make students wait for them, but students do not have the luxury of being late to class.

Second, time expresses liking. Studies reveal that the amount of time we spend with a person is an indicant of the amount of liking we have for that person. Of course, this is referring to time we choose to spend, not time we are assigned to spend with them. People can tell from the time we give them how we feel about them. If we consistently tell someone, "I only have a few minutes," they eventually will get the message. Parents must be very careful not to do this with children. Children need to know that they are important enough to warrant time with the parent.

Some studies suggest that time may be an important variable, although not the only one, in the physician–patient relationship. The amount of time a physician spends with a patient is related to the patient's willingness to continue the physician–patient relationship. The amount of time the patient is given to talk to the physician may determine the patient's feeling about whether the physician is concerned or cares about them. The actual amount of time interaction is less relevant than whether the patient feels that the amount of time taken is "enough." Being rushed in and out of the physician's office will probably lead to the perception that the physician did not spend "enough" time. Improving physicians' encoding and decoding of nonverbal behavior is critical to effective physician–patient relationship. Time is one variable that can be used to improve that relationship.

Third, the use of time communicates our cultural orientations. It is easy to tell the cultural upbringing of someone by their use of time and how they value time. We can also learn to understand others if we learn more about their time orientations.

Fourth, time communicates our personality orientations and background orientations. For example, Perry, Kane, Bernesser, and Spicker (1990) and Cinelli and Ziegler (1990) found some interesting results concerning Type A and Type B personalities. The Type A personality (aggressive, impatient, hostile, achievement-oriented, and time-urgent) was more likely to cheat on an exam than those who were Type B. In addition, Type A students were more likely to have more daily problems than Type B students. It seems that Type B people are time-conscious but not to the point that they are driven, whereas Type A people are driven, and often "drive" others, too.

Levine (1989) found that the thirty-six cities with the fastest paces also reported the highest rates of heart disease. Levine defined pace based on the walking speed of pedestrians; how long it took bank tellers to give change; how long it took postal clerks to explain the differences among regular mail, certified mail, and insured mail; and whether people wore watches. The following cities (presented from 1 to 36) had faster speeds, more watches worn, and higher coronary heart disease rates: Boston, MA; Buffalo, NY; New York, NY; Salt Lake City, UT; Columbus, OH; Worcester, MA; Providence, RI; Springfield, MA; Rochester, NY; Kansas City, MO; St. Louis, MO; Houston, TX; Paterson, NJ; Bakersfield, CA; Atlanta, GA; Detroit, MI; Youngstown, OH; Indianapolis, IN; Chicago, IL; Philadelphia, PA; Louisville, KY; Canton, OH; Knoxville, TN; San Francisco, CA; Chattanooga, TN; Dallas, TX; Oxnard, CA; Nashville, TN; San Diego, CA; East Lansing, MI; Fresno, CA; Memphis, TN; San Jose, CA; Shreveport, LA; Sacramento, CA; and Los Angeles, CA. Of course, many of these cities have several things in common: major highway and freeway systems, large populations, diverse populations, major businesses, major mass transit systems, and stimulus overload on a daily basis.

Lastly, we can teach and learn timing. This can help us to become better communicators. When is it a good time to ask for a day off from work? Get to know your boss's time orientations and decide what is the best time of the day to ask her or him. Timing is a most critical component of the communication process. If one doesn't know how to time communication, he or she might be perceived as an ineffective communicator.

A GLOSSARY OF TERMINOLOGY

Biological time orientation is how people feel and react physically to time and the affects of time on physical well-being.

Chronemics is how a culture perceives, uses, studies, structures, interprets, and reacts to messages of time.

Sooner or later, time runs out for everyone.

Cultural time orientation is the way in which different cultures manage, perceive, and use time.

Formal time is the way in which a culture keeps track or account of time.

Informal time is the most difficult cultural time orientation to understand and learn; it varies greatly from culture to culture. It is the casual time employed by a culture. It is often unconscious and determined by the situation or context in which it is used.

Monochronic time (M-time) is the norm in the North American culture. M-time emphasizes the scheduling of activities one at a time, the segmentation of work, and the promptness of work.

Polychronic time (P-time) is the norm for many Latin cultures. P-time emphasizes the involvement of many people and is less rigid about the ordering of events and scheduling. People functioning on P-time believe in managing several transactions at once.

Psychological time orientation is how people feel, think, or perceive time and how time affects daily communication and lives. Both individuals and cultures vary concerning psychological time orientations.

▲ 11

Immediacy

Two teachers, Candice and Christie, have approximately equal competence in their field and teach the same English course. Christie has trouble keeping her classes filled, but Candice has a problem because she has more students wanting the class than she can handle. Christie rarely smiles, rarely stands or positions herself close to students, uses closed body positions most of the time or stands behind a podium while teaching, has little eye contact with students, and does not appear to be interested in the class. Candice smiles often, stands or positions herself near the students, rarely uses closed body positions, never uses a podium, has eye contact with students, and generally appears to be interested in the class. You must take the English course. Which teacher do you choose, Candice or Christie?

For most students, this is not a difficult choice. Even if Candice taught at an inconvenient time, most would try to get in her class. With just the limited information about their nonverbal behavior provided above, we can make some very reliable predictions about how pleasant taking the English class will be, depending on which teacher we choose. Clusters of nonverbal behavior such as those described above can significantly influence all interpersonal encounters, not just classroom interactions. The previous chapters have reviewed the effects of individual nonverbal behavior on interpersonal relations. This chapter reviews the collective effects of nonverbal behavior on interpersonal relations. Such collective effects are a function of perceived immediacy.

Nonverbal behaviors of immediacy demonstrate enjoyment in one another's company.

IMMEDIACY DEFINED

Immediacy is the degree of perceived physical or psychological closeness between
people. The concept may be best understood in terms of the immediacy principle as
outlined by the person who introduced this concept into the literature, Mehrabian
(1971): "People are drawn toward persons and things they like, evaluate highly, and
prefer; they avoid or move away from things they dislike, evaluate negatively, or do
not prefer" (p. 1).

We cannot always physically approach people or things we like or move away
from things or people we don't like. However, we do communicate our feelings
most of the time by our nonverbal behaviors. For example, if someone is saying
something nice about us, we are likely to stand closer, listen more attentively, have
more eye contact, perhaps even touch. On the other hand, if someone is saying
something unpleasant about us, we are likely to lean away from that person, have little eye contact, remain silent, and not touch (unless it is to punch them out!). Therefore, we use "abbreviated forms" of approach or avoidance behavior. These
abbreviated forms of nonverbal behavior imply the degree of psychological closeness between people. The more forms of approachlike nonverbal behavior we use,

the more we are perceived as nonverbally immediate. The more we use avoidance-like behavior, the more we are perceived as nonverbally nonimmediate.

Behavior can be placed on a continuum from avoidance-oriented to approach-oriented (See Figure 11–1). Clearly we would like to avoid the person who wants to use physical violence or be verbally hostile (also defined as verbal nonimmediacy) with us. We might approach or let someone approach us who displays neutral behavior, and we are very likely to approach or allow someone to approach us who uses immediacy behavior.

Thus, on the avoidance–approach continuum, most of us feel comfortable with most other people in interpersonal encounters at only one point—the immediacy point. At the avoidance end, we do not feel comfortable or want to communicate with someone who is abusive either physically or verbally. At the extreme approach end, most of us do not feel comfortable communicating on an intimate basis with more than a few people. The neutrality point also makes us uncomfortable after a while because there is very little responsiveness by the neutral person. Nonresponsiveness usually is interpreted as a negative response, so we end the conversation.

In conclusion, nonverbal behaviors that denote immediacy are those that improve and encourage interpersonal encounters and communication. Scholars suggest that some common immediacy behaviors include smiling, touching on the hand, arm, or shoulder, moving close to another, making eye contact, facing another, using warm vocalics, and leaning toward someone. The remainder of this chapter reviews these and other nonverbal behaviors and how each can be used to increase immediacy and improve interpersonal relations. To understand immediacy and its relationship to interpersonal communication, it is important to look at specific behaviors that express varying degrees of immediacy.

VERBAL IMMEDIACY

What people say can cause us to feel either closer or more distant from them. Increased immediacy is produced by verbally immediate messages that show openness to the other, friendship for the other, or empathy with the other. Such simple things as the use of the pronouns "we" or "us" rather than "you" or "you and I" can increase the feeling of immediacy. For example, when trying to denote verbal immediacy to a friend, say "we can do this together" rather than "you should try this."

Physical Violence / Verbal Hostility / Neutrality / Immediacy / Intimacy

---

FIGURE 11–1　**Continuum of Avoidance-Oriented to Approach-Oriented Behaviors**

One of the most important ways of increasing immediacy in a relationship is sending verbal messages that encourage the other person to communicate. Such comments as "I see what you mean," "Tell me more," "That is a good idea," and "Let's talk more about this" create increased immediacy. Contrast these statements with the following comments: "Oh, shut up," "Stuff it," "Stick it," "I thought of that," and "That is just dumb." If you were to hear any of the latter comments, would you want to communicate more? Probably not. You would not feel very close to the person who made such comments, unless it was clear they were joking. Of course, addressing an individual by the name they prefer is more likely to denote immediacy than addressing them by another name such as "Hey You!"

Clearly, a most direct way to communicate feelings of immediacy is through verbal messages. However, there are many nonverbal behaviors that can accomplish the same outcome. Although immediacy is communicating both verbally and nonverbally, the nonverbal component is far more important in most cases. This is because the nonverbal may exist independent of any verbal message, but verbal messages are usually accompanied by a variety of nonverbal messages. Furthermore, if a verbal message suggests immediacy while nonverbal messages are contradictory, receivers tend to disregard the verbal and respond to the nonverbal.

The importance of the nonverbal message is illustrated in some recently reported research conducted by Blackman and Clevenger (1990). They centered their attention on computer-mediated interactions engaged in during electronic conferencing. Each person in such interactions is sitting alone at her or his computer terminal. All normal nonverbal message systems are unavailable. Nevertheless, the interactants usually feel a need to explain their verbal statements, much as they would if they were engaging in face-to-face conversation.

Figure 11–2 includes a simulated electronic interaction provided by the researchers to illustrate what occurs in these mediated interactions. Many types of messages are included in this brief illustration. Verbal descriptions of nonverbal behavior, particularly kinesic (Hugs, Chuckie.; <ducking>; SWAT!; winks) and vocalic (OUCH!!!, <YUCKS>, *TA-DA*!!!) behavior, and representations of facial expressions turned on their sides [:-(, :)] are most common.

In their careful analysis of more than 4,000 messages of this type, Blackman and Clevenger can identify twenty-two categories of nonverbal surrogates (see Figure 11–3). All of the major categories of nonverbal behavior we have outlined in previous chapters are represented except space, time, and scent. Clearly, surrogates for these could be represented in such interactions, as the authors noted, but did not happen to be in the particular interactions studied.

There is a strong need to use nonverbal messages to express relational feelings with verbal messages in both oral and mediated written interactions. An analysis of personal letters might well permit the same conclusion. Most of these nonverbal messages, as well as their surrogates, contribute to increases or decreases in perceived immediacy between interactants. The next section reviews some important nonverbal messages in this context.

NONVERBAL IMMEDIACY

Most categories of nonverbal behavior can be used to increase or decrease immediacy. Let us consider each in turn.

Physical Appearance

It is clear from the review in Chapter 2 that a person's general physical appearance communicates. What is communicated varies depending on the attractiveness of the person, their body, their scent, their hair, their dress, and their use of artifacts.

Attractiveness.   We know that attractive people are perceived by others as more likable, sociable, outgoing, friendly, popular, persuasive, successful, and happier than unattractive people. Research clearly shows that in most situations attractive people are more likely to be responded to favorably than unattractive people. For example, the attractive male is more likely to get the high-powered sales job than the unattractive male, particularly if their qualifications are equal. There have even been reports of people being refused employment because they were "too ugly." Being perceived as attractive might produce two immediacy-related results. First, because attractive people are perceived by others as more likeable and sociable, then they also might be perceived as more approachable. If they are responded to in an immediate fashion by others, then they will most likely respond in kind. Second, because attractive people have been treated as if they are more responsive and sociable, they will probably exhibit more immediate behavior. For most of their lives, attractive people have been approached by others, often simply because of their looks. Therefore, they have learned to be immediate with others, which makes them even more attractive. This is not to suggest that unattractive people are not immediate. Many unattractive people have learned that immediacy is one means of increasing their attractiveness.

   Consider the following. Would you rather talk with a less-than-attractive person who rarely smiles, nods, has eye contact, and moves toward you while interacting? Would you rather talk with a less-than-attractive person who smiles, nods, has eye contact, and leans toward you while interacting? Most people would prefer the latter. Many less-than-attractive people have learned these behaviors and use them to appear more attractive, sociable, and likable. Regardless of one's basic attractiveness level, the person who employs immediacy behavior is perceived as more attractive. In addition, making yourself physically attractive increases the likelihood that others will approach you and perceive you as more sociable and immediate.

Body Shape and Size.   As discussed previously, body shape and size communicate important information about a person. Endomorphs are usually perceived as sociable, friendly, and jolly. Mesomorphs are usually perceived as confident, competent,

SURROGATES FOR NONVERBAL BEHAVIOR IN ON-LINE COMPUTER CONFERENCING

If you were to sign on to certain electronic conferencing services, such as Compuserve's CB Simulator, your computer screen might show a series of messages like Figure 11–2. Each member of the dramatis personae is an individual sitting alone at his or her computer terminal. The computer system's public conferencing software brings them together and enables them to communicate.

Chuck:	Hi, everybody.
Mary:	Hugs, Chuckie.
Don:	You didn't give me a hug, M. (ducking)
Mary:	Don . . . (SWAT!)
Don:	Missed . . . (OUCH!!!)
Chuck:	Just back from the Big Apple—broke:-(
Jack:	Chuck—wine, women, or sushi? (YUCKS)
Chuck:	Har de har, Jack, Funnnneeeeee.
Mary:	Who writes your material, Jack!
Jack:	<======= [*TA-DA!!!]
Don:	S'okay, Jack. You can stay anyway.
Chuck:	I wanna vote. (winks at Mary)
Mary:	(winks back) Didja see Phantom?
Chuck:	Nope. Saw Cats.
Mary:	I haven't yet . . . any good?
Chuck:	Better than the Dallas Production.
Don:	Quite a kulcha klatch.:)
Jack:	Snarf.

Watching the monitor display, one is struck by the impression that Chuck, Mary, Don, and Jack are using their computers for something much like interpersonal communication. Several characteristics of their interaction stand out:
1. They take short turns, communicating with one another in brief messages marked by frequent changes of sender.
2. Many of the messages are directed from one individual to another.
3. The subject matter is "personal." It involves the feelings of the interactants and their relations with one another.
4. The tone of the interaction is spontaneous, the style relaxed and informal.
5. Many messages are responses to immediately preceding messages, giving evidence of feedback in the interaction.

FIGURE 11–2 **Simulated Electronic Interaction**

outgoing, energetic, and dominant. Ectomorphs are usually perceived as tense, anxious, awkward, and sensitive. Based on the above results, evidently endomorphs and mesomorphs are perceived as more immediate and approachable. Because of the perceptions associated with their body shape, ectomorphs are generally perceived as less immediate. Therefore, ectomorphs could dispel this perception by being immediate and using behavior that makes them seem as if they are approachable.

KINESIC SURROGATES
1. Kinesic Descriptions
2. Kinesic Pictographs
3. Self-Pointing

VOCALIC SURROGATES
Emphasis Indicators
4. Multiple Punctuation Marks
5. All Caps
6. Asterisk Bracketing
Duration and Rate Indicators
7. Extended Letter Repetition
8. Spaces Between Letters
9. Run-together Words
Pause Indicators
10. Ellipsis
11. Blank Spaces in Line
Vocalizations
12. Vocal Characterizations
13. Vocal Segregates
14. Interjections

HAPTIC SURROGATES
15. Touch Descriptions
16. Haptic Pictographs

PHYSICAL APPEARANCE SURROGATES
17. Appearance Descriptions
18. Handle Pictographs

ARTIFACT SURROGATES
19. Object Displays

ACTION SURROGATES
20. Action Descriptions
21. Sound Effects

MISCELLANEOUS
22. Conventional Symbols

FIGURE 11–3 **Outline of Nonverbal Surrogate Categories**

Scent.   Body scent can cause others to perceive you as immediate or nonimmediate. Consider, for example, the person who wears a very heavy scent to the office. Generally, others will avoid the person with the heavy scent because it is offensive to the olfactic senses. People are less likely to approach someone with an offensive scent. On the other hand, many people use scent for keeping others from approaching them.

Posted notices can be nonimmediate and
still communicate a message.

In conclusion, an individual can enhance her or his perceived nonverbal immediacy by using pleasant but not overpowering scents. One can appear to be nonimmediate by employing offensive scents to keep others away.

Hair.   The length, style, and color of one's hair can be used to foster immediacy or
nonimmediacy. For example, the person with the acceptable hair length, style, and
color is much more approachable than the person with the unusual length, style, and
color. Many rock stars may be perceived by the one segment of the population as
very approachable or immediate, but another portion of the population may perceive
them as outlandish and unapproachable. Much of it has to do with hair length, style,
and color.

Dress and Artifacts.   Dress and the artifacts one chooses can communicate immediacy or nonimmediacy. Informal but not sloppy dress usually communicates that
one is approachable. Often, people are intimidated by very formal dress. Formal
dress is one method of denoting higher status, and heightened status decreases
immediacy. In some situations, people want to be perceived as having higher status
and want decreased immediacy. For example, during job interviews, interviewers

want to establish who is the interviewee and who is the interviewer. This is often accomplished by the style and quality of dress of the interviewer.

Artifacts are items that adorn a person's body, such as jewelry, clothing, glasses, makeup, pipes, briefcases, books, and so on. We can think of instances of when someone's use of an artifact suggested that they were immediate or nonimmediate. For example, the person who wears a T-shirt that says "Take me, I'm lonely" is probably communicating something different from the person whose T-shirt reads "Get outta my face." Reflective sunglasses that do not allow you to see the wearer's eyes also generally denote nonimmediacy.

Gesture and Body Movements

The study of kinesics provides information about immediacy. As suggested in Chapter 3, a person's gestures and body movements convey considerable information. This section discusses how gestures and body movements are related to nonverbal immediacy.

Emblems.   Emblems are gestures that have a direct verbal translation that conveys a specific message that is understood by most people in the culture. For example, in North American culture, the "OK" sign is commonly used and the meaning is generally understood by all. Emblems, unlike many other gestures, generally have a very precise meaning. Therefore, emblems can be used to convey immediacy or nonimmediacy. For example, gestures that mean the following would generally be interpreted as nonimmediate gestures: get lost, stop, shame on you, and zip it. Most of these messages would not be interpreted as meaning someone is immediate. Most of us would avoid approaching someone who was using these gestures; they do not denote friendship or liking.

On the other hand, some emblems do convey liking, friendship, and immediacy, such as waving the hand in greeting, nodding the head to acknowledge another, slapping someone on the back for a job well done, smiling, and signing peace. Emblems can convey the message of immediacy or nonimmediacy. You might try to generate a list of emblems that convey immediacy and those that do not.

Illustrators.   Illustrators are gestures that are linked to spoken language and help in illustrating spoken language. With illustrators we generally can convey more or richer meaning than we can with the verbal message alone. For example, if we are very excited and pleased about something, we will use more illustrators to help us in telling others our pleasure. In a similar vein, if we are angry or displeased about something, we will use illustrators that stimulate that meaning. If we are bored with something or are communicating simple messages, we will use fewer illustrators. This means that illustrators that stimulate feelings of pleasure or excitement are much more likely to increase immediacy than illustrators that stimulate feelings of anger or boredom.

Regulators. Regulators are gestures that help to control the flow of communication in interpersonal interactions. They can be movements such as head nods, hand and body movements, eye behavior, touch, or the use of the voice. Regulators that increase immediacy in conversation include positive head nods, eye contact, silence, a relaxed posture, some positive vocalic behavior, and touch. All of the above encourage another to continue speaking and simultaneously convey the message that you are interested in what they are saying.

Illustrators that might decrease immediacy are movements such as negative head nods, little eye contact, slouching posture, leaning back, pressure on the arm, and dull-sounding vocalic behavior. Generally, the above behavior conveys to another that you are either bored with them or what they are saying or simply don't care. In either case, these behaviors usually decrease immediacy.

Affect Behavior. Affect behaviors are movements that reflect the intensity or strength with which we feel an emotion. These behaviors often display our emotional state. Affect behaviors can be displayed by any part of our body. The most easily recognizable affect displays are happiness, sadness, anger, disgust, interest, tension, contempt, restlessness, and relaxation. Let's take tension as an example. Someone who is preparing to give his or her first public speech generally displays behavior such as a tense body position, perhaps clenching and unclenching fists, and taut neck and face muscles. In contrast, someone who has finished a speech has a relaxed posture, perhaps even slouching, relaxed face and neck muscles, and relaxed hands. As we can see from the above, the emotional state of the person often determines their movements. Therefore, the emotional states of happiness, interest, and relaxation probably convey immediacy more than the other states.

Adaptors. Adaptors are unusually unintentional behaviors that are linked to negative feelings about a person or situation or feelings of anxiety. Such behavior can be movements such as picking one's nose, squeezing a pimple, playing with one's hair, tapping a pencil on a desk, scratching one's crotch, fiddling with one's clothing, picking lint off another's collar, and so on. Most adaptive behaviors do not increase immediacy. They may decrease immediacy because they make the other person uncomfortable.

People who are generally anxious and people who have a fear of communicating with others tend to have more adaptive behavior. People who are generally anxious usually are easy to pick out in a crowd. They are the ones who are chewing on their hands, scratching their head, picking at their clothing, and engaging in various other adaptive behavior. Because these people never appear to be relaxed, they do not convey immediacy to others. They usually convey only anxiety.

Posture. Good posture is more than standing straight. Researchers have long felt that posture communicates a whole range of perceptions about you to others. It seems that whether we slump, slouch, stand erect, stand swaybacked, hunch over, pose like a model, recline, move with vigor, or drag ourselves around, our carriage conveys to others how we feel about them, ourselves, and the situation.

Based on the above, it is relatively easy to define the postural stances that encourage or denote immediacy. Obviously, a hunched over, slumped shoulder stance does not encourage immediacy. However, an erect—not rigid—body position with a forward lean is much more likely to encourage communication and give the perception of immediacy. When one crosses her or his arms and leans backwards, this communicates noncaring and nonresponsiveness. Therefore, to create immediacy, one must have a posture that suggests openness, interest, and attention. Such postural movements are forward leans, relaxed body position, and direct body orientation.

In summary, gestures and body movements denote the degree of perceived physical or psychological closeness between people. It is also evident that immediacy can be increased by manipulating nonverbal movements. Increased immediacy normally leads to more effective communication.

Facial Expression and Eye Behavior

The face is perhaps the best indicator of affect and feeling. Your face and eyes communicate a plethora of information. For example, we make assumptions about people based totally on their facial expressions. We have been taught how to tell the "bad people" from the "good people." The bad people always have scars, tattoos, pimples, and shifty eyes, wear frowns, and have body and facial disfigurements. The good people have clear complexions, nice clear eyes, smiles, and no body or facial disfigurements.

Research shows that based on facial expressions, people can make fairly accurate judgments about a person's sex, race, nationality, age, personality, and emotional state. The last two judgments are more difficult. However, there are cues for making judgments about them (as we learned in Chapter 4).

Because no one area of the face reveals emotions or states best, we have to view the entire face when discussing immediacy. It is nearly impossible to convey immediacy if one is not smiling, has little eye contact, and is frowning. Because the smile is the most common universal expression, smiling clearly denotes immediacy or at the least friendship. Other factors that suggest immediacy include having an interested look, direct eye contact, and mutual glances. One might also watch for dilated pupils as a sign of interest. However, this is not a very valid predictor because light can cause eyes to constrict. Perceptions of immediacy are increased by the type and length of eye contact. People who have more eye contact with others are seen as more attractive, interested, sincere, honest, confident, and immediate. They are also perceived as more skilled or competent communicators. Therefore, eye behavior is a primary means of increasing immediacy.

In summary, both facial and eye behaviors have a significant impact on the perception of immediacy or nonimmediacy. People who have a positive facial affect and greater eye contact are perceived as more immediate than people who have negative facial affect and little eye contact.

Vocal Behavior

How do you feel when you have to communicate with or listen to someone who speaks in a monotone voice? How do you react when you have to listen to or communicate with someone who speaks with a harsh, strident, shrill, or nasal voice? In each case you probably want to be far away from the person speaking, but each for different reasons. The monotone voice bores you to death, and the harsh voice grates on your nerves. As Malandro, Barker, and Barker (1989) suggest,

> *Your voice is one of the most important factors affecting your image. The minute you begin to speak, your spoken image becomes dominant and overrides your visual image. (p. 232)*

Vocalics are useful in projecting an image, regulating conversation, relaying emotions, identifying socioeconomic status, ethnic group, age and sex of communicator, increasing credibility, improving affect, and creating immediacy.

What are the common vocal qualities that increase immediacy? Vocalic behavior such as increased rate of speaking (not abnormally fast), variety in pitch, confident tone, few pauses, and high vocal expressiveness tend to increase immediacy. Slow or extremely fast speech, little variety in pitch, antagonistic or aggressive tone, feeble tone, many pauses, sneering sounds, sarcasm, and extended silence decrease immediacy. Many of these behaviors even give the perception that the speaker is anxious or nervous, which also makes people uncomfortable. In fact, the anxious speaker usually exhibits many adaptive behaviors besides nonresponsive vocalic behavior. In addition, people who sound weak, bored, angry, disgusted, or uninterested tend to decrease immediacy, whereas people who are animated, dynamic, interested, and pleasant-sounding increase the likelihood of immediacy.

Spatial Behavior

The use of space involves both personal space orientations and territoriality. The first section reviews personal space orientations and their impact on immediacy.

Let's look at two examples. Decide which person has the appropriate space orientations to promote immediacy.

1. Bill always rushes to acquaintances and folds them into his arms. He usually gives an extended hug and a kiss. His behavior is predictable by his friends. He exhibits the above behavior with both males and females.

2. Lee rarely greets acquaintances with even a handshake. He usually stands back and asks about their health. His behavior is predictable by his friends. He exhibits the above behavior with both males and females.

You guessed it: Neither behavior promotes immediacy. Bill's behaviors are too immediate, moving into the intimate range, and make the average person very uncomfortable. Lee's behaviors are overly nonimmediate and tend to make the average person very uncomfortable. These sets of behavior increase the likelihood that people will want to avoid both Bill and Lee, but for totally different reasons. When people are with Bill they feel as if they are being mauled, whereas when they are with Lee, they feel as if they are being frostbitten. Simply being close to someone does not necessarily promote immediacy; it can hinder it. The key is the amount of closeness appropriate for the situation.

As suggested in Chapter 6, the amount of space appropriate for conversational settings is different from the amount of space appropriate for intimate communication. Therefore, we must learn to exhibit behaviors that are acceptable for individual situations. Most of us know the appropriate behavior for an intimate setting, so we will not dwell on it. The conversational setting is the most common communication setting in everyday life, so we will deal with it.

Sommer (1969) suggests that the "best way to learn the location of invisible boundaries is to keep walking until somebody complains" (p. 26). In general in this culture, people who stand or move closer to or lean toward another are perceived as more immediate than those who stand back and do not lean toward another. The person who moves closer to another in conversation is perceived as more approachable and immediate up to a certain point. When someone takes up more of the another's personal space than he or she should, they could be perceived as a space invader. They could also be perceived as aggressive, obnoxious, rude, and overbearing. Therefore, you should stay far enough away from the other person so that you cannot breathe the other's breath. This is Bill's problem; he never gives people room to breathe on an interpersonal level. Taller people must be concerned about being perceived as dominant simply because their height makes them appear to be more dominant. Therefore, taller people should be careful not to lean over someone, but they can lean toward the other person if they stand just a bit farther away.

How a person chooses to arrange her or his environment tells the other whether they want to increase communication or keep it to a minimal level. Let's look at two living rooms. The first one has the couches and chairs arranged so plenty of eye contact is possible for participants and it is arranged in a semicircle so all participants can see one another. The furniture looks comfortable and seems to have been used recently. The second living room has the couches and chairs arranged so little eye contact is possible for participants and it is arranged in a L-shape so all participants can see the view from the window. The furniture looks as if it is brand new and has never been used. Which room makes you feel as if conversation is encouraged? Obviously, the first room. This living room conveys warmth and comfort and gives the image of perceived immediacy. It says "Come in, you're welcome here." The other one says "Don't stay long."

The way one uses territory can either promote the feeling of immediacy or decrease it. If you want to increase conversation, then arrange your territory in a way that promotes conversation. If you want to decrease conversation, then arrange your territory in a way that limits conversation. A good means of creating space that promotes conversation is to arrange the environment so that all people can have eye contact with the others in the room. Two of the authors of the book were invited to a friend's home where the furniture was arranged in a circle with a large coffee table in the center. All participants seated around the table could easily converse with the others. They also had several other seating areas, all arranged similarly, only smaller. If you arrange your territory in a nonimmediate fashion, people will perceive you as nonimmediate. However, if you arrange your territory in an immediate fashion, people will perceive you as more immediate.

Tactile Behavior

Touch and the use of personal space go hand-in-hand. How one uses personal space often suggests one's touch orientations. Let's go back to the examples of Bill and Lee. How does each use touch? You guessed it. Bill caresses a person's back and neck while hugging. On the other hand, Lee rarely squeezes someone's hand when shaking it. Both have inappropriate touch behaviors for promoting immediacy. Bill's behavior suggests intimacy. He makes both males and females uncomfortable. Lee is perceived by others as cold, distant, and unfriendly. So the question becomes, How is touch used to increase immediacy? The answer is not so easy. We could say that you know it when you see it. However, let's look at some touch behavior that communicates immediacy.

Touch can be perceived differently by different people. We need to understand the context. However, there are still some touch behaviors that can be used in almost any situation to communicate immediacy. It is appropriate and acceptable to touch most people on the hand, forearm, shoulder, and middle to upper back. It is the type of touch that determines how people interpret it. Touch behavior in the above body areas that denotes warmth, caring, and concern for the other person generally increases immediacy and communication. Patting a shoulder or a slight squeeze of the shoulder lets the other know that you acknowledge them as a person and that you are listening. They will perceive you as more immediate without perceiving you as intimate. Touch behavior in the above body areas such as patting and squeezing usually promotes immediacy. In contrast, rubbing, caressing, and extended pressure can communicate many things, but immediacy is not one of them.

Environmental Factors

We noted in Chapter 8 that aspects of the environment can have a major influence on social interaction. Some areas seem to drive people apart, to be nonimmediate.

Other areas seem to be so immediate that they bring people closer together. In this section, we center our attention on characteristics that distinguish between areas that are perceived as immediate and those that are seen as nonimmediate.

All settings influence perceptions of immediacy and, as a result, the nature of the communication that occurs in that setting. For example, most churches are intentionally constructed to convey reverence and respect. This means that the environment is constructed so that a minimal amount of communication is encouraged (fixed or hard-to-move seating all pointing in one direction, dull colors, and very high ceilings). However, many classrooms within churches are constructed to encourage communication (moveable chairs, bright lighting, and bright colors). Many church facilities, then, are prime examples of both immediate and nonimmediate environments within one structure. Many apartment buildings and dorms also have both immediate and nonimmediate areas one structure. The rooms are constructed so people can have privacy, but the building also includes open areas or areas designated as social areas. Talk is encouraged in the social areas, whereas each individual resident has the option to leave that area and go to the privacy of her or his own room.

Clearly, the total structure of a facility can go a long way toward determining the amount of immediacy people perceive while in that facility. However, other elements in the environment also promote immediacy or nonimmediacy, such as use of seating arrangements, color, lighting, sound, and general attractiveness of the environment.

The shapes of tables have been found to affect communication through their impact on perceptions of power, attraction, and immediacy. As noted in Chapter 8, round tables denote equality for all because there is no "head" at which someone can sit. Square tables can also denote equality because all sides are equal. The various seats at rectangular tables can denote differences in status. However, research reveals that, whatever the shape of the table, when participants want to increase psychological closeness and have the feeling of immediacy, they should sit side-by-side, use corner seating, or use face-to-face seating. These are more immediate seating arrangements and, as noted in Chapter 8, these types of seating arrangements suggest openness to cooperation and conversation. These types of seating arrangements are also associated with higher degrees of affiliation and liking, whereas sitting in some nonimmediate positions, such as at the opposite ends of a table, can denote feelings of competition. Research also shows that the closer one sits to another, the higher the perception of psychological closeness. Research also suggests that in a seating arrangement where physical closeness is limited, increased eye contact can signal immediacy and increase psychological closeness.

Obviously, unpainted, dirty walls do not promote a feeling of immediacy. This type of environment can even encourage people to feel psychologically distressed and behaviorally aggressive. People react to colors emotionally and physically. Black has consistently been associated with darkness, evil, mystery, and power. White has consistently been associated with purity, joy, and innocence. Perhaps this is one of the reasons why newborns are always wrapped in white blankets.

Can you imagine the reaction of a new mother if her baby were brought to her in a black blanket?

Colors of walls and furnishings can affect how much we want to stay in a room and communicate with others. A room dominated by light and medium blues tend to give most people a warm, immediate feeling. People like to be in an environment with this decor. They enjoy talking to others and like those others more. In contrast, a room dominated by bright oranges and red can excite its inhabitants. Studies have found that bars with this color scheme are much more likely to host loud arguments and physical assaults—distinct responses to a nonimmediate environment. Clearly, color does affect the perceptions people have of others and the surrounding environment.

What colors are likely to promote immediacy or psychological closeness? Research clearly shows that colors that promote feelings of warmth, security, closeness, tenderness, calmness, and happiness also promote communication and feelings of psychological closeness. Bright colors such as red and orange within a context of darker wood tones stimulate interaction and may allow for the feeling of immediacy. However, as we noted above, too much bright red or orange could stimulate too much conversation of the wrong type. Colors such as deep blues, reds, and browns and promote a feeling of security and immediacy. Many nightclubs and similar intimate settings have tailored the interiors of their clubs to stimulate a certain mood in the customer. For example, clubs that want people to linger use darker, richer shades and colors. Environments such as McDonald's that want people to eat and exit quickly are more likely to use active tones such as bright oranges and loud reds.

Lighting can be used to promote a feeling of psychological closeness. Darker illumination is conducive to intimacy as well as feelings of immediacy. Again, many bars and clubs use this type of lighting to evoke certain feelings in their customers. High levels of illumination are nonimmediate and can cause fatigue, irritation, and even aggressive behavior. Moderate levels of illumination are best for task-oriented environments. This is where you want only moderate immediacy, but a lot of work.

Sounds that promote immediacy are usually of lower volume and pitch. For example, ballads generally tend to increase immediacy and marches tend to decrease it. Have you ever tried being immediate with another while Mötley Crüe is blaring "Shout at the Devil?" Music of this type evokes excitement and intensity, but rarely immediacy.

Lastly, the general attractiveness of the environment can communicate a feeling of psychological closeness or nonimmediacy. The unattractive environment (dirty, cluttered, unpleasant odors) generally evokes feelings of dislike, aggression, hostility, and even depression. More attractive environments (clean, uncluttered, pleasant odors, good colors) evoke feelings of happiness, lightheartedness, warmth, and security. In general, the attractive environment evokes feelings of immediacy and positive communication and the negative environment evokes nonimmediate feelings, negative communication, and a desire to flee.

Scent and Smell

It is clear from the research that smell can evoke emotional and even physical responses from people and animals. For example, a skunk emits a nasty odor as a form of defense. Few animals or humans want to be immediate with a skunk. Much of the scent released by animals is instinctual. However, humans have learned to manipulate scents to produce certain reactions. Musk is a common scent that has been credited with drawing people together. Scents that are inoffensive and pleasant are much more likely to increase conversation and perhaps lead to immediacy than offensive and unpleasant odors. Researchers generally agree that overpowering scents, such as those of many perfumes, do not lead to immediacy; they lead to non-immediacy. Be careful. The dollar value of a scent is not necessarily related to its immediacy value. Some most expensive scents are also the most offensive to others. Most scent companies have learned that, at least in this culture, scents must be unobtrusive and pleasant to increase psychological or physical closeness. Obviously, scents such as body odor, dirty feet, and bad breath decrease immediacy.

Temporal Factors

Some people tend to take time for granted. This is a mistake. People make judgments and attributions about us based on our use of time. People who are constantly late in this culture are perceived in a very negative manner. They are often perceived as uncaring, lazy, slow, uninteresting, and uncouth. People who are on time or even a little early in this culture are perceived as caring, bright, energetic, interesting, and acculturated.

Time and immediacy are inextricably related. Appropriate use of time determines whether you will be perceived as immediate on a social and task level. In this culture, it is expected that when someone asks you should respond almost immediately, either verbally or nonverbally. An immediate response generates a feeling of closeness, whereas a slow response generates feelings such as anxiety and tension. In conversations, the latency of response time is crucial to perceptions of psychological closeness. Immediate responses are (redundantly speaking) immediate. To spend more time with a person is to be more immediate with that person. Possibly the most nonimmediate gesture in a normal conversation is raising ones' wrist to look at a watch. It signals, often unintentionally, that a person has no more time to spend with their interaction partner. Clearly, time can be used to increase or decrease perceptions of psychological closeness. How one uses time determines how others perceive her or him.

OUTCOMES OF IMMEDIACY

It is clear from the preceding review of immediacy that positive outcomes in relationships can be stimulated by immediacy cues. For example, being verbally immediate, standing close to another, leaning toward another, smiling, having eye contact, facing another, touching, using positive gestures, and using time and smell appropriately allows one to make a favorable impression on the other person. Table 11–1 depicts the verbal or nonverbal category and the behavior normally used to achieve immediacy or nonimmediacy. The remainder of this section explores several outcomes of immediacy cues in relationships.

Increased Liking, Affiliation, and Affect.   Mehrabian (1971, 1981) confirmed that as immediacy increases, so does liking in interpersonal encounters. He suggested that "immediacy and liking are two sides of the same coin. That is, liking encourages greater immediacy and immediacy produces more liking" (1971, p. 77). He and others have suggested that people normally communicate with persons for whom they have positive affect. As they communicate more with people they like, the use of immediacy can improve the affect even more. Research from many areas clearly indicates that the more a person likes another, the more they will use affirmative cues such as leaning closer, touching, mutual gaze, smiling, and nodding—all immediacy cues. On the other side of the coin, Mehrabian (1971) says that "opportunities for increased immediacy can foster greater liking" (p. 77). If one wants to be liked by another, one should use the immediacy behaviors that are likely to increase liking. For example, Mehrabian (1981) states,

> *greater liking is conveyed by standing close instead of far, leaning forward instead of back while seated, facing directly instead of turning to one side, touching, having mutual gaze or eye contact, extending bodily contact as during a handshake, prolonging goodbyes, or using gestures during a greeting that imply a reaching out toward the other person who is at a distance. (p. 42)*

He suggests that the above behaviors not only increase liking or affect for another but also increase the approachability of the person.

More Approachable Communication Style.   The person who exhibits immediacy behavior is perceived as having a more approachable communication style than the person who exhibits nonimmediacy behavior. For example, are you more likely to approach someone who is smiling at you or someone who is frowning at you? This is a simple example, but normally out of 100 people, at least 90 percent are more comfortable approaching the person who is smiling. If the simple distinction between smiling and frowning can make such a big difference in whether one will approach another or not, imagine what a cluster of immediate or nonimmediate behaviors can do. Immediacy cues not only give a person a more approachable communication style, but they also help to decrease uncertainty about the person and the situation. Often we infer how a conversation will go based on the nonverbal cues given off by others. Immediacy cues help to decrease uncertainty about communication situations.

TABLE 11-1 Immediacy/Nonimmediacy Behavior Chart

CATEGORY	IMMEDIACY BEHAVIORS	NONIMMEDIACY BEHAVIORS
Verbal Immediacy	Pronouns like we, us. Talk with others. Statements that infer liking (e.g., I like your dress). I really like that. You are right.	Use of you, you and I, I. talk to/at others. Guarded statements of liking (Your dress is OK). That's dumb. That's a stupid idea.
Appearance	Attractive; Clean, Neat; Informal clothing but not sloppy; Appropriate hairstyle.	Unattractive; Dirty, Unkempt; Formal clothing; Inappropriate/unusual hairstyle.
Gesture and Body Movement	Leaning toward another. Open body position. More gestures. More positive affect displays. Relaxed body position. Calm movements. Positive head movements.	Lean away from another. Closed body position. Fewer gestures. More negative affect displays. Tense body position. Nervous movements. Negative head movements.
Face and Eye	Eye contact and mutual gaze. Facial expressions that show pleasure. Smile a lot.	Limited eye contact. Avert eye gaze. Facial expressions that show displeasure. Frown a lot.
Voice	Short pauses. Few silences. Positive vocal inflections. Vocal variety. Relaxed tones (calm). Sounds confident. Dynamic, animated, interested; Friendly vocal cues.	Lengthy pauses/silences. Sarcasm. Monotonous, dull, irritated tones. Nasal. Harsh sounding. Sneering sounds. Bored, unfriendly vocal cues.
Space	Move closer to a person. Stand closer to a person. Sit closer. Orient more directly. Lean forward while seated.	Lean away from a person. Sit farther away. Lean away/back while seated. Stand farther away. Indirect body orientation.
Touch	Touch on hand, forearm, shoulder, Pat; Friendly handshake; Frequent touch; Hugging.	Avoid or withdraw from touch. Clammy/distant handshake. Seldom touches. Slapping, hitting, striking another.
Environment	Warm, secure, pleasant environments. Soft colors. Movable chairs. Moderate to soft illumination.	Cold, distant, ugly environments. Bright illumination. Fixed seating. Ugly rooms. Ugly colors.
Scent	Pleasant, inoffensive scents. Familiar scents. Scents of one's own culture.	Unpleasant, offensive scents. Unfamiliar scents. Scents from other cultures.
Time	Short latency of response. Promptness. Spending more time with another. Spending time with another when they choose.	Long latency of response. Delinquent about being on time. Spending little time with another. Often glances at watch/clock.

More Responsiveness, Understanding, and Assertiveness. Responsiveness is the capacity to be sensitive to the communication of others, to be seen as a good listener, to make others comfortable in communicating, and to recognize the needs and desires of others. Considerable research suggests that people who exhibit immediacy behavior are perceived as more responsive and understanding of others. Ask yourself whether you'd rather communicate with a responsive person or a nonresponsive person. A responsive individual not only knows when and how to listen to another but they know how to respond in a given situation. They know the appropriate nonverbal and verbal communication behavior to use to improve communication. These are immediate behaviors.

Assertiveness is the ability to take a stand, defend one's beliefs, and express oneself without attacking or becoming verbally or physically aggressive. Immediate people are perceived as likely to be assertive as well as responsive.

Increased Solidarity Between Participants. Solidarity is the perception of closeness derived from similarity in sentiments, behavior, and symbols of that closeness. As immediacy increases between persons, so does solidarity; as solidarity increases, so does immediacy. We are much more likely to develop a solid relationship with an individual who uses immediate cues with us than someone who uses nonimmediate cues with us. In addition, as we become closer to another, immediacy tends to increase.

Decreased Anxiety. In most relationships, there is a high degree of anxiety or tension associated with the initial acquaintance stage. However, as the relationship develops, the anxiety lessens. Some of this decrease in anxiety results from verbal communication. Most of it results from nonverbal cues. Immediacy behavior tends to relax and calm another person so he or she can communicate without high anxiety. This does not mean that immediacy is the cure for anxiety; it is simply one method of alleviating tension in relationships.

Decreased Status Differences. Status is the societal level of a person. The higher the difference in status between two people, the less likely the persons will communicate effectively. One proven method of reducing status differences to improve communication is to use immediacy behavior. People of higher status in organizations have learned that to communicate more effectively with subordinates, they must reduce their status without giving up the authority. Immediacy enables them to do this. A supervisor can be friendly and immediate without giving up her or his power.

Increased Perceptions of Communication Competence. Although researchers disagree on the definition of communication competence, several communication variables emerge from the literature as characteristics normally considered necessary for a competent communicator. The most common of these are assertiveness, responsiveness, and versatility. In order to be perceived as competent, one must be assertive (able to stand up for one's rights), responsive (good, understanding listener), and versatile (knowing when to be assertive and when to be responsive). Immediacy behavior can be part of each of these characteristics. People can be assertive while being immediate. People who are responsive are definitely immediate. Lastly, the versatile communicator knows when immediacy is appropriate and when it is not. They also have the option to use it whenever they need to. Many incompetent communicators know what immediacy is, but cannot do the behaviors when they need to. Therefore, immediacy skills help people to be perceived as a more competent communicator.

Buhr, Clifton, and Pryor (in press) showed that immediacy behavior enhanced perceptions of a public speaker's likability, competence, trustworthiness, and similarity. They state:

> *Speaker immediacy appears to affect information processing, such that receivers rehearse more positive and neutral thoughts, and fewer negative thoughts about the speech and speaker. . . . [T]he nonimmediate delivery promotes more speech- and speaker-relevant thoughts, [and] these thoughts are predominantly of a negative kind. This negative affect toward the speaker apparently leads to more negative thinking about the speech itself. (p. 5)*

Immediacy behavior is one of the most valuable communication tools a person can have. By this point in the chapter, it may seem that immediacy is the answer to all the worlds' problems! Well, as with anything else, if it looks too good to be true then it probably is. There are drawbacks associated with being immediate. The drawbacks usually are not nearly as serious as those of being nonimmediate, but they can create some problems.

DRAWBACKS OF IMMEDIACY

The first drawback deals with perceptions. Occasionally, people mistake or misread immediacy cues for intimacy cues. You may have experienced the following. You're in a bar and someone smiles at you and, because you want to seem friendly, you smile back. Before you can count to ten, they are at your side asking if you'd like to go home with them. All you did was smile! There are instances where immediacy is misread for intimacy, and people who mistake immediacy cues for intimacy cues. Over time, as you use immediacy behavior, you will learn when and where you can use it appropriately.

The second drawback deals with anxiety. Some people are not more relaxed or less anxious when someone is being immediate. These people like to avoid communication as much as possible. Communication avoidants are more anxious, not less,

Instructions: Below are a series of statements that describe the ways some people behave while talking with or to others. You are asked to indicate how well each statement applies to your communication behavior. For each statement, choose the number that most closely describes your behavior. Write that number in the space before the statement.

1 = Never;   2 = Rarely;   3 = Occasionally;   4 = Often;   5 = Very Often

_____1. Use hands and arms to gestures while talking to people.

_____2. Use monotone or dull voice while talking to people.

_____3. Look at people while talking to them.

_____4. Frown while talking to people.

_____5. Have a very tense body position while talking to people.

_____6. Move away from people while talking to them.

_____7. Use a variety of vocal expressions while talking to people.

_____8. Touch people on the shoulder or arm while talking to them.

_____9. Smile while talking to people.

_____10. Look away from people while talking to them.

_____11. Have a relaxed body position while talking to people.

_____12. Am "stiff" while talking to people.

_____13. Avoid touching people while talking to them.

_____14. Move closer to people while talking to them.

_____15. Am animated while talking to people.

SCORING: Complete the following steps:

Step 1.   Add the scores for items 2, 4, 5, 6, 10, 12, and 13.

Step 2.   Add the scores for items 1, 3, 7, 8, 9, 11, 14, and 15.

Step 3.   Add 42 to your total for step 2.

Step 4.   Subtract your total for step 1 from your total for step 3.

The total from Step 4 is your SRIB score. It will be between 15 and 75. If it is below 15 or above 75, you have made a mistake in your score. The higher your score, the more immediate you see your communication behavior to be.

FIGURE 11–4   **Self-Report of Immediacy Behavior (SRIB)**

when someone is being immediate with them. Immediacy usually increases communication, and communication avoidants want less. Therefore, their anxiety level increases. This is easily recognizable. If you are being immediate and someone else is not responding and seems anxious, the best thing you can do is be less immediate.

Let the other person figure out the conversational flow. Being less immediate with communication avoidants might help them be less anxious.

The last drawback could be interpreted as a positive or negative. Immediacy promotes more communication between people. Sometimes this can be very rewarding. However, occasionally it is not. More communication requires more time. For example, the nurse who is immediate with her or his patients might find that this increases communication. This may require that he or she spend more time with patients than is possible in a day and still carry out other duties. Therefore, one has to learn how to withdraw gracefully from a communication relationship when they need to move to another one. Many people in sales are very adept at this sort of thing. They can be immediate even as they shake your hand to say goodbye.

In conclusion, the drawbacks to immediacy can create problems. However, the perceptions created in the mind of another by not being immediate are likely to be even more severe. Nonimmediate people are perceived by others as less friendly, less responsive, less outgoing, less likeable, cold, aloof, and even hostile. Therefore, the advantages of immediacy outweigh the drawbacks.

Before we conclude this chapter, take a moment to complete Figure 11–4 and get your score. The Self-Report of Immediacy Behavior (SRIB) tells you how immediate you see your communication behavior to be. If your behaviors are less immediate than you'd like them to be, try a few of the immediacy behaviors we have discussed in this chapter. Pick ones you think you would find easy to use and see whether this improves your relationships with others. After you try two or three, try a few more until you have behaviors you feel comfortable using in interpersonal encounters. Not everyone can use all the immediacy behaviors, so you have to select the ones that are most suitable for you. Not everyone can be immediate in the same way, but the effects of immediacy do not depend on which methods you use, just on whether you do use some.

A GLOSSARY OF TERMINOLOGY

Immediacy is the degree of perceived physical or psychological closeness between people.

Nonverbal immediacy is the use of nonverbal behavior that increases the immediacy between interactants.

Verbal immediacy is the use of language that increases the immediacy between interactants.

▲ 12

Female–Male Relationships

Two children are walking down a street. Both are about the same height and the same age, four. Both are wearing similar clothing and have the same length hair. Their faces are not visible, only their backs. Child A moves with a swagger down the street, with arms swinging and taking long strides. Child B sways down the street, with the whole body seeming as if it is one smooth swaying motion. Can you tell the gender of each child?

If you said child A is male and child B female, you are tuned in to common differences in the walking behavior of most males and females. As early as age four, or even sooner, there are distinct nonverbal differences in the behavior of males and females. Males tend to exhibit a typical male walk and females tend to exhibit a typical female walk, each similar to our four-year-olds described above.

Males and females differ about this and many other nonverbal behavior. Given that such differences are real, our concern in this chapter is twofold. First, how do males and females develop different nonverbal behavior? Second, how do these different behaviors affect communication?

DEVELOPMENT OF NONVERBAL BEHAVIOR IN MALES AND FEMALES

Research suggests three theoretical explanations about why males and females develop different nonverbal behavior. They are genetics, modeling, and conditioning or reinforcement.

Couples sometimes have very similar expressions.

Genetics.   Some scholars suggest that genetics plays no role in the development of different male and female nonverbal behavior, but we disagree. Biological research has shown that males and females inherit different bone structures and body types. It is even possible to identify the gender of a person whose skeleton has been buried for hundreds of years. These skeletal differences are critical in the performance of some nonverbal behavior. Inherited traits such as body type and structure usually cannot be significantly altered, tend to determine our walk, gestures, and posture, and can influence other nonverbal behavior such as the smile.

The shape of our bodies determines many of our nonverbal behaviors. For example, the average woman typically has larger breasts than the average man. This influences a woman's posture. A man usually has a larger shoulder span than a woman. This is a contributing factor in determining the man's posture. However small the role, genetics cannot be discounted as at least a partial explanation for the differential development of nonverbal behavior in males and females. This fact, of course, does not deny the existence of other causal factors, possibly even much more important ones.

Modeling.   If you ask parents how their children develop nonverbal behavior, they will give the explanation of modeling. We learn many of our behaviors by observing others and imitating their behavior. This is modeling. Children are very careful observers of their parents, siblings, teachers, and peers. Little boys and girls learn how to act like "big" boys and girls by observing others in their environment and modeling their behavior. A little girl will play dress up and model her mother, and a little boy will try to be like his dad.

This modeling explanation of differences in nonverbal behavior of males and females suggests that children observe the behavior of others in their environment and attempt to emulate it. This theory certainly helps to explain why children in one culture grow up with behavior typical of the adults in that culture whereas children in another culture grow up with different behavior typical of the other culture. This also explains, at least in part, why males and females differ in their nonverbal behavior within a single culture.

In conclusion, we cannot confirm that modeling is the primary reason for the development of male and female nonverbal behavior. However, it is probable that modeling makes a significant contribution.

Reinforcement or Conditioning.   Another popular explanation for the development of different nonverbal behavior by males and females is reinforcement or conditioning. The basic premise of reinforcement theory is that behavior that is reinforced or conditioned will increase, but behavior that is not reinforced will decrease. If a role model reinforces a child for walking with a sway or for wearing clothing suitable for that gender, the child is likely to continue the behavior. If a child is not reinforced for the walk or clothing, the behavior might not continue. The culture in which we live reinforces or punishes children for appropriate or inappropriate behavior. Little boys often are punished for playing with dolls, but little girls usually are not.

Although reinforcement plays a large role in the development of nonverbal behavior of males and females, it is not the definitive explanation. As much as many people wish it were otherwise, there is no single, definitive explanation for these differences. All three explanations outlined above are credible explanations, and no one explanation precludes the validity of the others. Most likely, these factors contribute to the development of nonverbal behavior of males and females. The degree to which each contributes is unknown and, for the present at least, unknowable.

DISTINCTIVE CHARACTERISTICS

Simply to distinguish female nonverbal behavior from male nonverbal behavior is no easy task. One must first look at the characteristics of males and females that determine why they employ certain nonverbal behavior.

Many writers believe that we must understand the differential gender-role expectations that society holds for men and women before we can understand their differential nonverbal behavior. Such role expectations are primarily a function of culture, and as such can change only as a culture changes. Writers describing Western culture say that expectations for women in this culture are characterized by reactivity whereas expectations for men are characterized by proactivity. This means that women in Western culture are expected to be sensitive, responsive to others, emotionally expressive, and supportive. In contrast, men are expected to be independent, self-assured, confident, and decisive.

Along the same line of thinking, Mehrabian (1981) suggests that the male in this culture is expected to have a dominant social style, whereas the female is expected to have a submissive social style. He concludes that women generally have more pleasant, less dominating, and more affiliative social styles than men. Males are more aggressive and dominant in their social styles. In a similar vein, Henley (1977) and Eakins and Eakins (1978) suggest that nonverbal behaviors differ between women and men because men in this culture generally are in superior positions and women are in subordinate positions. Society expects subordinates (women) to behave submissively (to perform the subordinate role), and society expects supervisors (males) to behave in a dominate manner (to perform the superior or assertive role).

We hasten to note that we are not advocating the desirability of such stereotypical gender-role identifications (after all, the senior author of this book is female!). Rather, we are presenting this information in the hope of identifying where these stereotypes come from. Many people, both female and male, may wish such stereotypical norms would just go away, but they will do so only if the culture changes sufficiently to make such stereotypical behavior dysfunctional in everyday life. That has yet to happen.

The distinctive differences between male and female communication behavior seem to be distinctions based on what are deemed the appropriate societal roles of women and men. Men tend to be more assertive, women more responsive. The assertive role suggests that males are more aggressive, outgoing, demonstrative, and dominant. The responsive role suggests that women are more expressive, sensitive, other-oriented, submissive, and immediate. Bernard (1968) said it quite well: Women are expected to "stroke" others and give "reassuring smiles and silent applause." Therefore, the stereotypical gender roles (assertive or responsive) may explain the gender differences in nonverbal behavior. The remainder of this chapter reviews the differences in nonverbal behavior of men and women that result from these culturally defined assertive and responsive functions.

Appearance and Attractiveness.   In this society, the person who is perceived to be physically attractive and has an attractive appearance is more highly rated than one who is not attractive, despite the gender. This society does not value being unattractive. Although beauty is in the eye of the beholder, there are still several conclusions that can be drawn from the research on general attractiveness of males and females. Attractive people are perceived by others as more sociable, more outgoing, more likeable, more intelligent, and happier. Less-than-attractive people, on the other hand, are perceived as less sociable, less extroverted, less likeable, less intelligent, and not very happy.

From informal observations of many females, and according to one formal study, females may have to meet higher attractiveness standards to be perceived as credible than do males. Eakins and Eakins (1978) report a study in which they found significant differences as a function of attractiveness of males and females presenting a well-reasoned talk. They had two women and two men give persuasive speeches about the merits of debate. Each gave her or his speech twice. Once, the speaker was made to appear attractive; the next time, the speaker was made to appear unattractive. Clothing was held constant. The talks were set up as follows: The first speech favoring debate was cogent and well-reasoned, the first speech opposing debate was poorly reasoned and dogmatic, the second pro speech was poorly reasoned and dogmatic, and the second con speech was cogent and well-reasoned. The raters were college students who had already completed a pretest on their attitudes on the subject who would complete the posttest.

The results revealed that differences in attractiveness of the speaker did affect the receivers' acceptance of the speaker's arguments. The results further revealed the following:

> *Both speakers of the well-reasoned talks had a greater persuasive effect when made up in their attractive state, as was anticipated. An interesting result was a difference in persuasiveness that occurred between the females and males in their unattractive states, whether they gave the poorly reasoned or well-reasoned talk. The males made up unattractively were only slightly less effective than in their attractive state. However, there was considerable difference in the influence of the females, depending on physical state. Unattractiveness in the female caused a decidedly more negative reception of her views. In fact, in one of the videotaped versions the unattractiveness of the female who delivered the cogent pro talk weighed so heavily that the attractive female who answered with the poorly reasoned and ill-constructed con speech had the greater impact on the listeners. Both females and males seemed more accepting of arguments or views from an unattractive male than from an unattractive female. Males were most negative toward the unattractive female's stand. (p. 166)*

Notice that unattractiveness did have a negative impact on male speakers. The difference between male and female speakers was one of degree: Both were hindered by unattractiveness, but the female a bit more so. In other research, which involved ratings of the credibility of individuals based on their photos alone, it was found that despite the gender of a speaker, attractive people are rated higher on the character dimension of credibility than unattractive people. Although the research in this arena is still sparse and does not give precise conclusions, Eakins and Eakins suggest that "the views of unattractively made-up males were accepted more readily than those of unattractively made-up females" (p. 167). It is then safe to conclude that regardless of gender, one should always try to present a good first impression, but even more so if a person happens to be female. The culture has not changed much over the last several years.

Clothing styles change quickly, often before any conclusions can be made about how one particular style affects communication, but it is safe to conclude the following: Dress for the occasion. If the occasion demands a business suit, then wear whatever is appropriate for your gender. If the occasion demands formal wear, then wear what your gender is expected to wear. If one chooses *not* to follow the norms on dress for each gender, one can expect to encounter ridicule and even expulsion from certain groups. To be perceived as credible and sociable, one must wear the cultural garb expected for their gender.

Gesture and Movement.   As early as preschool, small children are finding and using the body movements and gestures of their gender. Research has found that in preschool, little girls have more pronounced bodily movements when paired with little girls than when paired with little boys. When with little boys they tend to become shyer and more reserved in their body movements. Gender differences in behavior are very evident in preschool children. Children learn the behavior expected of young men and young women very early.

Birdwhistell (1970) in some of his studies of young children concluded that sex-role differentiation begins at a very early age. He cites the following example:

> [O]ne female infant . . . by the age of 15 months had learned portions of the diakinesic system . . . of the Southern upper-middle-class female. She had already incorporated the anterior roll of the pelvis and the intrafemoral contact stance which contrasts sharply with the spread-legged and posteriorly rolled pelvis of the 22-month-old boy filmed with her. (p. 49)

Males tend to use more dominant or commanding gestures and movements when communicating with females. Similarly, as compared to their male partners, females tend to use more submissive or acquiescent gestures. The results of several studies reveal that females may be predisposed to do the following when communicating with a male:

> Take up less space, shrink or pull in their bodies, tilt head while talking or listening, arrange or play with hair more often than males, put hands in lap or on hips, tap hands, cross legs, cross ankles, yield space, lower eyes, blink more, and keep legs and feet together while sitting.

Males may be predisposed to do the following when communicating with a female:

Stare more, point, take up more space, keep head straight, stretch hands, stand with legs apart, or sit with legs stretched out with ankles apart, knees spread while sitting, stroke chin more, use larger and more sweeping gestures, more leg and foot movement, and hold arms away from body more.

In sum, the research consistently indicates that in female–male interactions there is a greater display of dominant gestures by males and a greater display of acquiescing gestures by females. These behavioral patterns do not seem to be simply each gender's reaction to the other, because these same patterns are seen in both genders while interacting with another member of their own gender, but on a somewhat less extreme scale. This suggests that the observed pattern in male and female gestures and movement is probably due in large part to the role each gender plays in society, cultural stereotypes, and perceptions of what is appropriate for males and females. Essentially, each gender learns the appropriate "survival skills" for the culture in which they live.

Face and Eye Behavior.   Studies reveal that men tend to mask or hide their emotions more than women. It seems that our culture allows women to be very facially expressive but punishes the male for doing so. In one study, males and females were shown slides that should arouse emotions and strong expression. Included among the slides were scenes of burn victims, happy children, scenic views, and sexual displays. Coders watched the subject's facial expressions and then judged the emotion displayed. Coders found it much easier to code the accurate emotion based on the women's facial expressions. The men seemed to internalize or hide their emotions. In other words, they did not display their emotions on their face. Researchers suggest that this is because our culture tells boys that it is not appropriate for them to cry or show emotion in public. Therefore, males learn to internalize their emotional responses whereas females remain free to externalize their emotions through facial expressions.

Most of us have heard the song, "Smile, and the whole world smiles with you." Well, this is partially true. Women have learned that in this culture they should smile whether they are happy or not. Research suggests that women smile more often than men, in general, although both genders smile more when seeking approval. Women smile more than men when a woman and a man greet each other and when the two conversing are moderately acquainted. Women smile and laugh more than men, and women smile to mask or hide anxiety or nervousness. Research also suggests that women smile more than men even when they are alone. Perhaps the best explanation for why women smile more often is that it is a means of being responsive and acculturating oneself to one's culture. Western culture expects women to be sensitive and responsive. The smile is the international sign of friendship and understanding. Therefore, women are conditioned to smile more often because it is the communication expected of them.

Men often mask their emotions more than women.

Children respond differently to male and female smiles. The reason for this is that males smile primarily when amused or happy, whereas females smile even while sending negative messages. Therefore, children can interpret the male's smile as one of friendliness, but they may have to completely understand the situation to interpret the female's smile correctly. Why do women smile more even when sending a negative message? Society has socialized women to send negative messages with the public smile. They are conditioned to look pleasant and sensitive, not harsh and demanding. The smile is the form of socially ingratiating behavior that women have learned to use even when delivering negative messages. Therefore, women smile when being valuative of their children or even when scolding them.

The old saying "the eyes tell all" is somewhat true. The authors of this book have a friend who rarely makes eye contact with her friends and acquaintances. In this culture, people find it very frustrating to communicate with someone who is looking everywhere but in one's eyes. Our friend rarely looks at her students when teaching. They also find it equally frustrating and feel that she is an unresponsive teacher. Her behavior is not typical for females or males in general. When someone is not looking at you while conversing, you feel as if you are not really a part of the conversation. Males and females have similar functions for eye behavior; however, their use of eye behavior differs. It usually differs in terms of amount, frequency, and duration.

Research reveals that women look more at the other person in a conversation than men do. They also look more at one another more than men do and hold eye contact longer with each other than men do with each other. In general, women look at their conversational partner more and longer than men do. As with facial expression, the primary explanation for this behavior is that women feel that this is a method of establishing and maintaining interpersonal relationships.

Society expects women to be affiliative, and eye contact and gazes show affiliative tendencies. Another explanation is that females are stereotyped as in the subordinate position and males are stereotyped as in the superior position. The person in the subordinate position is expected to give the superior position more attention, but the person in the superior position is not expected to follow suit. An exception to this pattern occurs when the female and male are positioned a considerable distance from one another. Both males and females look more when distances increase between the two. This is simply an attempt to reduce the physical distance, but it tends to overpower the affiliative situational demands that exist in closer proximity. In interpersonal relationships, women gaze more and men stare more. Women lower their eyes when conversing with a male who is staring at them. This seems contradictory to the above. If women look more and hold gaze longer, then why do they lower their eyes more than males? The answer is quite simple. Most of a woman's eye behavior consists of mutual gaze. The women break the mutual gaze but also engage in mutual eye contact more than males. Women also tend to engage in fleeting glances at the other's face while the other is gazing elsewhere. Because women are more often listeners than speakers in female–male interaction, they watch the other more because eye contact is closely associated with attentiveness. In the acquaintance stage of a relationship, the male is usually the one who establishes eye contact with the female first. Rarely is it the other way around. Again, the male is seen as the asserter, the female the responder.

Recently, McAndrew and Warner (1986) studied male and female undergraduates who were randomly paired in same-sex (male–male, female–female) or mixed-sex (female–male) dyads and were asked to maintain silent mutual gaze for as long as possible over two or three trials. The students first completed the Mehrabian Arousal Seeking Scale. Then they were asked to engage in a staring contest. They were to look or stare into the other's eyes for as long as they could without breaking gaze. The length of visual engagement was timed with a stopwatch. When one of the two subjects had "won" two out of three staring encounters, the experiment was ended and subjects debriefed.

The results yielded the following. When subjects were divided into "winners" and "losers" on their performance in the gazing encounter, it was discovered that in the "male–male dyads the person with the higher score on the arousal seeking scale won the encounter 100% of the time, and that in the female–female dyads the high arousal seeker won 90% of the time" (p. 170). Only in one out of twenty dyads did the individual with the low arousal-seeking score come out the winner. Therefore, high arousal-seeking persons in same-sex dyads can hold gaze longer than low arousal-seeking persons. This type of nonverbal gaze behavior can give them a certain amount of power in a relationship.

In mixed-sex dyads (female–male), "this advantage of high arousal seekers over low arousal seekers did not hold up as well" (p. 170). In these dyads,

> *high arousal seekers dominated only four of the ten dyads while low arousal seekers won six times. The influence of the arousal-seeking tendency may have been moderated in these dyads by an apparent advantage of females over males in these encounters, as females were the winners in seven out of the ten pairs. (p. 170)*

McAndrew and Warner (1986) concluded that "individual differences in arousal seeking do in fact predict how well a person can maintain mutual gaze when no one is speaking, especially in same-sex dyads" (pp. 170–171). High arousal-seekers can hold gaze longer in same-sex dyads. However, there seems to be a strong influence of gender on this behavior. "Research has repeatedly shown that females look more than males on all measures of gaze, especially mutual gaze" (p. 171). This would serve as an explanation for the mutual gaze situations being "less novel and unsettling" for females than males in the mixed-sex dyads, "leading to the females' greater willingness to maintain eye contact. In same-sex dyads where this gender difference is absent, arousal seeking would become a more salient variable" (p 171).

In sum, women and men differ in their use of eye behavior. The differences in large part are due to the cultural stereotypes of how males and females should behave.

Vocal Behavior.   If we like the sound of a person's voice, we are more attentive, more open to listening, and more likely to engage in an extended conversation with that person. Some voices are more pleasant than others. Some accents are more pleasant than others. Some people find the New York (Bronx) accent to be strident and offensive, and others find the Southern drawl to be slow and dumb-sounding. We read people's voices as indicators of their personalities, and as we noted in Chapter 5, to some extent at least the voice is an accurate projection of personality. However, the primary differences between female and male voices are hormonal in origin, not personality-induced.

Children learn that their voice should sound the way society says a male or female voice should sound. For example, our culture does not respond well to the female with a deep bass voice. In a similar vein, our culture does not respond well to the male with a high-pitched, feminine sounding voice. Our society does not respond well to someone who uses incorrect grammar, informal speech, or a regional accent. However, our society is less critical of the male who uses incorrect grammar, informal speech, or a regional accent than they are of females who exhibit these characteristics. The research is clear that females begin talking earlier than boys and acquire mature articulatory skills before boys. What then are the acceptable vocal qualities for males and females?

Addington (1968) completed a most impressive study on the judgement of the voice. Two males and two females simulated nine vocal characteristics and listeners rated the personalities of the speakers. Addington found that certain voice qualities were acceptable for both males and females. For example, both females and males could use increased rate and still be perceived in a positive fashion. Nasality was perceived by listeners as having a wide array of socially undesirable characteristics for both males and females. However, the male who had a high-pitched voice was seen as dynamic, feminine, and aesthetically inclined. In contrast, the female with a high-pitched voice was seen as more dynamic and extroverted. The female with the orotund vocal characteristic was perceived as humorless yet lively. The male with orotund vocal characteristic was seen as energetic, proud, and interesting. The female with the throaty vocal characteristic was seen an ugly, boorish, and uninteresting, whereas the male with the throaty vocal characteristic was seen as older, mature, and well-adjusted. The female with the tense vocal characteristic was seen as young and emotional. The male with the tense vocal characteristic was seen as older and more unyielding. Males and females with flat vocal characteristics were not seen a very positive light. Females with a thin voice were seen as emotionally and socially immature while simultaneously getting ratings of increased sense of humor. There were no significant correlations for the male with the thin voice. Females with the breathy voice were seen as feminine and shallow, whereas males with the breathy voice were seen as younger and more artistic.

It is difficult to suggest any definite conclusions based on the above results. These vocal differences exist whether a person is communicating with their own or the opposite gender, and therefore are not a function of cross-gender communication. Clearly, very different perceptions of females and males can be based on the same vocal characteristics.

A few differences have been noted specifically within the context of female–male interaction. These differences are, again, consistent with the distinction in stereotypical gender roles. Males tend to use greater intensity and talk louder than do females. Females tend to raise their pitch and speak in quieter tones when talking to men.

Space.   As early as the second grade, children are using the space norms of their culture. Elementary school children sit farther away from others and touch others less than preschool children. Lomranz, Shapira, Choresh, and Gilat (1975) had three-, five-, and seven-year-olds sit next to an unknown peer and perform a task. The three-year-olds sat closer than the other two groups and even touched the unknown peer. When children enter school, they start becoming more aware of the adult space norms. They find out it is no longer appropriate to sit in one another's lap and that the teacher wants space of her or his own. Although children usually learn the space norms of their culture by third or fourth grade, males and females still use space differently.

Young boys seem to need more space then young girls. This probably depends on conditioning and cultures because it occurs before the boys become physically larger than the girls. Most parents and other adults in the society reinforce boys for playing with toys that require more space (trucks) than those girls play with (dolls). The type of toy often determines the amount of space needed for play. Therefore, boys may learn the need for more space than girls do. However, the possibility of a biological impact should not be totally rejected. Some research has indicated that boys prefer to spend more time outside than girls, play in more areas than girls, and require as much as fifty percent more space than girls. As boys and girls mature, these noticeable spatial differences do not disappear.

Piercy (1973) may have described the spatial differences of males and females best when describing movement to a theater group:

> *Men expanded into available space. They sprawled, or they sat with spread legs. They put their arms on the arms of chairs. They crossed their legs by putting a foot on the other knee. They dominated space expansively. Women condensed. Women crossed their legs by putting one leg over the other and alongside. Women kept their elbows to their sides, taking up as little space as possible. They behaved as if it were their duty not to rub against, not to touch, not to bump a man. If contact occurred, the woman shrank back. If a woman bumped a man, he might choose to interpret it as a come-on. Women sat protectively using elbows not to dominate space, not to mark territory, but to protect their soft tissues. (p. 438)*

These observations suggest that women require less space, protect their bodies by using space, and are more likely to have their space invaded. The rest of this section examines each of these behaviors.

Research on gender differences concerning space has revealed several interesting distinctions. The personal space bubble surrounding women appears to be smaller than the personal space bubble for men. In public settings, female dyads stand closer together than male dyads. Male–female dyads, however, stand closest of all. The reactions of men and women placed in crowded versus uncrowded rooms for periods of one hour have been found very different. Women felt the experience was pleasant, they liked others more, and found others to be friendlier than the men. Men found the situation to be an unpleasant experience, liked others less, and found others to be less friendly. In waiting-rooms, female pairs sit closer to each other than male pairs. Women are approached more closely than men by both males and females in initial interaction situations.

It seems that women require less space than men and do not become as upset if less space is awarded to them. This might be because women are more used to having their space invaded or having to share their space with another. In the typical household, it is the mother who gives up space to the children and her husband. Rarely is it the man who gives up space. When a new child is born, it usually is the mother who gives up her space and time to spend time with the child. Another reason for women requiring less space could be that of the difference in the male–female status roles. By virtue of having been granted higher status in the society, the male may have been granted the right to more space in the perceptions of men and women alike.

Given the abundance of research evidence showing major differences in the use of space by males and females, it should come as no surprise that females and males use space differently when encountering one another. Silveira (1972) found that when male–female pairs approach one another on the street, the female is expected to yield the space. Nineteen mixed-sex pairs were observed. In twelve of the nineteen cases, the woman moved out of the man's way. In four of the seven remaining cases, both sexes moved to make way for the other. In only three of the cases did the man move to make way for the woman.

So what does this body of research suggest? In typical female–male interactions, the male may command the bulk of the available space. The female may not contest for more of the space. Although in spatial invasion studies involving strangers it is usually the woman who flees the scene, in female–male interactions the female is unlikely to perceive her loss of space during an interaction as an invasion. Perhaps women feel that to be perceived as affiliative they must not fight over space. Perhaps they feel it is easier to give in than to either fight or flee. Perhaps they simply need less space, so they don't even notice that the male takes more. In any event, the negotiation of space in female–male interaction usually is a smooth process, requiring the conscious attention of neither. To the extent that occupation of more space reflects dominance, we again find the male exerting a dominant position in interaction with the female.

Touch.   It is sad but true that in this society, human touch diminishes from infancy on. Think of all the songs associated with touch. Our culture sings a lot about touch, but rarely engages in the act itself. This society is very selective about whom, when, and where we touch. In the eyes of many, it is almost a crime for two males to touch each other, except in the context of a sports event. If two males touch in this society, people immediately read something negative into it. As early as infancy, there are differences noted in female–male touch. Female babies receive more touch than male babies, but that starts to diminish around two years of age. Boys are encouraged to touch less and learn to need touch less.

Women seem to be more concerned about the type of touch than men. Nguyen, Heslin, and Nguyen (1975) asked unmarried college students what a pat, a squeeze, a brush, and a stroke meant when directed to different body parts by someone of the opposite sex. The differences between the two sexes were striking. Males understood the differences among patting, stroking, and squeezing, but were not concerned with the body part being touched. Men felt that warmth, love, sexual desire, and pleasantness all had the same meaning. On the other hand, women were very concerned about the body part involved. They felt that touch on the hands, head, face, arms, and back meant love and friendlessness. However, women felt that touch in the genital areas and breasts was a sign of sexual desire. Hence, women distinguish the type of touch and part of body being touched to mean either friendship or sexual desire. Men associated friendship and sexual desire with similar touch. Such perceptual difference in the meaning of touch portends problems within female–male interactions.

In male–female relationships, it is often the man who initiates the touch. Women are taught that for them to initiate the touch could mislead the man into thinking the woman is loose or promiscuous. Society is quite clear on this. Men should be allowed to initiate touch, not women. However, when women are approaching others, they often stop out of the touching range. In the male–female relationship, the man usually moves in on the woman and touches first. It is rarely the other way around.

In conclusion, until our society eliminates some of its cultural taboos on touching behavior (male touching male, female initiating touch with male) we will remain a very noncontact-oriented society. We have been conditioned from childhood not to reach out and touch someone. Touch between males and females in this society is reserved mostly for intimate relationships, and the touch is seen most often as sexual in nature. What little occurs outside this narrow range generally is initiated by the male (command again?) and accepted by the female (acquiescence?). Unlike many nonverbal behaviors we have discussed in this chapter, however, touch is much more likely to occur at the conscious than the nonconscious level. Touch between members of the opposite gender in this society carries such strong sexual overtones that it is virtually impossible for touch to occur without being noticed by one or both of the interactants.

In this section, we have enumerated many distinctions between females and males in nonverbal communication behavior. Table 12–1 provides a brief summary of some more important ones. You may find it a useful guide to a review of this material.

LIKING AND COURTSHIP OF THE AMERICAN MALE AND FEMALE

Scheflen (1965) studied the American courtship rituals and how they related to liking and disliking. He did a content analysis of films of various encounters and found some similar behavioral patterns across interpersonal encounters that related to dating or courtship. He called these behaviors *quasi-courtship cues* and classified them into four categories.

The first category Scheflen called *courtship readiness cues*. He said that this category included such things as reduced eye bagginess, higher muscle tone,

TABLE 12–1   **"Sterotypical" Nonverbal Behaviors of Males and Females When Communicating with One Another**

PERFORMED PRIMARILY BY MALES	PERFORMED PRIMARILY BY FEMALES
Stares	Lowers eyes
Frowns	Smiles
Holds head erect	Tilts head
Points	Doesn't point
Takes more space	Takes up less space
Moves in on other's space	Moves out of way of other/yields space
Initiates touch	Accepts touch
Has erect posture	Pulls body in
Stands/sits with legs apart	Stands/sits with legs together
Initiates looks	Bats eyelashes
Hands on hips	Hands at sides or in lap
Strokes	Cuddles

reduced jowl sag, little slouching, no shoulder hunching, and decreased belly sag. He concluded that both males and females engage in courtship readiness behavior. After all, no one is attracted by a saggy belly in either a male or female.

The second category was called *preening behavior.* This category is characterized by behavior such as stroking one's hair, fixing makeup, fixing clothes, looking in a mirror, leaving buttons open on shirts or blouses, adjusting suit coats, pulling up socks, and adjusting a tie. Obviously, both males and females engage in some of the above, depending on the situation.

The third category consisted of what Scheflen called *positional cues.* These cues are reflected in seating arrangements. A person positions herself or himself so that others know they are not open to conversation with anyone other than the person they are already talking to. For example, arms, legs, and bodies are arranged so that others cannot enter the conversation without great difficulty.

The fourth category is *actions of appeal or invitation.* These are cues such as rolling the pelvis, flirtatious glances, holding another's gaze, crossing a leg to expose thigh, over-the-shoulder breast thrust, showing wrist or palm, and flexing muscles. Obviously, all of the above categories are related to male–female quasi-courtship behavior. Both genders use cues from each category to attract the other sex.

In a similar vein, Birdwhistell suggested that there are twenty-four steps from initial male–female contact to a fully intimate sexual relationship, and that there is a sequence to the steps. For example, if a female does not reciprocate a male's eye contact, then he should not progress to the next step. Both females and males are labeled as fast or slow depending on whether they follow the steps. If steps are ignored or skipped, then someone is labeled as fast. If someone does not respond to steps or chooses to ignore steps, then he or she is labeled as slow. However, at certain steps it is expected that the female will slow the process. For example, a young man expects the woman to block him, as least for a while, when he starts for her breast.

Perhaps Morris gave us the most popular view of the courtship ritual. He suggests there are twelve steps that couples in Western culture go through, from initial contact through intimacy. He indicates that the steps have an order and that order usually is followed in female–male relationships. The steps are as follows: (1) eye to body, (2) eye to eye, (3) voice to voice, (4) hand to hand, (5) arm to shoulder, (6) arm to waist, (7) mouth to mouth, (8) hand to head, (9) hand to body, (10) mouth to breast, (11) hand to genitals, and (12) genitals to genitals or mouth to genitals. One who skips steps or fails to respond to a step may be seen as fast or slow.

The first six steps of the twelve steps can be classified as immediacy-like behavior. However, the last six are definitely intimate behavior. Therefore, because immediate behaviors often foreshadow subsequent intimate ones, immediacy often can be mistaken for an overture to intimacy. Recognize that although we see the first six steps as within the immediacy range, another individual may see everything from step 3 on as intimate.

We have taken the time to outline the Scheflen, Birdwhistell, and Morris examinations of male and female behavior not because of a particular interest in courtship behaviors, but because many of these same behaviors frequently are used in female–male interactions that are not intended as courtship. Certainly the first few of the Morris steps and nearly all of the Scheflen behavior occurs in noncourtship encounters between females and males. They are common behaviors exhibited every day in offices, stores, classrooms, libraries, hospitals, and virtually everywhere else where females and males come in contact.

Clearly, these behaviors are an invitation to communicate, even if they are not intended as an initiation of courtship. Rejection of such an invitation, if made quietly—by simply turning away for example—usually terminates the invitive behaviors if they are unwelcome. Sometimes, however, the outcome is not so easy or positive. People differ greatly in their sensitivity to the nonverbal behavior of others. Some, as an extreme example, see sexual harassment in what others see as a flirtatious glance. People are also sometimes insensitive to their own nonverbal behavior and cannot understand when someone else takes offense.

How can these problems be avoided? It is not likely that they can be avoided completely. However, becoming aware that these behaviors exist and can be subject to multiple interpretations goes a long way toward keeping the number of problems down. Remember, meaning is in people's minds. It is not in words, and it is not in nonverbal behavior. When we find a person's words offensive, we can tell the person so they can try to avoid the problem in the future, we can ignore the offense and go on to something else, or we can avoid that person so we don't have future interactions. We have similar options with offensive nonverbal behavior. If we offend others, similar options are available. If we, or they, choose the confrontation route, serious conflict is most likely to occur. The relationship between the two individuals will be damaged, possibly very severely, and friends of the parties most likely will become involved. Obviously, prevention is better than cure, and appropriate instruction in nonverbal behavior and communication is the best preventive system found to date.

Nonverbal Sensitivity.   We alluded to the fact that some people are more sensitive to nonverbal cues than others. Is it possible that one gender is more sensitive than the other? Some observers claim that females are more sensitive to nonverbal cues than males. On at least one measure of nonverbal sensitivity, the Profile of Nonverbal Sensitivity Test (PONS), females do score higher. Women have been found to be more accurate in judging various emotional states than men. Most of the literature suggests that women are more responsive nonverbally than men. For example, they look at others more, give up space to others, allow others to touch them more, and can interpret facial expressions more easily than men.

Are females more nonverbally sensitive than males? It seems that they may be, but the reason for any difference is not clear. Perhaps males are less sensitive because they have not been encouraged in this culture to be responsive. If men were encouraged to be more responsive, they might be as sensitive to nonverbal cues as women. Responsiveness in large part is cued to the nonverbal behavior of others, so it is hard to be responsive without developing nonverbal sensitivity.

Women tend to show emotions more than men in this society. It is acceptable for women to externalize their emotions but not for men. Men are taught that to show emotions or to be expressive is a sign of weakness or failure. Therefore, men have learned not to be too expressive. Perhaps this why men have more difficulty recognizing the implications of the nonverbal behavior of others. They may simply see such behavior as meaningless and not in need of interpretation.

Apparently, women generally are perceived as more nonverbally immediate than men. Women are more responsive nonverbally and more sensitive to nonverbal cues. They smile more often, use more pleasant facial expressions, allow others to touch them more, and allow others to approach them more. Throughout this chapter, we have alluded to the "commanding" male as the initiator of more of the interaction between females and males. Could it be that the true initiator is the female? Mehrabian's (1972, 1981) research on affiliative tendencies and approach behavior indicates that women definitely have more affiliative tendencies and approachable behavior than men. Affiliative tendencies are behaviors that show others how friendly we are. Women definitely display more affiliative, responsive tendencies than men. Men display more dominating tendencies than women. Who really initiates and controls female–male interactions?

ADVANTAGES OF IMMEDIACY

Because males and females who appear more immediate are perceived as more pleasant and friendly than males or females who appear to be nonimmediate, they are perceived as more approachable. Males and females who appear to be more immediate are also perceived as more likeable than males or females who appear to be nonimmediate. Others want to be closer to likeable people, talk to them more often, and even spend more time with them.

More immediate males and females are perceived as more popular than males or females who appear to be nonimmediate. Popular people usually appear to be more approachable and friendly, so immediacy increases popularity.

Males and females who appear to be more immediate receive more communication from others than nonimmediate males or females. People approach and want to communicate more with people who give off cues that say they are approachable. The immediate person, through her or his nonverbal behavior, says that he or she is open to communication and welcomes it. The nonimmediate person discourages communication through her or his nonverbal cues. For example, are you more likely to approach someone who has an open body position to ask the time or someone who has her or his arms folded across their chest and is looking at the ground? Obviously, most of us would approach the open person and ask the time.

Notice that all of these advantages are common to all kinds of relationships. They are not unique to female–male relationships. We reemphasize them here, however, because immediacy is critical to the development of relationships between females and males. Immediacy in these relationships may also have certain disadvantages.

DISADVANTAGES OF IMMEDIACY

Immediacy leads to more communication. This is something that many people do not want. Increased communication means increased interaction with someone despite their gender. Therefore, if one wants to decrease communication in a female–male relationship, he or she should be nonimmediate. There are times when we do not want more communication.

Immediacy can lead to misperception. For example, the female who smiles constantly at many males might be perceived as an easy target. She might simply be immediate. The nonverbal behavior of immediacy could be misjudged as cues suggesting an intimate relationship. Think of some immediate behavior and see how this might happen. Imagine you're in a restaurant and the person two tables away smiles at you and has direct eye contact. You might misperceive their behavior.

Immediate behavior can cause some negative perceptions for both males and females. For example, the immediate male might be perceived by other males as effeminate or girlish, whereas the immediate female might be perceived as easy or friendly but dumb. One must be cautious not to be too immediate and decide what situations dictate immediacy and what situations do not. Clearly, not all female–male relationships call for increased immediacy.

THE ANDROGYNOUS PERSON

The term *androgyny* is a combination of the Greek words *andros,* meaning man, and *gyne,* meaning woman. An androgynous person is one who can associate with both masculine and feminine characteristics. In terms of psychological gender orientation, this type of individual can adapt to a variety of roles by engaging in either responsive or assertive behavior, depending on the situation. At present, the responsive role in this society is primarily defined as the female's role and the assertive role is primarily defined as the male's role. Androgyny is the answer for those who want to be more assertive while still being responsive and for those who want to be more responsive while still being assertive. The androgynous person can be warm, compassionate, sincere, helpful, sympathetic, and acquiescent in one situation, and in another situation be competitive, risk-taking, assertive, independent, and dominant. An androgynous male might be a weight lifter (stereotypical male) who works in a home for underprivileged children on weekends. An androgynous female might be a home economics teacher (stereotypical female) who enjoys watching professional football and playing pool.

Typically, the androgynous person is highly flexible in her or his behavior. The individual does not feel limited in her or his verbal or nonverbal communication with others. He or she is fully aware of and adaptable to the affiliative and control needs of others. Thus, the androgynous person can sense another's needs and adapt to them. This type of person recognizes when an interaction partner requires affiliative behavior and can provide it. They also recognize when someone needs to exert dominance and adapt to that situation. People who are gender-role stereotyped (can only perform typically male or female behavior) are not as flexible in their verbal and nonverbal communication. They respond in the stereotypical ways. They are also less responsive to the needs of others. In sum, the androgynous individual is likely to be more sensitive nonverbally than the stereotypical male or female.

Bem (1974) and Richmond and McCroskey (1989) and others who have researched the area of androgyny have found that the androgynous male and the androgynous female are more flexible and adaptive to situations than males and females who follow the traditional roles assigned by society. Societal norms dictate that the female must usually react in a responsive manner in some situations and do not allow for assertiveness on her part. Similar norms dictate that the male must react in an assertive or dominant way in some situations and do not allow for responsiveness on his part. People who follow these societal norms are gender-typed. Their communication behavior corresponds closely to the normative descriptions we have provided in this chapter.

Some individuals, however, find these norms an impediment to their full development as females or males. They see each of the stereotyped gender roles as representing only half a person. Unfortunately, the solution advanced sometimes is as bad as the problem. Females sometimes attempt to assume the behavior role of males or males that of females. All that is accomplished in such attempts is to exchange one half a person for the other half, and the new half usually does not work as well as the old one did.

There are situations that call for the male to be responsive and situations that call for the female to be assertive. One should remember that the traditional roles developed because they were functional in some ways. There will remain situations where males should be assertive and females should be responsive. Therefore, individuals should strive to develop some nonverbal skills that help increase responsiveness in males and assertiveness in females, whichever is needed, without sacrificing the alternate skills that already have been developed. The androgynous person is much more likely to be able to respond appropriately across contexts than the gender-role stereotyped individual. To respond appropriately, one must be able to assess the situation. If the situation calls for assertive behavior, then be assertive. If the situation calls for responsive behavior, then be responsive. Competent communicators are capable of both types of behavior and smart enough to know which is appropriate.

A GLOSSARY OF TERMINOLOGY

Androgyny is a combination of the Greek words *andros,* meaning man, and *gyne,* meaning woman. An androgynous person is one who can associate with both masculine and feminine characteristics. Such individuals can adapt to a variety of roles by engaging in either responsive or assertive behavior, depending on the situation.

Quasi-courtship cues are nonverbal cues used to show intention to courtship. They are classified into four categories: courtship readiness cues, preening behavior, positional cues, and actions of appeal or invitation.

▲ 13

Supervisor–Subordinate Relationships

The relationship between supervisors and subordinates is best characterized by the dominance–submissiveness continuum. This indicates the degree to which a person feels in power, in control, or influential versus feeling weak, controlled, or dominated (Mehrabian, 1981). Mehrabian continues by suggesting that the power metaphor underlies the "inference of dominant–submissive feelings" (p. 58). In this and other cultures, we can learn the relationship between two people by watching their approach or avoidance behavior. In many relationships, it is clear who is the supervisor and who is the subordinate. The person of higher status is given more space, allowed to touch the person of lower status more, and is considered the dominant person in the relationship.

What is status? It is generally defined as a person's rank in a group. Therefore, in most relationships someone is usually of higher status and someone is of lower status by virtue of age, experience, training, education, or other factors. Mehrabian (1981), citing Lott and Sommer (1967), suggests that it is easy to identify high-status and low-status persons in a visitor situation:

> The clue to status and dominance differences is the degree of hesitation and discomfort shown by the visitor at each stage as he is about to approach the person he visits. If the status differential is significant, he must wait for permission before he makes any major move in coming closer, or risk offending the higher status other. He will be hesitant to presume familiarity by casually dropping into a seat, as this implies relaxation and an intention to stay on. Indeed, even when invited to sit, the visitor will

In many instances, you can determine who is the subordinate and who is the superior simply by observing nonverbal cues.

> *still behave in a way that is consistent with his status in the situation as he sees it. If there is more than one visitor's chair, he will tend to sit at a distance from his host. If the two are intimate or are peers, however, the visitor will feel free to take a seat without being invited to do so, one close to the person he visits. (p. 58–59)*

In conclusion, although we like to think all people are equal, we know better. There are high-status persons and low-status persons in almost any relationship. For example, in the teacher–student relationship, the teacher is generally perceived as the higher-status person. In the work environment, the supervisor is generally the higher-status person, the subordinate the lower-status person. The remainder of this chapter discusses supervisor–subordinate relationships in the work environment. It looks at the distinctive characteristics of the supervisor–subordinate relationship and reviews the nonverbal characteristics in such relationships.

DISTINCTIVE CHARACTERISTICS

What makes the supervisor–subordinate relationship in the work environment different from any other supervisor–subordinate relationship? Let's look at the distinctive characteristics from a practical standpoint. First, a supervisor in the work environment has the legitimate right to request that certain job responsibilities be carried out by the subordinate. In the stereotypical male–female relationship, the male (stereotypically the dominant one) may ask the female (stereotypically the submissive one) to carry out certain duties. Does the male have a legitimate right to require the female to do certain things? He might think so, but usually he does not. It depends on whether the female grants him the right to insist that she do certain things. Most organizations, however, have certain job responsibilities that are delegated to each person and that person must carry them out. Therefore, the supervisor in an organization can ask, will ask, and expects his or her subordinates to carry out certain tasks.

Second, the supervisor–subordinate relationship demands that a certain amount of respect be given to the supervisor because of his or her higher position or title. A coauthor of the text encountered a student who always addressed her as "Teach," rather than by an appropriate title. The informality implied that the student knew the teacher better than the other students, and thus created a problem in the classroom for her. To cure the student of the behavior, the teacher simply ignored him when he used the name "Teach." Once, the teacher found out that the student did not like being called Charles but wanted to be called Chuck. She called the student Charles in front of the student's peers. The student asked the teacher not to call him Charles anymore and she agreed if the student would refrain from calling her "Teach." The relationship was restored to its proper supervisor–subordinate level. The teacher received the respect she had earned and the student received respect from the teacher.

Third, in supervisor–subordinate relationships, the supervisor can bestow rewards or punishments on the subordinate. Most organizations grant any supervisor a certain amount of rewards and punishments to use as motivators for employees. For example, many organizations allow supervisors to dock an employee's pay if he or she does not complete a job. Many organizations allow supervisors to rate employees on the quality of their work. If the quality is rated low, the subordinate might be asked to leave. Thus, the higher-status person in an organization generally has the control over the rewards and punishments distributed to the lower-status persons. The higher-status person may not directly be in control of rewards and punishments. However, he or she may be asked to participate in assessing what types of rewards and punishments should be given.

In summary, the three main distinctive characteristics in the supervisor–subordinate relationship in the work environment are as follows: The supervisor has the legitimate right to ask her or his subordinates to perform certain job responsibilities; the supervisor has a right to higher status; and the supervisor can often bestow rewards or punishments on the subordinate. These unique relational characteristics establish the power (dominance–submissiveness) feelings in a supervisor–subordinate relationship.

ROLE OF NONVERBAL MESSAGES

As with any other relationship, the nonverbal messages primarily help in defining the supervisor–subordinate relationship. Nonverbal messages such as touch, seating, tone of voice, use of time, use of space, and artifacts and objects all contribute to defining who's the boss and who's the employee. They also help define how "big" the boss is and how low the status of the employee is. Korda (1975) proves the power metaphor in the supervisor–subordinate relationship. He states,

> *it isn't necessary to be six feet tall and built like a football tackle, but there are some physical signs that hint at power—a certain immobility, steady eyes, quiet hands, broad fingers, above all a solid presence which suggests that one belongs where one is, even if it's somebody else's office or bed. (p. 19)*

A stranger who understands status hierarchies when entering an organization can figure out who is higher status and who is lower status by looking at the various symbols. Common status symbols are found in many organizations: job titles, pay, clothing, size and location of desk or office, type of car assigned (if cars are assigned), secretaries, privacy, furnishings, privileges (such as not having to punch a time clock), ceremonies of induction, and possessions such as a home, private automobile, or stereo.

The role of nonverbal messages in organizations is to define the status of the individuals in the organizations. This helps a newcomer to know how to communicate with an individual. It is critical that statuses are somewhat clear so that people can adapt their communication accordingly. When a higher-status person is offended by the communication of a lower-status person, it can have dire consequences both for the lower-status person and the organization. In conclusion, the following quotation from Flippo illustrates how important nonverbal messages of status are in organizations:

> *With the company, however, many of the symbols are within the control of the management, and constitute the basis for many bloody battles. Executives have gotten down on hands and knees to measure and compare sizes of offices. Windows are counted, steps from the President's offices are paced off, secretaries are sought, parking space is fought for, and company cars are wrangled. (p. 219)*

Although we joke about status symbols, we are still uneasy about our own status. Everybody wants some status. Those who say they want none are kidding themselves. Through nonverbal messages, we establish or communicate our status to others. The rest of this section reviews each nonverbal message and how that message communicates status or power (dominance–submissiveness) in the supervisor–subordinate relationship.

Physical Appearance. Two men enter the executive vice president's waiting room. Both are there to be interviewed for the same position: assistant to the executive vice president. They approach the secretary simultaneously. Applicant A is wearing a solid-colored gray suit with a pale blue shirt and a blue-, gray-, and black-striped tie. Applicant B is wearing a black and red plaid suit coat with a solid black shirt and a red tie. The secretary says to Applicant A, in a very pleasant but professional tone, "Ms. Smith will be with you in a few minutes. Please be seated." The secretary says to Applicant B, in a very sneering tone, "Ms. Smith is very busy and will see you in a little while. You'll have to wait over there."

Which applicant is likely to get the job? Applicant A has the edge over Applicant B because his dress and appearance fit the expectations of the organization. Applicant B may be more qualified, but his appearance is going to hurt his chances. According to Korda (1975), the "overriding essential of all corporate business clothing is that it establish power and authority" (p. 230). Plaids do not establish power and authority. Solid colors do.

Clothing often determines how the receiver reacts to the wearer. Korda (1975) suggests that "people who look successful and well educated receive preferential treatment in almost all of their social or business encounters" (p. 12). The employee who dresses for success is more likely to be successful. Business clothing should establish power and status. People who dress accordingly are much more likely to be considered for better jobs, get promotions, and receive preferential treatment. We know that in the supervisor–subordinate relationship, the type of dress is often determined by the organization, the job in the organization, and the status of the person. For example, a machinist will most always been seen in a pair of coveralls. However, if he or she appears at a company party or function in an outfit that denotes power and status, he or she might be the next job boss in the machinist unit. Therefore, it is important not only on the job but off the job to appear as if one belongs to that organization.

Granted, styles for men and women are not always the same, and styles for different organizations vary. For example, a college professor can dress more casually than an IBM executive. The college professor can dress more casually than can her or his chairperson or a dean or president of the university. Employees must remember to dress for their role if they want to receive the proper respect. Clothing serves as a symbol of status. If people fail to dress as expected, their occupational mobility might be hindered. People dress according to their jobs to impress others. Others associate our clothing with socioeconomic status, achievement of goals, and satisfaction. Molloy (1975) suggests that what you wear to the office suggests whether you are there for business or monkey business. Molloy suggests that women who want to move up the executive ladder should not wear sweaters initially, because sweaters denote lower status. Sweaters that are soft and tight are also seen as sexy; few women want to get ahead by being seen as sexy. A sexy image will not get them the respect they might have earned. Molloy suggests that for women in business, the matching skirt and jacket is the look that says "I am a professional and want to be

People usually wear clothing that complements their jobs and organizations.

treated as one." Women, perhaps more than men, must be cautious about what they wear to the office. Primarily this is because the work world is just becoming used to the higher-status female executive. Therefore, unless they own the corporation, women should strive to adapt to clothing norms of the professional businesswoman.

Men should also wear the clothing dictated by the organization. Every organization has an image to uphold. People who do not fit the image will not move ahead unless they are unusually bright and irreplaceable. For example, the authors of this book have an eccentric friend who dresses rather casually: His shirt is always coming out of his slacks, usually unbuttoned too far, and has food stains from lunch. This person is employed by a large organization as a computer expert and analyst. They allow him to have his idiosyncratic dress because he is so good at his job. He is such an expert they are not interested in what he wears. This is an unusual case. His wife, on the other hand, is also very good at her job. She always wears a professional business outfit to work. This is because she is in an upper-level management position that few women ever have a chance to attain. Therefore, to command respect and liking from her subordinates, she must dress in the professional style dictated by the organization.

The color one chooses for clothing often denotes certain traits or moods. People who wear brighter colors typically want to be perceived as active. Timid or shy people often wear more drab colors so as not to call attention to themselves. However, research suggests that males and females both should avoid unusually bright colors in the work environment.

Bovee and Thill (1983) noted the top ten negative factors that may lead to rejection in an employment interview. Five of the top ten factors are nonverbal factors. Below is their list of the top ten negative factors:

* * *1. Has poor personal appearance*
* * *2. Is overbearing, overaggressive, conceited, has a superiority complex, seems to know it all*
* * *3. Is unable to express self clearly—poor voice, diction, grammar*
*   *4. Lacks planning for career—no purpose or goals*
* * *5. Lacks interest and enthusiasm—passive, indifferent*
* * *6. Lacks confidence and poise—nervous, ill at ease*
*   *7. Has failed to participate in extracurricular activities*
*   *8. Overemphasizes money—interested only in the best-paying job*
*   *9. Has poor scholastic record—just got by*
*   *10. Is unwilling to start at the bottom—expects too much too soon*

The factors marked by asterisks deal with various facets of nonverbal behavior, including physical appearance, kinesics, haptics, paralanguage and vocalics, chronemics, facial expressions, and eye behavior. These nonverbal behaviors are crucial for competing in the job market.

Lewis (1980) stresses that one's body type might determine how he or she is treated in the work environment. He suggests that endomorphs are often not hired because they are judged by their body type as lazy or unqualified. However, the ectomorph is usually perceived as intelligent and might have a better chance at a job. Being an ectomorph can have its drawbacks. People might perceive an ectomorph as high-strung and anxious. Mesomorphs are the most likely to be hired, promoted, and retained. They are perceived by employers as dependable and confident.

Artifacts such as briefcases, watches, glasses, and jewelry denote a person's status or power in an organization. Higher-status persons usually have more expensive briefcases and watches than lower-status persons. Glasses denote intelligence. One must be careful not to overdo jewelry. Too much jewelry detracts from one's overall appearance. Although jewelry can be a sign of wealth, it can also be a sign that someone is insecure about her or his position. Jewelry should be kept at a minimum for both males and females in the work world.

Based on the research on general physical attractiveness, it is safe to conclude that the employee who is generally attractive is more likely to get the better positions and opportunities. There have been instances where people have not received jobs because they were so physically unattractive. Employees who are unattractive should strive to make themselves more attractive so they can reap the same benefits as their attractive counterparts.

The following are conclusions that we can safely draw about appearance and dress in the supervisor–subordinate relationship. The higher people are in an organization, the more status their clothing denotes. The higher people are in an organization, the more idiosyncratic they can be about their clothing styles and appearance. Lower-status people must conform to the clothing and appearance norms of the organization more than the extremely high-status persons. The dress for male and females varies from one organization to another. More attractive personnel are more likely to receive preferential treatment. Less attractive personnel are more likely to receive negative treatment. The person who adapts to the image and appearance norms of the organization is likely to be accepted more readily, liked more, given better opportunities, and given more preferential treatment.

Gesture and Movement.   Gestures and movement can indicate the relationship between boss and subordinate. When two strangers meet, it is relatively easy to figure out which one is of higher status by looking at the posture of each. The person with the relaxed body position is the one who is perceived as having higher status by both. In ongoing relationships, similar postural cues suggesting relative status often are present also. The higher-status person in an organization (the supervisor) can assume a relaxed stance or posture. The lower-status person assumes a watchful, tense, cautious posture. The higher-status person is already in control; the lower-status person is trying to get some control over her or his own world.

When speaking with a higher-status person, a lower-status person is likely to exhibit more adaptive nonverbal behavior. This is primarily because he or she is anxious about communicating with a higher-status person. As the higher-status and lower-status persons become more familiar with each other, the lower-status person may exhibit less adaptors. People who exhibit too many adaptors are perceived by others as anxious and tense. Therefore, whether one is of higher or lower status, he or she should try not to exhibit adaptive behavior. Chewing on one's nails does not convey confidence or competence.

In sitting positions, the higher-status person is allowed to assume the more relaxed posture. For example, the higher-status person can slide back and relax in her or his chair, whereas the lower-status person almost "sits at attention." If the lower-status person is familiar with the higher-status person, he or she may sit in a more relaxed position. When in doubt, always assume the more rigid, upright posture when communicating with someone of higher status. Relaxation by the subordinate can be perceived by the higher-status person as a sign of disrespect or apathy. Relaxed posture can also be a sign of defiance or arrogance. However, if an employee assumes the relaxed posture without knowing her or his supervisor well, it usually is simply a sign that the subordinate does not know what is acceptable and what is not.

People with higher status usually keep their heads raised and shoulders straight when conversing with people of lower status. People with lower status lower their shoulders and may keep their heads lowered during the interaction. In other words, the higher-status person projects the image of the more dominant and the lower-status person projects the image of the less-dominant person. The higher-status person might lean over the lower-status person if he or she is seated. If both are seated, the higher-status person might lean backward in the chair while the lower-status person leans toward the higher-status person. This does not mean that the lower-status person looks cowed or belittled. It only means that one assumes the role of dominance and one assumes the nonverbal behavior of submissiveness. LaFrance and Mayo (1978) suggest that while sitting or standing, the higher-status person will exhibit arm positions different from those of the lower-status person. The higher-status person will have one arm in his or her lap and the other over the back of the chair. Lower-status people sit with their hands together or their arms at their sides. LaFrance and Mayo conclude:

> *The posture of the person with the higher status is marked by a sideward and backward tilt of the torso, crossed legs, loosely extended fingers, and the head resting on the back of a chair or couch. The lower-status member of the encounter sits upright, with both feet flat on the floor and hands clasping some object or clenched together. (p. 99)*

Think carefully: When was the last time you interviewed for a job? Did you sit or stand casually or as if you were interested and at attention? Think of the time you had to go see a teacher about a problem you were having in her or his class? How did you sit or stand? Probably in a very tentative, rigid pose, waiting for them to set the pace of the interaction.

In conclusion, persons of higher status are afforded the right to have a more relaxed body position. Persons of lower status usually have a more tense body position when interacting with someone of higher status, and usually exhibit more adaptive behavior. Persons of lower status who assume a relaxed or casual body position in the presence of a person of higher status might be perceived as disrespectful, uninterested, or defiant. Therefore, in the organizational environment, until one is sure he or she knows what is acceptable with the supervisor and what is not, one should assume the nonverbal behavior that denotes respect, interest, attention, and submissiveness.

Face and Eye Behavior.   The face plays just as important a role in the supervisor–subordinate relationship as it does in any other. For example, the person who is considered the supervisor is likely to be able to express facial expressions more freely than the subordinate. The subordinate learns to mask or disguise certain expressions when talking with a supervisor. For example, the subordinate learns not to look sad, bored, disgusted, or uninterested when the supervisor is introducing a new way of doing things in the work environment. If the subordinate looks interested, he or she might be asked for information and can influence the supervisor about the decision.

Someone who looks bored or uninterested is much less likely to be asked for ideas. Therefore, facial expression can be used to the subordinate's advantage.

Persons of higher status usually receive more direct and prolonged eye contact with persons of lower status than vice versa. Persons of high status look at persons of lower status less and often avert their eyes when speaking with someone of lower status. The higher-status person controls the eye behavior in an interaction with a person of lower status. They control when it is the lower status person's turn to talk, to stop talking, to continue talking, or to remain silent. A higher-status person might use a steady gaze or stare to make the lower-status person uncomfortable or unsure. A higher-status person might stare to reinforce the oral communication. Looking at a high-status person while he or she is interacting can be a means for the low-status person to show respect and interest. Looking away can also be a means for the low-status person to show respect. However, if the low-status person looks away too long, he or she might be perceived as uninterested in what the higher status person is saying. In conclusion, higher-status persons can control the supervisor–subordinate relationship by using eye contact. Higher-status persons feel less compelled to look directly and longer at low-status persons, whereas low-status person feel more compelled to look directly and longer at high-status persons.

Vocal Behavior.   A person can use her or his voice to sound more authoritative and in control. For example, a lower-status person using a self-assured, confident voice is more likely to be promoted and given preferential treatment than a lower-status person who has a thin, squeaky, mousy-sounding voice. Whether you are male or female, voice qualities such as assuredness, confidence, maturity, animation, and extroverted tones denote authority. Other vocal qualities, such as shallowness, nasality, whininess, and unhealthy voices denote powerlessness. In other words, the voices that denote authority also denote higher credibility and status; voices that denote powerlessness also denote lower credibility and status. The monotone voice usually denotes boredom. People have been known not to be hired in certain professions because their voices did not fit the job. A man with a high-pitched, thin voice would not make a credible sports announcer. A woman with a throaty, deep voice might not make a good receptionist.

When communicating with a higher-status person, the lower-status person is likely to sound anxious and have more filled and unfilled pauses than normal. A higher-status person, when communicating with a lower-status person, will sound more assured and authoritative. As anxiety decreases, the lower-status person will display less disfluencies and filled and unfilled pauses.

When discussing vocal behavior, the use of silence must always be considered. Silence can mean many different things in a supervisor–subordinate relationship. Most generally, silence by the subordinate suggests they are paying attention to what the supervisor is saying. Silence can also mean that the subordinate knows better than to interrupt the supervisor. In most supervisor–subordinate relationships, the subordinate is generally silent more often than the supervisor, but there are exceptions. For example, if the subordinate is presenting a new idea to the supervisor, then he or she might be talking more than the supervisor. Silence from the supervisor might indicate that he or she is processing the subordinate's ideas.

In the supervisor–subordinate relationship, the supervisor is rarely judged on her or his voice qualities. However, the subordinate might be. The subordinate who sounds bored and lazy might be perceived negatively. Lastly, silence can be used to improve the supervisor–subordinate relationship. Silence on the subordinate's part might show respect or interest. Too much silence on the subordinate's part, however, might show that he or she is timid or shy.

Space. Perhaps more than other nonverbal behaviors, the use of space defines who is in the dominant role and who is in the submissive role. Studies reveal that higher-status persons within organizations are more likely to invade lower-status persons' interpersonal space than vice versa. The organizational structure informally says it is OK for the supervisor to invade or enter the subordinate's work area or personal space zone. Read the following from Whyte (1949) and see whether you have encountered similar instances of space invasion by supervisors.

> *In the heat of the rush hour, we have seen pantry supervisors running up and down stairs, trying to get orders, trying to find out what is holding up things in the kitchen. Since they have supervisor status, the kitchen workers do not resist them openly, but the invasion of an upstairs supervisor tends to disrupt relations in the kitchen. It adds to the pressure there, for it comes as an emergency and lets everybody know that the organization is not functioning smoothly. (p. 302)*

In organizations, supervisors are responsible for and are supposed to know how their subordinates are performing their job tasks. Therefore, they are given the power to invade the subordinate's domain and privacy. They may even invade their interpersonal space by standing closer to them.

Jorgenson (1975) found in one company that although pairs of equal and unequal status did not stand closer or farther apart, they did display different body orientations. People of equal status faced each other more and at a more direct angle, whereas people of unequal status did not. Mehrabian (1981) notes that the "prerogative to approach the other belongs to the one with higher status" (p. 63). He cites several studies in support of this conclusion. Sommer (1969) concludes that "higher-ups have more and better space, as well as greater freedom to move about" (p. 25). He suggests that this is obvious not only in our interpersonal relations but in the layout of businesses and corporations. This layout aspect is reviewed further in the section on environment.

Touch. The boss enters the subordinate's work area and stops to chat with a few subordinates about how things are going. As the boss is leaving, he or she pats each subordinate on the shoulder or squeezes their arm. Is this sexual harassment or is it simply a boss being a boss? Most people would agree that it is the latter. This supervisor is trying to let her or his employees know that he or she is pleased with their work and touch is one major means of doing so.

Lately, it has become increasingly more difficult for a higher-status person to touch a lower-status person of the opposite gender, and, occasionally, of the same gender. Touch has always been a means of letting subordinates know that you are pleased with them. Many supervisors complain that they are afraid to use touch as a means to communicate with their subordinates. Sexual harassment laws and policies have made touch a touchy issue in the work environment.

How do you know sexual harassment when you receive it? Well, it's like pornography; you think you know it when you see it, but there is no universal agreement on what it is. Let's look at another example. Supervisor John walks into Jane's office and saunters behind her desk and asks her how things are going. As she is answering he puts his hand on her neck and caresses it. He then goes on to tell her she could do better in his organization if "you know what I mean." Jane says "No" while moving away from his touch. This is a case of sexual harassment. If Supervisor John had entered Jane's office and sat across from her and asked how things were going and touched her on the arm when she answered, this would probably not be sexual harassment. This is probably the case of a higher-status person trying to encourage a lower-status person by touch.

That, of course, does not mean that Jane will see it that way. Consequently, our advice to supervisors is to keep hands off unless a very well-established, positive, but nonintimate relationship exists between you and your subordinate. Although research from a couple of decades ago showed that higher-status persons were freer to touch lower-status persons, times have changed. There are many other immediacy cues that can be used to indicate reassurance and friendship. Touch is not required to accomplish this objective, and in today's organizational environment, its use invites needless risk of misperception.

Environment.   This section views two major aspects of the environment: How much space or territoriality is granted to persons in organizations, and how furnishings convey status. Higher-status persons find positions from which to observe or view what is going on around them, and higher-status persons who seek such "head positions" or central positions are assumed by others to be of higher status or more dominant. In almost any organization in this country, you can enter any unit and distinguish the higher-status positions from the lower-status positions. One organization has a supervisor who has his office right in the middle of all the subordinates, and his office has glass walls. He can see every transaction that takes place and is considered by all as having the highest-status position. Many of us wouldn't want to be in the center of things, but he does. Many other supervisors have their territory protected by barriers such as other offices and secretaries to guarantee their privacy.

The higher-status person is more likely to move in on a subordinate's space than vice versa. It is assumed that the higher status person has the legitimate right to invade the space or privacy of a subordinate. Therefore, the higher-status person often moves in on the subordinate's space and the subordinate thinks nothing of it. The higher-status person also has territorial rights to more space than lower-status persons. Those with more space are viewed by others as being of higher status. The higher up someone is in an organization, the better protected their territory might be.

Korda (1975) suggests that "office furnishings have strong symbolic value. . . . Power lies in how you use what you have, not in the accoutrements per se" (pp. 230–231). We'd like to suggest that one can design an office or environment to reflect power and status, or immediacy, or both. The office that reflects both power and immediacy is the optimal environment. It allows one to assume a power or status position when needed and yet it allows one to assume an immediate, responsive position when needed. Most successful organizational leaders have both in one office.

In a large office, Korda suggests, furnishings should be arranged so that a person has to walk by several objects and walk the length of the office to reach the supervisor. Korda suggests the following for small offices where people want to convey power:

> *However small the office, it is important to have the visitor's chair facing toward you, so that you are separated by the width of your desk. This is a much better power position than one in which the visitor sits next to the desk, even though it may make access to your desk inconvenient to you. When a small office is very narrow (and most are) it is often useful to have the desk placed well forward in the room, thus minimizing the space available for the visitor, and increasing the area in which it is possible for you to retreat, at least psychologically. (p. 232)*

Earlier, we suggested that the optimal office is one that allows one to assume a power position or an immediate position. Korda has designed office space that he refers to as having *semisocial space* and *pressure space*. This is similar to our concept of the office that allows for status and immediacy. In the pressure area, people are focused strictly on business. In the semisocial area, people can be more at ease and relaxed.

Figure 13–1 gives an example of an office that includes both an area of power or status and an area of immediacy. Note that the higher-status person can stay behind the desk or come out from behind the desk and assume a more immediate role. This office is the optimal for a higher-status person. It allows her or him to break down the status barrier or to establish the status barrier needed when communicating with some persons.

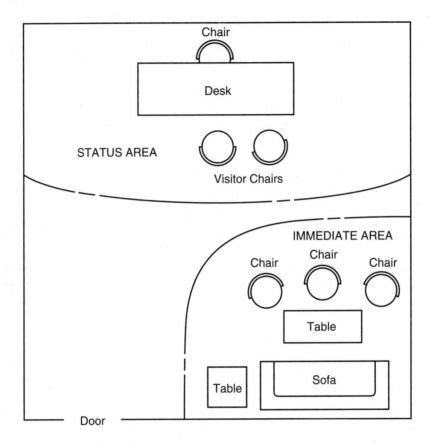

FIGURE 13–1 **Status Area vs. Immediate Area**

Other furnishings, such as the type of desk, the objects on the desk, the accompanying furnishings (such as chairs and sofas), windows, and color all enhance or inhibit status. People with large, imposing desks are usually perceived as having higher status. The objects on the desk denote status. The pictures on the wall denote status. The offices with windows in most organizations are considered the higher-status offices. The color, lighting, and carpeting all denote the rank of a person in an organization. The higher-status persons in organizations generally have more and better space than lower-status persons. American organizations use this as incentive to strive to do better or as a reward when one has done a job well. As an example, in our department, the full professors get their choice of the offices before associates and assistants. They also get their choice of furniture. When our department became computerized, the full professors received the computers and word processors before the associates and assistants.

Not surprisingly, then, higher-status persons usually have better territory than lower-status persons. Higher-status persons are usually given more space and better furnishings than lower-status persons. Office space and territory are a means that American organizations use to reward people for jobs well done. Lastly, the optimal office is one that allows for status and immediacy simultaneously.

Time.   Use of time communicates a person's feelings and attitudes toward an organization. Often, subordinates are judged by their supervisors on how they manage their time. Several years ago in our department, at the first faculty meeting of the year, the newest member of the faculty showed up a half-hour late and informed the rest of us that he couldn't stay more than an hour because his wife was picking him up and he had to leave. No one said a word—his career in the department was decided from that point on.

Gordon (1975) notes that during an interview, time can be a relevant factor in judging the interviewee. If an interviewee is late for the interview, this can suggest a lack of interest on her or his part. Gordon also notes that an interviewer can use time to advantage. The interviewer can use a chronemic technique to control the length of pauses and rate of speech of her or his own conversation. He or she can also control the length of time to wait to respond to the interviewee's comments. He calls the first technique *pacing* and the second technique *silent probe.* Both techniques might encourage the interviewee to talk more and thus give more information for the interviewer to use in evaluating the interviewee.

Time is a respected element in most organizations. It is a means of judging others. Those who are prompt are respected and rewarded. Those who are late are not respected and are often considered lazy and unreliable and are sometimes ejected from the organization. The time clock (whether real or imaginary) is part of an everyday American's work life. In business, time is money, and an employee who is casual about his or her use of time can cost an organization a fortune. Therefore, it is easier to fire and replace a time waster than to try to train the person to use time wisely.

Time and status are related. Higher-status persons are allowed to abuse time (be late or demand that others be on time) more than lower-status persons. Lower-status persons are expected to wait for higher-status persons. If a lower-status person leaves before the higher-status person arrives (although he or she is already late) the lower-status person is more likely to be in trouble than the higher-status person. Hall (1959) suggests that Americans of equal status allow a person five minutes of tardiness before an apology is expected. This culture demands that people be on time. Higher-status people are the only ones allowed to deviate from the norm.

Higher-status people can also demand more time from lower-status people. For example, the supervisor can ask her or his employees to put in extra time on a project, but the employees cannot ask a supervisor to do the same.

In organizations that use flextime, which allows employees to work their schedule around their daily lives, higher-status persons are allowed to choose the time schedules that fit them more than lower-status persons. For example, if a higher-status executive is a night owl, he or she will be allowed to choose a later schedule, whereas lower-status employees might still get the nine-to-five routine until they have earned the right to ask for a better schedule. This is not uncommon in hospitals, post offices, and similar organizations where night shifts are used. Most people do not want to work the 11 P.M. to 7 A.M. schedule, so the newest employees usually are assigned these schedules.

Time communicates many messages about status in supervisor–subordinate relationships. Higher-status persons are given more control over their time and subordinate's time, and can choose better time schedules. Lower-status persons must adapt to the higher-status person's time and are expected to devote more of their time to the higher-status person's assignments if asked.

CONCLUSIONS ABOUT SUPERVISOR–SUBORDINATE RELATIONSHIPS

Table 13–1 illustrates the supervisor's use of nonverbal codes that we have discussed in relation to the subordinate's use of these same codes. The superior role is the higher-status person or the one who is dominant or more powerful. The subordinate role is the lower-status person or the one who is submissive or less powerful. It is clear from Table 13–1 that the dominant or higher-status person can control the nonverbal codes to make himself or herself more dominant and more powerful. This has one big drawback: Communication between supervisor and subordinate will be influenced in a negative manner.

The greater the status differential between persons in an organization, the less effective the communication between supervisor and subordinate. The smaller the status differential between persons in organizations, the more effective the communication between supervisor and subordinate. Status differentials are always needed, but they don't need to be so large as to create major communication barriers. Status differentials can be reduced to a manageable level through interpersonal solidarity between supervisor and subordinate.

Wheeless (1978) suggests that solidarity is interpersonal closeness that forms favorable perceptions of the other and includes mutual trust. Higher solidarity exists when there is a high level of trust and mutual liking between persons. Therefore, as solidarity increases, effective communication increases between supervisor and subordinate. As solidarity increases, status decreases. We do not mean that one has to be buddy-buddy with one's subordinates, but a closer, more communicative relationship will improve the information flow between supervisor and subordinate. How does one increase solidarity? By increasing liking and trust. A good method is by using nonverbal immediacy. The supervisor who is immediate with her or his subordinates is perceived by them as caring, responsive, and trying to build solidarity while still maintaining her or his status. Let's look at the advantages and disadvantages of immediacy in the supervisor–subordinate relationship.

TABLE 13–1   **Superior and Subordinate Nonverbal Relationships**

NONVERBAL CODE	SUPERIOR (HIGHER STATUS)	SUBORDINATE (LOWER STATUS)
Appearance	Solid colors communicate power. Looks successful. Clothing should establish higher status. Can have idiosyncratic dress.	Looks less successful. Clothing states rank. Dress matches organizational standards. Must dress for respect.
Gesture and Movement	Relaxed body position. Calm, relaxed stance/pose. Relaxed posture. Fewer adaptors. Relaxed when seated. Head held high. Straight shoulders. Leans over others.	Tense body position. Watchful stance/pose. Tense posture. More adaptors. Sits at attention. Slightly bowed head. Lowered/slumped shoulders. Folds into self.
Face and Eye	Allowed to express facial expressions more freely. Looks at others more and longer. Controls turn-taking with eyes. Allowed to stare.	Learns to mask facial expressions (e.g., boredom). Gives more eye contact, but will also look away/down first. Watches superior for turn-taking cues. Does not stare.
Vocal Behavior	Sounds authoritative. Tries to sound like one with higher status and more credibility. Less anxious tones. Fewer disfluencies. Uses silence to communicate authority.	Sounds submissive. Tries to sound interested in what superior is saying. More anxious tones. More disfluencies. More filled and unfilled pauses. Uses silence to appear to be listening.
Space	Invades subordinate's space and privacy. Prerogative to approach. More and better space. More freedom to move about organization.	Cautious about entering superior's space or invading privacy. Lets superior approach. Less and not as good space. Less freedom to move about organization.
Touch	Initiates touch more. Controls relational touch. Freer to touch.	Receives touch from superior. Accepts touch. Never initiates touch. Reciprocates touch when appropriate.
Environment	Territorial rights on space. Central positions. Head positions. Erects barriers to keep others out of territory. Given more space. Better furnishings. Large desk.	Takes what space is assigned. Assumes low status space. Space is invaded by superiors. Given less space. Leftover furnishings. Smaller desk.

Continued

TABLE 13–1   *Continued*

NONVERBAL CODE	SUPERIOR (HIGHER STATUS)	SUBORDINATE (LOWER STATUS)
Scent	More freedom granted them on scents.	Less freedom granted them on scents.
Time	Abuse and use time more casually. Can arrive late or leave early. Freedom to deviate from time norm. Allowed to select optimal time work schedule. Can call unscheduled meetings.	Must be prompt. Not allowed to abuse time. Must follow time norms of organization. Follows time work schedule assigned. Must attend unscheduled meetings.

IMMEDIACY IN THE WORKPLACE

Advantages of Immediacy

The immediate supervisor is perceived as more accepting, responsive, and sensitive. Research shows that employees want a supervisor to be sensitive, warm, accepting, responsive, and immediate. Subordinates feel they can work better for that kind of supervisor. The supervisor who is immediate is more likely to gain cooperation from her or his subordinates without using coercive power. Cooperation is a key to any organization's success. Immediate supervisors generate more cooperation.

A supervisor's use of immediacy suggests an interest in and concern for the employee. Subordinates usually respond similarly. Immediacy promotes immediacy. Most subordinates will never be as immediate with their supervisors as their supervisors are with them because there still is the status barrier. Immediacy from the supervisor opens the channels for immediacy from the subordinate.

Lastly, immediacy improves communication between supervisor and subordinate. The relaxed subordinate feels freer to express her or his feelings to a supervisor than the anxious one. Immediacy helps subordinates relax and feel more comfortable with the supervisor.

Disadvantages of Immediacy

A supervisor who is immediate might be perceived by her or his boss as not being in control or being too easy with subordinates. This creates a double bind for the supervisor. How can one be immediate without being perceived as not being in control or being too friendly with one's subordinates? Simply put, do not be too immediate when the boss is near. Keep the status role distinct between supervisor and subordinate. Resume immediacy when the boss is gone.

Some subordinates try to use the boss who is immediate to their advantage. They think that the immediate supervisor is a pushover and can be manipulated. Remember, just because a supervisor is immediate does not mean that he or she cannot carry out orders and reprimand others.

Lastly, immediacy opens the lines of communication. Therefore, the supervisor might receive more communication than he or she can handle effectively, so, he or she has to learn what communication to handle and what to delegate or screen to others.

On balance, immediacy has more advantages for both the supervisor and the subordinate than it has disadvantages. It is only when immediacy is taken to excess that real problems are likely to arise.

A GLOSSARY OF TERMINOLOGY

Status is a person's position or rank in a group or organizational structure.

Supervisor is the manager or boss, the one who monitors, controls, and supervises others.

Subordinate is the employee.

▲ 14

Teacher–Student Relationships

The nonverbal component of the communication process is as important to the teacher–student relationship as the verbal component, and often much more important. Within the past twenty years, researchers, scholars, and practitioners have come to realize the relevance of nonverbal communication to the classroom environment. Earlier research on communication in the classroom was primarily on the verbal interaction between student and teacher.

The authors of the text have spent collectively almost fifty years working with and training teachers on how to be more effective communicators in the classroom environment. They have stressed the importance of both verbal and nonverbal communication. They have communicated with more than 40,000 teachers about what usually works and does not work in the typical classroom. Much of this chapter is devoted to discussing their conclusions about nonverbal communication and its impact on the teacher–student relationship.

DISTINCTIVE CHARACTERISTICS

Menges suggested the teacher is a controller, manager, and helper. The teacher acts as a controller by getting students to acquire certain behavior and knowledge. Teachers act as managers by selecting student activities and deciding what is the student's responsibility and what is the teacher's responsibility. Lastly, the teacher acts as helper by helping student understanding and expression of emotions and feelings. We would add to this list one other teacher responsibility. The instructor is

Teachers and students can have productive communication.

also responsible for being an entertainer. Teachers must know how to present material in an interesting and entertaining fashion. Students will then attend to it and retain it longer.

Society has (either implicitly or explicitly) established the above characteristics that make the student–instructor relationship distinctive. Teaching is perhaps the only profession in which people are allowed to have nearly total control over others (students). Parents often take their children to school the first day and say, "Handle Johnny (or Joanie) however you feel is best." We know that sometimes some teachers are not really trained or qualified to have such a high level of responsibility. Society expects teachers to control, manage, help, and entertain students and keep them happy. All of the above roles demand effective communication between teacher and student.

Instructors have a bigger responsibility to be effective communicators than any other group we discuss in this book. Teachers have control over children who have not yet formed their attitudes and ideas. If teachers are not effective communicators, they cannot control, manage, help or entertain their students. In fact, they will turn many students off to school before the students complete the elementary grades. This turning off can happen at any level. Teachers can either turn on or turn off students to school by their communication.

It is no wonder why so many students become alienated from school. In no other context within a free society are individuals required to spend more than six hours a day, five days a week, for months at a time listening to one other person. Yet this is what we demand of young children. We expect one person to hold the attention and maintain the interest of all those captive listeners. He or she must ensure that those captives learn all they need to know to become contributing adults in our society. An easy task? Society must think so, for in many areas we pay our teachers less than we do sanitation workers! Unfortunately, effective communication in the classroom may be the most difficult communicative task in society. Surprisingly, few teachers receive intensive training in communication. Most receive nothing more than an introductory class in public speaking, if they receive even that much. Only a small fraction receive any instruction in nonverbal communication.

ROLE OF NONVERBAL COMMUNICATION

As we learned in Chapter 1, nonverbal communication can function to repeat, contradict, substitute, complement, accent, or regulate the verbal. This is especially true of nonverbal communication in the classroom. In a survey of more than 10,000 teachers, we have found that most teachers feel that nonverbal behavior is a more effective communicative tool for improving student–teacher relationships than verbal. They feel this way because nonverbal communication permeates every facet of the classroom environment. In addition, many teachers are finding that nonverbal communication is more effective at helping them be better controllers, managers, helpers, and entertainers than verbal. Nonverbal communication is more subtle and can be used more often. Students get bored with instructor talk and eventually ignore it. Teachers can use nonverbal behavior to communicate to students without making a big point of it.

Ambady and Rosenthal (1993) completed a landmark study titled "Half a Minute: Predicting Teacher Evaluations from Thin Slices of Nonverbal Behavior and Physical Attractiveness." These researchers conducted three studies. In studies one and two, subjects were asked to rate college teachers' and high school teachers' nonverbal behavior and physical attractiveness based on ten-second silent video clips. In study three, they investigated whether strangers' ratings of teachers would predict nonverbal behavior and physical attractiveness from study one and two if even "more thinned slices of the video" were shown. The clips were reduced from ten seconds to five and two seconds. The results were astonishing. The results revealed the following:

> [T]here were no significant differences in the accuracy of judgments based on video clips 10s, 5s, and 2s in length. In addition, there were no significant differences in the accuracy of judgments for the two samples of

teachers. . . . Moreover, judgments based on 30s exposures (three 10s clips of each teacher) were not significantly more accurate than judgments based on 6s exposures (three 2s clips of each teacher). (pp. 437–438)

Ambady and Rosenthal (1993) suggest that the human ability to form impressions is strongly supported by their studies. In fact, as has always been suggested in the nonverbal literature, impression formation takes places very early in a relationship. Often, these initial impressions determine the communication that follows. They conclude that based on molar nonverbal behavior shown in very brief (under 30 seconds) silent video clips, we evaluate our teachers as accepting, active, attentive, competent, confident, dominant, empathic, enthusiastic, honest, likeable, not anxious, optimistic, professional, supportive, and warm. Subjects observed specific nonverbal behavior such as symmetrical arms, frowning, head nodding, head shaking, pointing, sitting, smiling, standing, strong gestures, head touching, upper torso touching, walking, and weak gestures. They conclude the following:

Teachers with higher ratings tended to be more nonverbally active and expressive. They were more likely to walk around, touch their upper torsos, and smile. Less effective teachers were more likely to sit, touch their heads, and shake rather than nod their heads. These results suggest that teachers with higher ratings showed more nonverbal expressiveness and involvement than less effective teachers. (pp. 436–437)

They also suggest that teachers "should be made aware of the possible impact of their nonverbal behavior and perhaps even trained in nonverbal skills" (p. 440). The researchers caution, however, that these judgments are most accurate for the affective side of teaching.

We have stated for years that the primary function of teachers' verbal behavior in the classroom is to give content to improve students' cognitive learning. The primary function of teachers' nonverbal behavior in the classroom is to improve affect or liking for the subject matter, teacher, class, and desire to learn more about the subject matter. One step toward that is the development of a positive affective relationship between the student and teacher. When the teacher improves affect through effective nonverbal behavior, then the student is likely to listen more, learn more, and have a more positive attitude about school. Effective classroom communication between teacher and student is the key to positive affect toward learning. As communication improves between teacher and student, so does affect. When teachers are trained to use verbal and nonverbal communication in the classroom more effectively, student–teacher relationships improve and so do the students' affective and cognitive learning. When positive affect is present, cognitive learning increases.

The nonverbal behavior of the teacher communicates meanings to students. For example, the teacher who rarely looks at a student when talking is communicating that he or she is not very interested in that student. Students' nonverbal behavior communicates meanings to teachers. The student who is always yawning might be bored, tired, or both. The teacher should review the context and determine whether the student simply is tired or whether the teacher is so boring that he or she is putting the student to sleep.

The remainder of this chapter focuses on discussion of the various types of non-verbal behavior and how each affects the student–instructor relationship. We direct primary attention to the teacher's behavior and how this might influence communication with the student. The reason we take this approach is that it is the student's perceptions of what the teacher does that determines how effective the communication is. If a student perceives that a teacher is using coercive power, then he or she will respond in a negative fashion. If a student perceives that a teacher is using immediacy, then he or she will be more responsive to the teacher. When a student perceives that a teacher does not like her or him, the student most likely will learn to dislike the teacher. The remainder of this chapter centers on how teachers and students can use nonverbal behavior to express affect and liking. All the examples discussed can be applied to the typical classroom setting.

Appearance. Appearance sends important messages in the classroom setting. An instructor's attire influences the way students perceive that instructor. Teachers who dress very formally are seen by students as competent, organized, prepared, and knowledgeable. Teachers who dress casually or informally are seen as friendly, outgoing, receptive, flexible, and fair.

We have found that when teachers dress very formally, it makes students feel as if the teacher is not receptive to their needs and not likely to communicate with them. The teacher is perceived as competent but not as receptive. The teacher who dresses casually is perceived as open, friendly, and more immediate but perhaps not as competent as the teacher who dresses more formally. Therefore, our advice is to dress formally for a week or two or until credibility is established. Then dress more casually to project the image that one is open to student–teacher interaction. The teacher who always dresses formally may communicate that he or she does not want much student–teacher interaction, even though the dressing behavior may simply reflect the teacher's clothing preferences. Whatever the teacher's motivation, the students' perceptions are what counts.

Because instructors' dress affects the way students perceive them, how does student dress influence teachers' perceptions? Teachers make very definite judgments about students based on their dress. The student who is always sloppily dressed, never put together well, and does not seem to take any pride in her or his personal appearance is likely to be perceived by teachers as lazy, slow, and not very interested in school. One teacher told us about a sixth-grade student who always dressed in a sloppy, disheveled manner. After several years of being treated as if he were lazy and slow, he began to meet those expectations. The teacher found that he had above-average intelligence and exceptionally good reading skills. She started to reach him by letting him read whatever he wanted to read. Then she started getting him to pay more attention to his schoolwork. By the end of the sixth grade, the student was a strong B-student. She even managed to get him to take more care of his appearance and dress. Other teachers commented on how "something has really changed" him when they noticed his change of dress.

Students who dress in an unusual or weird manner might also be perceived in a negative manner by teachers. They often punish or criticize the student who does not fit the norm of school dress. Sometimes they criticize the student's dress so much that it impairs the student's learning and the communication between teacher and student. In the early sixties, many schools had very strict dress codes. These codes did not allow young women to wear slacks and young men had to keep their hair short. We know of one situation where one boy was persecuted so often and so much by his teachers, peers, and principals that he never finished high school. His great sin was that his hair touched his ears. He was suspended from school because the teachers and the principal felt he was a disturbance to the other students. Similar cases were reported across the United States, and many students were persecuted because of their appearance. Although appearance factors that are considered distracting today may be different from those twenty years ago, the response of teachers and school administrators often is not.

Students who have the neat, clean, acceptable appearance are generally accepted by instructors, peers, and administrators. They are often given more latitude than the sloppy or unusually dressed student. For example, students who dress as the teacher thinks they should dress are more attractive to the teacher and are likely to be helped more. The teacher will spend more time interacting with them and helping them with their schoolwork.

Malandro and Barker (1989) discuss how general attractiveness can affect the student–teacher relationship. They cite the following:

> *Darren, thirteen years old, decided to lose twenty-five pounds because he was tired of being left out of games and sports. He was called names and it was especially difficult for him to make new friends. Being unattractive at any age changes the way people perceive you and, ultimately, the way they treat you, as Darren found out. Schools provide the nesting ground for the differential treatment of attractive and unattractive children. An unattractive child is seen as a chronic problem, for example, while the same misbehavior by an attractive child is dismissed as only a temporary problem. (p. 35)*

It is sad but true that attractive children are given better treatment than unattractive children in the school environment. Unattractive children are discriminated against in the classroom and the social environment of the school. The attractive child is interacted with more often by teachers than the unattractive child. Teachers interact more positively, and peers also react more favorably to the attractive child. The unattractive child does not receive the amount or type of teacher–student interaction that the attractive child does. He or she is also perceived more negatively by peers than the attractive child.

Often without realizing it, the teacher will avoid the unattractive child and display nonimmediate cues with the unattractive child while being immediate with the attractive child. Unattractive children are commonly ignored by teachers, given less time to answer questions than their attractive counterparts, encouraged less to talk, given less eye contact, given more distance, and touched less by their teachers. This type of nonverbal behavior communicates to the unattractive child that he or she is not as good as the other students. They often receive lower grades than the other students. Much of this is because of the different nonverbal treatment given them by the teacher. They feel as if they are not liked or not as good as the other students and eventually they will tune out the classroom environment and learn less. We have heard teachers tell us hundreds of stories about this type of thing happening in their school. We have also heard students say things like, "Mrs. Jones doesn't like me." When asked how they can tell, the student says, "I can tell, it's the way she behaves" or "it's the way she treats me."

Unattractive instructors also have a more difficult time in the classroom than attractive instructors. Students are more immediate and receptive to the attractive teacher and less immediate and receptive to the unattractive teacher. Therefore, the unattractive teacher has to work harder at establishing credibility, similarity, and liking than the attractive teacher.

Body type determines, at least in part, how a person is perceived by others. The ectomorphic student is likely to be perceived by the teacher as high-strung, anxious, and nervous, but probably competent. They might be perceived by their peers as nerdy. They are not perceived as the star athletes unless they also happen to be six feet, ten inches tall! The endomorphic student might be perceived by the teacher as slow, lazy, and not too bright, but really nice and funny. They are not perceived as star athletes either. The mesomorphic student is usually perceived as dependable, intelligent, competent, dominant, and appealing by the teacher. They are also often perceived as the best athletes.

Teachers who are ectomorphic are usually perceived by students as anxious and less composed, but perhaps intelligent. The endomorphic teacher is generally perceived by students as slow, lazy, underprepared, and not dynamic in the classroom. Lastly, the mesomorphic teacher is perceived as credible, dependable, likable, and competent, but possibly tough and dominant.

In conclusion, the general appearance and attractiveness of a teacher or student can have a major impact on student–teacher communication. Generally, the more attractive student or teacher is given preferential treatment. The unattractive student or teacher must work harder to be perceived as competent and likable. Parents should be encouraged to help their children present a reasonably attractive appearance in school. Many cannot accomplish this alone, and it does make a difference in student achievement.

Gesture and Movement.   Small children often use gestures and movements to explain what they cannot say verbally. As they get older, they tend to use less simple hand gestures and increase their use of complex hand movements. In this culture, we tend to use more gestures when we are excited or giving complex messages. On the other hand, we use fewer gestures when we are bored or transmitting a simple message. Therefore, in the early grades children are likely to use more gestures and movements than verbal messages to communicate. However, about the time children reach twelve, they should be acquiring the adult norms and using more complex gestures and a wider variety of verbal messages.

In the classroom, adaptors are probably the most common gesture used by students. The classroom is an anxiety-producing situation for many children. Observe a typical classroom and you will find students chewing pencils, biting their nails, picking at their desks or notebooks, pulling at their hair, smoothing their clothing, and clicking their pens. A classroom that has an inordinate amount of student adaptive behavior is one in which the anxiety level is high or the teacher is boring. Students use more adaptors in classes where they feel anxious or bored. These behaviors are often perceived as a form of misbehavior and are punished. The student who is constantly clicking her or his pen is perceived by the teacher as disruptive. Students may not even realize they are engaging in such behavior until they are reprimanded for it.

Adaptors are more prevalent during the first few days of school, near holidays, and near the end of school. Students unintentionally use more adaptive behavior at these times. Teachers also tend to use more adaptive behavior the first few days of a new school year. It is anxiety-producing for most teachers when they are meeting new classes for the first time. Teachers who use more adaptors are perceived as nervous and anxious.

There are also people (both students and teachers) who gesture very little in the classroom. Students and teachers who gesture very little might be perceived by the other as boring and unanimated. Teachers should use illustrators and affect displays more with their verbal messages to keep the classroom lively and the content interesting. The teacher's delivery style should be animated and dynamic, and gesturing is one method of achieving this. The animated and dynamic teacher can keep the class interested in the subject for longer periods of time. Nonanimated, boring teachers put their classes to sleep.

Instructors who have an open body position communicate to their students that they are receptive and immediate, whereas teachers who fold in or keep a closed body position are perceived as nonimmediate and unreceptive. Students with similar positions are perceived in similar ways by their teachers. Students who slouch in their seats when talking to the teacher are perceived as bored, rude, or even arrogant. Teachers expect students to look interested. One of the best indicants of interest is body position.

Both students and teachers use adaptive gestures, but they shou'd strive to decrease their reliance on such activities. Teachers should consciously work to be more animated and dynamic. This will improve student–teacher interaction and make the classroom a more exciting environment.

Face and Eye Behavior.   The student or teacher with a glum, dour facial expression is perceived as less animated and less immediate than the student or teacher with a pleasing facial expression. The use of facial expressions communicates a lot in the classroom environment. People cannot always hide their real feelings. The teacher can unintentionally express her or his real feelings about a student through facial expression. Smaller children do not understand many facial expressions and sometimes perceive any expression that is less than positive as a negative one. The frown is often associated with negative facial affect. Children usually do not learn the facial expressions until around age twelve. Before then, they have difficulty discriminating among facial expressions of their teachers. Therefore, a small child might react to a thoughtful expression as if they had done something wrong. Teachers need to be very careful in controlling their facial expressions with young children.

Students' facial expressions also influence how teachers react to them. The student who is staring out the window and has a totally bored expression on her or his face is not likely to be called on by the teacher, except as punishment. They also are not likely to receive any preferential treatment from the teacher. An author of the text had a student who literally slept through several sessions of his evening class. There were 146 students in the class and he was the only one who looked bored. This bothered the teacher a lot, until one day the student approached the instructor and apologized for sleeping in class and looking bored. He explained that he worked at the post office from 11:00 A.M. to 7:00 P.M. and had difficulty staying awake in all of his evening classes.

Teachers' facial expressions can affect how students feel about the classroom environment. The teacher who has a dull, boring facial expression when talking is perceived by the students as uninterested in them and the subject matter. This type of teacher is likely to have more classroom disruptions because students become bored with the teaching style. Teachers must have pleasing facial expressions, ones that show that they are interested not only in the subject matter, but also in their students. Pleasing facial expressions are often accompanied by positive head movements.

The teacher who uses positive head nods in response to a student's comments is perceived as friendly, concerned about the communication between teacher and student, and immediate. An instructor who rarely nods, or uses more negative head nods than positive quickly stifles teacher–student communication. Not many students volunteer to talk when they realize that their teacher will not respond in a positive or at least encouraging fashion. Positive head nods are a means of stimulating student–teacher interaction and student responses. Students who use similar head nods help promote student–teacher interaction and it helps the teacher in knowing whether the students have understood the content.

Smiling has long been associated with liking, affiliation, and immediacy. The teacher who smiles and has positive facial affect is perceived as more immediate and likeable than the one who does not. Students react more favorably to the teacher who smiles than to the teacher who frowns a lot or does not smile much. Similarly, teachers react more favorably to the student who smiles than to the student who frowns or does not smile much. They each perceive the other as more open to communication. Therefore, the student–teacher relationship is improved by smiling. Students from kindergarten through graduate school respond better to teachers who smile.

Both instructors and students must use pleasing facial expressions. It improves the perceptions and the communication between teacher and student. The teacher or student with the pleasing facial expression is perceived as more immediate and approachable than the teacher or student who is dour or sour-looking.

Eye behavior of instructor and student can affect the interaction between the two. Students who look away, avoid teacher eye contact, or look down when the teacher calls on them are perceived as uninterested, shy, or unwilling to communicate. None of these are very positive perceptions. We know that people like to have eye contact when communicating with another. Eye contact might be one of the biggest indicators of student interest in the classroom environment. Students who do not have eye contact with the teacher are perceived as uninterested. Teachers are the same as other people. They want people to whom they are talking to look at them and to have eye contact with them. If that does not occur, it is taken as rejection of the content—and personal rejection as well.

Some instructors seldom have eye contact with their students. This usually suggests to the student that the teacher is not interested in her or him and that the teacher is not approachable. Teachers who have little eye contact with students often are very shy, and probably should not be in the classroom at all. When there is little eye contact between students and teachers, students do not know when to talk, when to ask, or how to approach the teacher. This is a common complaint on college campuses. It often is directed toward some international instructors. The students complain that the instructor never looks at them when lecturing. This behavior may be the result of the instructor's cultural upbringing. In some cultures, it is considered inappropriate for instructors and students to have direct eye contact. The continued employment of such individuals to teach the young people of this culture reflects the insensitivity of the education establishment in America to the importance of effective communication in instruction. It is one more example of the faulty assumption that content mastery is sufficient for preparing one to teach that content.

There is one situation in the classroom that can cause deviant eye behavior. This is test-taking time. Often teachers assume that students' wandering eyes are a sign of cheating. This is not always the case. Test time is a very anxious time for most students and they unintentionally look around or look up when processing information. Teachers need to be cautious about accusing a student of cheating because he or she looks around during a test. When processing information on a test, students have many conjugate lateral eye movements (CLEMS), which we discussed in Chapter 4. If a student is consistently and constantly looking at another's paper, we can safely assume that he or she is cheating. When a student is glancing left or right or looking up, he or she most likely is just processing information.

In conclusion, eye behavior is a significant indicator of the relationship between student and teacher. Students who have eye contact with their teachers are perceived as more interested and better students. Teachers who look at their students are perceived as more animated, more interested, and more immediate.

Vocal Behavior. Recently we surveyed students to determine the nonverbal behavior that students liked or disliked most about teachers. Overwhelmingly, students felt that the monotone voice was the most objectionable behavior of a teacher. They felt that the monotone voice projected the image of boredom, noncaring, and nonimmediacy. They also said they learned less when the teacher had a dull or monotone voice. They were less interested in the subject matter and liked the class less when the teacher had a monotone voice. Students want the teacher to have a lively, animated voice.

Of all voice qualities, monotone seems to draw the most negative criticism from both teachers and students. Both say that they perceive the person with the monotone voice as boring and dull. Students who use the monotone voice in class are not helping themselves at all. Instructors want students who sound interested in the class.

An author of the book had a professor who taught philosophy of education. He droned on and on in a monotone voice for two and a half hours every class period. The class had more than 100 people in it, and most dozed off. He was the worst model that an education department could employ to teach prospective teachers about how to be an effective teacher. The most significant criticism the students had about him was not his competence, but his monotone voice.

There should be a sign placed in all classrooms that says "Laughter is encouraged in this class." Students do not get the opportunity to laugh in our classrooms. No one ever said learning had to be boring. A really good teacher laughs with the students and encourages and allows laughter when something occurs that all can enjoy. For example, an author of this text was lecturing one day and during the lecture she moved backwards to reach for her notes. She tripped over the garbage can behind her and fell in and got stuck. The whole class was stunned and then broke up laughing. She also laughed and finally some students helped her out of the garbage can. Had she not laughed, or criticized them for laughing, the whole class would have suffered. Laughing also allows students to release tension and to relax. Research completed more than sixty years ago (Barr, 1929) studied good and poor social science teachers and found that good teachers laughed more and allowed laughter in the classroom, whereas poor teachers did not. Many things have changed since then, but it is certain that the role of laughter in the classroom has not. Teachers who laugh and encourage laughter from their students are still more immediate than those who do not.

Space. How a teacher or student uses interpersonal space with the other communicates how they perceive the other. The teacher who stands behind the desk or podium and rarely approaches students or allows them to approach her or him is perceived by students as unfriendly, unreceptive, unapproachable, and nonimmediate. This does not help improve student–teacher relationships.

The student who backs away when the teacher approaches, or will not allow a teacher to stand or sit close to them, will be perceived in a similar manner by the teacher. The student might even be perceived as uninterested in learning and hostile to the classroom environment.

Some people simply do not like being approached by others. These people are touch-avoidants. When someone approaches them, they move away or back to avoid contact. We must be cautious to not judge the person who draws away from interaction too harshly. He or she might simply be a touch-avoidant.

There is also some research that suggests students who are abused at home have greater space needs than nonabused children, and they may behave like a touch-avoidant. Some research also shows that disruptive students have greater spatial needs than nondisruptive students. Their disruptiveness may stem from their feeling closed in and pressured.

Differences in size might make a big difference in how students and teachers feel about their space. For example, elementary teachers tend, even if they are only five feet tall, to tower over their students. Hence, we suggest that a simple means of getting closer without intimidating the student is to let them stand close while the teacher is seated. The teacher could also occasionally sit or kneel on the floor so that he or she is closer to the students. Students in college and high school often tower over their teachers. They should strive not to do this. Teachers do not like to feel as if a student is trying to intimidate them. The tall student is probably unaware of this. The easiest solution to this is for the student to stand farther away from the teacher. This reduces the towering-over effect and makes communication easier for both.

In summary, space communicates in the classroom environment. The teacher who withdraws from students is perceived as nonimmediate and noncaring. The student who withdraws from the teacher might be perceived as uninterested or hostile. We need to look beyond these perceptions to find out whether another problem is present.

Touch.   It is unfortunate that there is very little expressive touch in our classrooms today. Much of the touch that is present between student and teacher is as a punishment or reprimand. Teachers are reluctant to touch students because of the insinuations that others might make. Students, above the lowest grade levels, have always been reluctant to touch teachers because of the status differential.

Studies reveal that human touch helps people grow and adapt better in society. However, our schools have adopted the noncontact philosophy that our society perpetuates. If you survey most school children from kindergarten through the twelfth grade about the kind and amount of touch they receive from the teacher, most will say that they get less touch as they get older and much of what they receive is associated with a reprimand. Some students cannot recall the last time a teacher touched them in an expressive fashion.

Touch is a form of communication that can be very useful in establishing and maintaining an effective teacher–student relationship. Touch can be used by the instructor to reinforce a student for a job well-done. It can be used by the teacher to substitute for the verbal reprimand or control without ever saying a word. For example, the teacher who walks up and touches the child on the shoulder who is misbehaving has gotten her or his attention. The child knows that he or she should stop what they are doing. Touch should be an acceptable form of communication in the teacher–student relationship. Touching a student on the arm, hand, shoulder, or upper back should be acceptable. This type of touch can be a very effective means of communicating a message without ever uttering a word.

In the early grades, touch is an essential component to establishing an effective student–teacher relationship. Most small children are used to receiving much touch at home. They expect the same at school. The elementary teacher is often seen as the surrogate parent, and the children expect touch from that teacher. There is nothing wrong in giving it. If a teacher does not touch them, often the children feel as if there is something wrong with them, or they feel unloved. A teacher must be cautious not to touch one or two more than the rest. Even small children see this differentiation and wonder why the one or two get more touch than the rest. Touch is such an important communication variable that one has to use it in a fair manner in the classroom environment.

The younger children may also touch the teacher in places that are unacceptable for the older child to touch. Younger children usually learn the touch norms about age twelve. For example, when a child is in the first grade, it is not unusual for her or him to hug the teacher around the thigh. The teacher should be prepared for and accepting of such touching behavior. However, when the child is in the seventh grade, or a sophomore in college, it is highly unusual and generally unacceptable to initiate such touch! In the upper grades, older children expect less touch and receive less. However, touch should still be used as a reinforcer. Older children can be touched on the back or shoulder for doing good work.

Teachers should remember that some students are touch-avoidant and are very uncomfortable when touched. A teacher who encounters a touch-avoidant student should leave him or her alone and not try to relax the student. In addition, some teachers are touch-avoidant and do not want to be touched. These teachers should not teach at the elementary levels. The student or teacher who is the touch-avoidant might be perceived as nonimmediate and perhaps even aloof. If a person is touch-avoidant, other nonverbal cues can be used to communicate immediacy and establish an effective student–teacher relationship.

In conclusion, teachers or students who withdraw from another's touch might be perceived as nonimmediate. Teachers and students should both be aware of the touch norms in schools and communities and be cautious about following them. Teachers should use touch as a form of reinforcement, not a punishment. Lastly, many classes such as physical education, art, and music, allow for a great deal of touch. Teachers in these classes should use touch as a form of communication.

Classroom environment can affect student–teacher interaction. Often, students' and teachers' performance is affected negatively by ugly classrooms.

Environment. We acknowledge at the outset that many classrooms are not conducive to student–teacher interaction. We also acknowledge that many schools have drab and dreary classrooms and very little can be done to improve the environment. Much of what we discuss here, however, can be adapted to any classroom in any school.

Attractive classrooms are much more likely to keep students and teachers attentive and reduce hostility. Many studies have revealed that ugly environments produce hostile communication among participants. Think of the worst schoolroom in which you had a class. Think of all the ugly aspects and how you felt while in that environment. The authors of this text have taught in a variety of ugly environments. It is more difficult to keep students' attention when the environment is ugly, too hot or cold, not well illuminated, painted dark brown or industrial green, or is unclean. Darth Vader could have designed many classrooms in this country. They are dark, foreboding environments that say to students "don't plan on any fun here—shut up, sit, and listen forever."

It is a shame that in a country so affluent, many classrooms are still in the dark ages. Teachers and students usually must continue to accept this. However, many teachers redecorate their rooms at their own expense to make the environment more conducive to learning and enjoyment of learning.

There are optimal seating arrangements for different types of teaching. Traditional row and column arrangements (see Figure 14–1) are useful for listening, note taking, and lecturing. Modular seating is best for student group interaction; this arrangement allows the teacher to move from group to group to give assistance (See Figure 14–2). Figure 14–3 is the circular, horseshoe, or open-square arrangement. This is particularly useful for encouraging classroom discussions between students and teachers. If a teacher can use the above arrangements in different learning situations, it will improve student interest and communication between student and teacher. Some of these classroom settings do, however, increase the noise level, which must also be considered.

Music can be used to counteract student boredom and to establish a comfortable classroom atmosphere. We have found in our research that teachers can use music as an effective reinforcer for good behavior, as a reward for completing a task, and for relaxing the students. Elementary teachers have long known the power of music in the classroom. They use it to relax students, to generate conversations, to reward, to excite, and to lull students to sleep. Teachers at any level can use music on occasion to create a better classroom environment. For example, if a teacher wants to spice up a unit on French history, he or she might play the music of the age. If a teacher wants to teach a unit on careers and employment, then he or she can play records about various positions people have held.

"The only good classroom is the quiet classroom." This is the motto of many school systems. Many bright, energetic children enter Darth Vader's halls and eventually turn into little Darth Vaders after they are placed in drab classrooms and told to be quiet. Students at any age should be encouraged to participate in classroom discussions and talk on occasions. The teaching strategy of teacher lecturing and student learning has long since lost its appeal for both segments. Teachers who allow some student talk are perceived by students as more responsive to their needs and more immediate and approachable. We do not mean that classrooms should be noisy without any purpose, but student talk is essential to student growth and development. The teacher should set up situations in which students can talk without being reprimanded. Group exercises, projects, and similar activities allow for student talk without decreasing the content. Of course, the teacher should not use such activities for content. They should be used as a means of teaching content.

Whether the students are younger or older, allowing for student–teacher interaction is an effective means of improving communication between teacher and student. Talk can also be used as a reward for good behavior. If students sit and listen, and take notes as they should, then the teacher should do a group exercise or open the class for discussion. Allowing for talk time gives students a chance to relax and release tension, and makes them feel better about the classroom environment. Those

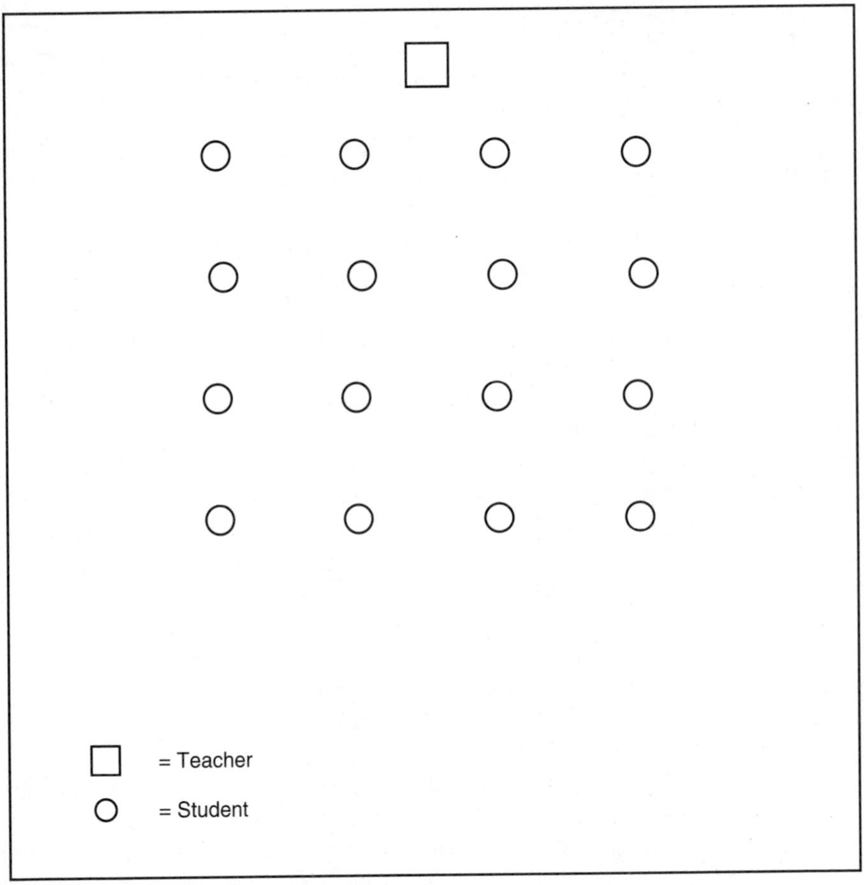

FIGURE 14-1 **Traditional Seating**

who do not want to talk, however, should not be forced to or punished for not talking.

Color can be used in the classroom to denote warmth or coldness. Recall the Ketcham (1958) study on school attractiveness we discussed in Chapter 8. Schools should never be painted dark brown, industrial green, or battleship gray. Younger children probably function better with the warmer colors such as soft blues, yellows, and pinks. Older students probably function better with the cooler colors such as blue and blue-green. Bright colors such as iridescent reds, yellows, greens, and oranges should not be overdone. A room painted in such colors might overstimulate the students. However, a single wall of bright color may create a bright, active environment.

Clearly color and decor can influence the school environment. It can affect how students feel about school, the teacher, and the total learning environment. There are

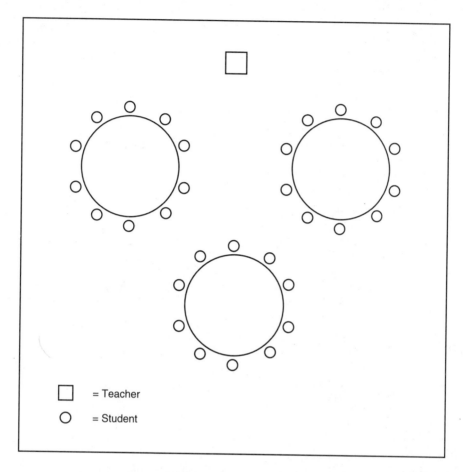

FIGURE 14–2 **Modular Seating**

many schools where the art teacher, the industrial arts teacher, the custodians, administrators, and some students help paint the school's interior. For example, they paint the hallways in warm colors and then paint geometrical designs on the warm colors. These schools have found over the past ten years that students in their build- ing take more pride in their school than students at other schools. They rarely have writing on the walls or smears or smudges. It is not unusual to see a student cleaning a wall if it gets marked. Student involvement can help guarantee that students will take care of the classrooms.

Lighting can also influence the relationship between teacher and student. A classroom that is poorly lit or too bright can cause fatigue and eye strain. Eventually, even boredom and hostility emerge. Thompson (1973) gave three guidelines for lighting in the classroom.

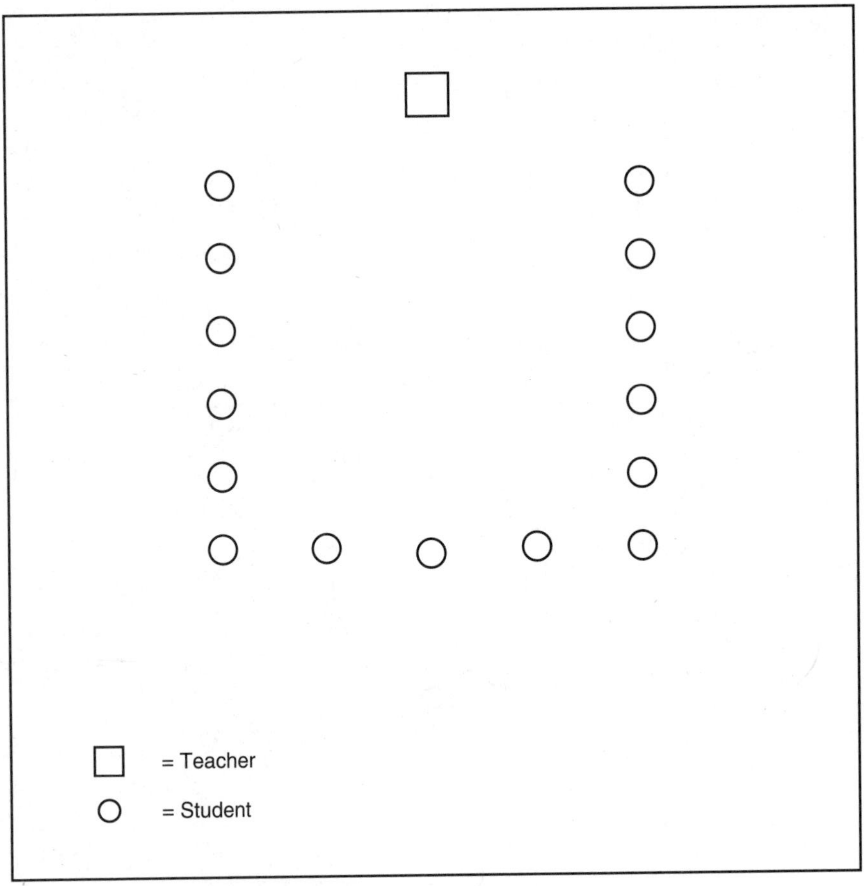

FIGURE 14–3   **Circular, Horseshoe, or Open-Square Seating**

Maintain high levels of illumination. When students must expend energy just to see, they will have little left to understand what is being said. All areas of the room should be balanced in brightness. Factory and assembly-line workers have their work well illuminated. Industry has known for a long time that eye fatigue plays havoc with production schedules. To avoid sharp contrast, the visual field around the task should be only one-third as bright as the work area. No part of the visual field should be brighter than the immediate vicinity of the task. Avoid glare either from direct light sources or from reflecting surfaces. (p. 81)

Imagine sitting in a classroom and trying to absorb content when the temperature is 90 degrees with 90 percent humidity. About all you can do is sit very still and keep wiping the perspiration from your body. Many classrooms are kept too warm, both in the summer and in the winter. In the summer, they are too hot because they are not air conditioned and the humidity is high. In the winter, they are hot and dry. Both climates are disruptive to the learning and communication process between student and teacher. When a room is too hot, people become antsy and irritable. When a room is too cold, people cannot concentrate either.

The optimal classroom temperature is 66 to 72 degrees. This assumes that the room is not too dry or humid. Many classrooms do not have temperature controls, but if the room is painted a cool color, it will seem cooler. However, we know that when it's 90 degrees outside and 100 degrees inside, no one will feel cool even in a light blue room.

During the winter, humidity should not fall below 30 percent or be allowed to rise above 50 percent. As humidity moves above or below these levels, student illness and absenteeism increase. Todd-Mancillas (1982) summarizes Green's (1979) results drawn from 3,600 students in grades one to eight in eleven different schools in Saskatoon, Canada:

> *Results indicated that children attending schools with classroom humidities ranging between 22% and 26% experienced nearly 13% greater illness and absenteeism than children attending schools with classrooms having humidity levels ranging between 27% and 33%. . . . Green also cautions against excessive humidity, as allied research also indicates that increased respiratory infections result from humidity levels in excess of 50%. (p. 85)*

If teachers cannot control the temperature in their classrooms, then they should vary activities so that students do not notice the temperature as much. In other words, they should give the students plenty to do and think about other than the temperature. In cold months, if the room is too cold they should have the students move around and talk a lot. In warmer months, if the room is too hot they should have group discussions and activities that help direct attention away from the temperature.

The furnishings in a classroom can often determine how students feel about the environment. Ugly furnishings do not improve communication between student and teacher. Granted, many schools do not have money to purchase new desks, chairs, equipment, and curtains. However, schools that are more attractive are generally taken better care of by the students. Teachers and students can improve the classroom by bringing in artifacts to improve the environment. Plants and homemade decorations can improve the climate in a classroom.

In conclusion, the instructor who makes optimal use of the space he or she has is likely to get along better with the students. Affect will improve for the teacher who cares about the classroom environment. Maximal use of space, seating, lighting, color, sound, noise, temperature, and furnishings improves communication between student and instructor.

Scent.   The odor a person exudes can encourage others to approach or avoid that person. Teachers should avoid wearing overpowering scents in the classroom. Overpowering scents can affect student attentiveness, learning, and health. Some students have allergies and cannot be near strong scents or odors. Teachers should be sensitive to this even if other students are not.

There is always one student in every class who has an offensive odor. Teachers need to learn not to avoid this student. Teachers still must be immediate with the student who doesn't smell like the others. A teacher we work with told us the following story: She sent home a note to the student's parents explaining that Joey had body odor and it was causing a problem in the classroom. Joey's mother wrote back and said, "Joey ain't no rose, don't smell him, just learn him." Sometimes there is little or nothing anyone can do about scent, except learn to live with it. Perhaps health teachers and physical education teachers can discuss odor with students, but other teachers probably cannot. However, all teachers can take care not to introduce noxious odors into the classroom. Some plants give off odors that some people cannot smell, but others find overpowering. Take care to avoid having such plants in a classroom.

Time.   Teachers must use time to their advantage. Time can be used to reward students for good behavior, to control students, to make the classroom more interesting, and to learn about others. Teachers often spend too much time on one unit. Most adults can only listen effectively for about thirty minutes, so why should we expect children to pay attention for longer periods of time? Teachers must structure activities to meet student's time needs. Inflexible schedules are harmful to owl students. Owls function best later in the day, whereas sparrows function best early in the morning and fade in the afternoon. Therefore, teachers must be sensitive to student's body schedules. Optimal learning occurs for the owl in the afternoon, whereas optimal learning occurs for the sparrow in the morning. To the extent possible, teachers should vary the time in which subject matter is taught and the time when tests are given. Rigid schedules make for tight organization, but if they are not adapted to student differences, they are not tools for effective teaching or testing.

Students are less aroused during the lunch period if they have a recess before lunch. Allowing children to let off steam before eating reduces problems in the lunch room. Once the students have eaten, then they are ready to go back to the classroom. Teachers also should avoid punishing students by taking away their recess. Teachers who ignore this caution may be, in effect, punishing themselves. Students who have recess taken away cause bigger problems in later classes than they would normally. This happens because they missed the opportunity to burn off their excess energy. Sometimes a few minutes devoted to recess will save many minutes for instruction.

Instructors should allow for free time or talk time. If students complete projects early, let them have some time to do whatever they want. This also helps teach them responsibility.

Teachers who use their time wisely have fewer classroom problems and student problems. They also have students who learn more and better. For example, testing should be rotated so that owls and sparrows both have a chance to do well. Teachers must be sensitive to the student's time needs. Around holidays, spring, and the beginning of school, students are more restless. The instructor must be more innovative and creative to keep the students' attention. Instructors can use time to understand their students better and to understand how to prepare lessons more effectively. Time can also be used to reward or punish students.

ADVANTAGES OF TEACHER IMMEDIACY

Throughout this chapter, we have discussed possible teacher and student nonverbal behavior that denotes immediacy or nonimmediacy. Obviously, the immediate teacher is perceived more positively than the nonimmediate teacher. There are significant advantages to be gained from teacher immediacy in the classroom.

Students have better affect for immediate instructors than for nonimmediate instructors. Immediate teachers are perceived as approachable, friendly, open, and responsive to students' needs.

Immediate teachers are also able to get their students to have better affect for the subject matter and content than nonimmediate teachers. This is particularly important because this might determine the student's future career goals. For example, how many of us decided that math was an undesirable subject because of the boring presentations of our math teachers?

Immediate teachers have increased student–teacher and student–student interaction in the classroom. In other words, communication is improved between student and teacher.

Immediate instructors can hold students' attention longer, thereby increasing the chances that cognitive learning might improve. Immediacy leads directly to increased cognitive learning by increasing student attentiveness.

Lastly, immediacy leads to better overall student–instructor relationships. This is one thing that most students and instructors want. Immediacy is the key.

DISADVANTAGES OF TEACHER IMMEDIACY

Immediacy has a plethora of positive results. However, the garden is not all roses. There are some thorns. Immediate teachers might encounter some personal or professional problems with their colleagues. They might be perceived as not having control over their classrooms.

Immediate teachers might seem as if they are pushovers to some students. Immediacy does not mean "let the student do whatever he or she wants." It means "be approachable." Immediate teachers must still be firm and have standards.

Lastly, not everyone can be immediate in the same way. Select the behaviors you are most comfortable with and use those. To be immediate, you do not have to perform all the behaviors we have identified as immediate in this chapter, but you do need some of them. If you try to use behavior that makes you uncomfortable, you will appear awkward and uncomfortable rather than immediate. False immediacy is worse than none at all.

A GLOSSARY OF TERMINOLOGY

The primary function of teacher's verbal behavior is to give content to improve students' cognitive learning.

The primary function of teacher's nonverbal behavior is to improve students' affect or liking for the subject matter, teacher, and class, and to increase desire to learn more about the subject matter.

▲ 15

Intercultural Relationships

Advances in modern transportation and electronic communications systems are making it possible for people all over the world to communicate more readily and over longer distances. People's perceptions are that the globe is shrinking and a melding of human cultures is taking place. Although our transport and electronic systems are rapidly advancing, it is arguable that they are only leading to more miscommunication among peoples of the world. Our human systems generally have failed to keep up with the advances of our technical systems. This chapter reviews the distinctive characteristics of intercultural communication, discusses the relevance of nonverbal behavior to communication across cultures, and examines some nonverbal messages from various cultures.

As we become more likely to come into contact with people from cultures very different from our own, there is a need for increased awareness about appropriate versus inappropriate behavior in intercultural contacts. Yousef (1976) confirms this in three illustrations of "funny people." The first illustration is about an American named John Smith who just returned from a vacation in Puerto Rico. He bragged to his friends about how he understood and spoke Spanish and said he had no problems communicating while in Puerto Rico. However, Smith related the following incident. He went into a large department store around noon in San Juan. As he approached a counter, the salesperson was talking to two native customers. The salesperson stopped talking to the native customers and asked if he could help. John Smith thanked him and told him to serve the others first. The salesperson returned to the conversation with the native customers. Other people arrived, interrupted, and were waited on and left while Smith stood angrily by. The salesperson never

Structures can communicate cultural values.

acknowledged Smith. Smith concluded to his friends that Puerto Ricans "don't have any sense of order or business."

The second illustration took place in Dammam, Saudi Arabia. Jim Ralph was sent by the U.S. head office to present a seminar for the native personnel in the branch of one of *Fortune* magazine's 500 corporations. He noticed that "These people are strangely nervous and jerky. Every time I come close or talk to one of them, the man bolts up and tenses in his seat. I wonder what kind of managers they will be."

The third illustration took place in an elementary classroom in Compton, California. Mary Moore was shouting at little Johnny, an African child. She shouted, "For the hundredth time, you look at me and listen when I talk to you! Is that clear?" Johnny proceeded to look up at her, then down at the floor, and turned and looked sideways while Moore stood by helplessly.

Yousef (1976) suggests that although these illustrations might seem to be describing "funny people," they are describing cultural misunderstandings because people are not aware of the nonverbal communication of the culture. John Smith did not understand the polychronic temporal orientations of Puerto Ricans. They will wait on many people at once, whereas in this culture, we are monochronic. Ralph thought the native personnel in Saudi Arabia were jittery. He was wrong. Their behavior demonstrated respect and deference for one of higher rank. They made conscious and deliberate moves to appear to be paying attention and listening. Lastly, Mary Moore misperceived Johnny's behavior. The difference in the cultural background was the problem; Johnny was not disinterested or bored. Johnny had learned that students should show respect for a teacher by looking down when spoken to. He never really understood why Mary Moore didn't like him. In all three situations, people appeared intolerant, but were really ignorant of the other culture. They expected people to respond using the general North American standard.

It is clear from Yousef's illustrations that all peoples need to be educated in some basic principles of intercultural communication. Perhaps the nonverbal aspects are more critical than the verbal aspects, because we readily recognize that other people speak a language different from our own. What we fail to recognize is that other people's nonverbal messages are even more vastly different from our own than are their languages. Before we continue, we must define intercultural communication and look at some of its variations.

DEFINING INTERCULTURAL COMMUNICATION

Rich and Ogawa (1972) define intercultural communication simply as "communication between peoples of different cultures" (p. 24). Communication is intercultural when one interactant is from one culture and the other interactant is from another culture. Klopf and Park (1982) note that "one will encode a message based on her or his cultural background; the other will decode it from the framework of her or his culture" (p. 15). Klopf (1991) defines *intercultural communication* as "the communication between people of different cultures, and it occurs when a person (or persons) from one culture talks to a person (or persons) from another" (p. 39). He defines a subculture as "collections of people who possess conscious membership in identifiable units of an encompassing, larger cultural unit" (p. 36).

Although culture always influences interaction between people, the more the cultures of two people are alike, the less likely culture will cause problems in their interactions. People from cultures that have similar languages, hygiene, foods, rituals, folklore, etiquette, ethics, backgrounds, religion, and schools, live in similar geographical regions, and have similar governments (Americans and English-Canadians) have a less difficult time communicating. The similarity between cultures makes communication easier. On the other hand, cultures that are very different in terms of language, hygiene, foods, rituals, folklore, etiquette, ethics, athletics, background, religion, schooling, geographical region, and governments have a more difficult time communicating (Western versus Asian cultures). Klopf and Park (1982) suggest

> *Nevertheless, the possibility of misinterpretation always exists when messages encoded by persons of one culture are decoded by persons of another. There is a need, therefore, to study intercultural communication to reduce or attempt to   eliminate any misunderstandings that might result from cultural modification. (p. 16)*

To avoid confusion, several variations of intercultural communication must be explained before we continue. We will use the distinctions drawn by Klopf and Park (1982). *Cross-cultural* and *transcultural* communication are terms generally used interchangeably with *intercultural communication.* However, there are other terms that have different referents. *International communication* is communication "between official representatives of nations and usually is political in nature" (p. 17). *Interracial communication* is communication between people "with racially identifiable physical differences, Koreans and Caucasians, for instance" (p. 17). This form may or may not be intercultural. Communication between a third-generation Korean-American and a third-generation Italian-American is interracial, but probably not intercultural. Both have been acculturated into the North American culture and probably have similar values. Communication between a native Korean and an American-born Korean would be intercultural. *Interethnic communication* is communication between "people of the same race but not the same ethnic background" (p. 17). For example, English-Canadians and French-Canadians have the same predominant culture and race, yet they speak different languages and have different objectives and viewpoints. Lastly, a *subculture* is a "racial, ethnic, social, regional, or economic group which displays certain behavior patterns differentiating it from the dominant culture" (p. 17). Some examples would be Texans, Mexican-Americans, senior citizens, homosexuals, handicapped people, residents of Beverly Hills, New Yorkers, and so on.

Despite the definitions, intercultural specialists suggest that certain universals are important to understanding communication practices across cultures. Hall's "map of culture" shows what he believes are culture's constituent parts, prominently featuring communication. His map has 100 universals classified in the ten categories listed:

1. Communication: vocal qualifiers, kinesics, language
2. Society: class, caste, government
3. Work: formal work, maintenance, occupations
4. Sexes: masculinity versus femininity, biological sex, technical sex
5. Space: formal and informal, boundaries
6. Time: sequence, cycles, calendars
7. Enculturation: rearing, informal learning, education
8. Recreation: playing games, fun
9. Protection: formal and informal defenses, technical defenses
10. Material systems: contact with environment, motor habits, technology

Clearly, communication behaviors, both verbal and nonverbal, are prevalent in all cultures and across cultures. To communicate effectively, we must understand the verbal as well as the nonverbal. Because intercultural communication is growing, persistent, enduring, and omnipresent, we must become more aware of and acquainted with intercultural communication, particularly the influence of nonverbal communication. Because cultures are made up of smaller units, or subcultures, we often have to learn the larger culture first, and then the subculture, to be effective.

NONVERBAL BEHAVIOR

A person's nonverbal behavior communicates the beliefs, attitudes, and values of that person's culture to others. Klopf and Park suggest that "what a person does nonverbally is always important in intercultural communication" (p. 73). Because nonverbal messages are always present, we must not ignore their importance or impact. Because we cannot learn the meaning of thousands of nonverbal behaviors, it is important that we at least "realize that the meanings are likely to change from culture to culture" (Klopf, 1991, p. 236). Often today communication scholars are educating people about the importance of effective cross-cultural communication. What if two countries have a nonverbal misunderstanding? Could it lead to war? It's probably less likely today than it was in the 1950s, but who knows? It is better to be safe than sorry.

Clearly, nonverbal behaviors are not pancultural. Most meanings attributed to nonverbal behavior are based on the attributer's culture. The motivation for given behaviors is not universal; it varies from culture to culture. Thus, the meaning we can reasonably attribute to any given behavior is culturally determined. Nonverbal behavior is differentially learned from one culture to the next. How well one learns about her or his own nonverbal culture and understands the nonverbal culture of another determines how effective communication will be between people of different cultures. The remainder of this section reviews some intercultural nonverbal behaviors and what they are likely to communicate.

Appearance. Whether we like it or not, people judge others by their appearance and perceived attractiveness. However, what is attractive in one culture may not be attractive in another culture. This has always been a source of communication misunderstandings. In ancient Rome, a culture of dark-haired people, the blonde-haired woman could either be royalty or a prostitute. Originally, only prostitutes had blonde hair. Then Messalina, the third wife of Emperor Claudius, started wearing blonde wigs. Soon many other women were wearing blonde wigs. It became nearly impossible to tell the prostitutes from the "in-crowd."

Roman men kept their hair short-cropped, whereas slaves or barbarians had long hair. When the long-haired Europeans conquered Rome, they thought the men with short hair were slaves. Around the time of Charlemagne, 800 AD, the noblemen kept their hair short. At the same time, the Japanese shaved the tops of their heads. Egyptians shaved off all of their hair.

For centuries, women have seemed to be more conscious of their appearance than men. American women spend far more on cosmetics and related items than American men. Women worldwide have always tried to alter their appearance to adapt to their culture. For example, binding the feet of baby girls was a common practice in China for nearly a thousand years. The size of the woman's foot was related to how wealthy she was. The smaller the foot, the greater the wealth. The girl's family would place her shoe in the window so that suitors might see the size. Foot binding was a very painful experience. Infants would cry for weeks and months as their foot muscles and bones were squashed into smaller sizes. It is still common practice in some remote areas of China to bind women's feet.

How else do people mutilate their bodies to be attractive? How about reshaping heads? Mangbettu females in the Congo had their heads wrapped tightly during early childhood so that they would become elongated. The Mayans would flatten their heads by tying boards to each side of the head in early childhood. They would also file their teeth into points and place valuable jewels in them. Some Burmese girls have several one-inch-thick rings placed about their necks to lengthen them, and their necks sometimes reach fourteen inches. In the Saras-Djinges tribe of Africa, girls have their lips stretched with wooden discs. Sometimes their lips stretch to fourteen inches around. They can consume only liquids. In Africa, the Masai use cow dung on their hair to make it stiff. Native American tribes used to paint their faces to represent various rituals.

Before you conclude that behaviors such as these occur only in far-off lands, consider some North American mutilations that are popular today. A popular fashion in North American culture is to have a small tattoo somewhere on the body. However, rather than enduring the pain of applying a permanent tattoo, some individuals have developed paints for the body and paste-on tattoos. Have you ever heard of ear piercing? Long the province of females in the United States, now many males do it too. Even serious surgical procedures are not beyond the North American—nose jobs, face lifts, breast implants, liposuction, and the list goes on. All in the name of improved physical appearance. No wonder that plastic surgery is the fastest growing medical specialization in the United States today.

For men to have longer hair in the late sixties and early seventies was acceptable. The crewcut was acceptable in the fifties in this culture. In the eighties, the well-groomed appearance was the most acceptable for men and women. We no longer have hippies; we have yuppies. Yuppies dictate the wearing apparel and hair length for the young upwardly mobile professional class. Therefore, the yuppie style is what this country probably will be modeling for some years to come.

This culture more readily accepts tall, large women than some Asian countries. The average height of a woman in this country is about five feet five. This is considered huge in Japan. Japanese women are very small and petite. Many Chinese women have small builds. An American woman of average height looks like a giant in either country; she towers over both men and women. Preferred body type and height vary from culture to culture. Some cultures prefer hearty, hefty women who can do strenuous chores. Anorexic-looking, fashion model–type women would be rejected in such cultures.

In conclusion, physical appearance and attractiveness are highly influential in intercultural communication. Those who do not look like they belong to the culture will not be listened to, will not be able to persuade others, and often will not successfully communicate with others. Anyone who does not fit the physical norm of the culture will have trouble communicating in that culture. When in other cultures, we should try to respect and conform as much as possible to the norms of that culture.

Gesture and Movement.   Axtell (1991) says, "gestures and body language are not only powerful communicators but . . . different cultures use gestures and body language in dramatically different ways" (p. 1991). People from different cultures learn the gestures and movements of their culture.

For example, North Americans use the OK hand sign to mean everything is all right. Several years ago, a U.S. vice president visited a country in South America. While he was deplaning, someone from below asked, "How was the trip?" The vice president didn't think he could be heard over the crowd, so he used the North American OK sign. In that country, the sign was interpreted the way "flipping the bird" is interpreted here. The local paper printed a picture of our vice president giving the equivalent of the bird to that country. Needless to say, the people of the country were not too pleased.

Axtell (1991) suggests that gestures can also a be a valuable form of public opinion polling. He says, "according to *People* magazine, at least one U.S. politician had his system of gauging his popularity. . . . 'I watch the crowds waving to me and I count the number of fingers they're using' " (p. 16).

People from different parts of the world differ substantially in their gesturing. The biggest differences are in the use of emblems, which you will recall are gestures that can substitute for language equivalents. Cultures have very different emblems that they use to communicate the same meaning. Some emblems are shared by two cultures, but they represent different meanings. Also, there are emblems employed by one culture for which another culture may have no equivalent and vice versa.

The use of our hands can mean many different things in different cultures. For example, Ethiopians put one finger to her or his lips to show silence when motioning to a child, but uses four fingers when motioning silence to an adult. It is disrespectful to use only one finger to show silence in Ethiopia when motioning to an adult. In the United States, we use one finger to the lips for both children and adults. The OK sign references totally different meanings in different cultures. In Japan, it references money. It could represent female genitalia if a man uses it in front of a woman he is attempting to seduce. When directed toward a man, it can be an indication about what another thinks of his masculinity. Therefore, the OK emblem can be interpreted many different ways. It depends on the culture. It is also clear that this one emblem could create many communication misunderstandings across cultures.

Morsbach (1976) suggests that in Japan, the little finger pointed straight up can refer to a girlfriend, wife, or mistress. Rapidly crossing the index fingers refers to a fight. Lastly, licking an index finger and then drawing it over an eyebrow is a way of suggesting that someone is a liar. He says that instead of eyebrow-saliva, the word *mayutsuba* can be uttered in the appropriate context and this enables the Japanese to imply lying and deception without saying the equivalent of the word *liar.*

A smile is welcomed nonverbal communication in
almost any cultural setting.

The use of the head often creates communication misunderstandings. In some
parts of the East and parts of Africa, a person nods her or his head when in disagreement and shakes her or his head when in agreement, whereas in the United States we
nod when in agreement and shake our head when in disagreement. An author of this
text, while lecturing to large number of students several years ago, encountered the
situation described above. As he was lecturing, many students would nod in agreement. One student would shake his head while the others were nodding. This confused
the instructor, and after class he approached the student who had been shaking his
head in apparent disagreement. He found out that the student was from a part of India
where shaking one's head meant agreement. Therefore, he had agreed with the other
students, and he was using the gesture appropriate for his culture to signify agreement.

In Japan, the head nod may only mean continued attention, not necessarily
agreement. You might find that a Japanese person totally disagrees with you, but he
or she will nod out of respect until you have finished speaking. Jakobson (1976)
found that Bulgarians throw their heads back and then return their heads to an
upright position for "no." Many Westerners could misinterpret this to mean "yes." In

Korea, shaking one's head horizontally means "I don't know." In North American culture, shrugging one's shoulders means "I don't know."

Certain meanings are derived from movements that require more from the body than just the head or hands. For example, the Japanese bow involves most of the body. There is a pecking order for who should be bowing to whom. The rule is that women bow to men, and juniors bow to seniors. The rules are even more complicated than one would think. For example, how often one should bow, how long, and how deep all have to be considered in a relationship. Bows are usually reciprocated.

The bow is usually a form of greeting or respect. Americans typically learn to bow even when they have only been in Japan for a few hours. However, they never really learn the exact way of doing it. The Japanese would never criticize a guest in their country. They are simply amused by the Americans trying to imitate them. When bowing, one must be careful to move one's head slightly to the right so as not to strike the other's head. Americans often forget this. The handshake as a form of greeting is a Western import to Japan. Cosmopolitan Japanese and Americans often shake hands and bow simultaneously. Brault (1962) found a very complicated routine in France for communicating exquisiteness. The French pinch the fingers of the right hand together, point toward and raise to lips, kiss the fingers and raise them into the air. The chin is held high and the eyes closed slightly. Brault suggests that Americans use it for more than expressing exquisiteness. The French reserve it only for very exquisite things.

Ishii (1973) explored the posture of the Japanese. He found that *teishisei* or low posture is a sign of acceptance or respect. People who have modest *teishisei* are often trusted, loved, and accepted. People who have *teishisei* and are quiet or smile often in public are seen as successful. Japanese do not stand up immediately to greet an American or European when they enter a room. Japanese women have been taught to keep low posture and remain quiet when greeting seniors. Japanese at American parties usually stay reserved and quiet and may sit quietly in a corner or talk to other Japanese.

Klopf and Park (1982) suggest that younger Japanese people no longer use the Oriental form of squatting down to relax. Many in the older generation still do. Younger Japanese males sit in a chair with their legs crossed.

It is clear from the above discussion that gestures and body movements have different meanings from one culture to the next. It is also clear that successful communication across cultures can only take place if one understands the nonverbal behaviors of both cultures. See Table 15–1 for a summary of such nonverbal behavior.

Face and Eye Behavior.   In any culture, faces communicate emotions, personality, and obvious demographic characteristics such as age, ethnic group, nationality, and sex. Ekman, Friesen, and Ellsworth (1972) and Izard (1969) suggest that the basic facial emotions are transmitted by the same facial expressions across Western Europe, South America, and even parts of New Guinea. The Ekman studies found that people can identify correctly the primary emotions of sadness, happiness, anger,

---

TABLE 15–1 **Gestures and Body Movements from Axtell**

Greetings

Americans—good, firm grip, looking straight in the eye.

Middle East—*salaam* (right hand sweeps upward, first touching the heart, then the forehead, and finally up and outward, perhaps a slight nod of head and words, meaning "Peace be with you").

Eskimos—bang the other party with a hand on either the head or shoulder.

Maori tribespeople in New Zealand—rub noses.

Some East African Tribes—spit at each other's feet.

South America—handshake and hearty clap on back.

Farewells

Americans—goodbye wave (hand up, palm out, wrist stiff) with a back and forth motion of forearm and hand.

Europeans—arm up and extended out, with the palm down and the hand bobbing up and down at wrist.

Italians and Greeks—arm extended, palm up, curling all the fingers back and forth toward themselves.

Beckoning

Americans—raise a hand (with index finger raised) about head high or a little higher, or raise the hand with the full open palm; wave back and forth to attract attention.

Much of Europe and many Latin American Countries—extend the arm, hand out, palm down, and then make a scratching motion with the fingers.

Colombia—clap the hands lightly.

Insulting (Perhaps Obscene) Gestures (Meaning Equivalent)

Americans—single middle finger salute.

Arabs—extending the hand, palm down, fingers splayed outward, with the middle finger directed down.

Russians—bend back the middle finger of one hand with the forefinger of the other.

Yugoslavia—bend the arm at the elbow, make a fist (with knuckles away from face) and shake the fist once.

North America, Latin America, and parts of Europe—the forearm jerk (right arm is bent at the elbow and the left hand comes chopping down into the crook of the elbow while the fist of the right hand is jerked upward).

---

surprise, disgust, and fear. Izard found that both adults and children in a primitive culture of New Guinea could identify most, but they confused fear with surprise. Ekman found that most people are fairly good encoders and decoders of the basic facial expressions. Ekman (1975) also showed that decoders from the United States, England, Germany, Spain, France, Greece, Switzerland, and Japan can interpret facial expressions as displaying the same expression or emotion. He also found that people are fairly accurate at judging the intensity of an emotion.

However, this does not mean that facial expressions are pancultural. Although many cultures recognize the primary facial expressions, we must remember that in every culture there will be culture-specific differences based on the context (Ekman and Friesen, 1969). For example, females in North America are allowed to be more expressive than females in Iran or Japan. The Japanese culture is conditioned to mask emotions. We have all heard the phrase "the inscrutable Japanese." They may not use many facial expressions, but they can recognize them. Children in North America can be more expressive and questioning than children in many Eastern cultures. Ekman (1971) suggests that it is "likely that there is much more cultural variability in blends of facial expression than in facial expressions of primary emotions" (p. 223).

According to Klopf and Park (1982), Koreans usually have fixed, rigid facial expressions when meeting new people. However, they are very warm and receptive to their friends. In public, Koreans are cold and distant, but in private they are more warm.

Klopf and Park (1982) also discuss the smiling behavior of the Japanese. They suggest that the "Japanese smile is not always a spontaneous expression of amusement or friendliness as it is among Americans" (p. 88). The Japanese smile is an acculturated dimension of their culture. They are taught to smile as a form of etiquette. They will even smile when it seems inappropriate. Klopf cites the following incident in history:

> *The smile of the Japanese ambassador to the United States announcing the imminent attack on Pearl Harbor to American officials was completely misinterpreted by millions of Americans who saw newspaper photographs of the scene or read about it in the papers. The ambassador was observing Japanese custom when he smiled. Children are taught in Japan to smile as a social duty even in case of sorrowful circumstances. Rather than show sorrow, cultural ritual requires the smile. The ambassador personally opposed the attack and did not like the news he was forced to deliver. Custom dictated that he smile. That smile was misunderstood by much of the world. It helped spur the American forces to a greater war effort. Photos of the smiling ambassador were tacked up in armament factories, military barracks, and the cockpits of American bombers to help motivate the nation to win the war. (p. 88)*

Eibl-Eibesfeldt (1972) found some similarities across cultures in social greetings. He found that Europeans, South American Indians, Samoans, and South American bushmen will give an eyebrow flash when greeting a friend at a distance. An "eyebrow flash" involves moving their eyebrows up and down slightly while keeping the eyebrow raised at the highest level for about one-sixth of a second. This would look very strange to us in greeting. However, we use the eyebrow flash many times when we are surprised or questioning something.

Eye behavior takes many forms in different cultures. In this culture, we are taught not to stare. It is considered impolite in most circumstances. This tells us how important people feel eye behavior is. We have learned to use the unfocused stare when we need it. When we walk through shopping malls and don't really want any eye contact, we use the unfocused stare. When we don't want to confront someone, we use an unfocused stare. Students use this on teachers in the classroom. The unfocused stare is looking at nothing, intently. In many cultures, staring is much more customary, particularly staring at strangers or attractive women. Americans traveling in such countries can become very uncomfortable and often find the people in those cultures to be very impolite.

In North American culture, eye contact is a significant part of the courtship dance of the male and female. Eye-to-body contact is the first step, eye-to-eye is the second step. If the female does not hold the male's eye contact, she has essentially said "get lost" or "bug off." If the male cannot take the lack of eye contact as the cue, then she will tell him in step three to "get lost." Many people in this culture do not follow nonverbal cues. A male may continue staring. A female may respond when she should not.

In Japanese culture, the male and female engaging in courtship rarely look one another in the eye. Japanese males look elsewhere while they say romantic phrases. Japanese females usually act very shy and do not have much eye contact. In Japanese culture, eye contact is relevant, but in a different way than in American culture. In this culture, we place much value on direct eye contact. For example, if someone doesn't look us in the eye we feel disliked, as if they are inattentive to what we are saying, and we might even think they are trying to deceive us.

It is not customary in Japan to look others in the eye. It makes people uneasy and uncomfortable to have much eye contact in Japan. Therefore, Japanese and Americans often misperceive each other because the nonverbal behaviors are so distinct. The Japanese often look down or at other things when talking with each other. This is very disturbing to Americans. However, downcast or closed eyes in the Japanese culture at a meeting or conference are signs of attentiveness and agreement, not rejection and disagreement. Americans often misinterpret downcast or closed eyes as signs of disagreement, disinterest, or rejection.

In Nigerian culture, prolonged eye contact with a superior is considered disrespectful. Klopf and Park (1982) cite the example of an American Peace Corps volunteer in Nigeria who kept telling his class to look at him. He had many problems with the students and their parents. He finally learned that in Nigeria, it is disrespectful for students to look at teachers. As an American, he needed and wanted eye contact from his students. The Nigerian students felt it very disrespectful to have prolonged eye contact with him, so they looked down.

Puerto Rican children are also taught as a sign of obedience and respect not to share eye contact with adults. To show respect in Asian cultures, one does not look the other in the eye. In addition, Asian men do not stare at women and vice versa. A woman who makes her living on the streets is allowed to stare at men. In France, it is quite common for men to stare at women and appraise their bodies.

In conclusion, clearly facial expressions and eye contact communicate various meanings across cultures. We definitely need to educate ourselves as to the various meanings so we can more fully understand people from other cultures and not offend them when communicating with them.

Vocal Behavior.   Everything about our voices communicates. Our vocal variety, rate, volume, pauses, and even silence communicates. It is not only how we talk that matters, it even matters whether we talk.

The general North American culture respects talkativeness. People are evaluated more positively the more they talk, up to a very high amount. The Amish use the absence of talk as a punishment. They use silence as means of shunning, or punishing, someone for inappropriate behavior. Japanese culture, in contrast, respects quietness. The Japanese are a very silent people when listening to someone they respect. Sometimes they will not disagree with you even if they feel you are wrong. Silence, of course, should not be perceived as noncommunication. Silence can be have a variety of functions, such as creating interpersonal distance, showing respect for others, punishing others, and avoiding embarrassment for others.

In many cultures, it is appropriate to make vocal noises of enjoyment while eating. It is not uncommon for Koreans to belch at the dinner table. This signifies enjoyment of the meal. Americans and English find this behavior rude and intolerable. Both Koreans and Americans find it appropriate to blow one's nose at the dinner table, but this would be gross in some cultures.

Japanese hiss or inhale their breath while talking to others as a sign of respect. It gives the other person time to think. This is difficult for Westerners to deal with. On the other hand, Westerners use many filled and unfilled pauses, as well as ahs and hums. This is difficult for the Japanese to respond to. Germans and Russians have very strong, demonstrative vocalic tones that say to Americans and Asians, "I am right, do not disagree." This prompts perceptions of rudeness and arrogance.

Thus, it is easy to understand why people have difficulty communicating across cultures. Not only do the languages differ substantially, but the vocal behaviors are varied as well.

Space.   Space talks. How we use space and territory tells something about our culture. On occasions, our culture dictates how we use space. South Americans, Greeks, Arabs, and Italians establish a much closer proximity when interacting than North Americans. For example, Arabs like to be able to "breathe each other's breath" when talking. Shuter (1976) found that Costa Ricans establish closer proximity when communicating than Panamanians or Colombians. Shuter also found that German men prefer greater distances when interacting whereas Italian men prefer closer distances when interacting. Jones (1971) found that Chinese in New York City interact at greater distances than Puerto Ricans and Italians. In general, Asians, Pakistanis, Native Americans, North Americans, and Northern Europeans prefer greater distances when talking than Southern Europeans, Arabs, and South Americans.

Space preference is influenced by cultural norms. Besides cultural norms, such things as economic background and density of population influence spatial norms. For example, it is not unusual in Japanese culture to find families sleeping in one bedroom even if they have extra bedrooms. Many sections of Japan are densely populated, but this does not seem to be the reason for families sleeping in one room. Japanese family norms dictate close family bonding. Therefore, Japanese often sleep in one bedroom to have closeness. Of course, larger families share more rooms.

The use of space by different cultures can communicate various meanings. For example, standing too far away from one who expects you to stand close might be perceived as aloofness or coldness. Standing too close to another might be perceived as pushiness or aggressiveness. Klopf and Park (1982) make the point well:

> *The South American automatically tries to step closer to the North American while the latter backs away. Each attempts to establish what he feels is the "correct" distance. In doing so, each produces a nonverbal message. The South American begins to believe that the North American is distant and remote and perhaps even downright unfriendly. In such an extreme situation, space becomes a powerful nonverbal communicator, and the verbal message tends to become completely overshadowed and virtually inconsequential. (p. 78)*

Touch.   Like space and other nonverbal behaviors, touch differs from culture to culture. Touch is a relevant form of communication in every culture. It has been said that touch may very well be the most intimate form of communication in North American culture. This is primarily because we are very selective about where and whom we touch. North American culture is considered a noncontact-oriented culture. Despite the culture, touch can communicate love, caring, warmth, anger, happiness, sadness, or a variety of emotional states. This section reviews the various forms of touch and what they suggest in a variety of cultures.

Frank (1982) says that "each culture builds upon the early tactile experience of the infant and child a more or less elaborate series of patterns of adult conduct in which tactile surrogates and symbolic fulfillments are provided" (p. 288). For example, we teach our children how others say "don't touch," what certain touching means, and how to respond to touch. Frank suggests that it would take much "time and space to do more than mention the cultural patterning of person-to-person tactile communications" (p. 287). This is because of the variety of touching behaviors in cultures. He cites several such touching behaviors: handshake; removing a glove; dancing; rubbing noses or foreheads; clasping arms, shoulders, and waists; embracing knees; kissing; laying on of hands; slapping; and spanking. We do not try to look at every tactile experience in a culture; we review only a few common touch patterns here.

Courtship takes place in every culture in the world, and the rituals for courtships vary from culture to culture. As noted in Chapter 12, the male is typically the pursuer in North American culture and the female is typically the pursued. The type, amount, and duration of the touch between males and females determines how far the courtship will go. If the female does not respond to the male's arm around her waist, then he should realize he has gone as far as he is going, at least for a while. The North American female is more accessible to touch than the North American male. In Ireland, a couple may not hold hands until a considerable amount of acquaintance time has passed. Unmarried Muslim couples in Malaysia are forbidden to embrace or hold each other or have similar close contact. If they are caught, it is a $25 fine. Depending on your social status or class, some countries still require chaperons for the females. Jourard (1968) studied couples in cafes in four different cities in the world. He found that the average couple in Paris came into physical contact 110 times during an hour. In San Juan, Puerto Rico, couples patted, tickled, and caressed 180 times in an hour. The typical London couple never touched at all, and the American couple patted once or twice in an hour's time. Cross-sexual contact is not widely used or accepted by adults in most Oriental cultures. Tactile forms such as kissing, holding hands, patting, and hugging are reserved for private situations. Therefore, there is very little contact in Oriental cultures between men and women in public. Sechrest (1969) studied cross-sexual student couples on college campuses. He found that the Oriental cross-sexual couples touched less than the Caucasian couples.

It is not unusual to find much same-sex touching in other cultures. However, United States culture has made it almost taboo for males to touch other males except in very unusual circumstances. For example, when the American men's basketball team won the Olympics in 1984, the men were hugging, kissing, and patting one another. If we saw two men hugging, kissing, and patting on Main Street, USA, we would assume they were homosexual. In Korea, both men and women often hold hands, link arms, or walk hip-to-hip with the same sex as they walk though the streets. Walking close demonstrates friendship, not sexual interest. Touch that means affection between sexes is reserved for private places in Korean culture. In Japan, is it not uncommon to see men and women touching as they walk in the street. Young women even walk arm in arm and boys touch and jostle each other on the street. Italian-Americans touch more often than Anglo-Americans. It is common for African, Arab, and Southeast Asian males to hold hands as a sign of friendship. Among European females, the handshake is very common.

Touch plays an important role in the home. Welch (1979) asked 2,200 children from ages seven to eleven how they were rewarded for good behavior. Almost two-thirds of the children said they were hugged. They also said they liked it. Kaleina (1979) reported that pets get more loving strokes than humans in the United States. He suggests that North American culture has more loving contact with its pets than its family members. In American culture, we allow our touch to decrease from early infancy on. Senior citizens receive less touch than any other group in our culture. Research suggests that the American mother has more vocal contact with her infant than tactile, whereas the Japanese mother has more tactile contact with her infant than vocal. The Jewish and Italian subcultures in the United States probably give their children more tactile experiences than the Anglo subculture. In fact, mothers in the Anglo subculture are encouraged to leave their children alone or not touch after a certain age, particularly with boys. Girls in the Anglo culture receive more touch than boys from their parents.

Americans, Germans, and English are more offended by accidental touch by strangers than people in Oriental cultures. This is because of the amount of space each culture is granted. Many Oriental cultures have limited space, so they ignore, or at least are not offended by, accidental touch. However, Americans, Germans, and English are used to demanding more space and getting it, so they are often offended by accidental touch of a stranger.

In general, we can classify cultures by their orientations toward tactile communication. The Caucasian North American, German, English, and many Oriental cultures are generally noncontact-oriented cultures. The Japanese exhibit less contact than any of the other cultures. Southern Europeans, Jews, Italians, Greek-Americans, Arabs, and Puerto Ricans are generally more contact-oriented. Often this difference can create communication misunderstandings. When two people communicate who have different touch orientations, the communication can be misunderstood. Klopf and Park (1982) suggest,

> What is "normal" for one group is not necessarily "normal" for another. As a result, serious misunderstandings can occur. An Anglo-American can be perceived as reserved and distant . . . an Italian-American or a Greek-American can be judged as too assertive and pushy. (pp. 90–91)

It is clear that we need to understand and accept the touch norms of other cultures.

Environment. People are always surrounded by the environment. Its smells, colors, lighting, seating, and artifacts all influence our communication with one another. It is the same across cultures. When one enters a new culture, the environment assaults one's communication. Imagine how you would feel taking a bath in a public place with other men, women, and children. This is quite common in parts of Japan. Public baths are and have been an acceptable way of life for many Japanese, whereas people in other cultures take baths literally once a month. Let's look at another example. Imagine how people from another culture react to Las Vegas. Some view it as wasteful, frivolous, and brassy. Others see it as the most marvelous place in the world. It depends on what a culture values.

An author of the text recently visited Korea and was taken aback by the odor of garlic. He found out that garlic is the main ingredient in their national food, Chim Chee. He was there for a week, and by the end of the week had adjusted to the odor of garlic. Think of how the Korean must feel on a street in the Italian section of Manhattan. He or she must adjust to the odor of Italian food.

Air conditioning is very unique to North America and American hotels abroad. Most other countries do not have central air and heat as we do. They have learned that to keep the American tourist satisfied, they must have air conditioning and heat. Even in countries such as England and France, they often do not have central heat or air in their own homes. Many hotels install them to accommodate the American tourists.

In the Philippines, many upper-class citizens have complete and very elaborate bathrooms that do not function because they do not have modern sewage systems. To meet American standards, they have bathrooms in their homes that are not usable. They love to show Americans their bathrooms, but they are only for show.

When visiting another culture, it is essential to find out as soon as possible what is acceptable and what is not. It is very easy to offend someone in another culture by attacking the environmental cues.

Scent. We touched briefly on scent in the environment section, and we look at it more thoroughly here. Scent communicates different things in different cultures. This culture is more concerned about smelling good than any other culture. Many cultures accept bodily scents that we do not tolerate. Italians do not cover up their body scents. Often, the women in Italian culture do not shave their legs or under their arms. Many other cultures do not have the bathing facilities to stay as clean as we do. They take sponge baths or simply try to not get dirty. Therefore, their odors may be stronger than ours. In another culture, we have to be careful not to offend people by being too concerned about their personal hygiene habits. We must continue to communicate with them and accept their ways. After all, our ways and odors are strange to them.

Time. Time communicates and affects our communication with others. Even in this culture, we judge others based on their use of time. Southern people in the United States are more casual about time than Northerners. This creates an immense amount of negative stereotyping. Northerners perceive Southerners as slow, lazy, and dumb, but really nice. Southerners perceive Northerners to be pushy, aggressive, and too fast. Hawaiians and Mexicans have less concern about time and meeting a time schedule than most North Americans. If the above relatively small differences create negative perceptions, imagine how other cultural time orientations that are very different can foster misperceptions.

Many Latin Americans and Arabs prefer to conduct several business meetings and activities simultaneously. Therefore, they will schedule several meetings at one time. This insults the American businessperson who believes that you can do only one thing at a time. This misunderstanding of time can lead to negative perceptions. The Arabs and Latin Americans could perceive the American as demanding and selfish. The American could perceive the Latin Americans and Arabs as unconcerned about her or his business.

In conversations, Americans talk faster and more, pause less often, fill silent pauses, and interject comments more often and more quickly than the Japanese. The Japanese use silence more. To the Japanese, silence can be used a means of respect for the other or to show that one is thinking. To Americans, the talk time must be fast-paced. The Japanese like talk time to be well-managed and thoughtful. Ishii (1975) surveyed businessmen and female secretaries in Japan about silence and eloquence. The survey revealed that 76 percent of the respondents believed that silent men were more likely to succeed than eloquent men. It also revealed that 65 percent of the secretaries would select silent men to marry. Thirty-six percent of those who felt they were eloquent would rather be perceived as silent, whereas only 22 percent of the silent men wanted to be eloquent in the future.

American culture is very time-oriented, perhaps even more time-oriented than the Swiss and Germans. Americans emphasize scheduling and segmentation. The clock is the controller. Americans, Swiss, and Germans hate to be kept waiting. They like people to be on time. They judge people by how punctual or late they are. In this culture, we expect people to actually be early, not on time or late for an appointment. Latin Americans are usually late. In fact, it is a sign of respect to be late or to start things later than scheduled. If a Latin American sets a party for a given time, it will not begin until much later. The Japanese call before they visit. According to Klopf and Park (1982), the Japanese "may arrive not at a specified hour but anytime during the day" (p. 83).

Obviously, when having contact with people from another culture, one can never take time for granted. It may be a very serious breach of etiquette to treat time as one would in one's own culture. Be sure to find out ahead of such contact, if possible, how the other culture's time system is arranged. Do not be surprised if it makes no sense to you. Just try to adapt as best you can.

GOALS TO SEEK

In today's world, it is highly likely that all of us will have contact with people from other cultures. Many educated Americans hold jobs that require extensive intercultural contact. From this chapter, it should be clear that learning to control our nonverbal communication behavior when interacting with a person from another culture is no simple task. It is difficult for us to decide how much effort to put into such learning unless we know it will be critical to our futures. Most people in the past have chosen to devote very little time indeed.

While traveling in Europe, an author of this text noted some graffiti scrawled on a restroom wall in Amsterdam. It read as follows:

Speaks 3 languages = trilingual
Speaks 2 languages = bilingual
Speaks 1 language = American

His own lack of skill in any language other than American English had been fully impressed on him in his early stops on his trip. The humor of the graffiti was tempered with a recognition of the truth it suggested. Very few Americans are truly bilingual. Far fewer are bicultural.

Knowledge of a language does not provide an understanding of a culture. For example, many cultures speak Spanish, but the cultures differ from each other in extreme ways. The nonverbal behaviors of a culture are as important, if not more important, to understanding the culture as is the language of the culture. Many believe that the study of the nonverbal behavior of various cultures is much more valuable to the American who may need to travel widely than is the study of foreign languages. Although English is not a universal language, it is now the most common language in international commerce. It usually is possible to find someone who speaks English in almost any part of the world. People accept the fact that one cannot know all of the languages of the world. What they do not accept is rude and discourteous behavior—the nonverbal social blunder that occurs when one is not familiar with the nonverbal norms of a given culture. In recognition of this fact, more business organizations are developing training programs for their employees who must venture abroad on behalf of the company.

There are essentially three types of people in today's world: monocultural, bi- or multicultural, and acultural. The vast majority of the people on Earth fit in the first category—they are a product of a single culture and have little or no understanding or appreciation of any other culture. People in the second group are a product of one culture but have learned to adapt to the ways of one or more other cultures. Such people can flow from one culture to another and be accepted by the culture in which they find themselves. They have mastered not only the language but also the nonverbal behaviors of more than one culture. Most of us envy such people and wish we could be like them, but few of us are willing to devote the years of effort and study required to make that wish a reality.

The third category of people often is not recognized as different from the second, but they are very different. These people are acultural. By this we mean that they are not the product of any given culture. The best example of such a person is one who is born and spends many years in one culture and then moves to another culture and spends many years in that culture. Many immigrants fall into this category. Sometimes their children do also. They may move back and forth between two cultures, but they are never fully accepted in either because they cannot fully adapt their language or nonverbal behaviors in the transitions. They become a hybrid that doesn't really fit anywhere except with similar hybrids. Many children of American military families who move all over the world report feeling that they are in this category.

Because most of us are destined to remain in our monocultural world, becoming bi- or multicultural is not a realistic goal and, because we do not want to give up our own culture to become acultural, we need to consider what goal we can set that will help us to communicate with people from other cultures, who may be just as monocultural as we are. Ruben (1977), Harris and Moran (1991) and Klopf (1991) have suggested seven skills that we can learn that will aid in our cultural awareness:

1. Be nonjudgmental; avoid moralistic, value-laden evaluative statements; listen.
2. Be tolerant of differences and ambiguity; recognize differences.
3. Show respect; verbally and nonverbally convey positive regard and interest.
4. Personalize remarks; recognize your own values (say "I think," or "I believe").
5. Empathize; try to think as the other person or share his or her feelings and emotions.
6. Take turns; try to have some conversational turn-taking. Don't try to control the conversation; share and learn from one another.
7. Be patient—it takes time to fully understand another and for them to understand you.

Although such skills probably are best fostered by traveling and living for periods of time in another culture, we can also improve our skills by taking the time and effort to seek out people from other cultures in our own environment with whom to interact. Remember, most people from other cultures are just as interested in learning about our culture and how to adapt to us and we are in learning about their culture and how to adapt to them. Such mutual learning can occur anywhere on the globe.

A GLOSSARY OF TERMINOLOGY

Intercultural communication is the communication between people of different cultures, and it occurs when a person from one culture talks to a person from another.

Subculture is a collection of people who possess conscious membership in an identifiable unit of an encompassing, larger cultural unit.

▲ References

Chapter 1

Andersen, P. A., Garrison, J. P., and Andersen J. F. (1979). Implications of a neurophysiological approach for the study of nonverbal communication. *Human Communication Research, 6,* 74–89.

Birdwhistell, R. L. (1970). *Kinesics and context: Essays on body motion communication.* Philadelphia: University of Pennsylvania Press.

DeVito, J. A., and Hecht, M. L. (1990). *The nonverbal communication reader.* Prospect Heights, IL: Waveland Press.

Harrison, R. P. (1974). *Beyond words: An introduction to nonverbal communication.* Englewood Cliffs, NJ: Prentice-Hall.

Hecht, M. L., and DeVito, J. A. (1990). Perspectives on nonverbal communication. In J. A. DeVito and M. L. Hecht (eds.), *The nonverbal communication reader* (pp. 3–17). Prospect Heights, IL: Waveland Press.

Hickson, M. L., III, and Stacks, D. W. (1993). *Nonverbal communication: Studies and applications* (3rd ed.). Dubuque, IA: Wm. C. Brown.

Katz, A. M., and Katz, V. T. (eds.) (1983). *Foundations of nonverbal communication: Readings, exercises, and commentary.* Carbondale: Southern Illinois University Press.

Knapp, M. L., and Hall, J. A. (1992). *Nonverbal communication in human interaction* (3rd ed.). New York: Holt, Rinehart & Winston.

LaFrance, M., and Mayo, C. (1978). *Moving bodies: Nonverbal communication in social relationships.* Monterey, CA: Brooks/Cole.

Leathers, D. G. (1992). *Successful nonverbal communication: Principles and applications* (2nd ed.). New York: Macmillan.

Malandro, L. A., Barker, L., and Barker, D. A. (1989). *Nonverbal communication* (2nd ed.). New York: Random House.

Manusov, V., and Rodriquez, J. S. (1989). Intentionality behind nonverbal messages: A perceiver's perspective. *Journal of Nonverbal Behavior, 13,* 15–24.

McCroskey, J. C. (1993). *An introduction to rhetorical communication* (6th ed.). Englewood Cliffs, NJ: Prentice-Hall.

McCroskey, J. C., and Richmond, V. P. (1992). *Introduction to interpersonal communication.* Edina, MN: Burgess International Group.

McCroskey, J. C., Richmond, V. P., and Stewart, R. E. (1986). *One on one: The foundations of interpersonal communication.* Englewood Cliffs, NJ: Prentice-Hall.

Mehrabian, A. (1981). *Silent messages: Implicit communication of emotions and attitudes* (2nd ed.). Belmont, CA: Wadsworth.

Richmond, V. P. (1992). *Nonverbal behavior in the classroom.* Edina, MN: Burgess International Group.

Richmond, V. P., and McCroskey, J. C. (1993). *Communication: apprehension, avoidance, and effectiveness* (3rd ed.). Scottsdale, AZ: Gorsuch Scarisbrick.

Chapter 2

Abravanel, E. D., and King, E. A. (1985, August). What's your body. *New Woman,* 78–82.

Aiken, L. R. (1963). The relationships of dress to selected measures of personality in undergraduate women. *Journal of Social Psychology, 59,* 119–128.

Andersen, P. A., Jensen, T. A., and King, L. B. (1972, April). *The effects of homophilous hair and dress styles on credibility and comprehension.* Paper presented to the International Communication Association.

Baber, E. (1939). *Marriage and family.* New York: McGraw-Hill.

Berger, C. R., and Calabrese, R. J. (1975). Some explorations in initial interaction and beyond: Toward a developmental theory of interpersonal communication. *Human Communication Research, 1,* 99–112.

Berscheid, E., and Walster, E. H. (1969). *Interpersonal attraction.* Reading, MA: Addison-Wesley.

Berscheid, E., and Walster, E. (1971, June). Adrenaline makes the heart grow fonder. *Psychology Today, 5,* 46–50, 62.

Berscheid, E., and Walster, E. (1972). Beauty and the best. *Psychology Today, 5,* 42–46, 74.

Berscheid, E., and Walster, E. H. (1978). *Interpersonal attraction* (2nd ed.). Reading, MA: Addison-Wesley.

Berscheid, E., Walster, E., and Bohrnstedt, G. (1973). Body image: The happy American body. *Psychology Today, 7,* 119–123, 126–131.

Bozzi, V. (1986, January). Beautiful name, beautiful face? *Psychology Today, 20,* 70.

Brislin, R. W., and Lewis, S. A. (1968). Dating and physical attractiveness: Replication. *Psychological Reports, 22,* 976.

Buckley, H. M., and Roach, M. E. (1974). Clothing as a nonverbal communicator of social and political attitudes. *Home Economics Research Journal, 3,* 94–102.

Cash, T. F., and Janda, L. H. (1984). The eye of the beholder. *Psychology Today, December,* 46–52.

Compton, N. H. (1962). Personal attributes of color and design preferences in clothing fabrics. *Journal of Psychology, 54,* 191–195.

Cortes, J. B., and Gatti, F. M. (1965). Physique and self-description of temperament. *Journal of Consulting Psychology, 29,* 434.

Dion, K., Berscheid, E., and Walster, E. (1972). What is beautiful is good. *Journal of Personality and Social Psychology, 24,* 285–290.

Efran, M. G. (1974). The effect of physical appearance on the judgement of guilt, interpersonal attraction, and severity of recommended punishment in a simulated jury task. *Journal of Research in Personality, 8,* 45–54.

Findlay, S. (1984, September 7). Northeastern kids tend to be tubbier. *USA Today.*

Freedman, D. G. (1969). The survival value of the beard. *Psychology Today, 3,* 36–39.

Gibson, J. E. (1985, August 4). Is beauty in the mind of the beholden? *Family Weekly,* p. 11.

Gladstone, V. (1986, January). Anorexia then and now. *Psychology Today, 20,* 76–77.

Hamid, P. N. (1968). Style of dress as a perceptual cue in impression formation. *Perceptual and Motor Skills, 26,* 904–906.

Heilman, M. E., and Stopeck, M. H. (1985). Being attractive, advantage or disadvantage? Performance-based evaluations and recommended personnel actions as a function of appearance, sex, and job type. *Organizational Behavior and Human Decision Processes, 35,* 202–215.

Hewitt, J., and German, K. (1987). Attire and Attractiveness. *Perception and Motor Skills, 64,* 558.

Hickson, M. L., III, Powell, L., Hill, S. R., Jr., Holt, G. B., and Flick, H. (1979). Smoking artifacts as indicators of homophily, attraction, and credibility. *Southern Speech Communication Journal, 44,* 191–200.

Hoult, T. F. (1954). Experimental measurement of clothing as a factor in some social ratings of selected American men. *American Sociological Review, 19,* 324–328.

Infante, D. A., Rancer, A. S., Pierce, L. L., and Osborne, W. J. (1980). Effects of physical attractiveness and likableness of first name on impressions formed of journalists. *Journal of Applied Communication Research, 8,* 1–9.

Jourard, S. M., and Secord, P. F. (1955). Body-cathexis and personality. *British Journal of Psychology, 46,* 130–138.

Knapp, M. L., and Hall, J. A. (1992). *Nonverbal communication in human interaction* (3rd ed.). New York: Holt, Rinehart & Winston.

Korda, M. (1975). *Power: How to get it, How to use it.* New York: Ballantine.

Langley, M. (1981, August 14). More fat people are going to court, charging employers with job bias. *Wall Street Journal,* p. 25.

Leathers, D. G. (1992). *Successful Nonverbal Communication: Principles and Applications.* (2nd ed.). New York: Macmillan.

Lenz, E. (1993). Mirror, mirror. *Modern Maturity, August–September,* 24, 26, 28, 80.

Levy, D. (1993). Obesity affects economic health. *USA Today,* September 30, Section D.

Levy, R., and Poll, A. P. (1976). Through a glass, darkly. *Dun's Review,* 107, 77–78.

Malandro L. A., Barker, L., and Barker, D. A. (1989). *Nonverbal communication* (2nd ed.). New York: Random House.

McCroskey, J. C., Larson, C. E., and Knapp, M. L. (1971). *An introduction to interpersonal communication.* Englewood Cliffs, NJ: Prentice-Hall.

McCroskey, J. C., and McCain, T. A. (1974). The measurement of interpersonal attraction. *Speech Monographs, 41,* 261–266.

Mills, J., and Aronson, E. (1965). Opinion change as a function of the communicator's attractiveness and desire to influence. *Journal of Personality and Social Psychology, 1,* 173–177.

Mitchell, C., and Burdick, T. (1985, August). First impressions last. *Savvy,* p. 32–35.

Molloy, J. T. (1975). *Dress for success.* New York: Warner Books.

Molloy, J. T. (1978). *The women's dress for success book.* New York: Warner Books.

Molloy, J. T. (1983). *Molloy's live for success.* New York: Bantam Books.

Molloy, J. T. (1988). *The new dress for success book.* New York: Warner Books.

Morris, D. (1977). *Manwatching: A field guide to human behavior.* New York: Harry N. Abrams.

Morris, D. (1985). *Bodywatching.* New York: Crown.

Paterson, J. (1993). Comfort or bust. *USA Today,* November 17, Section D.

Pellegrini, R. J. (1973). Impressions of the male personality as a function of beardedness. *Psychology, 10,* 29–33.

Pellegrini, R. J. (1973). The virtue of hairiness. *Psychology Today, 7,* 14.

Reyes, K. W. (1993). Eye of the beholder. *Modern Maturity, August–September,* p. 22–23.

Richmond, V. P. (1992). *Nonverbal communication in the classroom.* Edina, MN: Burgess International Group.

Richmond, V. P., and Robertson, D. L. (1977). Women's liberation in interpersonal relations. *Journal of Communication, 27,* 42–45.

Roach, M. E., and Eicher, J. B. (1973). *The visible self: Perspectives on dress.* Englewood Cliffs, NJ: Prentice-Hall.

Roppatte, V., and Cohen, S. S. (1985). *The looks men love.* New York: St. Martin's.

Rosenblatt, R. (1993). Secret admirer. *Modern Maturity, August–September,* pp. 25, 29, 80.

Rosencranz, M. L. (1962). Clothing symbolism. *Journal of Home Economics, 54,* 18–22.

Rosenfeld, L. B., and Plax, T. G. (1977). Clothing as communication. *Journal of Communication, 27,* 24–31.

Sabatelli, R. M., and Rubin, M. (1986). Nonverbal expressiveness and physical attractiveness as mediators of interpersonal perceptions. *Journal of Nonverbal Behavior, 10,* 120–133.

Satran, P. (1984, December). Dressing for a male or female interviewer. *Glamour,* p. 142.

Sheldon, W. H. (1940). *The varieties of human physique.* New York: Harper and Brothers.

Sheldon, W. H. (1942). *The varieties of temperament.* New York: Hafner.

Sheldon, W. H. (1954). *Atlas of men: A guide for somatotyping the adult male of all ages.* New York: Harper.

Singer, M. S., and Singer, A. E. (1985). The effect of police uniform on interpersonal perception. *Journal of Psychology, 119,* 157–161.

Singh, B. N. (1964). A study of certain personal qualities as preferred by college students in their marital partners. *Journal of Psychological Researchers, 8,* 37–48.

Sporkin, E. (1984, November 19). We're making passes at high-fashion glasses. *USA Today,* Section D.

Stark, E. (1986, January). Bulimia: Not epidemic. *Psychology Today, 20,* 17.

Sybers, R., and Roach, M. E. (1962). Clothing and human behavior. *Journal of Home Economics, 54,* 184–187.

Taylor, L. C., and Compton, N. H. (1968). Personality correlates of dress conformity. *Journal of Home Economics, 60,* 653–656.

Thornton, G. R. (1944). The effect of wearing glasses upon judgments of personality traits of persons seen briefly. *Journal of Applied Psychology, 28,* 203–207.

Thourlby, W. (1980). *You are what you wear.* New York: New American Library.

Walker, R. N. (1963). Body build and behavior in young children: II. Body build and parents' ratings. *Child Development, 34,* 1–23.

Walster, E. V., Aronson, E., Abrahams, D., and Rohmann, L. (1966). Importance of physical attractiveness in dating behavior. *Journal of Personality and Social Psychology, 4,* 508–516.

Wells, W. D., and Siegel, B. (1961). Stereotyped somatotypes. *Psychological Reports, 8,* 77–78.

What women like in men. (1983, July 20). *USA Today.*

Widgery R. N., and Ruch, R. S. (1981). Beauty and the Machiavellian. *Communication Quarterly, 29,* 297–301.

Williams, M. C., and Eicher, J. B. (1966). Teenagers' appearance and social acceptance. *Journal of Home Economics, 58,* 457–461.

Wilson, P. R. (1968). Perceptual distortion of height as a function of ascribed academic status. *Journal of Social Psychology, 74,* 97–102.

Winner's guide to job-smart dressing. (1986, March). *Glamour,* pp. 302–307.

Zakahi, W. R., and Duran, R. L. (1984). Attraction, communicative competence and communication satisfaction. *Communication Research Reports, 1,* 54–57.

Chapter 3

Argyle, M. (1975). *Bodily communication.* New York: International Universities Press.
Birdwhistell, R. L. (1952). *Introduction to kinesics: An annotation system for analysis of body motion and gesture.* Louisville, KY: University of Louisville Press.
Birdwhistell, R. L. (1970). *Kinesics and context: Essays on body motion communication.* Philadelphia: University of Pennsylvania Press.
Cohen, A. A. (1977). The communicative functions of hand illustrators. *Journal of Communication, 27,* 54–63.
DePaulo, B. M. (1988). Nonverbal aspects of deception. *Journal of Nonverbal Behavior, 12,* 153–161.
DePaulo, B. M., and Kirkendol, S. E. (1988). The motivational impairment effect in the communication of deception. In J. Yuille (ed.), *Credibility assessment* (pp. 50–69) Belgium: Kluwer Academic Publishers.
Dittmann, A. T. (1971). Review of kinesics and context by R. L. Birdwhistell. *Psychiatry, 34,* 334–342.
Duncan, S. D., Jr. (1972). Some signals and rules for taking speaking turns in conversations. *Journal of Personality and Social Psychology, 23,* 283–292.
Duncan, S. D., Jr. (1974). On the structure of speaker-auditor interaction during speaking turns. *Language in Society, 2,* 161–180.
Eakins, B. W., and Eakins, R. G. (1978). *Sex differences in human communication.* Boston: Houghton-Mifflin.
Ekman, P. (1976). Movements with precise meanings. *Journal of Communication, 26,* 14–26.
Ekman, P., and Friesen, W. V. (1969a). Nonverbal leakage and clues to deception. *Psychiatry, 32,* 88–106.
Ekman, P., and Friesen, W. V. (1969b). The repertoire of nonverbal behavior: Categories, origins, usage, and coding. *Semiotica, 1,* 49–98.
Ekman, P., and Friesen, W. V. (1972). Hand movements. *Journal of Communication, 22,* 353–374.
Ekman, P., and Friesen, W. V. (1974). Detecting deception from the body or face. *Journal of Personality and Social Psychology, 29,* 288–298.
Fast, J. (1970). *Body language.* New York: M. Evans.
Harper, R. G., Wiens, A. N., and Matarazzo, J. D. (1978). *Nonverbal communication: The state of the art* (pp. 119–170). New York: John Wiley & Sons.
Henley, N. M. (1977). *Body politics: Power, sex, and nonverbal communication.* Englewood Cliffs, NJ: Prentice-Hall.
Hocking, J. E., Bauchner, J., Kaminski, E. P., and Miller, G. R. (1979). Detecting deceptive communication from verbal, visual, and paralinguistic cues. *Human Communication Research, 6,* 33–46.
Johnson, H. G., Ekman, P., and Friesen, W. V. (1975). Communicative body movements: American emblems. *Semiotica, 15,* 335–353.
Kearney, P., and McCroskey, J. C. (1980). Relationships among teacher communication style, trait and state communication apprehension and teacher effectiveness. In D. Nimmo (ed.), *Communication Yearbook 4* (pp. 533–564). New Brunswick, NJ: Transaction Books.
Kendon, A., and Ferber (1973). A description of some human greetings. In R. P. Michael and J. H. Crook (eds.), *Comparative Ecology and Behavior of Primates.* London: Academic Press.
Knapp, M. L., and Hall, J. A. (1992). *Nonverbal communication in human interaction* (3rd ed.). New York: Holt, Rinehart & Winston.
Knapp, M. L., Hart, R. P., and Dennis, H. S. (1974). An exploration of deception as a communication construct. *Human Communication Research, 1,* 15–29.

Malandro, L. A., and Barker, L. (1983). *Nonverbal communication* (pp. 111–143). Reading, MA: Addison-Wesley.

Mehrabian, A. (1969a). Measures of achieving tendency. *Educational and Psychological Measurement, 29,* 445–451.

Mehrabian, A. (1969b). Significance of posture and position in the communication of attitude and status relationships. *Psychological Bulletin, 71,* 359–372.

Mehrabian, A. (1971). *Silent messages.* Belmont, CA: Wadsworth.

Mehrabian, A. (1972). *Nonverbal communication.* Chicago: Aldine-Atherton.

Mehrabian, A. (1981). *Silent messages: Implicit communication of emotions and attitudes* (2nd ed.). Belmont, CA: Wadsworth.

Norton, R. (1983). *Communicator style: Theory, applications, and measures.* Beverly Hills, CA: Sage Publications.

Norton, R., and Nussbaum, J. (1980). Dramatic behaviors of the effective teacher. In D. Nimmo (ed.), *Communication Yearbook 4* (pp. 565–579). New Brunswick, NJ: Transaction Books.

Richmond, V. P. (1992). *Nonverbal communication in the classroom.* Edina, MN: Burgess International Group.

Richmond, V. P., and McCroskey, J. C. (1993). *Communication: apprehension, avoidance, and effectiveness* (3rd ed.). Scottsdale, AZ: Gorsuch Scarisbrick.

Rogers, W. T. (1978). The contribution of kinesic illustrators toward the comprehension of verbal behavior within utterances. *Human Communication Research, 5,* 54–62.

Rosenfeld, H. M. (1966a). Approval-seeking and approval-inducing functions of verbal and nonverbal responses in the dyad. *Journal of Personality and Social Psychology, 4,* 597–605.

Rosenfeld, H. M. (1966b). Instrumental affiliative functions of facial and gestural expressions. *Journal of Personality and Social Psychology, 4,* 65–72.

Rosenfeld, H. M. (1982). Measurement of body motion and orientation. In K. R. Scherer and P. Ekman (eds.), *Handbook of methods in nonverbal behavior research* (pp. 199–286). New York: Cambridge University Press.

Scheflen, A. E. (1964). The significance of posture in communication systems. *Psychiatry, 27,* 316–331.

Weitz, S. (ed.) (1974). *Nonverbal communication: Readings with commentary.* New York: Oxford University Press.

Chapter 4

Andersen, P. A., Todd-Mancillas, W. R., and Clementa, L. D. (1980). Effects of pupil dilation on physical, social, and task attraction. Australian SCAN: *Journal of Human Communication, 7-8,* 89–96.

Argyle, M., and Ingham, R. (1972). Gaze, mutual gaze and proximity. *Semiotica, 6,* 32–49.

Bakan, P. (1971). The eyes have it. *Psychology Today, 4,* 64–67, 96.

Barlow, J. D. (1969). Pupillary size as an index of preference in political candidates. *Perceptual and Motor Skills, 28,* 587–590.

Boucher, J. D., and Ekman, P. (1975). Facial areas and emotional information. *Journal of Communication, 25,* 21–29.

Breed, G., and Colaiuta, V. (1974). Looking, blinking, and sitting. *Journal of Communication, 24,* 75–81.

Brownlow, S., and Zebrowitz, L. A. (1990). Facial appearance, gender, and credibility in television commercials. *Journal of Nonverbal Behavior, 14,* 51–59.

Burkhardt, J. C., Weider-Hatfield, D., and Hocking, J. E. (1985). Eye contact contrast effects in the employment interview. *Communication Research Reports, 1,* 5–10.

Clark, W. R. (1975). *A comparison of pupillary response, heart rate, and GSR during decep- tion.* Paper presented at the meeting of the Mid-Western Psychological Association, Chicago.

Darwin, C. (1872). *The expression of the emotions in man and animals.* London: Murray. Reprinted in A. Dittmann (ed.) (1972), *Interpersonal messages of emotion.* New York: Springer.

Dovidio, J. F., and Ellyson, S. L. (1985). Patterns of visual dominance behavior in humans. In S. L. Ellyson and J. F. Dovidio (eds.), *Power, dominance, and nonverbal behavior* (pp. 129–150). New York: Springer-Verlag.

Duncan, S. D., Jr. (1972). Some signals and rules for taking speaking turns in conversations. *Journal of Personality and Social Psychology, 23,* 283–292.

Eibl-Eibesfeldt, I. (1970). *Ethology: The biology of behavior.* New York: Holt, Rinehart & Winston.

Eibl-Eibesfeldt, I. (1972). Similarities and differences between cultures in expressive move- ment. In R. A. Hinde (ed.), *Nonverbal communication* (pp. 297–314). Cambridge: Cam- bridge University Press.

Ekman, P. (1972). Universals and cultural differences in facial expressions of emotions. In J. Cole (ed.), *Nebraska symposium on motivation* (pp. 207–283). Lincoln: University of Nebraska Press.

Ekman, P., and Friesen, W. V. (1967). Head and body cues in the judgment of emotion: A reformulation. *Perceptual and Motor Skills, 24,* 711–724.

Ekman, P., and Friesen, W. V. (1969a). Nonverbal leakage and clues to deception. *Psychiatry, 32,* 88–106.

Ekman, P., and Friesen, W. V. (1969b). The repertoire of nonverbal behavior: Categories, ori- gins, usage, and coding. *Semiotica, 1,* 49–98.

Ekman, P., and Friesen, W. V. (1975). *Unmasking the face: A guide to recognizing emotions from facial cues.* Englewood Cliffs, NJ: Prentice-Hall.

Ekman, P., Friesen, W. V., and Ellsworth, P. (1972). *Emotion in the human face: Guidelines for research and an integration of findings.* New York: Pergamon Press.

Ekman, P., Friesen, W. V., and Tomkins, S. S. (1971). Facial affect scoring technique: A first validity study. *Semiotica, 3,* 37–58.

Ellsworth, P. C. (1975). Direct gaze as a social stimulus: The example of aggression. In P. Pliner, L. Krames, and T. Alloway (eds.), *Nonverbal communication of aggression* (pp. 53–76). New York: Plenum Press.

Exline, R. V. (1963). Explorations in the process of person perception: Visual interaction in relation to competition, sex, and need for affiliation. *Journal of Personality, 31,* 1–20.

Exline, R. V. (1971). Visual interaction: The glances of power and preference. In J. K. Cole (ed.), *Nebraska symposium on motivation* (pp. 162–205). Lincoln: University of Nebraska Press.

Exline, R. V., Ellyson, S. L., and Long, B. (1975). Visual behavior exhibited by males differ- ing as to interpersonal control orientation in one and two way communication systems. In P. Pliner, L. Krames, and T. Alloway (eds.), *Nonverbal communication of aggression* (pp. 21–52). New York: Plenum Press.

Exline, R. V., and Fehr, B. J. (1982). The assessment of gaze and mutual gaze. In K. R. Scherer and P. Ekman (eds.), *Handbook of methods in nonverbal behavior research* (pp. 91–135). Cambridge: Cambridge University Press.

Exline, R. V., Gray, D., and Schuette, D. (1965). Visual behavior in a dyad as affected by interview content and sex of respondent. *Journal of Personality and Social Psychology, 1,* 201–209.

Exline, R. V., and Winters, L. C. (1965). Affective relations and mutual glances in dyads. In S. S. Tomkins and C. E. Izard (eds.), *Affect, cognition, and personality: Empirical studies* (pp. 319–350). New York: Springer.

Harper, R. G., Wiens, A. N., and Matarazzo, J. D. (1978). *Nonverbal communication: The state of the art* (pp. 77–118, 171–245). New York: John Wiley & Sons.

Heron, J. (1970). The phenomenology of social encounter: The gaze. *Philosophy and Phenomenological Research, 31,* 243–264.

Hess, E. H. (1965). Attitude and pupil size. *Scientific American, 212,* 46–54.

Hess, E. H., and Polt, H. M. (1960). Pupil size as related to interest value of visual stimuli. *Science, 132,* 349–350.

Hess, E. H., Seltzer, A. L., and Schlien, J. M. (1965). Pupil responses of hetero- and homosexual males to pictures of men and women: A pilot study. *Journal of Abnormal Psychology, 70,* 165–168.

Hickson, M. L., and Stacks, D. W. (1993). *Nonverbal communication: Studies and applications* (2nd ed.). Madison, WI: Brown & Benchmark.

Hindmarch, I. (1970). Eyes, eye-spots, and pupil dilation in nonverbal communication. In I. Vine and M. von Cranach (eds.), *Social communication and movement* (pp. 299–321). New York: Academic Press.

Johnson, H. G., Ekman, P., and Friesen, W. V. (1975). Communicative body movements: American emblems. *Semiotica, 15,* 335–353.

Jordan, N. (1986, January). The face of feeling. *Psychology Today, 20,* 8.

Katsikitis, M., Pilowksy, I., and Innes, J. M. (1990). The quantification of smiling using a microcomputer-based approach. *Journal of Nonverbal Behavior,* 3–17.

Kendon, A. (1967). Some functions of gaze-direction in social interaction. *Acta Psychologica, 26,* 22–63.

Knapp, M. L., and Hall, J. A. (1992). *Nonverbal communication in human interaction* (3rd ed.). New York: Holt, Rinehart & Winston.

Knapp, M. L., Hart, R. P., and Dennis, H. S. (1974). An exploration of deception as a communication construct. *Human Communication Research, 1,* 15–29.

Knapp, M. L., Hart, R. P., Friedrich, G. W., and Shulman, G. M. (1973). The rhetoric of goodbye: Verbal and nonverbal correlates of human leave-taking. *Speech Monographs, 40,* 182–198.

LaFrance, M., and Mayo, C. (1976). Racial differences in gaze behavior during conversations: Two systematic observational studies. *Journal of Personality and Social Psychology, 33,* 547–552.

Malandro, L. A., Barker, L., and Barker, D. A. (1989). *Nonverbal communication* (2nd ed.). New York: Random House.

Mehrabian, A. (1972). *Nonverbal communication.* Chicago: Aldine-Atherton.

Mehrabian, A., and Williams, M. (1969). Nonverbal concomitants of perceived and intended persuasiveness. *Journal of Personality and Social Psychology, 13,* 37–58.

Morris, D. (1985). *Body watching.* New York: Crown.

Nielsen, G. (1962). *Studies in self-confrontation.* Copenhagen: Scandinavian University Books.

Russell, J. A., and Bullock, M. (1985). Multidimensional scaling of emotional facial expressions: Similarity from preschoolers to adults. *Journal of Personality and Social Psychology, 48,* 1290–1298.

Scherwitz, L., and Helmreich, R. (1973). Interactive effects of eye contact and verbal content on interpersonal attraction in dyads. *Journal of Personality and Social Psychology, 25,* 6–14.

Tomkins, S. S. (1962). *Affect, imagery, consciousness, Vol. 1: The positive affects.* New York: Springer.

Tomkins, S. S., and McCarter, R. (1964). What and where are the primary affects? Some evidence for a theory. *Perceptual and Motor Skills, 18,* 119–158.

Tucker, J. S., and Riggio, R. E. (1988). The role of social skills in encoding posed and spontaneous facial expressions. *Journal of Nonverbal Behavior, 12,* 87–97.

Van Hooff, J.A.R.A.M. (1972). A comparative approach to the phylogeny of laughter and smiling. In R. A. Hinde (ed.), *Nonverbal communication* (pp. 209–241). Cambridge: Cambridge University Press.

Vlietstra, A. G., and Manske, S. H. (1981). Looks to adults, preferences for adult males and females, and interpretations of an adult's gaze by preschool children. *Merrill-Palmer Quarterly, 27,* 31–41.

von Cranach, M. (1971). The role of orienting behavior in human interaction. In A. H. Esser (ed.), *Behavior and environment: The use of space by animals and men* (pp. 217–237). New York: Plenum.

Wagner, H. L., MacDonald, C. J., and Manstead, A.S.R. (1986). Communication of individual emotions by spontaneous facial expressions. *Journal of Personality and Social Psychology, 50,* 737–743.

Watson, O. M. (1970). *Proxemic behavior: A cross-cultural study.* The Hague: Monton.

Weitz, S. (ed.). (1974). *Nonverbal communication: Readings with commentary.* New York: Oxford University Press.

White, K. (1984, September). Eye power. *Glamour,* pp. 360–361, 399–402.

Wiemann, J. M., and Knapp, M. L. (1975). Turn-taking in conversations. *Journal of Communication, 25,* 75–92.

Chapter 5

Addington, D. W. (1968). The relationship of selected vocal characteristics to personality perception. *Speech Monographs, 35,* 492–503.

Addington, D. W. (1971). The effect of vocal variations on ratings of source credibility. *Speech Monographs, 38,* 242–247.

Blanck, P. D., Buck, R., and Rosenthal, R. (eds.). (1986). *Nonverbal communication in the clinical context.* University Park: Pennsylvania State University Press.

Boomer, D. S. (1965). Speech disturbance and body movement in interviews. *Journal of Nervous and Mental Disease, 136,* 236–266.

Bradford, A., Farrar, D., and Bradford, G. (1974). Evaluation reactions of college students to dialect differences in the English of Mexican-Americans. *Language and Speech, 17,* 255–270.

Bruneau, T. (1973). Communicative silences: Forms and functions. *Journal of Communication, 23,* 17–46.

Colquit, J. L. (1977). The student's right to his own language: A viable model or empty rhetoric? *Communication Quarterly, 25,* 17–20.

Davitz, J. R. (ed.) (1964). *The communication of emotional meaning.* New York: McGraw-Hill.

Davitz, J. R., and Davitz, L. J. (1959). The communication of feelings by content-free speech. *Journal of Communication, 9,* 6–13.

Diehl, C. F., and McDonald, E. T. (1956). Effect of voice quality on communication. *Journal of Speech and Hearing Disorders, 21,* 233–237.

Duncan, S. D., Jr. (1972). Some signals and rules for taking speaking turns in conversations. *Journal of Personality and Social Psychology, 23,* 283–292.

Duncan, S. D., Jr. (1973). Toward a grammar for dyadic conversation. *Semiotica, 9,* 29–46.

Duncan, S. D., Jr. (1974). On the structure of speaker–auditor interaction during speaking turns. *Language in Society, 2,* 161–180.

Flexner, S. B. (1976). *I hear America talking: An illustrated treasury of American words and phrases.* New York: Van Nostrand Reinhold.

Glasgow, G. M. (1952). A semantic index of vocal pitch. *Speech Monographs, 19,* 64–68.

Goldman-Eisler, F. (1968). *Psycholinguistics: Experiments in spontaneous speech.* New York: Academic Press.

Harper, R. G., Wiens, A. N., and Matarazzo, J. D. (1978). *Nonverbal communication: The state of the art* (pp. 20–76). New York: John Wiley & Sons.

Hickson, M. L., III, and Stacks, D. W. (1989). *Nonverbal communication: studies and applications* (2nd ed.). Dubuque, IA: Brown.

Jensen, M., and Rosenfeld, L. B. (1974). Influence of mode of presentation, ethnicity, and social class on teachers' evaluations of students. *Journal of Educational Psychology, 66,* 540–547.

Johnson, J. (1985, November). Laughs every day could keep the doctor away. *USA Weekend,* p. 23.

Kibler, R. J., and Barker, L. L. (1972). Effects of selected levels of misspelling and mispronunciation on comprehension and retention. *Southern Speech Communication Journal, 37,* 387–401.

Kimble, C. E., and Seidel, S. D. (1991). Vocal signs of confidence. *Journal of Nonverbal Behavior, 15,* 99–105.

Knapp, M. L., and Hall, J. A. (1992). *Nonverbal communication in human interaction* (3rd ed.). New York: Holt, Rinehart & Winston.

Kramer, E. (1963). Judgement of personal characteristics and emotions from nonverbal properties of speech. *Psychological Bulletin, 60,* 408–420.

Lalljee, M. G., and Cook, M. (1969). An experimental investigation of the function of filled pauses in speech. *Language and Science, 12,* 24–28.

Malandro, L. A., Baker, L., and Barker, D. A. (1989). *Nonverbal communication.* New York: Random House.

Markel, N. N. (1965). The reliability of coding paralanguage: Pitch, loudness, and tempo. *Journal of Verbal Learning and Verbal Behavior, 4,* 306–308.

McCroskey, J. C. (1993). *An introduction to rhetorical communication* (5th ed.) (pp. 125–139, 248–268). Englewood Cliffs, NJ: Prentice-Hall.

McCroskey, J. C., and Richmond, V. P. (1992). *Introduction to interpersonal communication.* Edina, MN: Burgess International Group.

McCroskey, J. C., Richmond, V. P., and Stewart, R. A. (1986). *One on one: The foundations of interpersonal communication* (pp. 117–158). Englewood Cliffs, NJ: Prentice-Hall.

Mehrabian, A. (1968). Communication without words. *Psychology Today, 2,* 52–55.

Mehrabian, A., and Ferris, S. R. (1967). Inference of attitudes from nonverbal communication in two channels. *Journal of Consulting Psychology, 31,* 248–252.

Mehrabian, A., and Williams, M. (1969). Nonverbal concomitants of perceived and intended persuasiveness. *Journal of Personality and Social Psychology, 13,* 37–58.

Miller, G. R., and Hewgill, M. A. (1964). The effects of variations of nonfluency on audience ratings of source credibility. *Quarterly Journal of Speech, 50,* 36–44.

Miller, N., Maruyama, G., Beaber, R. J., and Valone, K. (1976). Speed of speech and persuasion. *Journal of Personality and Social Psychology, 34,* 615–624.

Mulac, A., Hanley, T. D., and Prigge, D. Y. (1974). Effects of phonological speech foreignness upon three dimensions of attitude of selected American listeners. *Quarterly Journal of Speech, 60,* 411–420.

Newman, J. M. (1982). The sounds of silence in communicative encounters. *Communication Quarterly, 30,* 142–149.

Pearce, W. B. (1971). The effect of vocal cues on credibility and attitude change. *Western Speech Journal, 35,* 176–184.

Pearce, W. B., and Conklin, F. (1971). Nonverbal vocalic communication and perceptions of a speaker. *Speech Monographs, 38,* 235–241.

Perlmutter, K. B., Paddock, J. R., and Duke, M. P. (1985). The role of verbal, vocal, and non-verbal cues in the communication of evoking message styles. *Journal of Research in Personality, 93,* 31–43.

Phillips, G. M., Kougl, K. M., and Kelly, L. (1985). *Speaking in public and private.* Indianapolis, IN: Bobbs-Merrill Educational Publishing.

Ray, G. B. (1986). Vocally cued personality prototypes: An implicit personality theory. *Communication Monographs, 53,* 266–276.

Richmond, V. P. (1992). *Nonverbal communication in the classroom.* Edina, MN: Burgess International Group.

Rosenfeld, L. B., and Civikly, J. M. (1976). *With words unspoken: The nonverbal experience.* New York: Holt, Rinehart & Winston.

Sayer, J. E. (1979). The student's right to his own language: A response to Colquit. *Communication Quarterly, 27,* 44–46.

Scherer, K. R. (1982). Methods of research on vocal communication: Paradigms and parameters. In K. R. Scherer and P. Ekman (eds.), *Handbook of methods in nonverbal behavior research* (pp. 136–198). Cambridge: Cambridge University Press.

Scherer, K. R., Koivumaki, J., and Rosenthal, R. (1972). Minimal cues in the vocal communication of affect: Judging emotions from content-masked speech. *Journal of Psycholinguistic Research, 1,* 269–285.

Sereno, K. K., and Hawkins, G. J. (1967). The effects of variations in speaker's nonfluency upon audience ratings of attitude toward the speech topic and speakers' credibility. *Speech Monographs, 34,* 58–64.

Shuy, R. W. (1965). *Social dialects and language learning.* Champaign, IL: National Council of Teachers of English.

Snyder, M. (1974). Self-monitoring of expressive behavior. *Journal of Personality and Social Psychology, 30,* 526–537.

Soskin, W. F. (1953). *Some aspects of communication and interpretation in psychotherapy.* Paper presented at the meeting of the American Psychological Association, Cleveland. Cited in E. Kramer (1963). Judgment of personal characteristics and emotions from nonverbal properties of speech. *Psychological Bulletin, 60,* 408–420.

Starkweather, J. A. (1961). Vocal communication of personality and human feelings. *Journal of Communication, 11,* 63–72.

Trager, G. L. (1958). Paralanguage: A first approximation. *Studies in Linguistics, 13,* 1–12.

Wiemann, J. M., and Knapp, M. L. (1975). Turn-taking in conversations. *Journal of Communication, 25,* 75–92.

Williams, F. (1970). The psychological correlates of speech characteristics: On sounding "disadvantaged." *Journal of Speech and Hearing Research, 13,* 472–488.

Woolbert, C. H. (1920). Effects of various modes of public reading. *Journal of Applied Psychology, 4,* 162–185.

Zuckerman, M., and Driver, R. E. (1989). What sounds beautiful is good: The vocal attractiveness stereotype. *Journal of Nonverbal Behavior, 13,* 67–81.

Chapter 6

Altman, I. (1975). *The environment and social behavior.* Monterey, CA: Brooks/Cole.

Baxter, J. C. (1970). Interpersonal spacing in natural settings. *Sociometry, 33,* 444–456.

Becker, F. D., and Mayo, C. (1971). Delineating personal distance and territory. *Environment and Behavior, 3,* 375–382.

Bell, P. A., and Barnard, W. A. (1984). Effects of hear, noise, and sex of subject on a projective measure of personal space permeability. *Perceptual and Motor Skills, 59,* 422.

Carey, G. W. (1972, March/April). Density, crowding, stress, and the ghetto. *American Behavioral Scientist,* 495–507.

Conigliaro, L., Cullerton, K., Flynn, K., and Rueder, S. (1989). Stigmatizing artifacts and their effect on personal space. *Psychological Reports, 65,* 897–898.

Edney, J. J. (1976). Human territories: Comment on functional properties. *Environment and Behavior, 8,* 31–47.

Fisher, J. D., and Byrne, D. (1975). Too close for comfort: Sex difference in response to invasions of personal space. *Journal of Personality and Social Psychology, 32,* 15–21.

Fry, A. M., and Willis, F. N. (1971). Invasion of personal space as a function of the age of the invader. *Psychological Record, 21,* 385–389.

Galle, O. R., Grove, W. R., and McPherson, J. M. (1972). Population density and pathology: What are the relations for man? *Science, 176,* 23–30.

Gifford, R., and O'Connor, B. (1986). Nonverbal intimacy: Clarifying the role of seating distance and orientation. *Journal of Nonverbal Behavior, 10,* 207–214.

Greenberg, C. I., and Firestone, I. J. (1977). Compensatory responses to crowding: Effects of personal space intrusion and privacy reduction. *Journal of Personality and Social Psychology, 9,* 637–644.

Hall, E. T. (1959). *The silent language.* Garden City, NJ: Doubleday.

Hall, E. T. (1963). A system for the notation of proxemic behavior. *American Anthropology, 65,* 1003–1026.

Hall, E. T. (1966). *The hidden dimension.* Garden City, NJ: Doubleday.

Hall, E. T. (1968). Proxemics. *Current Anthropology, 9,* 83–108.

Hall, E. T. (1983). Proxemics. In A. M. Katz and V. T. Katz (eds.), *Foundations of nonverbal communication: Readings, exercises, and commentary* (pp. 5–27). Carbondale: Southern Illinois University Press.

Harper, R. G., Wiens, A. N., and Matarazzo, J. D. (1978). *Nonverbal communication: The state of the art* (pp. 246–317). New York: John Wiley.

Hickson, M. L., III, and Stacks, D. W. (1993). *Nonverbal communication: Studies and applications.* Madison, WI: Brown & Benchmark.

Hughes, J., and Goldman, M. (1978). Eye contact, facial expression, sex, and the violation of personal space. *Perceptual and Motor Skills, 46,* 579–584.

Kirmeyer, S. L. (1978). Urban density and pathology: A review of research. *Environment and Behavior, 10,* 247–269.

Knapp, M. L. (1980). *Essentials of nonverbal communication* (pp. 75–96). New York: Holt, Rinehart & Winston.

Knapp, M. L., and Hall, J. A. (1992). *Nonverbal communication in human interaction* (3rd ed.). New York: Holt, Rinehart & Winston.

Lett, E. E., Clark, W., and Altman, I. (1969). A propositional inventory of research on interpersonal distance. *Research Report No. 1.* Bethesda, MD: Naval Medical Research Institute.

Luft, J. (1966). On nonverbal interaction. *Journal of Psychology, 63,* 261–268.

Lyman, S. M., and Scott, M. B. (1967). Territoriality: A neglected sociological dimension. *Social Problems, 15,* 236–249.

Malandro, L. A., Barker, L., and Barker D. A. (1989). *Nonverbal communication.* New York: Random House.

McAndrew, F. T., Ryckman, R. M., Horr, W., and Soloman, R. (1978). The effects of invader placement of spatial markers on territorial behavior in a college population. *Journal of Social Psychology, 104,* 149–150.

Mehrabian, A., and Diamond, S. G. (1971). Seating arrangement and conversation. *Sociometry, 34,* 281–289.

Patterson, M. L. (1976). An arousal model of interpersonal intimacy. *Psychological Review, 83,* 235–245.

Pederson, D. M., and Heaston, A. B. (1972). The effects of sex of subject, sex of approaching person, and angle of approach upon personal space. *The Journal of Psychology, 82,* 277–286.

Richmond, V. P. (1992). *Nonverbal communication in the classroom.* Edina, MN: Burgess International Group.

Richmond, V. P., and McCroskey, J. C. (1993). *Communication: Apprehension, avoidance, and effectiveness* (3rd ed.). Scottsdale, AZ: Gorsuch Scarisbrick.

Rosenfeld, L. B., and Civikly, J. M. (1976). *With words unspoken: The nonverbal experience.* New York: Holt, Rinehart & Winston.

Russo, N. (1967). Connotation of seating arrangements. Cornell *Journal of Social Relations, II,* 37–44.

Sadalla, E. K. (1978). Population size, structural differentiation, and human behavior. *Environment and Behavior, 10,* 271–289.

Scheflen, A. E. (1976). Micro-territories in human interaction. In A. Kendon, R. M. Harris, and M. R. Key (eds.), *Organization of behavior in face to face interaction* (pp. 159–174). Chicago: Mouton-Aldine.

Scherer, S. E. (1974). Proxemic behavior of primary school children as a function of their socioeconomic class and subculture. *Journal of Personality and Social Psychology, 29,* 800–805.

Schaffer, D. R., and Sadowski, C. (1975). This table is mine: Respect for marked barroom tables as a function of gender of spatial marker and desirability of locale. *Sociometry, 38,* 408–419.

Shuter, R. (1976). Proxemics and tactility in Latin America. *Journal of Communication, 26,* 46–52.

Sommer, R. (1959). Studies in personal space. *Sociometry, 22,* 247–260.

Sommer, R. (1965). Further studies in small group ecology. *Sociometry, 28,* 337–348.

Sommer, R. (1969). *Personal space: The behavioral basis of design.* Englewood Cliffs, NJ: Prentice-Hall.

Watson, O. M. (1970). *Proxemic behavior: A cross-cultural study.* The Hague: Mouton.

Watson, O. M. (1972). Conflicts and directions in proxemic research. *Journal of Communication, 22,* 443–459.

Willis, F. N., Jr. (1966). Initial speaking distance as a function of the speakers' relationship. *Psychonomic Science, 5,* 221–222.

Chapter 7

Adler, R., and Towne, N. (1975). *Looking out/looking in.* San Francisco: Rienhart Press.

Andersen, P. A., and Leibowitz, K. (1978). The development and nature of the construct touch avoidance. *Environmental Psychology and Nonverbal Behavior, 3,* 89–106.

Andersen, P. A., and Sull, K. K. (1985). Out of touch, out of reach: Tactile predispositions as predictors of interpersonal distance. *Western Journal of Speech Communication, 49,* 57–72.

Argyle, M. (1975). *Bodily communication.* New York: International Universities Press.

Barnlund, D. C. (1975). Communicative styles of two cultures: Public and private self in Japan and the United States. In A. Kendon, R. M. Harris, and M. R. Key (eds.), *Organization of behavior in face-to-face interaction.* The Hague: Mouton.

Boderman, A., Freed, D. W., and Kinnucan, M. T. (1972). Touch me, like me: Testing an encounter group assumption. *Journal of Applied Behavioral Science, 8,* 527–533.

Burgoon, J. K., and Saine, T. (1978). *The unspoken dialogue: An introduction to nonverbal communication.* Boston: Houghton-Mifflin.

Clay, U. S. (1966). The effects of culture on mother–child tactile communication. Ph.D. dissertation, Columbia University. *Dissertation Abstracts,* 1967, *28,* 1770B.

Davis, F. (1978, September 27). Skin hunger—An American disease. *Woman's Day,* pp. 154–156.

Despert, J. L. (1941). Emotional aspects of speech and language development. *International Journal of Psychiatry and Neurology, 105,* 193–222.

Freedman, N. (1972). The analysis of movement behavior during the clinical interview. In A. W. Siegman and B. Pope (eds.), *Studies in dyadic communication* (pp. 153–175). New York: Pergamon Press.

Fromme, D. K., Jaynes, W. E., Taylor, D. K., Hanold, E. G., Daniell, J., Rountree, J. R., and Fromme, M. L. (1989). Nonverbal behavior and attitudes toward touch. *Journal of Nonverbal Behavior, 13,* 3–13,

Giffin, K., and Patton, B. (1974). *Personal communication in human relations.* Columbus, OH: Charles E. Merrill.

Goldberg, S., and Roshenthal, R. (1986). Self-touching behavior in the job interview: Antecedents and consequences. *Journal of Nonverbal Behavior, 10,* 65–80.

Hall, E. T. (1966). *The hidden dimension.* Garden City, NY: Doubleday.

Hammett, F. S. (1921). Studies of the thyroid apparatus: I. *American Journal of Physiology, 56,* 196–204.

Hammett, F. S. (1922). Studies of the thyroid apparatus: V. *American Journal of Physiology, 60,* 221–229.

Harlow, H. F., Harlow, M. K., and Hansen, E. W. (1963). The maternal affectional system of Rhesus monkeys. In H. L. Rheingold (ed.), *Maternal behavior in mammals.* New York: John Wiley.

Harlow, H. H., and Zimmerman, R. R. (1958). The development of affectional responses in infant monkeys. *Proceedings of the American Philosophical Society, 102,* 501–509.

Harper, R. G., Wiens, A. N., and Matarazzo, J. D. (1978). *Nonverbal communication: The state of the art.* (pp. 295–302). New York: John Wiley.

Henley, N. M. (1973). Status and sex: Some touching observations. *Bulletin of the Psychonomic Society, 2,* 91–93.

Henley, N. M. (1977). *Body politics: Power, sex, and nonverbal communication.* Englewood Cliffs, NJ: Prentice-Hall.

Heslin, R. (1974). *Steps toward a taxonomy of touching.* Paper presented at the Western Psychological Association Convention, Chicago.

Heslin, R., and Boss, D. (1976). *Nonverbal immediacy on arrival and departure at an airport.* Cited in M. L. Knapp, *Nonverbal communication in human interaction* (2nd ed.) (1978). New York: Holt, Rinehart & Winston.

Hickson, M. L., III, and Stacks, D. W. (1993). *Nonverbal communication: Studies and applications* (3rd ed.). Madison, WI: Brown & Benchmark.

Hite, S. (1977, July–August). What kind of loving does a woman want? *New Woman Magazine,* 75–76.

Johnson, K. L., and Edwards, R. (1991). The effects of gender and type of romantic touch on perceptions of relational commitment. *Journal of Nonverbal Behavior, 15,* 43–55.

Jones, S. E., and Yarbrough, A. E. (1985). A naturalistic study of the meanings of touch. *Communication Monographs, 52,* 19–56.

Jourard, S. M. (1966a). An exploratory study of body-accessibility. *British Journal of Social and Clinical Psychology, 5,* 221–231.

Jourard, S. M. (1966b). *The transparent self: Self-disclosure and well-being.* Princeton, NJ: Van Nostrand.

Jourard, S. M. (1968). *Disclosing man to himself.* New York: Van Nostrand Reinhold.

Jourard, S. M. (1971). *The transparent self* (rev. ed.). New York: D. Van Nostrand.

Jourard, S. M., and Friedman, R. (1970). Experimenter–subject "distance" and self-disclosure. *Journal of Personality and Social Psychology, 15,* 278–282.

Knapp, M. L. (1980). *Essentials of nonverbal communication* (pp. 146–160). New York: Holt, Rinehart & Winston.

Knapp, M. L., and Hall, J. A. (1992). *Nonverbal communication in human interaction.* New York: Holt, Rinehart & Winston.

Larsen, K. S., and LeRoux, J. (1984). A study of same sex touching attitudes: Scale development and personality predictors. *The Journal of Sex Research, 20 (3),* 264–278.

Lewis, M. (1972). Culture and gender roles: There's no unisex in the nursery. *Psychology Today, 5,* 54–57.

Malandro, L. A., Barker, L., and Barker, D. A. (1989). *Nonverbal communication.* New York: Random House.

Marler, P. (1967). Animal communication signals. *Science, 157,* 769–774.

Maurer, D., and Maurer, C. (1988). *The World of the Newborn.* New York: Basic Books.

Mehrabian, A. (1971). *Silent messages.* Belmont, CA: Wadsworth.

Mehrabian, A. (1981). *Silent messages: Implicit communication of emotions and attitudes.* Belmont, CA: Wadsworth.

Montagu, M.R.A. (1971). *Touching: The human significance of the skin.* New York: Columbia University Press.

Montagu, M.R.A. (1978). *Touching: The human significance of the skin* (2nd ed.). New York: Columbia University Press.

Morris, D. (1971). *Intimate behavior.* New York: Random House.

Morris, D. (1976). Please touch is message of Morris. In L. B. Rosenfeld and J. M. Civikly (eds.), *With words unspoken: The nonverbal experience* (pp. 129–132). New York: Holt, Rinehart & Winston.

Morris, D. (1977). *Manwatching.* New York: Abrams.

Nguyen, M. L., Heslin, R., and Nguyen, T. (1976). The meanings of touch: Sex and marital status differences. *Representative Research in Social Psychology, 7,* 13–18.

Nguyen, T., Heslin, R., and Nguyen, M. L. (1975). The meanings of touch: Sex differences. *Journal of Communication, 25,* 92–103.

Patterson, M. L., Powell, J. L., and Lenihan, M. G. (1986). Touch, compliance, and interpersonal affect. *Journal of Nonverbal Behavior, 10,* 41–50.

Pines, M. (1984, December). Children's winning ways. *Psychology Today,* pp. 58–66.

Pisano, M. D., Wall, S. M., and Foster, A. (1985). Perceptions of nonreciprocal touch in romantic relationships. *Journal of Nonverbal Behavior, 10,* 29–40.

Richmond, V. P. (1992). *Nonverbal Communication in the classroom.* Edina, MN: Burgess International Group.

Rosenfeld, L. B., and Civikly, J. M. (1976). *With words unspoken: The nonverbal experience.* New York: Holt, Rinehart & Winston.

Rosenfeld, L. B., Kartus, S., and Ray, C. (1976). Body accessibility revisited. *Journal of Communication, 26,* 27–30.

Schutz, W. (1971). *Here comes everybody.* New York: Harper & Row.

Shuter, R. (1976). Proxemics and tactility in Latin America. *Journal of Communication, 26,* 46–52.

Smith, A. I. (1970). *Non-verbal communication through touch.* Unpublished Ph.D. dissertation, Georgia State University.

Sorensen, G. A. (1979, May). *The effects of touch on interpersonal perceptions.* Paper presented at the Eastern Communication Association Convention, Philadelphia.

Storrs, D., and Kleinke, C. L. (1990). Evaluation of high and equal status male and female touchers. *Journal of Nonverbal Behavior, 14,* 87–95.

Thayer, S. (1986). Touch: Frontier of intimacy. In S. Thayer (ed.), *The psychology of touch* (A special issue of the *Journal of Nonverbal Behavior),* 10, 7–11.

Watson, W. H. (1975). The meanings of touch: Geriatric nursing. *Journal of Communication, 25,* 104–112.

Weitz, S. (ed.) (1974). *Nonverbal communication: Readings with commentary.* New York: Oxford University Press.

Willis, F. N., and Hofman, G. E. (1975). Development of tactile patterns in relation to age, sex, and race. *Developmental Psychology, 11,* 866.

Chapter 8

Abbott, A. G. (1947). *The color of life.* New York: McGraw-Hill.

Adams, R. S. (1969). Location as a feature of instructional interaction. *Merrill-Palmer Quarterly, 15,* 309–321.

Adams, R. S., and Biddle, B. (1970). *Realities of teaching: Explorations with video-tape.* New York: Holt, Rinehart & Winston.

Baker, J. (1985). What your favorite color says about you. *Cosmopolitan,* p. 232.

Baron, R. A., and Bell, P. A. (1976). Aggression and heat: The influence of ambient temperature, negative affect, and a cooling drink on physical aggression. *Journal of Personality and Social Psychology, 33,* 245–255.

Benson, T. W., and Frandsen, K. D. (1982). *Nonverbal communication* (2nd ed.). Chicago: Science Research Associates.

Birren, F. (1950). *Color psychology and color therapy: A factual study of the influence of color on human life.* New York: McGraw-Hill.

Bruneau, T. J. (1972, April). *Educational corridors: A field study and conceptualization of the non-verbal dimensions of spatiotemporal influences in a university hierarchy.* Paper presented at the annual convention of the International Communication Association, Atlanta.

Carr, S. J., and Dabbs, J. M., Jr. (1974). The effects of lighting, distance, and intimacy of topic on verbal and visual behavior. *Sociometry, 37,* 592–600.

Cook, M. (1970). Experiments on orientation and proxemics. *Human Relations, 23,* 61–76.

Decorating your office for success. (1979). By the editors of *Consumer Guide.* New York: Harper & Row.

Desk for success. (1984, February, 12). Cited in *Family Weekly.* p. 14.

Gergen, K. J., Gergen, M. M., and Barton, W. H. (1973). Deviance in the dark. *Psychology Today, 7,* 129–130.

Gifford, R., and O'Connor, B. (1986). Nonverbal intimacy: Clarifying the role of seating distance and orientation. *Journal of Nonverbal Behavior, 10,* 207–214.

Griffitt, W., and Veitch, R. (1971). Hot and crowded: Influences of population density and temperature on interpersonal affective behavior. *Journal of Personality and Social Psychology, 17,* 92–98.

Hall, E. T. (1966). *The hidden dimension.* Garden City, NY: Doubleday.

Hare, A. P., and Bales, R. F. (1963). Seating position and small group interaction. *Sociometry, 26,* 480–486.

Harper, R. G., Wiens, A. N., and Matarazzo, J. D. (1978). *Nonverbal communication: The state of the art* (pp. 285–295). New York: John Wiley.

Hickson, M. L., III, and Stacks, D. W. (1993). *Nonverbal communication: Studies and applications.* Madison, WI: Brown & Benchmark.

Howells, L. T., and Becker, S. W. (1962). Seating arrangement and leadership emergence. *Journal of Abnormal and Social Psychology, 64,* 148–150.

Huntington, E. (1915). *Civilization and climate.* New Haven: Yale University Press.

Ketcham, H. (1958). *Color planning for business and industry.* New York: Harper and Brothers.

Knapp, M. L. (1978a). *Nonverbal communication in human interaction* (2nd ed.) (pp. 83–113). New York: Holt, Rinehart & Winston.

Knapp, M. L. (1978b). *Social intercourse: From greeting to goodbye.* Boston: Allyn & Bacon.

Knapp, M. L. (1980). *Essentials of nonverbal communication* (pp. 53–74). New York: Holt, Rinehart & Winston.

Koneya, M., and Barbour, A. (1976). *Louder than words. . . : Nonverbal communication.* Columbus, OH: Charles E. Merrill.

Korda, M. (1975). *Power! How to get it, how to use it.* New York: Random House.

Kowinski, W. (1975, April). Shedding new light. *New Times, 4,* 48.

Malandro, L. A., Barker, L., and Barker, D. A. (1989). *Nonverbal communication* (2nd ed.). New York: Random House.

Maslow, A. H., and Mintz, N. L. (1956). Effects of aesthetic surroundings: I. Initial effects of three aesthetic conditions upon perceiving "energy" and "well-being" in faces. *Journal of Psychology, 41,* 247–254.

McClellend, D. (1976). *The achieving society.* New York: Van Nostrand Reinhold.

McCroskey, J. C., Larson, C. E., and Knapp, M. L. (1971). *An introduction to interpersonal communication* (pp. 93–122). Englewood Cliffs, NJ: Prentice-Hall.

Mehrabian, A. (1976). *Public places and private spaces: The psychology of work, play, and living environments.* New York: Basic Books.

Mintz, N. L. (1956). Effects of aesthetic surroundings: II. Prolonged and repeated experience in a "beautiful" and "ugly" room. *Journal of Psychology, 41,* 459–466.

Molloy, J. T. (1983). *Molloy's live for success.* New York: Bantam Books.

Richmond, V. P. (1992). *Nonverbal communication in the classroom.* Edina, MN: Burgess International Group.

Rosenfeld, L. B., and Civikly, J. M. (1976). *With words unspoken: The nonverbal experience* (pp. 161–185). New York: Holt, Rinehart & Winston.

Russo, N. F. (1967). Connotations of seating arrangements. *Cornell Journal of Social Relations, 2,* 37–44.

Sommer, R. (1965). Further studies of small group ecology. *Sociometry, 28,* 337–348.

Sommer, R. (1969). *Personal space: The behavioral basis of design.* Englewood Cliffs, NJ: Prentice-Hall.

Strodtbeck, F. L., and Hook, L. H. (1961). The social dimensions of a twelve-man jury table. *Sociometry, 24,* 397–415.

Sutton, T. (1985, March). Setting the tone. *Savvy,* pp. 74–82.

Walberg, H. J. (1969). Physical and psychological distance in the classroom. *School Review, 77,* 64–70.

Williams, R. (1954). *Lighting for color and form.* New York: Pitman.

Zell, F. (1984, August 14). Using hues and light to color our moods. *USA Today.*

Zweigenhaft, R. L. (1976). Personal space in the faculty office: Desk placement and the student–faculty interaction. *Journal of Applied Psychology, 61,* 529–532.

Chapter 9

Bell, C. (1983, December 25). Why foods feed your emotions. *Family Weekly,* p. 13.

Burton, R. (1976). *The language of smell.* Boston: Routledge & Kegan Paul.

Cain, W. S. (1981). Educating your nose. *Psychology Today, 15,* 48–56.

Davis, F. (1975). *Inside intuition: What we know about nonverbal communication.* New York: New American Library.

Erb, R. C. (1968). *The common scents of smell: How the nose knows and what it all knows.* Cleveland: World Publishing.

Hall, E. T. (1966). *The hidden dimension.* Garden City, NY: Doubleday.

Hickson, M. L., III, and Stacks, D. W. (1993). *Nonverbal communication: Studies and applications* (3rd ed.). Madison, WI: Brown & Benchmark.

Luka, T., Berner, E. S., and Kanakis, C. (1977). Diagnosis by smell? *Journal of Medical Education, 52,* 349–350.

Malandro, L. A., and Barker, L., and Barker, D. A. (1989). *Nonverbal communication* (2nd ed.). New York: Random House.

Manning, A. (1994, February 22). Doctors do tests to solve body fumes mystery. *USA Today,* Section D.

Miller, L. (1986, January). The cross-cultural nose. *Psychology Today, 20,* p. 68.

Ponte, L. (1982, June). Secret scents that affect behavior. *Reader's Digest,* pp. 121–123.

Richmond, V. P. (1992). *Nonverbal communication in the classroom.* Edina, MN: Burgess International Group.

Wiener, H. (1979). Human exocrinology: The olfactory component of nonverbal communication. In S. Weitz (ed.), *Nonverbal communication: Readings with commentary* (2nd ed.) (pp. 338–345). New York: Oxford University Press.

Winter, R. (1976). *The smell book: Scents, sex, and society.* Philadelphia: Lippincott.

Young, S. (1985, December). Bad breath: Learn how to leave home without it! *Glamour,* p. 268.

Chapter 10

Bloomfield, H. H., and Felder, L. (1985, June). Why are you always late for everything? *New Woman,* pp. 67–69.

Brophy, B. (1985, October). Conquering the time crunch. *USA Weekend,* p. 22.

Cinelli, L. A., and Ziegler, D. J. (1990). Cognitive appraisal of daily hassles in college students showing Type A or Type B behavior patterns. *Psychological Reports, 67,* 83–88.

DiMatteo, M. R. (1979). Nonverbal skill and the physician–patient relationship. In R. Rosenthal (ed.), *Skill in nonverbal communication: Individual differences* (pp. 104–134). Cambridge, MA: Oelgeschlager, Gunn & Hain.

DiMatteo, M. R., Prince, L. M., and Taranta, A. (1979). Patients' perceptions of physicians' behavior: Determinants of patient commitment to the therapeutic relationship. *Journal of Community Health, 4,* 280–290.

Fine, G. A. (1990). Organizational time: Temporal demands and the experience of work in restaurant. *Social Forces, 69,* 95–114.

Gray, P. G., and Cartwright, A. (1953, December, 19). Choosing and changing doctors. *Lancet,* pp. 1308–1309.

Hall, E. T. (1959). *The silent language.* Garden City, NY: Doubleday.

Hall, E. T. (1972). Proxemics: The study of man's spatial relations. In L. A. Samovar and R. E. Porter (eds.), *Intercultural communication: A reader* (pp. 205–220). Belmont, CA: Wadsworth.

Hall, E. T. (1973). *The silent language.* Garden City, NY: Doubleday.

Hall, E. T. (1976). *Beyond culture.* Garden City, NY: Anchor Press/Doubleday.

Hall, E. T. (1984). *The dance of life: The other dimension of time.* New York: Anchor Books.

Hickson, M. L., III, and Stacks, D. W. (1993). *Nonverbal communication: Studies and applications* (3rd ed.). Madison, WI: Brown & Benchmark.

Kasteler, J., Kane, R. L., Olsen, D. M., and Thetford, C. (1976). Issues underlying prevalence of "doctor-shopping" behavior. *Journal of Health and Social Behavior, 17,* 328.

Lakein, A. (1973). *How to get control of your time and your life.* New York: New American Library.

Levine, R. (1989). The pace of life. *Psychology Today, October,* 42–46.

Malandro, L. A., Barker, L., and Barker, D. A. (1989). *Nonverbal communication.* New York: Random House.

Perry, A. R., Kane, K. M., Bernesser, K. J., and Spicker, P. T. (1990). Type A behavior, competitive achievement-striving, and cheating among college students. *Psychological Reports, 66,* 449–465.

Potter, B. A. (1980). *Beating job burnout.* New York: Ace Books.

Richmond, V. P. (1992). *Nonverbal communication in the classroom.* Edina, MN: Burgess International Group.

Vuori, H., Aaku, T., Aine, E., Erkko, R., and Johansson, R. (1972). Doctor–patient relationship in the light of patient experiences. *Social Science and Medicine, 6,* 723–730.

Chapter 11

Andersen, J. F. (1979). Teacher immediacy as a predictor of teaching effectiveness. In D. Nimmo (ed.), *Communication yearbook 3* (pp. 543–559). New Brunswick, NJ: Transaction Books.

Andersen, P. A. (1985). Nonverbal immediacy in interpersonal communication. In A. W. Siegman and S. Feldstein (eds.), *Multichannel integrations of nonverbal behavior* (pp. 1–36). Hillsdale, NJ: Erlbaum.

Blackman, B. I., and Clevenger, T., Jr. (1990, April). *Surrogates for nonverbal behavior in on-line computer conferencing.* Paper presented at the annual convention of the Southern States Communication Association, Birmingham, AL.

Buhr, T. A., Clifton, T. I., and Pryor, B. (in press). Effects of speaker immediacy on receivers' information processing. *Psychological Reports.*

Christophel, D. M. (1990). The relationships among teacher immediacy behaviors, student motivation, and learning. *Communication Education, 39,* 323–340.

Malandro, L. A., Barker, L., and Barker, D. A. (1989). *Nonverbal communication* (2nd ed.). New York: Random House.

McCroskey, J. C., and Richmond, V. P. (1992a). *Introduction to interpersonal communication.* Edina, MN: Burgess International Group.

McCroskey, J. C., and Richmond, V. P. (1992b). Increasing Teacher Influence Through Immediacy. In V. P. Richmond and J. C. McCroskey (eds.), *Power in the Classroom: Communication, Control, and Concern* (pp 101–120). Hillsdale, NJ: Lawrence Erlbaum.

McCroskey, J. C., Richmond, V. P., and Stewart, R. A. (1986). *One on one: The foundations of interpersonal communication.* Englewood Cliffs, NJ: Prentice-Hall.

Mehrabian, A. (1966). Immediacy: An indicator of attitudes in linguistic communication. *Journal of Personality, 34,* 26–34.

Mehrabian, A. (1971). *Silent messages.* Belmont, CA: Wadsworth.

Mehrabian, A. (1981). *Silent messages: Implicit communication of emotions and attitudes* (2nd ed.). Belmont, CA: Wadsworth.

Osmond, H. (1957). Function as the basis of psychiatric ward design. *Mental Hospitals, 8,* 23–32.

Osmond, H. (1959). The relationship between architect and psychiatrist. In C. Goshen (ed.), *Psychiatric architecture.* Washington: American Psychiatric Association.

Plax, T. G., Kearney, P., McCroskey, J. C., and Richmond, V. P. (1986). Power in the classroom VI: Verbal control strategies, nonverbal immediacy, and affective learning. *Communication Education, 35,* 43–55.

Richmond, V. P. (1978). The relationship between trait and state communication apprehension and interpersonal perceptions during acquaintance stages. *Human Communication Research, 4,* 338–349.

Richmond, V. P. (1990). Communication in the classroom: Power and motivation. *Communication Education, 39,* 181–195.

Richmond, V. P. (1992). Nonverbal communication in the classroom. Edina, MN: Burgess International Group.

Richmond, V. P., Gorham, J. S., and McCroskey, J. C. (1986). The relationship between selected immediacy behaviors and cognitive learning. In M. L. McLaughlin (ed.), *Communication yearbook 10* (pp. 574–590). Beverly Hills, CA: Sage.

Richmond, V. P., and McCroskey, J. C. (1983). *Communication: Apprehension, avoidance, and effectiveness* (3rd ed.). Scottsdale, AZ: Gorsuch Scarisbrick.

Richmond, V. P., and McCroskey, J. C. (1990). Reliability and separation of factors on the assertiveness–responsiveness measure. *Psychological Reports, 67,* 449–450.

Sanders, J. A., and Wiseman, R. L. (1990). The effects of verbal and nonverbal teacher immediacy on perceived cognitive, affective, and behavioral learning in the multicultural classroom. *Communication Education, 39.*

Sommer, R. (1969). *Personal space: The behavioral basis of design.* Englewood Cliffs, NJ: Prentice-Hall.

Wheeless, L. R. (1976). Self-disclosure and interpersonal solidarity: Measurement, validation, and relationships. *Human Communication Research, 3,* 47–61.

Chapter 12

Addington, D. W. (1968). The relationship of selected vocal characteristics to personality perception. *Speech Monographs, 35,* 492–503.

Baxter, J. C. (1970). Interpersonal spacing in natural settings. *Sociometry, 33,* 444–456.

Bem, S. L. (1974). The measurement of psychological androgyny. *Journal of Consulting and Clinical Psychology, 42,* 155–162.

Berman, P. W., and Smith, V. L. (1984). Gender and situational differences in children's smiles, touch, and proxemics. *Sex Roles, 10,* 347–356.

Bernard, J. S. (1968). *The sex game.* New York: Atheneum.

Birdwhistell, R. L. (1970). *Kinesics and context: Essays on body motion communication.* Philadelphia: University of Pennsylvania Press.

Broverman, I. K., Vogel, S. R., Broverman, D. M., Clarkson, F. E., and Rosenkrantz, P. S. (1972). Sex-role stereotypes: A current appraisal. *Journal of Social Issues, 28,* 59–78.

Buck, R., Miller, R. E., and Caul, W. F. (1974). Sex, personality and physiological variables in the communication of affect via facial expression. *Journal of Personality and Social Psychology, 30,* 587–596.

Bugental, D. E., Love, L. R., and Gianetto, R. M. (1971). Perfidious feminine faces. *Journal of Personality and Social Psychology, 17,* 314–318.

Chesler, P. (1972). *Women and madness.* New York: Doubleday.

Dittmann, A. T. (1972). Developmental factors in conversational behavior. *Journal of Communication, 22,* 404–423.

Eakins, B. W., and Eakins, R. G. (1978). *Sex differences in human communication.* Boston: Houghton-Mifflin.

Evans, G. W., and Howard, R. B. (1973). Personal space. *Psychological Bulletin, 80,* 334–344.

Freedman, J. L. (1971). The crowd: Maybe not so madding after all. *Psychology Today, 5,* 58–61, 86.

Grady, K. E., Miransky, L. J., and Mulvey, M. A. (1976). *A nonverbal measure of dominance.* Paper presented at the meeting of the American Psychological Association, Washington, DC.

Hall, J. A. (1984). *Nonverbal sex differences: Communication accuracy and expressive style.* Baltimore: The Johns Hopkins University Press.

Hall, J. A., and Halberstadt, A. G. (1986). Smiling and gazing. In J. S. Hyde and M. Linn (eds.), *The psychology of gender: Advances through meta-analysis* (pp. 136–158). Baltimore: Johns Hopkins University Press.

Harper, L. V., and Sanders, K. M. (1975). Preschool children's use of space: Sex differences in outdoor play. *Developmental Psychology, 11,* p. 119.

Henley, N. M. (1977). *Body politics: Power, sex, and nonverbal communication.* Englewood Cliffs, NJ: Prentice-Hall.

Hickson, M. L., III, and Stacks, D. W. (1993). *Nonverbal communication: Studies and applications* (3rd ed.). Madison, WI: Brown & Benchmark.

Jenni, D. A., and Jenni, M. A. (1976). Carrying behavior in humans: Analysis of sex differences. *Science, 194,* 859–860.

Jones, S. E. (1986). Sex differences in touch communication. *Western Journal of Speech Communication, 50,* 227–241.

Jourard, S. M. (1966). An exploratory study of body-accessibility. *British Journal of Social and Clinical Psychology, 5,* 221–231.

Jourard, S. M. (1968). *Disclosing man to himself.* New York: Van Nostrand Reinhold.

Jourard, S. M., and Rubin, J. E. (1968). Self-disclosure and touching: A study of two modes of interpersonal encounter and their interrelation. *Journal of Humanistic Psychology, 8,* 39–48.

Knapp, M. L., and Hall, J. A. (1992). *Nonverbal communication in human interaction* (3rd ed.). New York: Holt, Rinehart & Winston.

LaFrance, M., and Mayo, C. (1978). *Moving bodies: Nonverbal communication in social relationships* (pp. 155–170). Monterey, CA: Brooks/Cole.

Lomranz, J., Shapira, A., Choresh, N., and Gilat, Y. (1975). Children's personal space as a function of age and sex. *Developmental Psychology, 11,* 541–545.

Malandro, L. A., Barker, L., and Barker, D. A. (1989). *Nonverbal communication* (2nd ed.). New York: Random House.

McAndrew, F. T., and Warner, J. E. (1986). Arousal seeking and the maintenance of mutual gaze in same and mixed sex dyads. *Journal of Nonverbal Behavior, 10,* 168–172.

McCroskey, J. C., and Richmond, V. P. (1992). An introduction to interpersonal communication. Edina, MN: Burgess International Group.

McCroskey, J. C., Richmond, V. P., and Stewart, R. A. (1986). *One on one: The foundations of interpersonal communication.* Englewood Cliffs, NJ: Prentice-Hall.

Mehrabian, A. (1972). *Nonverbal communication.* Chicago: Aldine.

Mehrabian, A. (1981). *Silent messages: Implicit communication of emotions and attitudes* (2nd ed.). Belmont, CA: Wadsworth.

Mehrabian, A., and Diamond, S. G. (1971b). The effects of furniture arrangement, props, and personality on social interaction. *Journal of Personality and Social Psychology, 20,* 18–30.

Morris, D. (1971). *In. mate behavior.* New York: Random House.

Mulac, A. Studley. L. B., Wiemann, J. W., and Bradac, J. J. (1987). Male/female gaze in same-sex and mixed-sex dyads: Gender-linked differences and mutual influence. *Human Communication Research, 13,* 323–344.

Nguyen, T., Heslin, R., and Nguyen, M. L. (1975). The meanings of touch: Sex differences. *Journal of Communication, 25,* 92–103.

Peterson, P. (1976). An investigation of sex differences in regard to nonverbal body gestures. In B. W. Eakins, R. G. Eakins, and B. Lieb-Brilhart (eds.), *Siscom '75: Women's (and men's) communication.* Falls, Church, VA: Speech Communication Association.

Piercy, M. (1973). *Small changes.* New York: Doubleday.

Richmond, V. P., and McCroskey, J. C. (1989). *Communication: Apprehension, avoidance, and effectiveness* (2nd ed.). Scottsdale, AZ: Gorsuch Scarisbrick.

Rosenthal, R., Hall, J. A., DiMatteo, R., Rogers, R. L., and Archer, D. (1979). *Sensitivity to nonverbal communication: The PONS test.* Baltimore: The Johns Hopkins University Press.

Scheflen, A. E. (1965). Quasi-courtship behavior in psychotherapy. *Psychiatry, 28,* 245–257.

Silveira, J. (1972). Thoughts on the politics of touch. *Women's Press, 1,* 13.

Widgery, R. N., and Webster, B. (1969). The effects of physical attractiveness upon perceived initial credibility. *Michigan Speech Journal, 4,* 9–15.

Willis, F. N., Jr. (1966). Initial speaking distance as a function of the speaker's relationship. *Psychonomic Science, 5,* 221–222.

Chapter 13

Bovee, C. L., and Thill, J. V. (1983). Business communication today. New York: Random House.

Cohen, L. R. (1983, January–February). Nonverbal (Mis) communication between managerial men and women. *Business Horizons,* 14–17.

Flippo, E. (1974). *Management: A behavioral approach.* Boston: Allyn & Bacon.

Gordon, R. L. (1975). *Interviewing: Strategy, techniques, and tactics.* Homewood, IL: The Dorsey Press.

Hall, E. T. (1959). *The silent language.* Garden City, NY: Doubleday.

Hall, E. T. (1966). *The hidden dimension.* Garden City, NY: Doubleday.

Heckel, R. V. (1973). Leadership and voluntary seating choice. *Psychological Reports, 32,* 141–142.

Henley, N. M. (1977). *Body politics: Power, sex, and nonverbal communication.* Englewood Cliffs, NJ: Prentice-Hall.

Hickson, M. L., III, and Stacks, D. W. (1993). *Nonverbal communication: Studies and applications* (3rd ed.). Madison, WI: Brown & Benchmark.

Hunsaker, P. L. (1980, March–April). Communicating better: There's no proxy for proxemics. *Business,* pp. 41–48.

Jorgenson, D. O. (1975). Field study of the relationship between status and discrepancy and proxemics behavior. *Journal of Social Psychology, 97,* 173–179.

Koehler, J. W., Anatol, K. W. E., and Applbaum, R. L. (1981). *Organizational communication: Behavioral perspectives* (2nd ed.). New York: Holt, Rinehart & Winston.

Korda, M. (1975). *Power! How to get it, how to use it.* New York: Ballantine.

LaFrance, M., and Mayo, C. (1978). *Moving bodies: Nonverbal communication in social relationships* (pp. 95–105). Monterey, CA: Brooks/Cole.

Lewis, P. V. (1980). *Organizational communication: The essence of effective management* (2nd ed.). Columbus, OH: Grid.

Lott, D. F., and Sommer, R. (1967). Seating arrangements and status. *Journal of Personality and Social Psychology, 7,* 90–95.

McCaskey, M. B. (1979, November–December). The hidden messages managers send. *Harvard Business Review,* pp. 135–148.

McCroskey, J. C., and Richmond, V. P. (1992). *An introduction to nonverbal communication.* Edina, MN: Burgess International Group.

McCroskey, J. C., Richmond, V. P., and Stewart, R. A. (1986). *One on one: The foundations of interpersonal communication.* Englewood Cliffs, NJ: Prentice-Hall.

Mehrabian, A. (1971). *Silent messages.* Belmont, CA: Wadsworth.

Mehrabian, A. (1976). *Public places and private spaces: The psychology of work, play, and living environments.* New York: Basic Books.

Mehrabian, A, (1981). *Silent messages: Implicit communication of emotions and attitudes.* (2nd ed.). Belmont, CA: Wadsworth.

Molloy, J. T. (1975). *Dress for success.* New York: Warner Books.

Oldham, G. R., and Rotchford, N. L. (1983). Relationships between office characteristics and employee reactions: A study of the physical environment. *Administrative Science Quarterly, 28,* 542–556.

Remland, M. S. (1984). Leadership impressions and nonverbal communication in a superior–subordinate interaction. *Communication Quarterly, 32,* 41–48.

Richmond, V. P., Davis, L, M., Saylor, K., and McCroskey, J. C. (1984). Power strategies in organizations: Communication techniques and messages. *Human Communication Research, 11,* 85–108.

Richmond, V. P., and McCroskey, J. C. (1992). *Organizational communication for survival.* Englewood Cliffs, NJ: Prentice-Hall.

Richmond, V. P., and McCroskey, J. C. (1993). *Communication: Apprehension, avoidance, and effectiveness* (3rd ed.). Scottsdale, AZ: Gorsuch Scarisbrick.

Richmond, V. P., McCroskey, J. C., and Davis, L. M. (1986). The relationship of supervisor use of power and affinity-seeking strategies with subordinate satisfaction. *Communication Quarterly, 34,* 178–193.

Richmond, V. P., Wagner, J. P., and McCroskey, J. C. (1983). The impact of perceptions of leadership style, use of power, and conflict management style on organizational outcomes. *Communication Quarterly, 31,* 27–36.

Sommer, R. (1969). *Personal space: The behavioral basis of design.* Englewood Cliffs, NJ: Prentice-Hall.

Street, R. L., and Buller, D. B. (1987). Nonverbal response patterns in physician–patient interactions: A functional analysis. *Journal of Nonverbal Behavior, 11,* 234–253.

Strodtbeck, F. L., and Hook, L. H. (1961). The social dimensions of a twelve-man jury table. *Sociometry, 24,* 397–415.

Sybers, R., and Roach, M. E. (1962). Clothing and human behavior. *Journal of Home Economics, 54,* 184–187.

Viteles, M. S. (1954, January). What raises a man's morale. *Personnel, 30,* 305–313.

Wheeless, L. R. (1978). A follow-up study of the relationships among trust, disclosure, and interpersonal solidarity. *Human Communication Research, 4,* 143–157.

Whyte, W. F. (1949). The social structure of the restaurant. *American Journal of Sociology, 54,* 302–310.

Chapter 14

Algozzine, R. (1976). What teachers perceive—children receive? *Communication Quarterly, 24,* 41–47.

Ambady, N., and Rosenthal, R. (1993). Half a minute: Predicting teacher evaluations from thin slices of nonverbal behavior and physical attractiveness. *Journal of Personality and Social Psychology, 64,* 431–441.

Andersen, J. F. (1979). The relationship between teacher immediacy and teaching effectiveness. In D. Nimmo (ed.), *Communication yearbook 3* (pp. 543–560). New Brunswick, NJ: Transaction Books.

Andersen, J. F. (1986). Instructor nonverbal communication: Listening to our silent messages. In J. M. Civikly (ed.), *Communicating in college classrooms: New directions for teaching and learning* (pp. 41–49). San Francisco: Jossey-Bass.

Andersen, J. F., Andersen, P. A., Murphy, M. A., and Wendt-Wasco, N. (1985). Teachers' reports of students' nonverbal communication in the classroom: A development study in grades K–12. *Communication Education, 34,* 292–307.

Andersen, P., and Andersen, J. (1982). Nonverbal immediacy in instruction. In L. L. Barker (ed.), *Communication in the classroom: Original essays* (pp. 98–102). Englewood Cliffs, NJ: Prentice-Hall.

Andersen, P. A., and Leibowitz, K. (1978). The development and nature of the construct touch avoidance. *Environmental Psychology and Nonverbal Behavior, 3,* 89–106.

Barr, A. S. (1929). *Characteristic differences in the teaching performance of good and poor teachers of the social studies.* Bloomington, IL: Public School Publishing Company.

Christophel, D. M. (1990). The relationships among teacher immediacy behaviors, student motivation, and learning. *Communication Education, 39,* 323–340.

Green, G. H. (1979). Ah-choo! Humidity can help. *American School and University, 52,* 64–65.

Kassinove, H. (1972). Effects of meaningful auditory stimulation on children's scholastic performance. *Journal of Educational Psychology, 63,* 526–530.

Kearney, P., Plax, T. G., Richmond, V. P., and McCroskey, J. C. (1984). Power in the classroom IV: Teacher communication techniques as alternatives to discipline. In D. Nimmo (ed.), *Communication Yearbook 4* (pp. 724–746). Beverly Hills, CA: Sage.

Kearney, P., Plax, T. G., Richmond, V. P., and McCroskey, J. C. (1985). Power in the classroom III: Teacher communication techniques and messages. *Communication Education, 34,* 19–28.

Kearney, P., Plax, T. G., and Wendt-Wasco, N. J. (1985). Teacher immediacy for affective learning in divergent college classes. *Communication Quarterly, 33,* 61–74.

Ketcham, H. (1958). *Color planning for business and industry.* New York: Harper and Brothers.

Malandro, L. A., and Barker, L. (1983). *Nonverbal communication.* Reading, MA: Addison-Wesley.

Malandro, L. A., Barker, L., and Barker, D. A. (1989). *Nonverbal communication* (2nd ed.). New York: Random House.

McCroskey, J. C. (1992). *Communication in the classroom.* Edina, MN: Burgess International Group.

McCroskey, J. C., and Richmond, V. P. (1983). Power in the classroom I: Teacher and student perceptions. *Communication Education, 32,* 175–184.

McCroskey, J. C., Richmond, V. P., Plax, T. G., and Kearney, P. (1985). Power in classroom V: Behavior alteration techniques, communication training and learning. *Communication Education, 34,* 214–226.

Menges, R. J. (1977). *The intentional teacher: Controller, manager, helper.* Monterey, CA: Brooks/Cole.

Naumann, N. (1977). Three cheers for the self-contained classroom. *Teacher, 95,* 86–89.

Plax, T. G., Kearney, P., McCroskey, J. C., and Richmond, V. P. (1986). Power in the classroom VI: Verbal control strategies, nonverbal immediacy and affective learning. *Communication Education, 35,* 43–55.

Richmond, V. P. (1990). Communication in the classroom: Power and Motivation. *Communication Education, 39,* 181–195.

Richmond, V. P. (1992). *Nonverbal communication in the classroom.* Edina, MN: Burgess International Group.

Richmond, V. P., Gorham, J. S., and McCroskey, J. C. (1986). The relationship between selected immediacy behaviors and cognitive learning. In M. L. McLaughlin (ed.), *Communication Yearbook 10.* Beverly Hills, CA: Sage.

Richmond, V. P., and McCroskey, J. C. (1984). Power in the classroom II: Power and learning. *Communication Education, 33,* 125–136.

Richmond, V. P., and McCroskey, J. C. (1985). *Communication: Apprehension, avoidance, and effectiveness.* Scottsdale, AZ: Gorsuch Scarisbrick.

Richmond, V. P., McCroskey, J. C., Kearney, P., and Plax, T. G. (1987). Power in the classroom VII: Linking behavioral alteration techniques to cognitive learning. *Communication Education, 36,* 1–12.

Richmond, V. P., McCroskey, J. C., Plax, T. G., and Kearney, P. (1986). *Teacher immediacy training and student learning.* Paper presented at the annual convention of the Speech Communication Association, Chicago.

Sanders, J. A., and Wiseman, R. L. (1990). The effects of verbal and nonverbal teacher immediacy on perceived cognitive, affective, and behavioral learning in the multicultural classroom. *Communication Education, 39.*

Sellers, J. (1978). How to improve lunchtime discipline. *American School Board Journal, 165,* 29.

Smith, H. A. (1979). Nonverbal communication in teaching. *Review of Educational Psychology, 49,* 631–672.

Sommer, R. (1977). Classroom layout. *Theory into Practice, 16,* 174–175.

Thompson, J. J. (1973). *Beyond words: Nonverbal communication in the classroom.* New York: Citation Press.

Todd-Mancillas, W. R. (1982). Classroom environments and nonverbal communication. In L. L. Barker (ed.), *Communication in the classroom: Original essays* (pp. 77–97). Englewood Cliffs, NJ: Prentice-Hall.

Wiemann, M. O., and Wiemann, J. M. (1975). *Nonverbal communication in the elementary classroom.* Urbana, IL: ERIC Clearinghouse on Reading and Communication Skills.

Chapter 15

Adler, P. S. (1974). Beyond cultural identity: Reflections on cultural and multicultural man. *Topics in Culture Learning, 2,* 23–40.

Axtell, R. E. (1991). Gestures: The do's and taboos of body language around the world. New York: John Wiley & Sons.

Brault, G. J. (1962). Kinesics and the classroom: Some typical French gestures. *French Review, 36,* 374–382.

Bruneau, T. (1973). Communicative silences: Forms and functions. *Journal of Communication, 33,* 17–46.

Bruneau, T. (1982). The time dimension in intercultural communication. In L. A. Samovar and R. E. Porter (eds.), *Intercultural communication: A reader* (3rd ed.) (pp. 290–299). Belmont, CA: Wadsworth.

Cambra, R. E., and Klopf, D. W. (1979). *A cross-cultural analysis of interpersonal needs.* Paper presented at the Speech Communication Association Intercultural Communication Conference, Honolulu.

Davis, F. (1978, September, 27). Skin hunger—An American disease. *Women's Day,* pp. 48–50, 154–156.

Eibl-Eibesfeldt, I. (1972). Similarities and differences between cultures in expressive moments. In R. A. Hinde (ed.), *Non-verbal communication.* London: Cambridge University Press.

Ekman, P. (1971). *Universals and cultural differences in facial expressions of emotion.* In Nebraska Symposium on Motivation (pp. 207–283). Lincoln: University of Nebraska Press.

Ekman, P. (1975, September). Face muscles talk every language. *Psychology Today, 9,* 35–39.

Ekman, P., and Friesen, W. V. (1969). Nonverbal leakage and clues to deception. *Psychiatry, 32,* 88–106.

Ekman, P., Friesen, W. V., and Ellsworth, P. (1972). *Emotion in the human face.* New York: Pergamon Press.

Frank, L. K. (1982). Cultural patterning of tactile experiences. In L. A. Samovar and R. E. Porter (eds.), *Intercultural communication: A reader* (3rd ed.) (pp. 285–289). Belmont, CA: Wadsworth.

Harris, P. R., and Moran, R. T. (1991). *Managing cultural differences* (3rd ed.). Houston: Gulf Publishing.

Harrison, R. P. (1974). *Beyond words: An introduction to nonverbal communication*. Englewood Cliffs, NJ: Prentice-Hall.

Horton, J. (1976). Time and cool people. In L. A. Samovar and R. E. Porter (eds.), *Intercultural communication: A reader* (2nd ed.) (pp. 274–287). Belmont, CA: Wadsworth.

Hur, S. V., and Hur, B. S. (1988). *Culture shock! Korea*. Singapore: Times Books International.

Iliffe, A. H. (1960). A study of preferences in feminine beauty. *British Journal of Psychology, 51,* 267–273.

Ishii, S. (1973). Characteristics of Japanese nonverbal communicative behavior. Communication, 2. Cited in Klopf, D. W. and Ishii, S. (1984). *Communicating effectively across cultures*. Tokyo: NAN'UN-DO.

Ishii, S. (1975). The American male viewed by Japanese female students of English: A stereotype image. *Speech Education, 3.* Cited in Klopf, D. W. and Ishii, S. (1984). *Communicating effectively across cultures*. Tokyo: NAN'UN-DO.

Izard, C. E. (1969). The emotions and emotion constructs in personality and culture research. In R. B. Cattell (ed.), *Handbook of modern personality theory*. Chicago: Aldine.

Jakobson, R. (1976). Nonverbal signs for 'Yes' and 'No.' In L. A. Samovar and R. E. Porter (eds.), *Intercultural communication: A reader* (2nd ed.) (pp. 235–240). Belmont, CA: Wadsworth.

Johnson, K. R. (1976). Black kinesics: Some nonverbal communication patterns in the black culture. In L. A. Samovar and R. E. Porter (eds.), *Intercultural communication: A reader* (2nd ed.) (pp. 259–268). Belmont, CA: Wadsworth.

Jones, S. E. (1971). A comparative proxemics analysis of dyadic interaction in selected subcultures of New York City. *Journal of Social Psychology, 84,* 35–44.

Jourard, S. M. (1968). *Disclosing man to himself.* New York: Van Nostrand Reinhold.

Kaleina, G. (1979, March 3). More than other folks, pets get loving strokes. *The Arizona Republic,* p. c-2.

Klopf, D. W. (1987). *Intercultural encounters: The fundamentals of intercultural communication.* Englewood, CO: Morton.

Klopf, D. W. (1991). *Intercultural encounters: The fundamentals of intercultural communication* (2nd ed.). Englewood, CO: Morton.

Klopf, D. W., and Ishii, S. (1984). *Communicating effectively across cultures.* Tokyo: NAN'UN-DO.

Klopf, D. W., and Park, M.-S. (1982). *Cross-cultural communication: An introduction to the fundamentals.* Seoul, Korea: Han Shin Publishers.

Hall, E. T. (1959). *The silent language.* Greenwich, CT: Fawcett.

Malandro, L. A., Barker, L., and Barker, D. A. (1989). *Nonverbal communication.* New York: Random House.

Martin, J. G. (1964). Racial ethnocentrism and judgment of beauty. *Journal of Social Psychology, 63,* 59–63.

Morsbach, H. (1976). Aspects of nonverbal communication in Japan. In L. A. Samovar and R. E. Porter (eds.), *Intercultural communication: A reader* (2nd ed.) (pp. 240-259). Belmont, CA: Wadsworth.

Rich, A. L., and Ogawa, D. M. (1972). Intercultural and interracial communication: An analytical approach. In L. A. Samovar and R. E. Porter (eds.), *Intercultural communication: A reader.* Belmont, CA: Wadsworth.

Richmond, V. P. (1992). *Nonverbal communication in the classroom.* Edina, MN: Burgess International Group.

Richmond, V. P., and McCroskey J. C. (1993). *Communication: Apprehension, avoidance, and effectiveness* (3rd ed.). Scottsdale, AZ: Gorsuch Scarisbrick.

Ruben, B. D. (1977). Human communication and cross-cultural effectiveness. *International and Intercultural Communication Annual, 4.*

Saitz, R. L., and Cervenka, E. J. (1972). *Handbook of gestures: Colombia and the United States.* The Hague: Morton.

Sechrest, L. (1969). Nonreactive assessment of attitudes. In E. P. Willems and H. L. Rausch (eds.), *Naturalistic viewpoints in psychological research.* New York: Holt, Rinehart & Winston.

Shuter, R. (1976). Proxemics and tactility in Latin America. *Journal of Communication, 26,* 46–52.

Shuter, R. (1977). A field study of nonverbal communication in Germany, Italy, and the United States. *Communication Monographs, 44,* 298–305.

Welch, M. S. (1979, July). Touching: Kissing, hugging, stroking, patting, grabbing, tickling, tweaking, brushing. *Glamour,* 70–71.

Yousef, F. S. (1976). Nonverbal behavior: Some intricate and diverse dimensions in intercultural communication. In L. A. Samovar and R. E. Porter (eds.), *Intercultural communication: A reader* (2nd ed.) (pp. 230–235). Belmont, CA: Wadsworth.

▲ Index